THE MacARTHUR HIGHWAY

RELATED TITLES FROM POTOMAC BOOKS

The First Resort of Kings: American Cultural Diplomacy in the Twentieth Century
by Richard T. Arndt

Imperial Footprints: Henry Morton Stanley's African Journeys
by James L. Newman

Paths Without Glory: Richard Francis Burton in Africa
by James L. Newman

Surviving Twice: Amerasian Children of the Vietnam War
by Trin Yarborough

THE MacARTHUR HIGHWAY & OTHER RELICS OF AMERICAN EMPIRE IN THE PHILIPPINES

JOSEPH P. McCALLUS

Potomac Books, Inc.
Washington, D.C.

Library of Congress Cataloging-in-Publication Data

McCallus, Joseph P.

The MacArthur Highway and other relics of American empire in the Philippines / Joseph P. McCallus. — 1st ed.

p. cm.

Includes bibliographical references and index.

ISBN 978-1-59797-497-4 (hardcover : alk. paper)

1. Philippines—Civilization—American influences. 2. Philippines—Colonial influence. 3. Americans—Philippines—History—20th century. 4. United States—Relations—Philippines. 5. Philippines—Relations—United States. 6. Philippines—History—1898–1946. 7. Philippines—Description and travel. 8. McCallus, Joseph P.—Travel—Philippines. I. Title.

DS685.M33 2010

959.9'03—dc22

2009039357

Printed in the United States of America on acid-free paper that meets the American National Standards Institute Z39-48 Standard.

Potomac Books, Inc.

22841 Quicksilver Drive

Dulles, Virginia 20166

First Edition

10 9 8 7 6 5 4 3 2 1

For my wife,
Juliet Adolfo McCallus

CONTENTS

PART 4. MANILA

PART 5. MAKATI

PREFACE

A t the turn of the twentieth century, the United States conquered and colonized the Philippines. Its stated goal was to build a modern nation by ripping down the foundation of European medievalism, that is, the legacy of Spanish colonialism. For almost fifty years the United States attempted to create a country and a people in the American image. The colonial relationship formally ended with Philippine independence in 1946, but the American influence did not. It still exists to varying degrees in the agencies the United States used to manage its colony.

In the following pages I will explore just what remains, both physically and conceptually, of the first American experiment in nation building. This is a broad task, and, admittedly, I could not address each aspect. The areas I do explore are politics, because the United States largely formed the system that now governs the nation; education, because the United States instituted an English-language public education system that remains a fair reflection of the U.S. public school system; religion, because the United States attempted to weaken the influence of Spanish Catholicism by exporting Protestant missionaries to the islands; and military presence, because despite the removal of U.S. bases in the Philippines, the country is still dependent on American aid and soldiers to fight communist and Muslim insurgencies. I also discuss the remains of American architecture, particularly in Manila, and I introduce a number of American expatriates I have known, persons who have lived for decades in the Philippines. These buildings and expatriates are evidence of the deep-rooted, ongoing influence of the United States in the daily lives of Filipinos.

In an effort to find these relics of American empire, I decided to retrace Douglas MacArthur's route from Leyte to Manila in the years 1944 and 1945. MacArthur's return to the Philippines is often shown to be a shining example of the moral goodness of the United States in that the man and his people kept their promise to their colonial subjects through fire and sacrifice. However, his "liberation" of the Philippines is one of World War II's great ironies. Vanquished and humiliated at Bataan, MacArthur did return to deliver the Philippines from the Japanese. But the cost in civilian lives and property was incredible. The nation's infrastructure was badly damaged. The city of Manila was destroyed, with 100,000 lives lost. Although most Filipinos celebrated MacArthur and the United States as liberators, not all did. In fact, for some Filipinos, the name of MacArthur and the country he symbolized came to denote devastation. MacArthur's liberation, like the American period itself, can be seen as a paradox, an ironic symbol constructed through the conflict of hope and disillusionment. Furthermore, it can and has been argued that the independence MacArthur brought in 1946 was largely a conditional one: the Philippine government could in no way act without Washington's approval, a constraint that some say continues today. Finally, and perhaps most poignantly, what arose from the ashes was not the great neoclassic republic that the American and Filipino leaders dreamed of in the 1920s and 1930s; rather, it was something less identifiable. Like the hasty rebuilding of postwar Manila, the Philippines has often been a confused, uncertain place during the sixty years since the general landed at Leyte beach. MacArthur's route, then, serves as both a symbolic and physical framework to view the remains of empire.

My journey took place in segments between the years 2004 and 2007, although some events I discuss, such as the Oakwood mutiny and my conversation with Eddie Woolbright, occurred earlier. I began the trek in Makati, the center of the megalopolis known as Metro Manila. From there I traveled to the Leyte-Samar area, where MacArthur landed in 1944 and where he had also served as a young officer in 1903. Moving back north, I toured the Lingayen beaches and then took the MacArthur Highway down through Luzon, stopping at major historical and contemporary points of interest such as Hacienda Luisita. The tour ends back in old Manila, a city that MacArthur loved but would find largely unrecognizable today.

A number of organizations and individuals helped me on my journey. Institutions such as the Filipinas Heritage Library in Makati, the American Historical Collection at the Ateneo de Manila University, and the MacArthur Memorial all provided me with invaluable resources and assistance. The Columbus State University's Simon Schwob Memorial Library, as always, was very supportive. In Manila, Leslie Murray of the Filipino-American Memorial Endowment was especially helpful, as was Edgar Krohn Jr., a founding member of the Memorare Manila 1945 organization. Merv Simpson was a critical component of the endeavor, and I am very thankful for his participation. John Melvin and the late Robert Robbins of the Elks Club Kapihan have always given friendship and assistance. In Pampanga, Lino Dizon of Tarlac State University and Rhonie Dela Cruz of the Bamban Historical Society gave much time and material. In the United States, Lia Scott Price supplied me with information and contacts concerning her ancestor, Walter Scott Price.

Finally, the title of this book may strike some as perplexing. I have often thought that the MacArthur Highway, at one time the major artery in central Luzon but now a road supplanted by more modern thoroughfares, stood as a symbol of the American era in the Philippines. In fact, it has become a relic of sorts. The term "relic" has several definitions. A relic can be a part of a dead holy person's body kept over the years in reverence; it is something essentially meaningless but holds strong connotations. A relic can also be an object or belief still existing but outmoded or obsolete, such as an old piece of technology. As I observed what remains of the American period, I was constantly reminded of these two definitions.

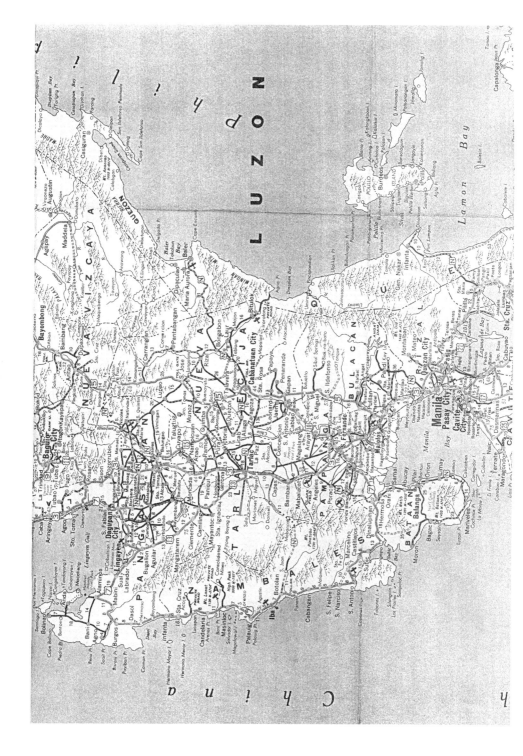

PART 1
MAKATI

1

THE FUTURE AND THE PAST

Bright and dazzling, the Ayala Center shopping complex stretches for several city blocks, a number of different malls interconnected. Within its superbly air-conditioned avenues, blue-eyed blondes stare and freckled, flaxen-haired children smile from giant posters in many stores. Pictures of colossal African American athletes provide an Olympian aura for the thousands of mostly young Asian faces flowing past. Girls in low-waist jeans and designer handbags glide by in schools. Young men sport super haircuts and wear shirts that pay homage to Old Navy and Abercrombie & Fitch. English competes well with Tagalog on the cell phones that almost everyone has pressed to their ears.

For an American visiting the Philippines for the first time, the Ayala Center provides the immediate comfort of recognizable icons. Yet, why should these American figures loom so large in a Philippine setting? Why are there so few Filipino faces in the advertisements? The answer is, of course, globalization, or what some call Americanization. Globalization is a palpable state of evolution, and here, as in so many other places around the world, the culture is a work in progress, an ongoing event that pulls and pricks at traditional identities.

Consider the mall's eateries. An Ilonggo restaurant serves up its ethnic fare, and there is a Jollibee, the nation's rice-instead-of-fries answer to American fast food. These restaurants, in turn, are challenged by a two-story McDonald's anchor, a Burger King anchor, a Chili's, a T.G.I. Friday's, a humongous KFC anchor, a Subway, and a Hard Rock Café, with presumably more American chains on the way. The coffee house, a cherished old Manila institution, has quite a few Filipino representatives in the Ayala; as to be expected, they are facing a terrific onslaught from Starbucks, Seattle's Best, and McCafé. The health minded can work off all this fare at the Gold's Gym.

Then there are the movies. The large Philippine film industry has an illustrious history dating back to the 1920s. The Ayala Center thus has multiple theaters. Perhaps it is not surprising that few contemporary Philippine films actually play in the Ayala or in most of the Metro Manila theaters or even most theaters in the country. As in many other parts of the world, Hollywood dominates film distribution here. Generations of Filipinos grow up watching Bruce Willis and Angelina Jolie successfully compete with their own culture's celluloid heroes.

There is much, then, that an American could identify with in Makati, for there is little difference between the Ayala Center and that of any mall in any town America, save perhaps for the frisking. Armed security guards regulate the complex's entrances. Customers must queue up by gender to be frisked or have an electronic wand go over them. Bags are sometimes opened and checked. The American visitor need not be alarmed by this process, however. At the Ayala, foreign-looking people, especially white people, are usually not frisked. In the Philippines, it is the foreigners who are trusted, which, given the country's history, is simply stunning.[1]

Filipinos are long used to dealing with foreigners. The indigenous peoples throughout the archipelago have encountered Arabian, Chinese, Spanish, British, American, and Japanese colonizers, all with an eye for plunder of some kind and all who have in some way left their mark on the islands. The Filipinos have had to live with being highly Westernized or, worse, the title of "little Americans," a barbed moniker assigned by other Asians. Through all the eras of colonization, Filipinos have shown the remarkable ability to take the foreign influence and adjust it to their own situation.

The original settlers of the islands came out of China more than fifteen thousand years ago, bringing with them hunting and planting skills. Roughly at the beginning of the Christian era arrived the Malays, an ancient people made up from many influences. In terms of race and temperament Filipinos share essential qualities with other Malays in the area. But a later migration of

Chinese, whose trade and piracy became extensive beginning roughly in the eleventh century, heavily influenced the local culture. Muslim Malays from nearby Sumatra and Java began to arrive and quickly spread their influence through Mindanao and the area that would become Manila. The Spanish in the sixteenth century brought with them Catholicism, architecture, progressive agricultural techniques, and a rough idea of nationhood. And finally the Americans came and brought English, public education, and democracy.

The successive conquests did much to temper the soul of the people, and, as in other colonized cultures, it did everything to establish a curious relationship between Filipinos and foreigners. Scholars such as Renato Constantino have noted that Filipinos suffer from the stereotypical colonial or now postcolonial identity: a warped sense of history, a national character either cloudy or xenophobic, and a near enslavement to Western ideas. Just as accurate, though, is that many Filipinos pragmatically see the advantage of foreigners as exemplified by the Filipinos' long-standing popular support of the former U.S. bases in Subic and Angeles City. On the other hand, a deep-seated, anti-Western nationalist movement has existed for centuries. This pulling and tugging between two basic forces has formed the Filipino approach to outsiders. In 1968, revered journalist Carmen Guerrero Nakpil wrote of foreigners:

> They are the best of friends, they are the worst of enemies; they are just and generous, they are tricky and tight with their money; they are so frank it is a pleasure to deal with them, they are so insincere one never knows where one stands; they are selfless and upright, they are only out for what they can get; they feel superior although there is no reason for it; they are physically and intellectually better endowed by nature, they are ugly and graceless and disease-prone; they are friendly and democratic, they are filthy snobs; they represent the best their countries have to offer, they are the dregs of their own societies; we like them, we can't stand them. The ambivalence of a love-hate relationship is indeed the average Filipino's attitude towards the foreigners in their midst.[2]

The center of gravity for most foreigners in the islands is Manila and, today,

Makati. Makati is the quintessentially planned postwar city. A small pueblo originally named San Pedro, Makati existed in the seventeenth century. The word "Makati" is from *mag kati na*, or "when the tide has receded." The Pasig River, which is on the city's northern border, is affected by the tides and commonly overruns its banks. In 1851 the powerful Roxas family purchased the pueblo. In 1914 it officially became Makati. Until the Second World War its only claim to distinction was that it was home to the American installation at Fort McKinley and that American John Canson built the Sta. Ana Cabaret, then considered to be the world's largest and raunchiest nightclub.[3]

The Second World War redefined the Philippines, Manila, and especially Makati. The prewar areas of commerce and residence, or the city of Manila proper, which included the Ermita and Malate areas, were the most heavily damaged. Indeed, they were essentially obliterated by Japanese incineration and U.S. artillery. The Battle of Manila left thousands unemployed. Power, water, and sanitation did not function. Inflation skyrocketed. Adding to the problem were the tens of thousands of migrants from the provinces who flooded the cities, hoping to escape the war's hardships and work for the U.S. Army. In 1941 the population of Manila was 450,000, and nearly 100,000 of its residents died in February and March 1945. But by 1948 the population swelled to two million.

Both long before and now more than sixty years after the war, a few powerful families have controlled the direction of Philippine culture and society. Today's Makati is the product of one such clan, the Zobel de Ayala family. Born in Manila the son of a Scottish father and a Filipina mestiza mother, Joseph R. McMicking married into the Zobel de Ayala clan (which had absorbed the Roxas family and thus owned most of Makati). McMicking's social circle included Gen. Douglas MacArthur, as well as Dwight and Mamie Eisenhower. A pilot in the fledgling Philippine Air Force, McMicking taught the future president how to fly. Because he was a citizen of the Commonwealth, he was inducted into the U.S. Army when the war broke out. As a colonel, he served on MacArthur's staff throughout the war, escaping to Australia with the general in 1942 and landing with him on Leyte two and a half years later. After the war, during which he suffered much personal loss, he went back to work with the Zobel de Ayala family.

In the immediate postwar years, McMicking looked at old Manila and saw the destruction, the human flotsam, and the one thousand hectares of open land owned by the Zobel de Ayala's known as Makati. He had a plan: he would make Makati into the ideal modern city. Over the next several years he laid out the modern city of Makati, one that would absorb the vast new arrivals from the provinces, who were squatters really. Makati was intended to be an urban center and a magnet to the affluent classes, where business would flourish. For McMicking, Makati was to be a holistic vision, a model city where social consciousness, industry, and wealth would burgeon. It was an ambitious undertaking.

In the 1950s Makati grew at an astonishing rate. Low-cost housing eased the plight of the workers, although much of it was thrown up quickly and in an ad hoc manner. Fifty years on, many of these areas can officially be called slums. Industry sprouted, with businesses forming nuclei in several places, and today, Makati's major street, Ayala Avenue, is the nation's financial center. The subdivisions sprang up one by one—Forbes Park, San Lorenzo, Bel-Air, Dasmarinas—housing the rich and nearly rich. Behind their high walls and armed checkpoints lies a world of quiet, tree-lined streets and manicured lawns; a world of servants and *ya-yas* (nannies); of investment brokers, CEOs, and ambassadors; of BMWs and Volvos; and, most importantly, of visas to other countries.

2

THE OAKWOOD MUTINY

Adjacent to the Ayala Center sits the large, twin-towered structure once known as the Oakwood Premier Ayala Centre Hotel. It is a pricey place, with a large international clientele. On July 27, 2003, it became the focal point of a unique aspect of Philippine political culture—the rebellion.

I awoke that Sunday morning to the roar of helicopters above my condo in Legaspi Village, several city blocks from the Ayala. One passed close overhead, shaking the room. Then another helicopter passed, after which the noise became constant. Having heard rumors of a coup in the making the night before, I quickly turned on the television and saw that soldiers had taken over the Oakwood building. A rebellion was taking place just down the street. I grabbed my camera and rushed out the door.

The streets were deserted, and a decided eeriness settled around me. When I arrived at the corner of Dela Rosa Street and Makati Avenue, a number of camouflaged troops and an armored personal carrier blocked my way. The soldiers carried M-16s. None wore helmets; a few sported soft hats. All, however, had white cloth bands around their left arms to distinguish them, as I was told later, from the mutinous troops inside the Oakwood. The soldiers looked very young. Some had plain, expressionless faces; others were obviously edgy.

I stood next to a twenty-something-year-old man holding several serious-looking cameras, and I assumed he worked for a branch of the Manila media.

We chatted. I asked him what was going on. He said that renegade soldiers were inside the Oakwood building, perhaps two hundred yards in front of us and right next to the Ayala mall complex. Perplexed, I asked why exactly soldiers would be taking over a condominium building. The young man shrugged his shoulders. "This is not serious. These guys [the soldiers near us] won't fire on the soldiers inside. No one will shoot at anybody. This is all a show. Nothing is going to happen here."

I asked for whom they were putting on the show, and he shrugged again. "Maybe the government. Maybe the media. Who knows? But if this was serious, they would not be trying to overthrow the government by taking over the mall on a Sunday morning."

I considered that point as I stood there, arms folded, waiting for something to happen. Presently soldiers escorted a group of people—men, women, and children—across Makati Avenue. These were the tenants and guests of the Oakwood, presumably released by the rebellious soldiers. Many appeared to be of either Indian or Chinese ancestry. A few seemed to be shaken, but most walked past us with calm reserve. Some had their luggage, but others did not. It became quiet again for a time.

Then a command was shouted, and a platoon suddenly began to march double-time in a single file along the side of a building, moving away from the Oakwood. They quickly disappeared around the corner. Both the cameraman and I took photos of this odd procedure, then looked at each other and shrugged. All was quiet.

After some time a civilian brought some bags of lunch for the soldiers in the personnel carrier. They ate rather leisurely. The sun rose higher. I noted the bizarre incongruity of seeing a machine of war with heavy guns sticking out of its turret parked in front of the shopping mall. Nothing happened.

For perhaps another hour I continued to watch nothing happen. Then, figuring I could run back in less than a couple minutes if something did, I went home. For most of the day I listened to helicopters roar overhead while watching the nearby spectacle on TV. Nothing happened.

The Oakwood Mutiny, as it was labeled, featured more than three hundred rebel soldiers led by two officers, Army Capt. Gerardo Gambala and Navy Lt. Antonio Trillanes IV of the Philippine Navy. They wanted to protest the alleged corruption in the administration of President Gloria Macapagal-Arroyo. If they assumed the people would rise up, they were sadly mistaken. No one offered them any support, and, after eighteen hours, they gave themselves up. Most of the leaders were court-martialed.[1]

But the story does not end here. Trillanes, while still in court hearings for his part in the rebellion four years later, ran for the Senate from his prison cell and won. On November 29, 2007, he and about twenty codefendants ran out of the courtroom where they were being tried and marched into the Peninsula Hotel. There they commandeered a luxury suite. After a six-hour standoff, the soldiers surrendered after elite army forces stormed the hotel. Two people were hurt, and the hotel suffered damage.

The nation has seen an extraordinary number of coup attempts since 1986, when a group of soldiers led by then–Secretary of Defense Juan Ponce Enrile and Gen. Fidel Ramos ousted President Ferdinand Marcos. There was a wave of coup attempts against President Corzaon Aquino between 1986 and 1989. One in 1987 killed fifty-three people, most of whom were civilian onlookers jeering at the rebels. Another in December 1989 nearly succeeded until the United States directly intervened and sent unarmed fighter aircraft to buzz rebel-held air bases. Ninety-nine people died and nearly six hundred were wounded. In 2001 a second popular uprising took out then-President Joseph "Erap" Estrada and placed Gloria Arroyo, daughter of former president Diosdado Macapagal, in the presidential seat. Rebellion has also marked her tenure. In February 2006 Arroyo declared a state of emergency after proclaiming she had foiled a coup plot hatched by Estrada supporters and former members of the Reform the Armed Forces Movement (RAM), the group that helped throw out Marcos. In other words, she was not going to be thrown out of office in the manner in which she gained office. Couple these attempts with a nearly forty-year-old communist insurgency and a protracted Muslim secessionist movement, and one might get the impression that the Philippine democracy, a form inspired and built upon the U.S. model, is being torn apart.

It is always interesting to speculate on the condition of Philippine democracy, particularly its development from colonial beginnings. In 2003 President George W. Bush, during a brief visit to bolster President Arroyo in Manila, cited the Philippines as a vibrant democracy, meaning an American type of democracy. In nearly every way, it is. The nation has a presidency, a Senate, a House of Representatives, and a Supreme Court. Its first constitution was virtually a carbon copy of the American Constitution. And while often violent and questionable, elections are popular and have large turnouts.

But how much of Thomas Jefferson's ideal is left, or was ever present, in Manila? It has been argued that in the decade after the colonial conquest, the United States built a democracy by wooing the Philippine elite class so that the masses would not rise up and revolt.[2] The result has been a century-old cacique (local political bosses') system that allows for landed families and wealthy upstarts to dominate the nation. The military does not stand divorced from that system. In the sixty-odd years since Philippine independence, the nation has endured an almost unbroken string of corruption cases, murdered politicians, a long period of martial law and ensuing dictatorship, popular uprisings, two deposed presidents, and a seemingly unending number of military coup attempts. All of this turmoil has occurred in what has been called America's showplace of democracy.

The resulting consequences are somewhat baffling. The country still marches on, regularly holding elections at all levels. With a few exceptions, lengthy jail time for corruption charges or coup attempts is rare. Deposed presidents have had to suffer little: Marcos was allowed to flee and live in splendor in Hawaii until he died; his wife, Imelda, cleared of racketeering charges in the United States, came home to run for president twice and eventually became a congresswoman from Leyte. Estrada spent a number of years under house arrest in his Manila mansion until receiving a full pardon from Arroyo in 2007. It seemed that the same people merely juggled power for temporary intervals. Thinking about why a group of military officers would valiantly attempt to take over a luxury condominium building, I could not help but remember the photographer's comment about it being all for show.

3

THE ELKS CLUB

Close to the Peninsula Hotel and right next to the Ayala shopping district sits the Corinthian Plaza, an attractive seven-story office building. It is ably guarded out front by busts of Julius Caesar and Aphrodite, both of whom sit just behind a revolving Rolex wristwatch streetlight. The lobby's marble floors shine. Against one wall stands a highly polished grandfather clock. To its right a smiling young woman usually issues a "Good morning, sir," and enters visitors' names in a book. There are giant framed prints of ancient Rome and of American yachts. Almost unnoticeable in opposite corners are small pictures of Lapu-Lapu, the Visayan chieftain, who defeated and killed Spanish explorer Ferdinand Magellan, and José Rizal, the late-nineteenth-century Filipino patriot, who was arrested and executed by the Spanish.

The second floor holds the American Chamber of Commerce in the Philippines, now brightly referred to as AmCham Philippines. According to its purpose statement, AmCham Philippines is there to serve the needs of U.S. businesses by acting as a conduit between the two countries. There is a security camera outside its locked doors, an aftereffect of 9/11. It is a busy office, and it has been for some time. The chamber was established in 1902 as the Manila Coffee Round Table—by a small group of American entrepreneurs who met regularly for coffee—and has seen wars, dictators, and coups come and go. For a century a round table—the original round table for the 1902 group—has been part of the Chamber's offices, despite being temporarily lost during World War II. It was apparently found in a Sta. Ana warehouse and now sits in the office.

Not much is known about the men who created and sustained the round table. Some of their pictures hang on the office walls, rows of black-and-white eight-by-ten-inch photos that probably do not capture the color of their lives. But actual scholarship or even written accounts about them are slim. There is, of course, the AmCham *Journal*, which goes back nearly to the beginning. Tom Carter, the AmCham historian who was instrumental in bringing the round table back to the AmCham office, recorded vignettes of businesses and businessmen here. Lewis E. Gleeck Jr., a former State Department officer who retired in the Philippines, wrote a number of books in the 1970s that documented the careers of some prewar American expatriates. American historian Michael Onorato captured some of their voices in oral histories. What they thought of themselves was perhaps presented best by Walter Robb. In 1939, Robb, an American teacher who settled in the country, wrote a flowery apotheosis to the American in the Philippines with a book titled *The Filipinos*. Consistently using a cowboy metaphor, he described these prewar businessmen and other Americans:

> Filipinos were accustomed enough to dealing with strangers, but these rugged and untiring pioneers were a new experience for them. On their part the Americans displayed a remarkable adaptability; without destroying what existed, they set to building upon it and to patterning for the Philippines a government of the American type that was effective against a Latin background. . . . The American businessman in the Philippines both stimulated and was stimulated by it. From the outset he grew in stature of business capacity. His associates demanded leadership of him, he responded with pioneer courage . . . his success, derived from his adaptability to circumstances he could not set aside, repeats the old idealization of the border and its material blessings waiting only the alchemy of the bold hand of the pioneer. . . . The American community in the Philippines has profoundly influenced society in the islands, always in the direction of democracy. . . . All that Americans took hold of, which in fact was everything, they bettered.[1]

There have been differing views of Americans in the islands. In contrast to the above, Florence Horn's 1940 book, *Orphans of the Pacific*, documented

Americans, and especially the Manila business community, in quite another way. She described the chamber and its members as "knights of the round table," a plain reference to the chamber's table and a metaphoric swipe at what she perceived as American pretentiousness. Her images have irked Americans in the Philippines ever since. For example, on the eve of war and the end of the American era, her portrait of Sam Gauches, a prewar luminary in the business community, is typically acidic:

> His speeches typify the old-timer's attitude. Gauches reminds the natives and anyone who will listen to his pontifications what a noble and splendid work the American businessmen have done in and for the Philippines; how they have opened up and developed the country; how many jobs they have created. After listening to Gauches, one gets, dimly, the impression that he and the other old boys got their patent of nobility direct from Almighty God. They labored hard for much more than six days, and at last 7,091 islands rose up out of the Pacific Ocean. On those islands were put some men who are now slowly being molded into the ways and habits of Americans. In all the dreary talk about the blessings brought by American business, the Filipino is given a patronizing pat on the head: "You too, my good fellow, have progressed well these forty years."[2]

After more than sixty years, one does not know whether Horn was an objective observer or just a caustic onlooker with some type of ax to grind. But her depiction of the American old-timer in Manila does correspond to the typical caricature of the Westerner in Asia—be it Singapore or India—persons whom Carlos Romulo, the Philippine reporter turned general turned diplomat, called "the triumph of the arrogant mediocre."[3] As for Robb, his portrait reflects precisely what overseas Americans thought of themselves before the war—pioneers on a Pacific prairie, rugged, hard working, and moral. It probably does not matter that both writers pour more heat than light on the subject, and, in any event, these Americans are long gone, ghosts of America's short-lived colonial era.

On Friday mornings, descendants of that era, however, can usually be found haunting the seventh floor of the Corinthian Plaza. Here is the Elks Club. The Manila branch is the only one outside the United States, and it has been in operation since 1902. Its membership, once in the thousands, is now so low it may not be sustainable. Friday mornings are the *kapihan* (coffee break) morning. This informal assembly, which has been meeting since 1990, evolved more or less from the original coffee club of a century before.[4] The members gather at seven thirty to discuss all things Philippine, business, American politics, and so on. There is a six-dollar donation fee for each meeting. The collection goes to a number of different charities, including the Philippine-American Guardian Association, which takes care of Amerasian children abandoned by American servicemen in the Olongapo and Angeles areas. Some of the money goes to the American Association of the Philippines, a half-century-old group that assists down-on-their-luck Americans in the Philippines. Several years ago, for example, they lobbied for and eventually won an early release for two American women convicted of drug smuggling. The association is also the trust for the American Historical Collection, a collection of materials from the American period that is housed in the Rizal Library at the Ateneo de Manila University.

In a dark, tastefully paneled room, enhanced by prints of nineteenth-century American art of the Old West, sits a small group of old men. Among them is Rob Robbins, in his late eighties, who has been here since 1972. He and his Filipina wife of thirty years produce high-quality baby clothes for export, but now, competing against the low wages of China and Vietnam, his business is off 50 percent. He walks pretty slowly these days (his wife finally convinced him to buy a cane), and you might not guess that in his military service he was highly decorated for piloting Allied ships into Marseille's harbor in 1944. There is John Melvin, in his mid-seventies, who owns an agricultural equipment company and manages an organization that provides schoolbooks for needy children. He came here during Eisenhower's first term. Sitting there also is a man who, with his wife, has for decades directed a home for severely handicapped children, many of whom are adopted by couples in the United States. Another is a former CEO of a company that predates World War II.

The kapihan meetings are pretty much the same each week: collecting funds to be used for the various projects, distributing handouts on health (especially geriatric) matters, and engaging in *tsismis* (gossip) about people they know, the friendly banter between Republicans and (the highly outnumbered) Democrats, and the usual cryptic discussion of Philippine business prospects. Today the Elks take up the fact that FedEx and Ford are both shutting down their Philippine operations and moving to China. It makes sense, they agree; how can anyone do business with the Philippine government hamstring-ing everything one does? They discuss the matter of the multinational call centers and their effect on Makati. And someone asks, Just what are all of these Koreans doing here? Some theorize the new migrants have small im-port shops, some think gangs, and others posit prostitution. None of the men seem to like the trend, but no one seemed to know what it was about, either. Then this meeting breaks up pretty in much the same manner as last week's: the old men shuffle out the door, with some walking to their offices down the street and others folding themselves into cars and heading off to other parts of Makati. One man, Merv Simpson, always stays behind; he is the manager the Corinthian Plaza.

Wearing a simply embroidered *barong* (translucent shirt) and slacks, this Westerner in the tropics now sat quietly at a table in the restaurant portion of the Elks Club. At eighty-three, Simpson has collected quite a few memories. It is seldom that a common man is historically significant, but Simpson is im-portant in that he is both a prewar and postwar expatriate, a cultural bridge within what is left of the American community. Simpson was born in 1921 in Hawaii. His father was an engineer who helped design sugar plantations in Hawaii and the Philippines. After his parents divorced early in his life, Simpson came to the Philippines with his then-remarried mother. His stepfather, John McFie, was a prominent American attorney in Manila. Simpson grew up in a typical expat American home of the time, with servants, a cook, a driver, and a nanny, on then-fashionable Dewey Boulevard (now Roxas Boulevard). He matriculated at the American School (now the International School). Every student and teacher was a Westerner. There he studied English, Spanish, biol-ogy, math, Latin, French, and American and world history, and nothing about the country in which he was living. For fun he and his friends went to the expat clubs of the day, especially the Polo Club. There were no Filipinos in the club, save for very high-profile personalities and, of course, the help. He remembers life in the 1930s:

> I think the Filipinos I got to know best before the war were the driver and a houseboy. We had a cook and a Chinese *ahma*. I didn't know any Filipino girls—too bad.
>
> Socially, there was not much [racial] interaction, but there were a lot of Filipino employees and Filipino companies. Mainly, they were Spanish companies. There were more Spanish people here at that time. Spanish was a very common language. A much stronger Spanish influence. I took Spanish in school before the war. It was a regular class; you had to take Spanish. I can still speak a reasonable amount of garden variety Spanish. But after the war gradually the Spanish influence faded. After that it was not a requirement to take Spanish anymore.
>
> [At home] we had no air conditioning. We all slept under mosquito nets. We were real careful when we got in at night that there weren't any mosquitoes inside. We had malaria and dengue fever. My brother got dengue but recovered. There were a lot more bugs around. We had to look in our shoes in the morning to see if there were any cockroaches there.
>
> Before the war we didn't play with Filipino kids or associate with them very much. It wasn't any snobbish thing; we just didn't do it.
>
> It was a sheltered life. I don't remember any crime, although there must have been. Of course, we didn't go walking around at nighttime. I didn't go down to Tondo. Even at that time Tondo was a good place to stay away from—a lot of gangs.
>
> It was pretty sheltered. We went to the American School. No Filipino kids [but some] mestizos. We had a driver who would take us everywhere. We did not talk to the driver at any time. We would get up in the morning and the cook would cook us an American breakfast. No Filipino food. The driver would take us to school even though it was not very far.
>
> School started at 7:30. It was pretty intense. School was only from 7:30 to 12:30. The driver would pick us up and take us home. My stepfather, who we called Uncle John, would come home for lunch, and then

everybody would take a nap. Except I didn't take a nap. I would do my homework, which was a lot of homework, too. After that we would just go out and play with the kids. I'd play baseball and, later, golf. We didn't have any Filipino friends—all expats.

It was a peaceful life. We had parties, or at least my parents had parties, but nobody got bombed, at least as I can remember.

My stepfather did very well; he was a very successful lawyer here. We weren't rich, but I never had to worry about money. I'd ask my mother—I'd want to go to the Polo Club, it would be Saturday morning—so she'd give me a peso. That was big dough back then. I'd take a taxi out there. The taxi would be about twenty centavos. At the Polo Club we used to swim, badminton, bowling, tennis—it was a nice life. We would just sign [for the bill], and my stepfather got really mad at me one time because one month I think I signed for fifteen pesos worth, and he was outraged I spent so much money. He banned me from the Club for three months.

[Through my parents and golfing] I met [MacArthur's chief of staff] Richard Sutherland. In fact, I beat him in the semi-finals of the Philippine Amateurs. He later became MacArthur's chief. I met MacArthur, too, one time. It was just a "hello sonny," that sort of thing. We were in the Manila Hotel, and I was with my parents. They knew MacArthur, and he shook hands with me: "hello sonny." He was impressive. Even at that time everyone [in the Philippines] knew of MacArthur. He wasn't the kind of guy to hide under anything.

Manila was very small. [For the American] there was Tom's Dixie Kitchen. There was the Santa Ana dance hall. That was the place to go but I never went there. We went to parties for young people in Ermita.

There were good relations between us and the servants. In fact, I was pretty lucky. Nobody [in the house] seemed to get mad. My stepfather would get a little pissed off once in a while, but no fights. We had no problems with the servants. They spoke English. Presumably they were well paid. Everything was pretty peaceful.[5]

Simpson's narrative reflects the American lifestyle in Manila during the

1920s and 1930s, a story filled with serenity, goodness, and de facto segrega-tion. But life for Simpson would soon change drastically. He graduated from the American School in 1939, the year he became the amateur golf champion of the Philippines. After a short stint at the University of Hawaii, he enrolled in the College of William & Mary. Then came the attack on Pearl Harbor. Simpson finished his degree and enlisted in the U.S. Army. He was accepted into the Air Corps and then trained as a navigator. In 1945 he was stationed on Guam, where he took off fourteen times in a B-29 for bombing runs over Japan. They were long flights, and Simpson would forever wonder why the Japanese never seemed to challenge the planes. He chuckled as he remem-bered eating six eggs after each mission.

During the time Simpson was in school and the service, his parents were interned with other Westerners at the Santo Tomas camp in Manila. At first, the experience for these people was tolerable. By 1944, however, food short-ages and the turn in the war made the Japanese guards irritable. Their mood was exacerbated when MacArthur landed in Leyte in October and then in Luzon in January 1945. He drove down from Lingayen to Manila, and the Western internees in Santo Tomas were rescued on February 3.

On February 7, 1945, General MacArthur, with Japanese troops still fighting in different areas of the city, paid a visit to the liberated Santo Tomas camp, shaking hands with the emaciated survivors and recognizing a few pre-war faces. Hours after MacArthur left, a Japanese shell hit one of the buildings at Santo Tomas. Merv Simpson's stepfather, John McFie, was killed.

After the war was over, Simpson returned to California and married a local girl in 1946. His mother, who survived the war in Santo Tomas, died in 1950. That year his father offered him a job in his acetylene business, and Simpson and his wife moved back to Manila. The Philippines had changed: it was now an independent nation. Manila had changed: in spite of the com-plete destruction of large parts of the city and a hundred thousand inhabitants killed, its population had grown to four times its prewar size. The Filipinos had changed: they had just undergone a catastrophe and were now trying to recover. The American community had changed: with their numbers mark-edly diminished, they now found themselves in a country where their once-sheltered, peaceful life had become tinged with social anxiety. And Simpson had changed: he had left a teenager and had returned to the Philippines as an adult war veteran. In the midst of a wrecked Manila, Simpson started a career. His marriage, like those of many Westerners in the Philippines, did not survive. He went on to marry one of the most famous women in the country, television personality Lelia Benitez.

Despite the wreckage that was Manila, both money and fun were to be had there. The Americans who came were more aggressively entrepreneurial, more seasoned, equipped with a cynicism-fueled drive that immediate post-war veterans felt. In this jumbled world of destroyed buildings and unlimited opportunity, Simpson made his mark. He earned some nice money and spent it in places such as the Elks Club, the Polo Club, and the much-venerated Swiss Inn restaurant and on Basque jai alai matches and Manila horse races. Both games, he claims with a laugh, were "crooked."

But if the American population had changed in the postwar period so did its host. Simpson, echoing a commonly held opinion, felt that the Japanese occupation had scarred the Filipino psyche. With the nation's independence in 1946 came a crass commercialism and well-entrenched corruption. A popular communist movement, the Hukbalahaps, or Huks, threatened the new nation in the early 1950s until, according to Simpson, his wife's sister's husband, Napoleon Valeriano, directed the operation to wipe them out. The vein of corruption within Philippine postwar society reached its zenith (but did not end) with President Ferdinand Marcos, whose fourteen years of martial law and dictatorial rule traumatized the land perhaps worse than the Japanese had. Only with his overthrow in 1986 could the nation really begin to realize the fruits of independence.

Simpson has seen it all, from the end of the American commonwealth period, through the war, through fifty years of independence. He sat, relaxed. Around us one or two waiters walked by, but we were the only two customers in the Elks this morning. Indeed, it is doubtful that the Elks Club gets much in the way of business anymore. I asked Simpson if he would make his career in the Philippines again.

> If I were thirty years old and starting a career I would not come to the
> Philippines; no, not now. The general financial structure here makes it

hard to get rich. It would be easier in the United States. I have had a whole bunch of American friends here who have had to go back to the United States. Filipino companies don't pay very well. There is no such thing as all the perks you get in the United States, like insurance. It's tough. Tougher if you're a girl. It's hard for a girl to do anything here except work in a bar.

The expat population has changed. Like Caltex: in the Fifties they had about sixty American guys on the payroll. Now maybe one, two. The Philippine guys have gotten a lot sharper and much cheaper.

But if you do get something going here, in some ways it's much better. There is very little pressure here. You don't have to do anything when you go home after work [because you have cooks and servants]; in the U.S. you are doing everything. Here it is easier to get together with your friends. It's cheaper, too.

On the whole, it's more fun. I have been very well off here and pretty poor. Both ways. But I am sure I have had more fun [here than] if I would have been back in the States. Whether the object of life is to have fun or not I don't know, but I think it's pretty important.

And, of course, if you have been in a place a long time you make a lot of good friends, which [in my case] are dropping like flies.[6]

Earlier at the kapihan, Merv Simpson had revealed that he had a dilemma. The board of the Corinthian Plaza is studying the possibility of bringing in a professional management company to run the building. If that happens, Simpson will most assuredly lose his job. What would he do then? Others at the table tendered suggestions. Most offered that going back to the United States with his wife would be the best thing. He does have wonderful adult children living there, and his Filipina wife, who is younger, could find work. People at the table discussed how much money a person can get by on in the States. Simpson looked concerned and asked where could an eighty-three-year-old man get a job in the United States. There was an awkward silence.

The kapihan is not what it once was. Friday's meeting pulled only five members. It was the same as last Friday and pretty much the trend for the past few years. Members are worried because the low turnout means less money to donate to American prisoners in Philippine jails and abandoned Amerasian children. Amid the old Western prints and the dark wooden walls, various remedies are discussed, and some sound promising. But the truth is the club is dying, not because of its activities, but because there are few Americans like these men in the Philippines anymore.

These men are, in no uncertain terms, cultural artifacts. Relics. You will not come across them ever again. They are, sometimes literally, sometimes philosophically, the descendants of the Americans who came and stayed in the Philippines during the years before MacArthur arrived. Today, the American one would meet on a Manila street is more than likely to be either a tourist or a multinational worker. Neither will stay in the country long, and neither will offer any real role in its development. The case of multinational workers is especially sour, given the lives and contributions of their predecessors like Simpson. Inside the trendy bars and clubs of Makati, they breezily call themselves expats, but this label is not appropriate. More fitting is the simple term "technocrats," which describes those who work in a global environment. Unlike the men at the kapihan, they will not put down roots in the Philippines or the next country they will live in or even in the one after that. They will stay perhaps two years at the most and then head off somewhere else. As is the case with most Americans and other Westerners here, they will live in a closed, well-guarded subdivision or high-rise in Makati, associating only with others of their kind; ironically, their lifestyle resembles that of the early colonialists. But the newcomers will not marry into the culture. They will sacrifice nothing; they will contribute nothing. They will leave nothing to remember them by.

Manila, and indeed the nation, just as other former colonial places, often wears its past as an uncomfortable uniform. Despite the open embrace of all things American as one sees in the mall and the movies, on TV, and through iPods, there are plenty of sensitive points. While many Filipinos have relatives in the United States and many more want to live there, some Filipinos, especially the nationalists, are suspicious of America. They feel America is not to be trusted, that America acts only in its own interests, and that America does not keep its word. To be sure, this is a minority viewpoint, but it is there and it is vocal.

Sewn on this nation's uniform is a patch that cannot be stripped off—the face of an American, Douglas MacArthur. For the young he is just a part of the historical landscape, a name in a history book, a face sometimes seen on a float during a fiesta, or even a character in a story told by the grandparents. There is no need to really understand his significance. For the older Filipino he is an icon and, more importantly, a bridge to a time of suffering, heroism, and pride. But he is also a connection to more confusing concepts, such as colonialism. It was a time when, as the old, old folks say, Filipinos did not run their own country, and there was discipline in both the streets and the home.

In many ways to understand MacArthur is to understand America's role in the Philippines. He was surely representative of the American colonial ideal, if not of its practice: a neoclassical patrician, he was progressive, generous, loyal. And his postwar abandonment of the Philippines in many ways mirrors the policies of the United States. A major key, then, to comprehending the present significance of America in the Philippines is to look backward to MacArthur, to the cataclysm that enveloped him and wrote his name forever in history.

MacArthur, the Elks Club, Merv Simpson—all fading from memory and representing a cultural era now nearly ended. To reach some appreciation of the surviving American cultural influence here, I decided I would retrace MacArthur's route during his 1944–45 liberation of the Philippines. I would begin in the Leyte-Samar area and then work my way down from Lingayen to Manila. I would look for all vestiges of America, large and small, physical and conceptual. The ghost of MacArthur would be the ghost of America.

PART 2
LEYTE AND SAMAR

4

THE RETURN

I t was shame that drove MacArthur to Leyte. He carried the shame of
losing his troops on the same island that his father had conquered years
before, the shame of his inglorious nickname "Dugout Doug" for his
failure to show himself in battle, the shame of his clandestine escape from
Corregidor, the shame of leaving his men to a hellish fate, and the shame of
Bataan, still the worst defeat in American military history. MacArthur's landing at Red Beach on Leyte, considered one of the high points of World War
II, was the culmination of his drive north from Australia as he defeated the
Japanese on island after island, the Philippines forever in his mind. At Leyte,
on October 20, 1944, MacArthur satisfied his promise to the Philippine peo-
ple and to himself that he would return. He had redeemed himself.

Since 1935 MacArthur had been charged with building the Armed
Forces of the Philippines (AFP) and became a field marshal for the Philippine
commonwealth, the first and only U.S. officer to hold the rank. In the summer of 1941 he was reinstated into the U.S. Army, never completing his
job of building the Philippine Army. After the attack on Pearl Harbor that
December and the subsequent Japanese invasion of the islands at Lingayen
and other points, as commander of the U.S. Armed Forces in the Far East,
MacArthur enacted the prewar tactic of War Plan Orange, which called for
the retreat into the Bataan Peninsula with enough provisions to wait out the
assumed siege until supplies could be sent. What followed was one of the epic
struggles in Philippine-American history. A force of about eighty thousand

27

Filipino and U.S. troops were backed into a mountainous jungle area perfectly formed for a defensive stand. However, through a series of blunders and poor judgment, these troops received little in the way of food or medicine. Washington officials never seriously contemplated sending help from the United States, largely because the Pacific Fleet, which was to come to their rescue, had been destroyed at Pearl Harbor. MacArthur, his family, President Quezon, and advisers escaped to the well-stocked and fortified Corregidor Island. During the three months of the battle for Bataan, MacArthur visited his starving troops but once. The beleaguered men on Bataan soon began singing a ditty to the tune of "The Battle Hymn of the Republic" named "Dugout Doug." Its chorus went:

> *Dugout Doug, come out from hiding*
> *Dugout Doug, come out from hiding*
> *Send to Franklin the glad tidings*
> *That his troops go starving on!*[1]

The Filipino and American forces fought on, often with great success, but the hunger continued unabated. Without outside help the outcome was certain. In early March 1942 Roosevelt ordered MacArthur to Australia. Under the cover of night, the general, his family, and his staff left in four PT boats for Mindanao, where they would take a plane to Melbourne. The men and women left on the islands would, like those on Bataan, become casualties or be taken prisoner.

In Australia MacArthur had assumed he would quickly be given forces to retake the Philippines; rather, the buildup of the attack army took another year. Then, getting back to the Philippines was no easy feat. MacArthur had to fight his way up from New Guinea, using the famous tactic of leapfrogging the Japanese outposts and cutting them off from their supply lines. Odd-sounding names like Truk and Tinian became burned into the nation's lexicon as great American victories. The tide seemingly had turned, and plans were being drawn up to deliver the deathblow to Japan. The best route, according to the U.S. Navy, was to attack and take Formosa, bypassing the Philippines. MacArthur was aghast at the plan, and he opposed it, saying it was a U.S.

obligation to free the Philippines. In July 1944 President Roosevelt and the Joint Chiefs of Staff held a meeting in Hawaii with MacArthur and his navy counterpart, Adm. Chester Nimitz. There was much to be said about the navy's plan to take Formosa: it would cut vital communication lines between Japanese-occupied China and Tokyo and would put U.S. troops and airplanes much closer to Japan and not Luzon. When the Formosa plan's proponents finished presenting their case to Roosevelt, MacArthur stood up. In a magnificent display of rhetorical prowess, he argued that the Philippines had to be retaken on the grounds that America did not abandon its allies. It was a moral duty to liberate the Philippines. Ultimately, MacArthur was allowed to keep the promise he had made in Australia in 1942.[2]

In September 1944 Leyte was selected as the entry point to the Philippines for a number of reasons, the most important being that its central location would give the landing force access to the belly of Luzon as well as all of the Visayas. At 2,785 square miles, it is the eighth largest island in the Philippines. Its shape has been compared to a molar tooth. A rugged, mountainous island with thick jungles, Leyte does have two large valleys—the Leyte in the east and the Ormoc in the northwest—that agriculturally serve the population. The control of these two valleys and their surrounding mountains were essential in the minds of U.S. war planners. The people were mostly of Waray stock, with a strong Chinese presence. In 1939, it was reported that there were fifty-six Americans living on Leyte and seventy-three Japanese.

Most appealing to U.S. military planners were the island's beaches. The shoreline along Leyte Gulf on the eastern side of Leyte held several beaches with firm sand, which was perfect for landing craft. Two main areas were especially attractive: the beaches around the city of Palo, just south of Tacloban, and the city of Dulag, twenty-odd miles south of Palo. Behind these beaches ran the north–south Highway 1, one of the island's few roads. Just below Palo, Highway 1 intersected with Highway 2, which ran west into the Leyte Valley. Moreover, these eastern beaches sat on Leyte Gulf, which offered superb anchorage for all types of vessels. The planners' strategy was fairly simple: take the beaches, jump on the highways, and move into the two valleys.

Since their invasion in 1942, the Japanese had kept relatively few soldiers on Leyte. In fact, in the mountainous southern portion of the island, there were few or no Japanese at all. But in early 1944, with Gen. Tomoyuki Yamashita (the Tiger of Malaya) now in command, the Japanese force was greatly enhanced, and the United States estimated that perhaps twenty thousand troops were there in October. With the increased number of Japanese came a more aggressive rule, including the commandeering of farm products. Relations between the Japanese and Filipinos, never good, became even more strained, and a resistance movement, which had formed in 1942 (but had been divided and ineffectual), began to assert itself. The movement was in part the product of U.S. intelligence.

The landing at Leyte was in no small way prepared by an American spy, whose story is the stuff of legend. Charles A. "Chick" Parsons came to Manila in 1922 as a young man seeking his fortune.[3] Unfortunately, he had no profession. He finally found both a vocation and wealth, first by becoming Gov.-Gen. Leonard Wood's stenographer, and then by working as a broker, a businessman, and an executive of a shipping company. He also became a prominent polo-playing Manila socialite, deeply involved in the development of Philippine baseball. Along the way he became an officer in the U.S. Naval Reserve. Unlike most American businessmen of the time, he knew well the country's topography, spoke Tagalog and a number of provincial dialects, and held dual Philippine-American citizenship. When Manila fell in January 1942, he used his superb Spanish to convince the Japanese that he was a Panamanian diplomat. This ruse was partly true: Panama, a neutral country, had made him an honorary consul after he helped register ships for that country. He even raised the Panamanian flag in front of his house. The Japanese considered him a neutral citizen, and Parsons was able to travel occupied Manila at will, with his eyes and ears wide open, mentally recording what he saw and heard. Eventually, however, he was arrested by the Japanese military police, the *Kempeitai*, and imprisoned in the old Spanish dungeon at Fort Santiago. After several months and through the assistance of a Swedish friend, he was released and deported with his family. In June 1942 the Parsons safely made it back to the United States.

The U.S. military quizzed Parsons, now a lieutenant commander, on the situation in the Philippines. The military liked what he had to say and decided that he should report to MacArthur in Australia, which he did in early

1943. After meeting with MacArthur, the swashbuckling Parsons was ordered to return to the Philippines as a spy. With supreme confidence and the code name Q-10, Parsons began his espionage career with a submarine landing in Mindanao, where he legitimized the command of Wendell W. Fertig, a contentious, peculiar American prewar engineer, who led a large force of irregulars. Later, Parsons traveled to Leyte, where he made contact with Col. Ruperto K. Kangleon, the island's guerrilla leader. He used Kangleon to settle the petty but damaging squabbles between guerrilla units in Leyte and Samar. Kangleon also went on to set up the radio network on Leyte. Parsons was instrumental in establishing coast-watching activities in the Visayas, and he eventually became the main link between its underground movement and MacArthur.

His most important mission occurred later that year. Parsons returned in a PBY flying boat on October 10, 1944, landing on a beach south of Tacloban. The once resplendent Manila sportsman had traded his polo breeches for tattered trousers, an old shirt, and a straw hat and sported a four-week-old beard. He arrived without shoes or a gun. He also carried a fifty-thousand-dollar price on his head, offered by the Kempeitai. Traveling in and around Tacloban, he observed the absence of underwater obstacles at the designated landing beaches, troop emplacements in the inland hills, and, perhaps most importantly, the lack of Japanese units in Tacloban. In fact, Parsons convinced U.S. planners to spare the city of Tacloban, which the preinvasion design had designated for complete destruction because of an assumed large enemy garrison. Parson put out the word to local guerrillas that a large bombardment was to occur soon and that local residents must evacuate. He was successful: not one Filipino died during the bombardment, and Tacloban suffered no damage during the invasion.

The U.S. flotilla, some seven hundred ships, moved into position around 11:00 p.m. on October 19. It had been a starless, sweaty, restless night. Black cloths had been hung over cabin lamps, and portholes had been blacked out. Many men had swapped the stifling bunks below for the sticky night air topside. Just after dawn the next morning, the American troops readied themselves for the attack. They were anxious, understandably, but they were eager as well. Most of them thought of the heroism and sacrifice of Bataan, by 1944 an anthemic image as well as a Hollywood movie. They all had heard of the fanfare, the champagne, and the kisses given to the troops who liberated Paris. Now they saw themselves as the liberators of the Philippines. It would be their day of headlines.

The sun broke over heavy clouds, the brief coolness giving way to the dull, oppressive heat of the Visayas. From various positions on the ships, soldiers and sailors could see the dark, misty mountainous island in the west, Leyte. They had finished their breakfast of steak and eggs, the traditional meal for those who were about to land on an enemy's beach. Throughout the ships, the soldiers knew this assault marked the return of MacArthur. They appreciated thoroughly that they were in the crux of a historical moment, for they were the keepers of his promise.

Searchlights blinked, and flags of all colors and designs began to wave. Small boats circled and jockeyed for various positions around larger ships. The constant roar of engines filled the ears of men who gazed at the now visible beach, postcard perfect with swaying palms and a green mountain behind them. Units were formed on deck. Chaplains said the final words. On some of the ships, loudspeakers were playing popular songs. Overhead, navy planes roared off to numerous locations in and around Leyte. Then it began: the troops began the terrifying climb down the Jacob's ladders fifty feet into the bobbing landing craft.

A survivor and escapee from Corregidor and aide to President Sergio Osmeña, Carlos P. Romulo was on the troop carrier *John Land* that morning. Romulo remembered seeing the men "going over the side, some of them grinned their clear young grins at me and flipped thumbs up. 'For Bataan!' . . . The whole screaming panorama beyond our deck was reprisal for Bataan."[4]

The actual invasion began as a virtual textbook exercise. The weather was perfect. The seas calm. The U.S. troops would land at color-coded beaches: to the north it was white near San Jose and red at Palo; orange, blue, violet, and yellow at Dulag to the south. At 8:00 a.m. three old battleships—the USS *Mississippi* and two veterans of Pearl Harbor, the USS *Maryland* and the USS *West Virginia*—opened fire with high-capacity explosives on the Red Beach and Hill 522, which towered a few miles behind the beach. Cruisers and destroyers joined in the bombardment. For an hour and a half, the shelling was frenzied. Then it suddenly stopped, and an eerie silence enveloped the scene. At 9:45 the transport ships, which had been moving into their assigned positions, began to move toward the beach. For the men aboard, it was a relief. The constant circling and the fumes from the engines had made many sick.

At first, it was an easy landing. No surf, no mines, no underwater obstacles, and little enemy fire. Leading the charge were eleven rocket craft, which discharged more than five thousand missiles onto the Red and neighboring White beaches. The 24th Infantry landed and took three hundred yards in seven minutes. Then things changed. For three months the Japanese had fortified Hill 522, impressing most of the men in Palo to build pillboxes and tunnels, and hid weapons in caves and trenches on the mountain. Mortar and sniper fire began to rain down from its slopes. Landing craft, especially the clumsy and thin-skinned LSTs (the landing ship tank carriers), were hit and began to burn. One fully loaded craft was hit and disintegrated. Some were beached. As the morning wore on, the casualties mounted. Two cruisers, the USS *Phoenix* and USS *Boise*, were called in. They delivered two hundred rounds into the mountain, but most of this firepower came too late to save the lives of the men in the beaching crafts.

MacArthur observed the panorama while standing on the bridge of the cruiser USS *Nashville*. It was a personal moment for him: he saw the troops begin to land at Red and White beaches. Despite enemy fire from Hill 522, the operation was going well. The third assault wave prepared to make a run at Palo. MacArthur climbed into a landing craft. Following him was his staff: Lt. Gen. George Kenney, Lieutenant General Sutherland, and Col. Roger O. Egeberg, and other brass. Sharing the craft was also Philippine president Sergio Osmeña and aide Romulo. The craft turned toward the shore. MacArthur wore a pistol in his belt to ensure he would not be taken alive.

The dash to Red Beach was as dramatic as any Hollywood picture show, with planes roaring overhead and the sound of naval shelling—"crump, crump"—accompanying the men ashore. As they came closer to the beach, they could hear the shouting of troops and the sounds of small arms. MacArthur was able to pick out the distinct signature of Japanese machine guns, accented by the acrid smell of burning palm trees. His men were already there, the beach was established, and the rough job of unloading supplies was in full swing.

When MacArthur's transport landed at Red Beach, it could not get entirely to the shore; rather, the party would have to wade into knee-deep water. MacArthur had changed into a fresh uniform and had no intention of getting it wet. As the story goes, one of the general's aides ordered a smaller craft from the beach master to carry the general and his staff the rest of the way. The beach master, responsible for landing hundreds of craft under Japanese sniper fire from Hill 522, reportedly told the aide to "let 'em walk." The general and company walked. The last few steps to the beach were immortalized on film as being one of the most heroic in American history, but the grim determination on the general's face may have been more the result of getting his new uniform soaked.

MacArthur later wrote that

> it took me only 30 to 40 long strides to reach dry land, but that was one of the most meaningful walks I ever took. When it was done, and I stood on the sand, I knew I was back again—against my old enemies of Bataan, for there, shining on the bodies of dead Japanese soldiers, I saw the insignia of the 16th Division, General [Masaharu] Homma's ace unit.[5]

General MacArthur had stepped off a ship and into iconography. After inspecting the beach he picked up to a microphone. Rain began to fall. Wet to the belt he spoke to the Philippine people. The short exhortation with the repeated religious references sanctified MacArthur, bolstered him with divine guidance, and, most importantly, washed away the sins of Bataan.

> To the People of the Philippines: I have returned. By the grace of Almighty God our forces stand again on Philippine soil—soil consecrated in the blood of our two peoples. We have come, dedicated and committed, to the task of destroying every vestige of enemy control over your daily lives, and of restoring, upon a foundation of indestructible strength, the liberties of your people.

At my side is your President, Sergio Osmena, worthy successor of that great patriot Manuel Quezon, with members of his cabinet. The seat of your government is now, therefore, firmly re-established on Philippine soil.

The hour of your redemption is here. Your patriots have demonstrated an unswerving and resolute devotion to the principles of freedom that challenge the best that is written on the pages of human history. I now call upon your supreme effort that the enemy may know from the temper of an aroused and outraged people within that he has a force there to contend with no less violent than is the force committed from without.

Rally to me. Let the indomitable spirit of Bataan and Corregidor lead on. As the lines of battle roll forward to bring you within the zone of operations, rise and strike! Strike at every favorable opportunity. For your homes and hearths, strike! For future generations of your sons and daughters, strike! In the name of your sacred dead, strike! Let no heart be faint. Let every arm be steeled. The guidance of divine God points the way. Follow in His name to the Holy Grail of righteous victory![6]

The general put down the microphone. Two leaf-stripped palm trees were crudely made into poles for the American and Philippine flags, which were raised. A short distance away, sitting on a fallen log under a tree, he calmly spoke with Osmeña for almost an hour about the problems of civil government that awaited them. About them were the snaps and pings of snipers from Hill 522. The dead Japanese veterans of Bataan lay grotesquely all around. MacArthur was sixty-four years old, and he had finally returned home.

✷ ✷ ✷

The Philippines really was home to MacArthur, in both a physical and emotional sense.[7] For nearly all his life, he lived in army camps and big city hotels, much of them in the Philippines. Indeed, he had planned to live out his life in the comfort of the Manila Hotel. Perhaps more importantly, for MacArthur the Philippines meant family and, specifically, his ability to meet the self-perceived challenges of family and receive the gratifications of family. For the MacArthur legacy in the Philippines began with the father, Arthur, a man whom Douglas adored and in at least some ways shaped the direction of the country.

Arthur MacArthur (1845–1912) had had a remarkable career in his own right. He was the renowned hero of Chattanooga, where at age eighteen he led the charge up Missionary Ridge and carried the day for the Union. It also won him the Congressional Medal of Honor and a place in the pantheon of U.S. military heroes. MacArthur spent a relatively uneventful professional career in the West before being sent to the Philippines in 1898. There he quickly capitalized on his opportunities. Shortly after the surrender of the Spanish forces, U.S. military commander Gen. Wesley Merritt chose him to serve as the provost marshal officer of Manila. In this capacity he was charged with bringing order to the chaos created by the loss of Spanish rule. The city's water supply, the sewage system, and even the food supply were in shambles, contributing to the constant outbreak of such diseases as malaria and dysentery. The task was daunting, but MacArthur soon had the disorder under control.

In performing this largely civil, police action, MacArthur equipped himself with a number of social and political perspectives that marked him as different from his contemporaries. For one, he publicly and privately interacted with Filipinos more than his commanders did and consequently had a better understanding of Filipino nationalism and the people's desire for independence. He realized the Filipinos would prefer self-government than being under another foreign rule, and he knew that their acceptance of America would take much time and expense. This insight served him well during his tenure as military governor. It also marked him as somewhat idiosyncratic within the military.

After months of simmering tensions, war broke out between U.S. troops and Filipino forces in early 1899. The U.S. commander, Gen. Elwell Otis, confronted Emilio Aguinaldo, chief of Philippine forces and president of the republic, in pitched battles around Manila. The results were predictable: with little training in marksmanship, poor supplies, and disastrous leadership, Filipino troops were continually routed. But they were not defeated. The spring and summer of that year showed Otis that land was easily taken, but the acquiescence of the civilians and, more importantly, the capture of Aguinaldo were not. In November, Otis embarked on a complicated three-part plan to flush

Aguinaldo into a trap set in northern Luzon. Maj. Gen. Henry W. Lawton's 1st Division would follow the Rio Grande River first north to San Isidro and then west to the Lingayen Gulf, flanking and sealing off Aguinaldo's escape route into the eastern mountains; Brig. Gen. Loyd Wheaton would land on the Lingayen coast and block roads heading north; and MacArthur's 2nd Division would travel northwest up the Angeles-Dagupan railway to push Aguinaldo into the pocket created by Lawton and Wheaton. While the plan failed to capture Aguinaldo (he was apprehended in 1901), the prolonged activity in the provinces convinced MacArthur that opposition to the U.S. presence was eroding quickly.

In May 1900, with nearly all formal resistance to the United States ended, MacArthur succeeded Otis as the military governor. Yet almost immediately guerrilla activity reached perhaps its highest point in the conflict, and MacArthur responded with force. During this period, a number of atrocities occurred, including that of the infamous Balangiga, Samar, massacre. Nearly fifty U.S. troops were killed, causing severe reprisals against barrios on the island. MacArthur had hoped that a compassionate approach to the occupation would succeed, and he was troubled that such force was necessary. Furthermore, he found himself at odds with the civilian leader and future president, William Howard Taft.

MacArthur was called to testify at a Senate hearing in 1902, where he spoke on a number of issues. Unlike many American politicians, he was optimistic about the Filipinos: he saw them as drawn to democracy, hard working, and demonstrating great potential for self-government. He did not see them as racially inferior, as most others did, but as the products of a corrupt Spanish colonial system. Indeed, MacArthur's racial views were progressive for the time, and he became indignant when asked to compare the characteristics of Filipinos and African Americans. Most importantly, he voiced his opinion that the Philippine Islands were a critical part of the U.S. Pacific defense perimeter, a view that is still accepted today.

Arthur MacArthur died in 1912, bitter toward the military for being passed over for the head of the chiefs of staff in Washington, D.C. His son remarked, "My whole world changed that night. Never have I been able to heal the wound in my heart." As Clayton James points out, the father's noble bearing, his excellence as a combat leader and peacetime administrator, his ability to gather and promote strong younger officers, and his sense of justice and magnanimity all impressed the young man. Other elements of the father would later become apparent in the son: his place within the military elite, his formal attire, and his conservative personal conduct. James also notes that Arthur bequeathed his son two striking liabilities: one was his disdain for the interference of civilian officials; another was his outspoken opinion on nonmilitary matters.[8] These inclinations would plague his son throughout his career.

The role of the Philippines in Douglas MacArthur's psychological development cannot be overstated. It should be remembered that between the Spanish-American War and World War I, the Philippines was the major training ground for the U.S. Army. For many young officers, it was their first overseas assignment, and the Filipinos were their first enemy. Carol Petillo, in her astute study of MacArthur's personality, writes that the young man found the Philippines a suitable proving ground for his psychological needs and professional ambitions. In the still unpacified Visayas and the politically treacherous Manila, the Philippines presented MacArthur with a superb opportunity to construct his heroic vision of himself. He had been too young to ride after the Sioux, and he had missed fighting the Spanish in Cuba, but here was his battlefield, and what he experienced in Leyte and Samar would remain with him the rest of his career. Petillo notes that

> the dangers he saw and experienced there [Leyte and Samar] encouraged his perception of the Islands as a place suitable for the heroic deeds which would support his view of himself as a brave warrior . . . on many levels of his consciousness, he perceived the Islands as the most appropriate stage upon which to act out both his personal and public dramas. There he could participate in adventures which would reinforce his shaky self-esteem in an arena made safe by his father's still-remembered presence, and the warm support of many Filipinos.[9]

From late 1903 through the spring of the following year, MacArthur spent his most adventurous days, a period that would distill his character. He was initially assigned to Camp Jossman on the small island of Guimaras, just off the larger island of Panay. Camp Jossman held a relatively large American presence; often these soldiers were sent to Leyte and Samar, where there was still a strong guerrilla movement. As an engineer, MacArthur had to oversee the improvement of a dock at the harbor in Buenavista. One day he took a work crew out to acquire wood for the dock's pilings. While they worked, he haphazardly wandered away into the jungle, where he was confronted by two *ladrones* (thieves). MacArthur killed both of them with his pistol, helping to create his sense of personal heroism and destiny. More importantly, as Petillo points out, it supported his identification with the heroes of the Old West, a critical ingredient in the MacArthur psyche.[10]

Other details in the Leyte-Samar area continued to form MacArthur's personal and professional identities. In November 1903 MacArthur went to Tacloban for the first time, helping to survey a reservation. Leyte was still being ravaged by the *Pulajanes*, groups of religious fanatics who attacked both Filipinos and Americans in the coastal areas. In January 1904, MacArthur was ordered to Samar, where he began to survey the reservation at Calbayog. Once again, MacArthur, as an engineer, took part in no combat, but in Samar he would have been in even closer proximity to danger than in Leyte. At the time the island was known as "bloody Samar," a hotbed of guerrilla and lawless activity. Here MacArthur would have seen the early attempts at "Filipinization," essentially replacing U.S. troops with the Philippine Constabulary's forces. It would take years before peace would come to the island.

In March 1904, MacArthur was back in Manila, enjoying both its cosmopolitan lifestyle and the mysteries of colonial politics. During the American imperial era, Manila was a heady place, reeling under the influx of the many nationalities that contributed to the already international atmosphere of the 300,000-person city. In contrast to the stark garrison routines in Leyte and Samar, MacArthur enjoyed European cuisine, vibrant newspapers, and the promenade around the Luneta, the park in which Manileños and foreigners alike gathered for music and socializing. The (presumed) end of the war brought social change and financial opportunity, and MacArthur seized them both. He went on to fame in World War I, returned to the Philippines in 1922 as the commander of the U.S. garrison, and came back in 1928 as the head of the entire military structure in the archipelago. In 1932, MacArthur earned dubious distinction during the veteran's pension march in Washington, D.C., and in late 1935 he returned to the Philippines to build the citizen army. Throughout all these trips, he nurtured his strong friendship with Manuel Quezon, the first Philippine president.

From an early age MacArthur believed that he was a person of destiny, a belief in no small part fostered by his parents. He placed enormous stress on personal honor. To him, the concepts of Christianity, democracy, and service to country were all synonymous. According to Michael Schaller, Christianity often seemed a metaphor for MacArthur's vision; he was not above comparing his struggle with that of Christ's. In fact, immediately after the war in occupied Japan, he dropped immigration restrictions on missionaries, causing the renowned evangelist Bob Jones to write MacArthur that eleven hundred of his followers were "learning how to load the Gospel Gun and how to shoot it."[11]

Undoubtedly, as MacArthur stood on Leyte beach and spoke into the microphone, he saw himself as the destined savior of the Philippines—a classical patrician, with a noble obligation to serve the people. But his destiny was hardly fulfilled; indeed, on a shell-marked hill nearby, a vicious fight was still undecided.

✳ ✳ ✳

As the general was creating history on the beach, U.S. troops were sweating on Hill 522. Hill 522 was vital: it commanded the view of Palo and Highway 2, the major artery into the Leyte Valley. Its capture was essential and was eventually accomplished, but the execution was a strange sort of affair. When the naval bombardment began, many of the Japanese defenders were ordered to the mountain's west side to escape the shelling. The U.S. advance at Red Beach was so swift that members of the 24th Infantry Division scrambled up the hill and captured the crest while the Japanese were still hiding on the western side. After the shelling ended, the Japanese were forced to mount a counterattack up the slope to recapture the hill.

One of the most interesting accounts of the engagement comes from one of the most controversial U.S. war correspondents, Jan Valtin. Born Richard Krebs, Valtin served as a rifleman for the 24th Division. He was a bona fide German Communist who had trained in Russia. Having operated as a Red organizer and spy in Germany and aboard merchant marine vessels, he became fluent in several languages, including English. He spent three years in San Quentin prison on a "botched" assassination of a Communist Party leader (it was argued he never meant to murder). Deported, he was arrested and tortured by the Nazis. He later defected and escaped to the United States in 1938, where he was destitute. In 1941 his autobiography, *Out of the Night*, was immensely popular, and probably on the strength that the United States allowed him to cover the war. His narrative of that night on Hill 522 is a compelling piece of war correspondence, even though it has been suggested that Valtin overembellished. What follows below is from his *Children of Yesterday*, an account of the 24th Division in the Philippines.

> Hill 522 is very steep. Trails up its side are winding. Fatigued from a long and hectic day the men looked toward the towering crest and clenched their teeth. At times they pulled themselves up bodily by grasping lianas and overhanging roots.
>
> They passed through the menacing mouths of tunnels half hidden by bamboo thickets. The tunnels were silent. They struggled over the last hundred yards, a ragged and drawn-out column rushing upward through an ominous patchwork of lengthening shadows and austere rock formations. The panorama below them was sweepingly beautiful—the beaches, the purple headlands, a great fleet at anchor, the silvery sea and the distant mountains of Samar. No one gave it a glance.
>
> At this time "Charlie" Company's scouts . . . saw swarms of bobbing helmets, a mass of bayoneted rifles in the hands of a mob of Japanese. The Japanese were muscling rapidly toward the crest.
>
> *"The Japs are coming up the other side!"*[12]

The attack at sunset was repulsed. The mountain became silent. The fleet was silent. All was silent save for the insects. The soldiers relaxed.

At 1:30 a.m. the Japanese attacked up the south slope of the mountain. Under a heavy machine-gun and mortar barrage they quickly made their way up 522. The scream of "banzai" was heard in a black night, but after more than an hour of fighting, the American gunners on the top repelled the Japanese, even though they made it to within a few feet of U.S. lines.

Throughout the night, pockets of Japanese infiltrators attacked numerous points along the mountain. At 4:00 a second strike came; unlike the earlier charge, it was not a wild, screaming affair but rather a highly skilled assault. Once again there was fear and cursing in the darkness, and once again the Americans held the mountain. The Japanese did not try again.

The Americans continued their advance. On October 21 they captured Tacloban, with MacArthur and Sergio Osmeña conducting the ceremony at the provincial capitol on the 23rd. The Philippines was proclaimed a nation, again. Then the battle for Leyte really began. The Japanese had suckered Adm. William "Bull" Halsey into chasing a mock fleet northwest of the Philippines, leaving the invasion force, much of it still on the beach, unprotected. In a series of actions that would later be called the Battle of Leyte Gulf and that are usually considered one of the most important naval engagements in history, an undermanned U.S. fleet valiantly held off Japanese forces. Its efforts saved not only the men on the beach but the actual invasion as well.

U.S. troops moved into the Leyte Valley, although MacArthur remained in his Tacloban headquarters. Despite ferocious attacks by U.S. air forces, Yamashita had been able to reinforce his garrison on Leyte. By December the Japanese contingent had sixty-five thousand men, its size tripled since the actual U.S. landing. For the Americans, Leyte became a nightmare. On a good day the terrain was rugged, but now monsoon rains and poor roads created rivers of mud that immobilized U.S. trucks and tanks. The Japanese air force was still active, hampering American supply efforts. In places like Breakneck Ridge on the northern quadrant, the fighting was sometimes hand to hand. Finally, Ormoc on the west coast was taken, and on December 26 MacArthur announced that Leyte was in U.S. control, save for some loose ends. MacArthur pushed on to Luzon, but the "mopping up" took four more months of horrible fighting. At its conclusion, the superior U.S. firepower nearly cost the Japanese its entire garrison. The Americans lost four thousand dead and fifteen thousand wounded, an expenditure MacArthur had not anticipated. Valtin recorded afterward that

> in Palo grown-ups and children had a liberation fiesta. On the town
> square the children staged a pantomime: an unwashed urchin wearing a

top hat paraded on the stage; around his neck hung a sign, "President of the Philippines." A second urchin jumped to the stage. He was disguised as a Japanese and he proceeded diligently to rifle the "President's" pockets. Then a third little boy, garbed as "Uncle Sam," stormed upon the stage. His bare brown foot lashed to the rear of "Nippon's" pants; "Nippon" fled. Whereupon the "President" shook "Uncle Sam's" hand. In Palo, too, the war had passed.[13]

For the Japanese, the decision to confront the United States on Leyte was nothing short of disaster. Their infantry was shattered. Their air forces, both naval and ground based, lost hundreds of planes and pilots. Their navy lost not only many warships but also cargo and transport ships, all irreplaceable. For the Filipinos, the island of Leyte, and the memory of MacArthur and America, was secure.

✳ ✳ ✳

Today, Red Beach has been built up. A large retaining wall shoulders the land against the tide. In a discerningly designed MacArthur memorial park, double-life-sized bronze statues of MacArthur and his entourage—Philippine president Sergio Osmeña, Lt. Gen. Richard Sutherland, aide Carlos Romulo, and others—depict the epic scene of wading ashore. The statues, well made and accurate, also have a semicomical quality: the heroic figures here wade through a small, motionless pool, and often local birds make good use of their heads. The statues' shoulders now wear different emblems. The grounds surrounding the memorial are kept trimmed, with huge palms standing sentry. For the historian, though, there is precious little that describes what actually happened here. Several plaques show the interest and presumed generosity of a number of politicians over the years, especially at the 1994 fifty-year celebration, but that is about it. There is nothing to explain just what political and military events caused this battlefield to even be here. In fact, the major analytical activity on the grounds seems to come from teenage couples who walk by hand in hand, then retire giggling to a convenient park bench.

Macarthur's return was not the only battle fought at Red Beach. In 1994 during the run-up to the landing's fiftieth anniversary, a vicious firefight erupted in the Manila media. Several University of the Philippines faculty, the renowned Renato Constantino among them, challenged a number of long-held beliefs about the war. One was that the U.S. return was not really necessary as the Filipino guerrillas, including the Huks, a group that will be discussed at length later, were on the verge of overthrowing the Japanese. Another was that the destruction of Manila and the huge loss of civilian life were actually the fault of the Americans. The media fight pointed to a number of threads within the Philippine culture: the tug between a nationalism that rightly or wrongly has proceeded to revise history, the unsettling resentment of the Japanese by older Filipinos against the positive views of Japan held by younger Filipinos, the accountability for the incredible loss of civilian life during the Battle of Manila, and, in general, the Philippines' relationship with the United States.[14]

While the media brawl rocked Manila, the celebration in Leyte moved forward. Advertisements by the Philippine Department of Tourism enticed people to be a witness to history, of a trip back in time. The festivities began on October 17, and they included a veterans' tree planting, the Leyte Landings oratorical contest, sunrise and wreath-laying ceremonies, the Fun Run from Tacloban to MacArthur Park, the coronation of Miss Liberation, the dedication of the Philippine Commemorative Rock Garden, and, of course, the reenactment of the landing. Performed by a group of Filipino and American personalities from Manila, the landing was highlighted by the actor who played MacArthur. Stepping proudly off a landing craft, corncob pipe clenched between his teeth, he immediately stumbled and fell to his knees in two feet of water.[15]

What was most striking about Red Beach was the row of dark mountains facing the beach to the west. One nearby crag with an oddly two-pronged shape seems particularly ominous. A quick query to the man selling fake samurai swords on the street outside the park revealed that this was Hill 522. He did not know exactly why it was important, but he knew it was somehow connected to MacArthur and the invasion.

Hill 522, also called Mt. Guinhandang, sits at the north end of Palo, a small town several miles south of Tacloban. There is a memorial to Americans at the top. A few of the many pedicab drivers circling the memorial were flagged down; they knew how to get to the mountain. Along with several friends from Samar, I decided to climb it. The convoy of pedicabs got us there for about a dollar and a half, pedaling a mile or so from Red Beach to the bottom of the small mountain. The drivers stopped at an intersection near an old steel bridge and below a narrow and steep set of cracked concrete stairs that marked the starting point of the climb.

Across the street from the steps a young boy stood in front of a *sari-sari* (convenience) store and rather disinterestingly stated that he would be our guide up the mountain for only ten pesos. We declined politely, and we began the climb. The stairs quickly disappeared, giving way to a muddy path covered in a wonderful shade. We soon passed two, perhaps three, nipa huts replete with dogs, chickens, pigs, and naked children, all content in the shady mud. A mother wearing a duster, the colorful and formless dress that is the uniform of seemingly all provincial women, watched our party and nonchalantly told us that we had no guide.

Several minutes past the huts, with the path rising more steeply with each foot, a remarkable site appeared on the left, the side facing west, away from the beach. It was concrete, perhaps ten yards in circumference, rising out of the earth in the shape of roughly a quarter of an egg. After a few moments of silent confusion, it became clear what the object was—a Japanese pillbox. While some greenish moss grew in places, it was perfectly formed and absolutely unscathed. The gun was gone, of course, surely collected decades ago for scrap metal. There was a second hole just below the barrel opening, with rusted metal rungs that descended into a dark hole filled with water and garbage. The stench was powerful.

The climb continued. The path was slippery, and at times it became so steep that we had to hold onto the vegetation for support. Five minutes past the pillbox, our shirts were completely drenched. The leather wristband on my watch was so wet it changed colors.

We heard voices. Then a group of six or seven men appeared, all carrying bolos, the eighteen-inch, one-sided blade used throughout the islands but revered in the Visayas and Mindanao. They were serious workingmen, clearing the large grass that grew off the path. One man did not seem particularly friendly; in fact, he was scowling. He asked why we didn't have a guide. Noting the bolo in his hand, we stuttered and searched for a polite answer.

Complicating matters was that the Waray our party spoke was the Samar brand, not the Leyte, marking us as outsiders. It was then that it dawned on us that we were *supposed* to have a guide, even though it was essentially impossible to get lost if we stayed on the path. We thought of the boy in front of the sari-sari store: maybe he was part of an unofficial tourist board, and perhaps we had created some type of Paloarian faux pas. It was a tense moment, and we attempted a smile and a thank you and walked on. Behind us we heard the muttering of the bolomen.

The path seemed almost vertical. Sweat was falling into our eyes. The cold bottled water we had purchased before the climb was now tepid. Someone at the head of the climbing party yelled that we were nearly there. Unexpectedly, the green canopy ended, and the full force of the sun blasted our skin. The land was sheltered only by tall grass and short shrubs. Now, for the first time, we could actually see how high we had climbed. Then a shout arose, "There it is!" And above us, at twelve o'clock, there it was—a large cross, plain and unadorned, standing at the knob of the mountain.

The last thirty yards were the most difficult. With neither breeze nor shade, the mountain seemed cruel and ugly. We lurched the last few steps, and, finally, at the summit, there was both joy and discomfort. The view was magnificent. The town of Palo lay below, with its superb sixteenth-century cathedral anchoring a sea of tin-roofed houses. To the west were the green-black mountains of central Leyte; today a cloudy halo hung over each peak. Beneath them spread a brilliant green plain, dotted by farms and houses. To the east were the beaches and the sea. Red Beach was almost directly below, open and vulnerable. Past them and over the San Pedro Strait was Samar, looking large and dark and somehow foreboding.

As a memorial to the sacrifices of American dead, the summit was something of a disappointment. I remembered seeing photos of the cross from the late 1960s when it stood alone on the peak, dominating the landscape. Now it was immersed in vegetation nearly as tall as the cross itself. The structure had no scripture, no plaque, no markings, nothing to identity its purpose. It was old and chipped; cracks appeared to have been spackled over. At its base was a simple altar that was in part burnt black and disfigured. Perhaps people had lit candles here at one time. Or perhaps someone needed a flat surface to cook a meal. In any event, the cross was intended to commemorate what happened on the mountain and below it sixty years ago. Considering the magnitude of that event, the cross seemed markedly inadequate.

With no shade and but a drop of water, our climbing party did not stay at the summit very long. After a few photographs and a few final wonderstruck shivers, we headed back down. The descent was faster and easier. The bolomen were taking lunch; some reclined in hammocks strung between trees. They were smiling now. One called out, "Did you kiss the cross?" "Yes, of course!" we lied, having no idea what this meant. If we would have had a guide, the significance of this inquiry would have been clear. At the group of nipa huts, the woman we had seen earlier was chatting to a neighbor. One of us mentioned the condition of the Japanese pillbox, particularly the smell, and the woman laughed and told us that the families in the area use the two holes of the gun emplacement as latrines.

We stumbled down the few steep steps and then back onto the barrio street. Our throats were dry, our skin was burned, and our legs were sore. The boy who had offered to be our guide was nowhere to be seen. We walked toward the highway, planning to grab the first jeepney to Tacloban. For those who have not had the pleasure of travel by jeepney, the vehicle is essentially an elongated, covered jeep, roughly the length of a pickup truck. Two benches placed in the back compartment can hold up to around twenty passengers, depending on how many the driver can squeeze in. Not only is the jeepney a cultural icon, it is the people's main mode of transportation. It is cheap, more or less reliable, and easy to find. Highly uncomfortable and usually smoky, a jeepney ride does offer close quarter companionship with your fellow travelers—if that is what you wish.

Just before leaving the base of the hill, I noticed the old, decrepit steel bridge that went across the river. I remembered a story about a long-dead American who had built a steel bridge in Palo, and that made me think about an old junkyard dealer who used to live here.

5

THE KING OF LEYTE AND
THE JUNKYARD OAKIE

Most Americans who seek their fortune in the Philippines do so in Manila. This makes sense: Manila is the center of commerce and culture. But a fair number have gone out into the provinces to earn their livelihoods. Two Americans who did make their careers in the provinces started out in Leyte. Although a half century separated them in age, they shared a number of commonalities. Both arrived in the Philippines as military men and took advantage of the calamity of war to build financial wealth. These two men underwent an incredible metamorphosis: they came from undistinguished middle- and working-class backgrounds and had uncertain futures while in America; in the islands, however, they hobnobbed with heads of state and had the ears of Philippine leaders.

Their transformation began in Tacloban, the capital of Leyte. The name is derived from the Waray word *taklub*, meaning "to cover," which was apparently an allusion to a particular method of fishing with bamboo. If the fishermen were asked where they were going, they would say, "Tarakluban" (going fishing with the bamboo device). This place eventually became Tacloban. The city is not unattractive; is a sizable place, with a quarter of a million people; and has an airport and easy access to the sea.[1] Tacloban serves first and foremost as the center of regional government and commerce. In this capacity it is similar to many other of the provincial capitals. It has several universities and does seem like a tropical college town. The city has another distinction: it is the ancestral home of Imelda Marcos. Born Imelda Remedios Visitacion

Romualdez in 1929, her clan was and is still the most powerful in Tacloban. At this writing the mayor is, in fact, Alfredo "Bejo" Romualdez, Imelda's cousin.

MacArthur entered Tacloban on October 21, 1944. He quickly set up Sergio Osmeña as the president of the Philippines. Manuel Quezon, the first Philippine president and one of MacArthur's closest friends, had recently passed away in New York, leaving the job to his vice president. They reestablished the Philippine government at the Leyte provincial capitol building. The ceremony, however, demonstrated the indifference MacArthur held for Osmeña. Standing on the steps of the capitol (the interior of the building had been reduced to rubble), MacArthur's words accentuated his own sense of destiny.

> On behalf of my government I restore to you a constitutional administration by countrymen of your confidence and choice. As our forces advance I shall in like manner restore the other Philippine cities and provinces until throughout the entire land you may walk down life's years erect and unafraid, each free to toil and to worship according to his own conscience with your children's laughter again brightening homes once marked by the grim tragedy of conquest.[2]

He turned to Osmeña and told him to perform his responsibilities as president. The Philippine president was then sworn in. After the brief ceremony, MacArthur and his staff piled into jeeps and drove away, leaving the Philippine president standing alone and bewildered on the capitol steps. An American lieutenant saw Osmeña and, after a brief conversation, found out that the U.S. military had not provided the president with a vehicle, lodgings, or food. Surprised and sympathetic, the lieutenant gave Osmeña his jeep, and the president drove off to find a place to stay.

I was surprised the first time I saw the capitol building. This splendid, classically inspired building was designed by Ralph Harrington Doane of Boston, the brilliant, young chief consulting architect for the Philippine government from 1916 to 1918. He also designed the capitol building at Pangasinan and did work with Malacanang Palace. Looking at the Tacloban building one sees America. Its white color, the classical columns, and the overall Greco-Roman design would be entirely appropriate on Constitution Avenue in Washington, D.C. Outside the building was a large plot of shell stone pavement, fountains, and symmetrical hedges. Lush ornamental vegetation framed different areas. A lion guarded the entranceway on one side, a late-nineteenth-century cannon the other. Between them stood a line of flagpoles that all flew the Philippine tri-color. It was an altogether impressive scene, propelled by the economy and decorum of Doane's design.

But there was something here that was clearly not part of the original design. The building had a large central structure, with two smaller wings to the right and left. Both of these wings had been altered. In 1964, as part of a restoration project, two huge bas-reliefs were added. One depicts the first Mass celebrated in the Philippines. The second shows MacArthur and his generals, plus Osmeña, grim faced and determined. The bas-reliefs were really quite notable, but, glued onto the structure as they were, the original design was compromised, and the total effect was awkward.

Doane was concerned about philosophical compromise. He addressed it in a 1919 article in the prestigious *Architectural Review*. As the consulting architect, he was responsible for designing the Philippines' public buildings. This burden, it would seem, would have been heavy. How does one actually reflect a nation and a people in a concrete and stone structure? Considering world history and the place of America and architecture within it, Doane wrote that

> if the architecture of the Philippines is to fittingly reflect the political transitions, American Colonial Architecture to be distinguished of course from Georgian work, must unmistakably indicate to posterity the Era when American democracy surplanted the exploitations of Spanish despots. . . . Here lies our first opportunity as a great nation to inaugurate a real colonial architecture.[3]

I was looking, then, at a neoclassical interpretation of the defeat of old Europe and the rise of young America. This building celebrated America extending itself to others. But Doane, just as other administrators of the time, saw American architecture here as something of a transitional period. In describing the country, on which he heaps significant praise, he writes, the overwhelming bulk of the inhabitants is a Christianized people who have in their veins such a mixture of Spanish and Chinese blood as to make the thoroughbred Filipino almost a curiosity. It is for this somewhat passive people, so picturesque in their colorful and fantastic dress and so admirably endowed with the communal idea, that an American Colonial Architecture is being developed which, in time, if the Filipino demonstrates sufficient genius, will give place to a distinct Philippine Architecture.[4]

The question might be raised: why would the Filipinos need American help, especially in terms of architecture? Doane provided this answer:

The fact that there is not, and never has been, a characteristically Philippine architecture is not necessarily a reflection upon the genius of the Filipinos. . . . America began its history, as the Philippines began theirs, without any native architecture, but has legitimately followed precedent in the solution of American architectural problems. The Philippines have been following the same policy, utilizing the best traditions of ancient and modern architecture. There is no more logic in refusing to erect buildings in the Philippines of a distinctive American character (with suitable modifications) than there would be in declining to use electricity there because of its American derivation.

The Filipino people must go through a long period . . . [of the] adaptation of foreign architecture and methods of construction before a distinctly characteristic Philippine style will appear.[5]

Doane, while an exceptional architect, was also a classic colonialist. As his writing demonstrates, he believed that it was America's responsibility to build up the Filipinos, who were colorful but passive. Because they did not have an indigenous architecture—that is, a Western one—the people would need to study and use American and European models. If such study were diligent, over a long expanse of time original thought might occur. His argument incorporates some basic tenets of Orientalism: because the Filipinos had no identifiable architecture (to Doane), the indigenous people had no "past," and because of this historical void, there was no hope for the future. With the arrival of the West and its art and science, there was the possibility of salvation through progress and enlightenment. This logic was employed before Doane became the consulting architect, and it would carry on afterward. Indeed, it would be on Doane's steps, literally, that MacArthur bequeathed sovereignty to the Philippines.

After the president's installation, MacArthur needed a home and head-quarters. MacArthur apparently claimed he knew of the biggest house in Leyte, and it was the residence of an incarcerated American, Walter Scott Price. The Price Mansion, as it is now commonly referred to on tourist maps, was then the largest residential building in Tacloban and located three blocks away from the capitol building. MacArthur used it as his general headquarters from October 1944 to early January of the next year. Just prior to MacArthur's arrival, the Japanese had used it as an officers' club. In the front yard the Japanese had built a huge air raid shelter, replete with electric lights, furniture, and other amenities befitting high-ranking officers. Against his subordinates' advice, MacArthur had this shelter filled in, saying that it spoiled the lawn. Probably nearer to the truth was the belief that MacArthur was still sensitive to the moniker "Dugout Dug," which he had acquired on Corregidor. Near the house, the U.S. military built four prefabricated houses, forty feet wide and one hundred forty feet long, for the staff's use. An elevated catwalk ran between them and the Price house.[6]

MacArthur should have thought twice about filling in the air raid shelter. Despite the fact that the Japanese did not know that MacArthur was living there, the mansion, the most modern structure in the provincial city, became a magnet for Japanese air and artillery attacks. One aircraft shell went through MacArthur's bedroom, and an American antiaircraft round—a dud—fired at a Japanese plane landed on a couch. Within a short time of his arrival, witnesses say MacArthur's headquarters at the Price house was perfectly pockmarked with bullet holes from being strafed. Through this chaos moved MacArthur, seemingly oblivious to the danger. Indeed, when several slugs from an enemy plane entered a window and slammed into a wooden beam above MacArthur's head, the general had them removed and sent to his young son in Australia, with a note saying the two bullets had been aimed at his daddy but had missed. He was seen continually pacing the veranda, pipe in mouth, lost in thought. The soldiers were now in awe of him; the days of "Dugout Doug" were long gone.

I was interested in seeing the Price house, obviously because of its association with MacArthur and because of its builder as well. A trike driver brought me to the corner of Justice Romualdez and Santo Niño streets, roughly in the center of Tacloban. Today what the soldiers once called the Big House is now the College Assurance Plan (CAP) Development Center, operated by an insurance and investing company focused on college students. My first impression of the building was somewhat disconcerting. The house had been lovingly restored in 1982. At some point after this restoration, an incredibly garish and totally nonsensical tower was added to the front of the house. It immediately threw the fine, economical lines of the building off-kilter. In a more aggravated sense, the house reminded me of the bas-relief glued onto the capitol, and it begged the question: was this an example of the symphony of American and Filipino architecture that Doane hope would develop? I would later learn that, the tower aside, the structure is essentially the same since Price built it and MacArthur used it. I entered the gate and walked thoughtfully through the well-manicured garden. A bronze statue of MacArthur and Osmeña (the latter having grown remarkably in height) stood roughly where the Japanese bomb shelter would have been located. No one was around. I wandered through the garden and into the house. The CAP offices were somewhere, but I did not see them. Eventually, a guide in a T-shirt, who was apparently also the gardener, greeted me and offered to show me around.

Built in 1908, the house was a beautiful example of a typical upper-class, two-story Spanish stucco design. Shell windows let in a diffused light that gleamed off hardwood and tile floors. Impressive chandeliers and candelabras gave a glimpse of the lighting used in MacArthur's day. Despite a fierce Visayan sun and no air-conditioning, the house was quite comfortable. The main rooms were vacant, but the master bedroom was furnished as a memorial, with an elegant, old four-poster as the centerpiece. There were many photographs of MacArthur, Osmeña, and even Rupurto Kangleon. A few were photographs of MacArthur during his 1961 return and farewell tour of the Philippines, when he stopped at the house and said hello to the aged Mrs. Price. A painting stood on an easel. The guide showed me the gaping hole in the wall where the Japanese shell had torn through. Surrounded by paintings, prints, photos, and plaques of the Leyte landing and the general, and accompanied by a relatively mute gardener-guide, I marveled that I was standing in the same room where MacArthur had once berated Adm. Thomas Kinkaid for not providing more support for the army. On this same wooden floor, MacArthur had planned the final conquest of Leyte, as well as the invasions of Mindoro and Luzon. Outside on the porch, MacArthur had paced, smoking his famous corncob pipe, sometimes sitting alone on a wicker chair underneath a naked fluorescent light, quite impervious to the danger posed by Japanese planes or snipers. All of this experience was quite fascinating; yet, there was virtually nothing on the house's namesake. Little or faulty information seems to surround Walter Price. James reported that at the time MacArthur occupied the house, its owner had already been killed by the Japanese, while Geoffrey Perret wrote that Price had been "killed by the Japanese early in the war."[7] Both were incorrect.

In its prewar days, the house was a social beehive, a lavish, happy place where the wealthy residents of Tacloban came to the court of an American known as the "King of Leyte." Walter Scott Price (1876–1945) was a vibrant example of the American expatriate who came to the provinces and succeeded in building a career.[8]

Price was born in Philadelphia, the eighth of eleven children. His parents were German immigrants. Price had little use for school, making it only to the seventh grade. At the outbreak of the Spanish-American War, the twenty-one-year-old joined the National Guard, hoping to see action in Cuba. Instead, he spent the entire war guarding powder works in New Jersey. As a consequence, he enlisted in the Fourth United States Army and was ordered to the Philippines. He arrived there holding the rank of second lieutenant.

His military career was mercurial. Almost immediately he saw action near the town on Imus, Cavite, where he acquitted himself well. Price was eventually reassigned to Camp Bumbus in Tacloban, where he was the military provost, which was basically the camp's commanding officer. The town was essentially deserted, for the citizens, terrified of the Americans, had fled into the hills. Somehow Price prevailed and implored the people to submit to U.S. governance. Shortly thereafter he accepted the surrender of Philippine Col. Leon Rojas, the leader of resistance in the area, who dramatically entered Tacloban on a white stallion, followed by four hundred bolomen and hundreds of townsfolk carrying the statue of the town's patron, Santo Niño. Price was well on his way to becoming a local legend.

By age twenty-five Price was an accomplished military professional who had packed more into his short life than most could in a lifetime. Then he began to think outside the box. In 1901, despite his brief but remarkable military career, he refused an officer's commission in both the regular army and the Philippine Constabulary and was mustered out. Price married a Leyte girl, Simeona Kalingag, from San Jose, Leyte, whose father was a relative of Emilio Aguinaldo, the general and president of the fledgling Philippine republic. A Filipino-American marriage was not unheard of, especially if the woman was of pure Spanish ancestry, but it was not common with women of the more "native" class. Despite the social taboo, the Price marriage was long and productive. Over the years, Simeona gave birth eighteen times, and eleven children survived. She died in 1973 at the age of 100.

Just as so many American expatriates who made a professional go of it, Price developed military ties that served him well. Right after becoming a civilian, he contracted with the army to load and unload transport ships that docked at Tacloban. For the next five years, he expanded into road building. Price bought a roller, and with no knowledge of civil engineering whatsoever, he began the trade of road construction. His success was immediate. Paved roads began to traverse Leyte. Isolated barrios became connected. Remarkably, in 1906 he even built the steel bridge in Palo, where he lived during its construction.

At the end of his first decade in the Philippines, Price was privately comfortable and professionally on the move. He joined with several other Westerners and formed the Leyte Transportation Company (Letranco) in 1911. With three new buses and one motorcycle, the company not only carried passengers but loads of the all-important *copra* (dried coconut meat) crop as well. With its fleet of about 140 vehicles, Letranco became virtually the only form of public transportation in Leyte until World War II. In the prewar years, Price also became a surveyor, a department store owner (the only store owner in Tacloban who was not Chinese), and the owner of coconut plantations; grew interested in rice production; invested in Baguio mining; and became an active player on the Manila stock market.

It would have been hard not to gravitate toward Manila, the center of Philippine commerce and society. Price began to visit the city, and he built his family a luxurious city house on Colorado Street, now Felipe Agoncillo Street, in the then fashionable district of Paco. This home supplemented his renowned mansion in the province. In Manila, Price became just as well known as he was in Tacloban. A carefree party giver and goer, he and his wife were often on the society page, and his exploits sometimes made it back to his hometown Philadelphia newspaper. He and Simeona were visitors to Malacanang Palace. The papal legate and the archbishop of Manila were guests in his Manila residence. He was, by all accounts, a successful American pioneer in the Pacific.

His exploits complemented his physical appearance and mannerisms. Price was a large 225-pound man. His personal style included fresh carnations or violets in his lapel, large diamond rings, and superb suits. He was often considered one of the ten best-dressed men in the Philippines.[9]

Just as all Americans living in the islands, he and his family were completely upturned by the war. When the Japanese attacked Pearl Harbor, Price and his wife were in their Manila home. They made it back to Tacloban in mid-December 1941, in time to see the city evacuated. The family moved to Carigara, Leyte, but each day Price and one of his sons would drive into Tacloban to check on the business and the house, now being run by the oldest son, Joseph. All went well until May, when the Japanese landed in Capoocan, just west of Carigara, along the northern Leyte coast. The Prices were forewarned and dodged the Japanese as they passed, ironically driving in commandeered Letranco buses.

The family was able to elude the Japanese for a short time, but Price, at the urging of a local politician, soon turned himself in. The Japanese treated Price quite civilly and even him allowed to remain under arrest in his Tacloban house. One night, however, he was caught in his office attempting to remove something from the safe. The Japanese beat him and sent him to the internment camp located in a nearby public school. He remained there for about eight months. From there he was sent to Santo Tomas in Manila, where the bulk of the Western civilians were kept.

According to Santo Tomas internee A. V. H. Hartendorp, whose recollections of the internee experience are probably the most detailed and comprehensive, Price arrived in the Santo Tomas camp on January 16, 1943.[10] Hartendorp describes Price as a "prominent and wealthy old-timer" from Tacloban, where he had been jailed since May. Price was with another affluent American, James R. McGuire from Samar, and they both had stories to tell of what was happening in the south. While incarcerated in Tacloban, Price was elected president of the small group of American internees; McGuire was elected vice president. One of their duties was to prepare daily reports for the Japanese.

A large internment camp located on the grounds of the oldest university in Asia, Santo Tomas held Westerners of many nationalities, but Americans were the predominate group. There is little to mention of Price's life here, save that he was alone. His wife and children, Filipino citizens, were not required to be interned, and they opted not to go. Records show that his wife and eight of the children—some of them in middle age with families of their own—remained in Tacloban while three stayed in the Paco residence. Price's name appears a number of times throughout the attendance logs kept for the Japanese in 1943 and 1944, but little is actually known of his internment. From the records we only know that his address on Colorado Street was 534, that his room in the camp was EB-114, and that he was described as a "businessman."[11]

In the summer of 1944 the Japanese began work on another internment camp at Los Baños, south of Manila. The camp would eventually hold about twenty-two hundred persons, many being Western religious personnel of all denominations. In Santo Tomas, the Japanese drew up a work detail to be shipped to help complete the construction of the Los Baños camp. When an old and sick man was called to go, Price, at age sixty-seven, volunteered to take his place and was sent south.

The new camp, although not nearly the horror suffered by military prisoners at such places as Camp O'Donnell, Cabanatuan, and Bilibid, was difficult. By the second half of 1944, food in the Philippines was scarce. Filipinos,

Japanese, and internees were all hungry. Price came down with common prison camp afflictions: beriberi and dysentery. As the Americans landed first at
Leyte and then Lingayen, the Japanese guards became more brutal. While
executions were rare, beatings were common.

On February 23, 1945, while the Battle of Manila was at its height, U.S.
paratroopers from the 11th Airborne Division and Filipino guerrillas liberated
the camp. The fight was fierce, but the surprise of an air attack so dumbfounded the Japanese that the operation was successful: not one American or
Filipino soldier was lost, and not one internee was killed. The prisoners were
evacuated over the Laguna de Bay by amphibious vehicles, with U.S. fighters flying cover overhead and Japanese troops shooting at them from nearby
Mount Makiling.

Price was among the rescued, but he was very sick. With the others he
was transported to the Muntinlupa Prison, where he was cared for by military authorities. His sons Robert, Joseph, and Walter found him there. Shortly
thereafter, he was transferred to the Santo Tomas hospital. His health began to
improve, and he was able to send a message, presumably to a family member
in Philadelphia: "Rescued from starvation and internment camp February 23
by the finest troops in the world—from the good old U.S.A. Doctors, nurses,
Red Cross doing everything possible for us. Health poor, but expect daily improvement. Brother Walter S. Price."[12]

But the years of severe treatment had taken their toll. His health re-
versed and quickly declined. A lifelong Baptist and Mason, he received the
last rites of the Catholic Church, and then on March 18, 1945, as Hartendorp
reported in his chronicle of the internees, the "transportation king of Leyte,
died of pneumonia." The man who developed roads and bus services in Leyte
and contributed so much to the development of the province had passed into
obscurity, without even a photograph in his house to invoke his memory.

As the 24th Infantry Division was busy on Hill 522 and while Price
faded in Los Baños, a young merchant marine officer was watching the smoky
coastline from his cargo ship in Leyte Gulf. His name was Eddie Woolbright,
and he became perhaps the most flamboyant, the most successful, and even
the most revered of all the postwar American expatriates.

I met Eddie Woolbright in August 1995. While working on an oral history of Americans in the Philippines, I had come down to Cebu from Manila, largely at the urging of American historian Michael Onorato, as well as from the guys in the Makati kapihan. Tom Carter, in particular, said that I just had to talk to Woolbright, the last of a special breed. Lewis Gleeck Jr., who then ran the American Collection at the Ateneo de Manila Library, also seemed interested in seeing what I could come up with on Woolbright. I had no idea what to expect, sitting there that noon at the bar of the just-opened Eddie's Heritage Hotel. Someone—I believe his son, as it turned out—told me to go to one of the hotel rooms; Eddie was there and waiting. I walked into the room and started from surprise and anxiety. Here, stretched out on the bed was an old man, fully dressed and nearly emaciated. A nurse was adjusting the oxygen tube that went from the large canister into his nose. He was, without question, in very bad shape. Yet, he was striking with his shiny, quick eyes and remarkable crop of black hair. He had a haggard, wrinkled, but friendly face. It was, as I would always recall, a decidedly American face, if such a thing is possible.

Woolbright hardly allowed me to introduce myself and my oral history project. Rather, he took the lead and immediately began telling me his story, as I desperately tried to set up my tape recorder. Despite a five-pack-a-day cigarette habit that caused his now terminal lung cancer, his voice was strong though hoarse, and, regardless of his half century in the Philippines, his Oakie accent was unmistakable; indeed, it was heavy. Lying flat on his back, with his oxygen attached and with all the appropriateness of a classical *partitio* (how a speech will be divided), he told me he would talk a while, then he would rest, and then he would like to take me for a little ride around Cebu.

Woolbright's life could be compared to a Horatio Alger story. He was born in Boswell, Oklahoma, near the Red River, in 1920. A son of the Dust Bowl, he found joy working as a soda jerk during the Depression. After graduating from Franklin Roosevelt's Civilian Conservation Corps, Woolbright entered the war as a merchant marine officer. During the Battle of the North Atlantic, he sailed to Russia. Woolbright remembered those days most vividly. He recalled the cold and the fear and the sight of German airplanes coming out of Norway that skimmed the water to drop their bombs. He encountered submarines, too. Fifteen ships in his group—thirteen in one day—were sunk, but they made it to the White Sea. They spent the winter frozen in Archangel until a Russian icebreaker got them out.

From the voice on the bed, people and places from half a century before floated up into the room like puffs of smoke. The old man then took a rest from talking. The nurse watched him. After a minute or so, he signaled he wanted to get up, and the nurse helped him to his feet. Standing, he seemed even thinner. But I remember thinking that he only needed a hat and a horse and he would have been a perfect cowboy from a Frederic Remington painting. The gaunt cowpoke motioned, and I followed him and the nurse to a waiting car in the street. He walked slowly but fairly well and without the use of a cane.

During the trip around Cebu City, he sat up front, directing the driver. Throughout the journey, a Filipina staff person, sitting in the back seat with me, kept fanning or massaging him. Sometimes he was hooked up to the oxygen canister, which also rode in the back seat. Cebu City slid past, providing an interesting but inconsequential backdrop for Woolbright's early life.

He was in Caracas, Venezuela, when the Japanese bombed Pearl Harbor. Patriotism immediately took control. At first he wanted to be a pilot but could not arrange it; so he settled on continuing his service in the merchant marines. After his harrowing 1942 trip to Archangel, he went to Australia and loaded up supplies again for Russia, but this time via Basra, Iraq. Then came the Sicilian invasion, then Naples. A ship he was on nearly cracked in half during an Atlantic storm, and he spent months in the Azores while the ship was under repair. In October 1944 he was on a supply ship out of New Guinea that met up with the giant convoy that formed the Leyte invasion fleet. After the landing, Woolbright got shore leave, and he recalled his first moments in the Philippines this way:

> I went from Leyte Gulf to Tacloban in late October, 1944, and that was the worst place I suppose I ever saw in the world. See the Army was there . . . hundreds and hundreds of trucks and all kinds of vehicles . . . tanks . . . bulldozers. All of them up and down the road. The roads were just muck. You couldn't even walk down the roads . . . I had to go in a jeep. Mud holes two or three feet deep in the town and all. Dirtiest, ugliest place in the world.

I went ashore there and met with some people. Talked to them. Met with them in a little place. We sat down and talked. We had a USO [United Service Organization] and had some beer served, and the Red Cross had some lemon juice [stands] all over the town. But not much to see in Tacloban. A couple of little Chinese restaurants, and we would eat Chinese food. But it was a dirty town because of so many people and so many vehicles of all types. I met a few people there and they all spoke English very, very well. And I enjoyed Tacloban, except that it was a dirty, dirty town because of the invasion.[13]

Woolbright's interaction with the local people was the birth of his Philippine business career. He went on to Manila with the fleet and saw the shattered city. There he and another merchant marine, as well as other soldiers, became involved in a scheme to carry thousands of worthless Japanese bills back to the United States and sell them for souvenirs, but the deal fell through. Disappointed, he sailed for other Pacific ports. Soon, though, the time came to return home: the war was over. His spell Stateside did not last long, and once again Woolbright found himself on a ship in Leyte Gulf. This time he decided to stay longer. Woolbright returned to a trick that that had worked for him in Brazil: he feigned sickness and asked his merchant marine captain to discharge him in Tacloban. The artifice succeeded. Woolbright, paid off, began his illustrious career, starting first as a junk dealer and then as a hotelier.

Because of the protean conditions, Americans who decided to set up business in the Philippines directly after the war often had incredible opportunities. Some of them made quite a livelihood. Most did not. Unlike Woolbright, few had any experience with metal and machines. Woolbright's father had been a machinist and owned a blacksmith shop. Eddie looked around and saw an island full of scrap metal, which he began to gather and sell. His life was set.

But with the war over, dramatic political changes were about to occur. At the end of the war, both countries wanted something from the other: the Philippines wanted independence, the United States wanted security. To complicate matters, the Philippines desperately needed financial assistance to rebuild its shattered cities and infrastructure. That assistance came but with a cost. In 1945 Senator Millard Tydings of Maryland, after visiting what remained of Manila, sponsored a bill to help the Philippines recoup war damages while setting the stage for future economic growth. Rep. C. Jasper Bell of Missouri opposed Tydings's bill. Instead, Bell sought to control the Philippines economically through a number of methods, including allowing Americans a near monopoly on exports to the islands while restricting their Philippine counterparts. Known as the Philippine Trade Act of 1946, it contained several controversial elements, one of which concerned parity rights. Parity rights allowed Americans in the Philippines to be treated as citizens in terms of economic matters, such as the ownership of mines and natural resources. Such a clause would require that the Philippines amend its Constitution, a document that strictly limited foreign investment. To the act's supporters, the parity rights clause meant that the war-torn country would now be open for development via U.S. dollars. Its detractors countered by saying that Washington would still control the country despite granting its independence. As Woolbright watched a new country being born, he worried if he would be able to continue in his business.

Woolbright did stay, unfettered by Philippine law and supported by U.S. politics. He spoke with intense pride at his early accomplishments in Tacloban. His enthusiasm was authentic, and his admiration for the Filipinos was sincere. I found that his comments on the Thomasites, the American schoolteachers who came early in the century and did much to introduce English and U.S. culture to the Filipinos, presented a view of a time and place now largely forgotten by both Filipinos and Americans.

In 1947 I had a hardware store, a spare parts store. Next to it I started the *Airline Hotel and Coffee Shop*. What made me open up a restaurant next to that was during my childhood days I used to work in a drug store, but at the soda jerk fountain, because all drug stores practically had soda fountains. This was a come-on call; this was advertisement for your store. So I put the coffee shop in Tacloban next to my auto supply store, and it really boomed. I had ice cream machines. I had normal electricity. Tacloban had brown outs all the time but I had my own generators.

So it became part of me. If anybody wanted to see me or buy something from me they would go to the *Airline Hotel and Coffee Shop.*

It was great to work with Filipinos. At that time it was so easy, because I didn't speak a word of dialect, and even now I speak very little. I know very few words. But at that time Tacloban was like me living in the States. Practically everybody spoke English. Because Tacloban was a place where there was a lot of old time Americans, those who landed there during 1898. They sent American schoolteachers after the Spanish-American war. The American schoolteachers were all over the islands. Every province had American schoolteachers. They brought their families over. It was like the USA. You could just walk out and everyone was right with you. Even the songs, music, parties . . . They all knew the American songs. You just felt at home. Really at home.

Despite his love of Tacloban and apparently the excitement it presented, the scrap metal business was beginning to show signs of weakening. During his stay in Leyte, Woolbright was befriended by Joseph Price, the eldest son of Walter Scott Price. Joe gave him sound business advice: get out of Tacloban. The friendship between Price and Woolbright was an interesting bridge between the old colonial order and the new postcolonial boom.

There was no law really in Tacloban. In the early days of Tacloban, see everybody had guns. Everybody protecting themselves. In Leyte [I] always had a .45 and machine guns. I had two or three machine guns. There was a lot of robbers. You had to protect yourself.

I had a junkyard out in the town of Palo. In those days it was rough. Anyone could get a gun there. A person needed protection. So I had five or six guards there with machine guns. In my house I had boxes of ammunition. . . . [the Communists] tried to force you to pay, give them something on the side. I always paid them off . . . Every afternoon we would go out in the yard and practice shooting revolvers and guns. It was the wild west. I had an armor plated jeep. . . . Always had a guy sitting with me and my German Shepherd dog. I had a German Shepherd well-trained, sitting in my armor plated jeep.

Until 1948, 1949 Tacloban was really a lively town. Because there was a lot of machinery, army equipment, left behind at the bases and that was being sold, and it was a boom in Tacloban. It wasn't that way before the war. After liberation time—'48, '49, '50—it got slowing down. . . . And I got a lot of information from a man named Joe Price. He was the son of one of the 1898 veterans. They had a transportation company there in Tacloban. Joe Price used to tell me, "Eddie, things are good here now but when the army equipment and all its surplus are gone this is a dead town. You should look for greener grass." He was like my father. He was about fifty-five, sixty at that time, and I was twenty-five. He taught me a lot, and I listened to the old man, and he was really right about the economy in Tacloban. In 1948, '49 it started to slack off. So I decided to start coming to Cebu once in awhile. And I decided to move over here to Cebu.

In 1949 Woolbright pulled up stakes and left for Cebu City. Once there, he essentially repeated his success in Tacloban. He opened up a restaurant that would become part of local legend, Eddie's Log Cabin.

We went to the Log Cabin, which was near the wharf in a decidedly seedy part of town.[14] Woolbright was clearly proud of it. He claimed he built it by importing logs from Mindanao and that he wanted to re-create an American pioneer home here on the Cebu waterfront, making me immediately think of Doane's philosophy and the Leyte capitol building. I suppose it was a log cabin in Cebu, but the place reminded me more of a great old bar I frequented when I was in graduate school. It was cool and dark and beery, with a well-seasoned sense of decadence. Woolbright said it was the first air-conditioned restaurant in Cebu, and it was at one time a haunt for local celebrities and politicians. In fact, it was on the campaign circuit: anyone running for president and visiting Cebu had to stop at the Log Cabin. Today there was but one patron, quietly sitting at a table with a coffee and a book. Woolbright introduced him as the former mayor of Cebu City. A friendly man, he told me that a much younger Eddie would sometimes swing from the chandelier right here in the Cabin. Everyone, he said, *everyone* loved Eddie. Woolbright and I left, and the mayor went back to his Herman Wouk novel.

We got back into the car and resumed our cruise throughout Cebu. During the 1950s and 1960s, Woolbright ventured into other areas, including construction, concrete, and real estate. It was real estate that won him his lasting fame in the area. He built Beverly Hills, still the most prestigious subdivision in Cebu. His financial success and standing within the Cebu community undoubtedly helped him land Annie Corrales, Miss Philippines 1957 and a Miss Universe contestant, whom he married.

The man even made his mark on Asian culture. According to an alumni group at the University of Singapore, a popular dice game called *balut*, played throughout the Far East, is accredited to Woolbright. As the story goes, one night shortly after the end of the war, a couple of U.S. soldiers were sitting in Woolbright's Tacloban Airline Hotel. They wanted to play poker but had no cards. Instead, they used dice, and the drinking/gambling exercise became known as poker dice. A couple of Europeans staying at Woolbright's hotel saw the game and then refined the rules to allow more than two people to play at one time. A new game had been invented. But it had no name. One day as Woolbright and the players left the hotel and went for a walk, they heard the ubiquitous egg vendors calling out their product: "Balut!" Woolbright and the others decided that this was the right name. Later, when Woolbright moved to Cebu City, he took the game with him, often playing at the British Club. It was an immediate hit. In the 1960s a British captain took the game to Singapore, and the later some Scandinavian expats introduced balut to Thailand. By 1972 the International Balut Federation was established, and today it has branches worldwide. What had been born in Woolbright's Tacloban bar had grown into a global sport, with a world championship held annually.[15]

Yes, Woolbright was an American sui generis, even after his death. His rise to fame, however, came with personal hardship, probably more than Woolbright would admit. In the first postwar days in Tacloban, he came to know the Romualdez family; the teenage Imelda Romualdez, later Imelda Marcos, would stop in his restaurant on the way home from school. They became friends. He remembered that at American parties she would sing American songs. She was a hit. When Woolbright moved to Cebu, he formed a close and costly friendship with the leading family of the city, the Osmeñas. Sergio Osmeña, he knew, had landed with MacArthur as president of the Philippines. As years passed, Woolbright prospered; Imelda married Ferdinand and set up house in Malacanang. At a party in Baguio he met Marcos, whom Woolbright determined was one smart boy. During the 1960s Sergio Osmeña Jr. began to challenge the president politically. Perhaps he could follow his father and become president. In 1972 martial law was declared, and Woolbright, probably because of his association with Osmeña, found himself in a difficult situation.

One day he received a phone call from the Cebu detachment of the Philippine Constabulary. He knew these guys pretty well. They invited him to a party that afternoon. A partygoer, Woolbright got dressed, hopped in his sports car, and drove over to the police station for the party. There was no party. The police told him he was under arrest.

"What's the charge?" a shocked Woolbright asked. But there was no charge; there would never be a charge. Like a character in a Kafka novel, he was just under arrest. It was martial law.

Woolbright was taken to the stockade in Cebu and kept with other political prisoners. With the help of the U.S. consul in Cebu, he began to kick up a fuss about not being charged. Finally, the authorities gave him a day pass, meaning that every other day he could leave the stockade during daylight but needed to be back by midnight. At once his experience turned around. He would leave the prison and return at night with food from the Log Cabin. He started poker games. Sometimes he would bring in singers. Coyly, he said they had some "action." His fellow prisoners loved him. His own testimony was this: "I was having a lot of fun. It was a good experience."

Leave it to Woolbright to turn incarceration into a romp. But after a couple months it wore thin, and at the urging of fellow prisoners, he finally contacted his old friend from Tacloban, Imelda Marcos. He sent her a cable saying he was tired and confused and wanted to go home. Within two hours, he was released, still without a charge or an apology. He claimed it was his only bad experience in the Philippines.

Throughout our drive around Cebu, one subject kept cropping up, scrap metal. Seemingly at every place we visited, Woolbright would comment on how much a piece of metal was worth, how much he could get for it, what he could do with it. He seemed consumed by the subject, determined, even with the end staring him in the face, that he would transform all unwanted metal into some type of profit.

We arrived shoreside, looking out to Mactan Island, Cebu's famous international vacation spot. The car pulled up to a pier, and we got out. Off in the distance we could see a skyline of hotels and resorts, where wealthy Asians and that week, according to the newspapers, a group of U.S. National Basketball Association (NBA) players came to relax and frolic. We were in a nearly deserted stretch of wharves and warehouses. There was a lonesome little dive shop owned by a couple of Swedish men. Woolbright went over and chatted with them. After a few moments he motioned for me to follow him to the boat. He was chuckling.

"Those Swedish boys, they're good boys. They didn't recognize me. Last time they saw me I was 190 pounds. Now I am 125."

We walked down the pier and up a plank into the boat. It was an abandoned commercial ship that Woolbright said he had towed down from Manila. I wanted to laugh: the ship looked like a floating disaster. Peeling paint and rusted metal. Broken machinery on the decks. Steps and railings that looked dangerous. It had no engine or at least not one that worked. It was junk, a giant floating pile of scrap metal. The whole structure appeared haunted, and I may have quietly said something like "Flying Dutchman" to myself. Woolbright, however, was optimistic about it; he was going to turn it into a restaurant or maybe a casino. At that point I realized what the ship meant to him: it connected all of his lifelong pursuits—the sea of his youth, the scrap metal that made him his livelihood, and the restaurant business that he had always enjoyed. Now, surely realizing he had but months to live, he had taken on the project that was going to tie everything together. I never found out if he got it up and running.

The last time I saw Eddie was in his house in Cebu. The family sat around in his bedroom, with Eddie in bed on oxygen, and I remember looking at a portrait of him on the dresser. In the portrait, done years before the cancer had set in, he reminded me somewhat of Charles Bronson: robust, tough, handsome. We ate local fruit, and I am sure we both felt we would never see each other again. He held out his hand and gave me some seeds for a tree whose genus I cannot recall. Eddie told me to plant them in America. I found the moment both moving and ironic. Here at the end of his life, a life of planting seeds in the Philippines, he wanted to grow things back home. I left with the seeds in my pocket. We would correspond over the next few months. Then Eddie died.

Price and Woolbright present a composite character of the old-time American in the Philippines. Restless men, they left their own culture for a foreign one, capitalizing on the confusion of war to build a fortune. In doing so, they became a part of their adopted community, albeit in a patriarchal way. Unlike today's global technocrats, however, they did put down roots, they did immerse themselves in the local culture, and they did give of themselves.

But the question is, what remains of their presence and of their labor? Some of it is still quite evident, such as the road infrastructure of Leyte or the suburbs of Cebu, physical foundations that will exist for years to come. But much of it is eroding, like their memory. Maybe they will continue as a reference in some obscure history book. They might carry on in an album of old bridges, buildings, and restaurants or perhaps in a photograph of a rusting boat. Or they might live in a reverential account of their deeds spoken by someone who admired them. One thing is certain: the Philippines will never see their type again.

6

THE SECOND BATTLE OF LEYTE

The Leyte Park Resort Hotel, the best and most expensive hotel in Tacloban, is the pride of Imelda Marcos and the Romualdez family, or so says the Philippine historical marker at the entrance. It overlooks the San Pedro Strait, which separates Leyte from the dark, craggy island of Samar to the east. Despite the years of tropical assault, the hotel still more or less maintains its initial splendor. Below the main building, private cottages look out over the water. The liver-shaped pool has a waterfall and an aqua bar. The lobby is noteworthy for its various forms of ornamental bamboo that cover the walls and for its thirty-foot cathedral ceiling. Its check-in counter is a faux nipa hut.

At noon, in the waiting area of the lobby, sat five or six members of an American missionary group. The entire contingent, perhaps twenty-five in all—mostly American and some Filipino men and women, nearly all of whom were younger than thirty—had arrived several days before. When the group first walked in to the hotel, they all wore blue T-shirts marked with crosses and scripture. They formed a line in the lobby. Group leaders barked directions and gave orders in loud, conspicuous American accents. The young people responded quickly and quietly, picking up their bags and going to their rooms. The next morning, large uniformed boxes containing (according to the hotel staff) either medicine or books were loaded into several large jeepneys and taken away. The fresh-faced apostles went with them and returned, smiling, at the dinner hour. Over the next several days not one of these young persons was seen in the swimming pool or at the bar. This spot was no rest and recreation resort for them.

Perhaps the oldest members and certainly the officers of the platoon sat within arm's reach of a newspaper rack, but no one held a paper. Several read their Bibles while the others leafed through three-ring binders. One white man, clearly the group's leader, sat close to a Filipino subordinate. The leader was tall and in his mid-forties. With sandy hair and a toothy smile, he wore a flowered shirt, shorts, and hiking shoes. As everyone else did, he kept a backpack handy.

He instructed the Filipino subordinate on scripture, something about leadership and training leaders. Leadership was connected to Jesus. He talked about building spiritual communities and planting churches. His voice became soft as he quoted from Proverbs. He and the Filipino closed their eyes together, and their lips moved silently and seriously. No one else seemed to notice them. After a few moments both opened their eyes, relieved. They smiled, and the leader said to the others, "We were just energizing." Some grinned in response.

"Do you have any children?" the leader asked the Filipino. "Yes. Two." He showed pictures. "Good," responded the leader. "Children are our future leaders." He held a short conversation with an American subordinate, whose reconnaissance reported that the Davao Hall, their next destination, held 750 seats.

There is a war going on in the Philippines, and the persons sitting in the hotel lobby are frontline soldiers. Today the battlefield is Tacloban. As with all wars, this conflict is about power and territory but is measured by the souls of the people; indeed, it is a spiritual war with all eternity as the prize. But it is also a war with an extended history and contemporary cultural and political ramifications. Beginning with the American invasion of the islands in 1899 and later with the arrival of fundamentalist Christian groups, first during the postwar years and more dramatically since 1980, the Catholic Church's dominance here has been under attack. The weapons are Bibles, food packages, and televisions. It is an invasion that will probably not end soon, and the final campaign is uncertain.[1]

The people of the Philippines have long been targets for missionary armies. The Muslims came first. During the fourteenth century, Islam arrived from Indonesia. Muslim forces had colonized much of Mindanao, with outposts in Cebu and what is now Manila. Through them a large Muslim population was established.

Catholicism came to the islands in the sixteenth century with Ferdinand Magellan and Miguel López de Legaspi, dedicated evangelists if ever there were any. The early Spanish conquerors must have sensed something vulnerable about the indigenous population. Soon thereafter, different Catholic orders washed up on the islands' shores. In 1565 the Augustinians arrived. The Franciscans landed in 1577. Both the Dominicans and the Jesuits disembarked in 1581. The Recollects came in 1606. By the time Cromwell sacked Ireland, nearly all parts of the Philippines were under Rome.

The conversion of the native population was relatively easy, and it was not done, as has been often been claimed, at the point of a sword. Rather, the Spanish used the highly evocative clerical garbs, statues, incense, and the mysterious ceremony of the Mass to win over a basically animist people. The Spanish set up pueblos all over the islands to better protect their interests and the local population from Muslim slave traders who plied the Malaysian waters. These towns, built around the church in the central plaza, were run by both a civil administration and the ecclesiastical order, with the real power wielded by the parish priest. Living in such towns, or being "under the bells," gave Filipinos concrete protection, but it also created a rhythm of life largely drawn on the liturgical calendar. Fiestas, holidays, weddings, baptisms, funerals, and other celebrations of life and death—all occurred under the bells.

Living outside Manila with little in the way of secular Spanish authority eventually changed the character of the Catholic orders, which evolved into what has been called a friarocracy. The orders, especially the Dominicans, Franciscans, and the Augustinians, exerted control over education, the police, health matters, and taxes. With a virtual monopoly on the social system, the friars eventually acquired vast landholdings (mostly in the agriculturally rich Central Luzon region). In turn, they leased out the land to planters, thus providing the orders with even more income. By the mid-nineteenth century, the friars were often seen living in palatial houses, much to the amazement of the Filipinos and the church officials in Manila.

It is important to note that the friars were at odds with the Catholic

Church itself. Canonical law states that the activities of all clergy must be supervised by the regional bishops; yet, the friars were able to thwart this authority and operate as essentially rogue parishes. This independence brought about friction between them and the church hierarchy. Moreover, the political ablation never healed. Another issue furthered the conflict: although church policy demanded that the parishes of colonized countries be eventually turned over to local priests, once again, the friars nullified the statutes of Rome and did little in the way of allowing Filipino priests into positions of authority.

The friars' unabashed racism, however, galled the Filipinos most. The friars regarded any aspect of Filipino authority or independence with open contempt. Because they held power over education and other forms of social control, they were chief targets of the Philippine independence movement of the late nineteenth century. A series of antifriar revolts occurred in the mid-nineteenth century. In 1887, José Rizal's universally acclaimed novel, *Noli Me Tangere*, which virulently attacked the friars, galvanized anti-Spanish sentiment and geared up a fledgling independence movement. Under the direction of Emilio Aguinaldo, a Filipino force defeated a number of Spanish contingents in the provinces and in 1898 had Manila encircled. At the same time, war between Spain and the United States broke out in Cuba. Comm. George Dewey was sent by President William McKinley to destroy the Spanish fleet stationed in Manila Bay. In late April, Dewey coaled his flagship, the USS *Olympia*, and with a small squadron sailed out of Hong Kong Harbor bound for the Philippines.

On May 1, 1898, Dewey's defeat of the Spanish navy signaled the end of official Catholic domination of the islands. Spain, devastated by defeats in Cuba, ceded the Philippines to the United States; however, there remained a popularly supported independence movement, with a seasoned and enthusiastic, if poorly armed and trained, military. President McKinley made the decision that independence was not a viable solution for the Filipinos, believing they were simply not capable of governing their own land. The independence movement had to be put down, and a large contingent of U.S. troops, mostly volunteers from the western states, was sent to do the job.

In the United States, there was substantial opposition to this decision. Should not the United States be freeing people from European oppression instead of conquering them? McKinley had the answer to this thorny conundrum. The Americans would not only create a new country for the Filipinos, one built in the image of its creator, but it would also replace the Spanish culture as well. One of the reasons why the United States had decided to send troops to the Philippines, at least according to McKinley, was to "Christianize" the Filipino people. In the company of a missionary committee from the Methodist Episcopal Church, he said that

> I went down on my knees and prayed to Almighty God . . . and [the decision to invade the Philippines] came to me this way . . . there was nothing left for us to do but take them [the islands] . . . and to educate the Filipinos, and uplift and civilize, and Christianize them, and by God's grace do the very best we could by them, as our fellow-men for whom Christ also died.[2]

American Protestant groups immediately picked up McKinley's concept of physical and spiritual conquest of the Philippines. Two weeks after Dewey's *Olympia* and its squadron had decimated the Spanish fleet off Cavite, the Presbyterian General Assembly offered this statement: "God has given into our hands, that is, unto the hands of American Christians, the Philippine Islands. . . . By the very guns of our battleships God summoned us to go and possess the land."[3] The war had commenced.

The fact that Filipinos had been worshipping Jesus Christ for roughly two hundred years before the Declaration of Independence seems to have been lost on McKinley and American religious denominations. No matter. The U.S. forces went in, and the fighting (replete with atrocities on both sides) was all over in about two or three years. Then came the difficult part—turning uncivilized and heathen Filipinos into good American Christians. One method was the creation of a mass education system. Throughout most of the Spanish period, education in the Philippines was limited only to the elite, and it had always been under the auspices of the Catholic Church. In the latter part of the nineteenth century, the Spanish did attempt a public education system, but it was largely controlled by the religious orders and was considered ineffective. Almost immediately after defeating the Filipino forces, the

United States recruited young American teachers—by and large Protestants and with a good number of ministers among them—to help the Filipinos better themselves through democracy. Collectively known as the Thomasites after the transport ship *Thomas*, in which an early batch of teachers arrived, the teachers came to the islands with high ideals and an evangelical spirit. Within a decade of their arrival, the Thomasites were successfully operating a nationwide public education system. In schools all over the country, children saluted Old Glory every morning and then proceeded to their American history and literature lessons. Of equal importance the public school system was being used to combat Catholicism. Despite the fact that the official U.S. policy instructed teachers to remain neutral regarding religion and refrain from opining their own religious views, many teachers saw the public school as an opportunity to reduce the Catholic cultural influence. As one Baptist missionary put it: "Every public school can be counted as an evangelical force in a Roman Catholic country."[4]

A second part of the plan to Christianize the Filipinos involved missionaries. Now under the subjugation of a U.S. administration, Filipinos were allowed religious freedom, and American officials enthusiastically welcomed and, in fact, recruited Protestant missionaries. Just as the Catholic orders before them, different Protestant churches arrived and began to spread out over the islands. Much like a good military plan, the comity agreements of 1901 formally divided the islands among the different denominations. The Presbyterian Church sent its missionaries to Manila and the Tagalog provinces that surrounded the city. The Methodist missionaries went to Pangasinan and Pampanga. The Baptists worked Manila and the Visayas. The Ilocos region received the United Brethren in Christ and the Mission of the Disciples of Christ. In late 1901 the Mission of the Protestant Episcopal Church went to both northern Luzon and southern Mindanao. The next year the Christian and Missionary Alliance was ordered to the islands of Mindanao and Sulu. The Seventh-day Adventist Church followed soon after in various cities throughout the country.

These missionaries faced, of course, an immediate and troubling situation. Missionaries are typically sent into the wild lands of the unbelievers to spread the word of Christ. But Filipinos had long worshipped Christ, believing in the same ideas of redemption and salvation. How was it possible to bring Christ to people who already had accepted Christ? How could the evangelical men and women justify their actions? The answer was based not so much in religion as it was in power and prejudice.

Realizing their ticklish moral situation, the missionaries had to address the righteousness of their purpose straight away. This effort lead to an uneven relationship with the Catholic Church that lasted throughout the colonial and commonwealth periods. During the first few years after the war, only the Episcopalians did not try to convert Catholics. Some missionaries saw that Catholicism had served at least some good purpose in the Philippines: it had defended the Filipinos against Islam, initiated an educational system, and raised the level of civilization. Catholic missionaries had introduced the story of Jesus Christ, even if it did come with the worship of Mary and the saints.

But all Protestant missionaries saw Catholicism as an acutely flawed form of religion. The prevailing thought among these missionaries was that Catholicism had little connection to true Christianity. They hated the power of the priest within parishes. Missionaries sometimes called Catholic Filipinos immoral, heathens, ignorant of Christian principles, and idol worshippers. More alarming, they found the Catholic Church had allowed folk rituals and superstitions into Christian ceremonies such as weddings and funerals. Doctrinally, Protestants felt that Catholic priests withheld the Bible from their flocks and kept the people uninformed. Early Protestant clergy consistently cited corruption among the priests, and as in America, an entire corpus of urban legends grew up concerning the morality of these men.

As the Protestant missionaries multiplied, they not surprisingly received opposition from Catholics. While no American missionaries were actually harmed, Filipino Protestants were physically harassed, and some were killed. Most of the opposition, however, came in the form of mental intimidation. Priests called for boycotts of Protestant businesses. Protestants were not allowed to be buried in public cemeteries and often were not allowed to rent land. Over the next decade, the animosity between the religions lessened but did not disappear. Some Protestant missionaries began a cordial working relationship with priests, many of whom were now young Americans who had been sent to replace the Spanish orders. Other missionaries refused such relationships and continued to see Catholicism as a threatening non-Christian religion.

Two issues troubled the Protestant clergy in the Philippines during the first two decades of American rule: how far should the Filipinos rise within the hierarchy of the church, and what was to be done about Philippine independence? Most missionaries were undecided or ambivalent about Filipino participation in the curacy of their respective churches. While some churches did promote local clergy in the church hierarchy, most often Americans firmly held control. The consequences were sometimes devastating to the congregations. The Methodist and Presbyterian churches both suffered major schisms when large groups of Filipinos left to start their own churches. The Seventh-day Adventists lost their most capable convert, Felix Manalo, who formed the Iglesia ni Cristo, which today holds considerable influence in the Philippines.

If, by and large, the missionary community were ambivalent about Filipinos taking positions within the churches, its members were clearly uncomfortable with the notion of Philippine independence. Some were virulently opposed to the idea, which had taken root as early as the initial volleys of the Philippine-American War. During the first decade after the war, when civil Governor William Howard Taft proposed that the Filipinos should have their own elected assembly, many missionaries became alarmed. Their perturbation, in some cases, turned into sharp commentaries. Charles E. Rath of Leyte said, "If they get their assembly they can pass a law after their own heart . . . we believe they now enjoy many more privileges and much more liberty and protection and safety than if they had their won independence."

Once the assembly's proposal was passed, a Methodist publication announced that America had been wrong to place responsibility in the hands of Filipinos because they were not capable of governing themselves and that they could not apprehend the "benefit accruing from the American Occupation." And when U.S. congressman William B. Jones introduced a bill that would eventually grant the Philippines independence, Stealy B. Rossiter of the Presbyterian Church in Manila told an American audience that Filipinos, and Malays in general, were unfit for independence because they lacked constitutional initiative. If independence were granted, Rossiter predicted that "grass would be growing in the streets of Manila and hogs would be in the front yards." By the end of the second decade of U.S. rule, however, many missionaries were resigned to the fact that independence would someday occur. By then their paternalistic attitude had caused marked damage to Filipino-American relations.[5]

If the goal of these early colonial churches was to counterbalance Catholicism, the results are mixed. During the first decades of the century, Protestant denominations made major contributions, such as establishing medical centers throughout the islands. They also provided educational opportunities. Silliman University, a Presbyterian school in Dumaguete, Negros Oriental, is one of many exceptional private schools of higher education. These works, as well as the close relationship between the churches and the ruling U.S. colonial administrations, attracted many middle-class, upwardly mobile Filipinos. But after World War II and with the removal of the U.S. government, participation in the Protestant churches began to wane. While a warm afterglow of affection for the United States continued for decades, rising middle-class professionals felt less and less compelled to associate themselves with American institutions, and membership in Protestant churches leveled off. In sum, the actual amount of conversions was much smaller than initially hoped. This rate was also impeded in part after the Catholic Church quietly instituted reforms that ended the friars' abuses. The missionaries' condescending attitude to Filipino nationalism also hampered growth. Finally, the Protestant churches split into many factions; indeed, shortly after World War II there were as many as two hundred denominations in the country. By the 1980s, only 3 percent of the population could trace its religious ancestry to the prewar American missionaries.[6]

As the postwar world divided itself into communist and noncommunist countries and as the United States slowly declined from a position of economic dominance, so rose fundamental Christianity. Just as the perpetrators of Manifest Destiny nearly a century before, fundamentalist groups in the United States and around the world have tied their belief in God to nationalism. Unlike the mainstream Protestant churches, the fundamentalists are more conservative in both theological and political senses and far, far more aggressive. The keystone in the fundamentalist dogma is the evangelizing of the world. All people must receive Jesus Christ on their terms; there is no other alternative. Because it is mandatory that everyone worship Christ in the manner the fundamentalists dictate, spiritual and political conquests are unavoidably joined. Individual salvation is stressed; social reform is not. The problems of the country are often attributed to the sins of man: if the people are lazy or, as in the case of the Philippines, idolaters, God will punish the nation. Poverty exists in the Philippines because the people have not walked the true path. Thus, the solution to the country's ills lies in a more obedient individual. Such groups also preach the notion of wealth and prosperity through the gospels. Like the Calvinists before them, postwar fundamentalists pronounce that faith and material blessings are inextricably linked. In the 1960s charismatic preachers such as Oral Roberts and others in the Pentecostal movement, and later the television evangelists Pat Robertson, Jim Bakker, and Kenneth Copeland, all professed how the gospels led to personal and thus national prosperity. It was and is a message quite appealing to poor and not-so-poor people because it reads simply: "Ask Jesus, and it will be given to you."

The fundamentalist movement is worldwide, and it has targeted third world nations. There can be no question that the Philippines is high on the list of fundamentalist objectives. The study conducted by Steve Brouwer, Paul Gifford, and Susan Rose shows that only Brazil has had more evangelical missionary activity than the Philippines. One of the reasons that the Philippines is so important to fundamentalist groups is that it falls within the "10/40 window"—in other words, that part of the world that extends from 10 degrees to 40 degrees north of the equator. Within this area are enormous populations of unevangelized people, such as Muslims, Hindus, Buddhists, Shintoists, and, as with the Philippines, Catholics. The Philippines is seen as particularly useful because of the high volume of overseas workers who leave the country and travel to the Middle East and other parts of world. Thus, a major component of the fundamentalists' plan is to first plant churches in the Philippines and then have Filipinos help take the word to other places, such as Saudi Arabia and Kuwait.

The growth of the fundamentalist movement in the country has had two stages. As with the wave of Protestant missionaries after the Philippine-American War, the fundamentalist invasion began in the confusion of the postwar period. American soldiers who were stationed in the islands right

after World War II became involved in evangelism, including the establish-
ment of Bible schools. From this body of military men, a group known as the
G.I. Gospel Crusade in the Philippines formed and eventually evolved into
SEND International, a global evangelical missionary organization. Although
the number of groups was not large, fundamentalism had a beachhead in the
Philippines.

The second stage has been complex and dramatic. The expansion of
American fundamentalism in the country since 1980 is startling. Between
1980 and 1990 there has been a 145 percent rise in the number of fundamentalist churches (13,600).[7] The reasons for this growth are directly tied to the
nation's political woes. After President Ferdinand Marcos declared martial law
in 1972, many civil liberties were suspended. This situation quickly accelerat-
ed two phenomena: the deterioration of the nation's economy, which by 1980
was on the verge of collapse (and has never really recovered), and the growth
of a small but vocal communist movement. Concurrently, as the years of repression dragged through the 1970s and into the 1980s, a good number of
Filipino Catholic priests publicly or privately embraced "liberation theology,"
a liberalized viewpoint inspired first by the Second Vatican Council in 1965
and probably more so by the Second Latin American Bishops' Conference
in 1968. The Latin conference demanded more direct and substantial efforts to help the poor of South America. Philippine priests condemned the
enormous disparities between the wealthy elite and the majority of Filipinos,
who were living well beneath the poverty line. These priests advocated an improvement in the Filipinos' lives though a collective approach: Base Christian
Communities (BCCs), cooperatives, labor unions, and civic projects. Their
many detractors, both inside and outside of the Catholic Church, saw this
philosophy as alarmingly close to communism.

The close connection between the church and civil rights activism could
be exemplified by the comments of Gordon Koller, a Jesuit priest from New
York who spent a lifetime in Mindanao. He first came to the islands in 1933, as
part of the church's effort to replace the Spanish influence with an American
one. In 1997, in a retirement home on the Ateneo de Manila campus, Koller
remembered how Marcos harassed, imprisoned, and murdered priests. He
recalled that in Mindanao in the late 1970s

[t]he bishop had a diocesan newspaper; they [the Marcos government] wanted to close that. We were influencing people. We were telling them about their rights and all that. We weren't going to take it sitting down. They suspected us of being with the communists. I heard this story that even in Central and South America money was poured in against the Church because they thought the Church was helping the communists. Well, we were in that sense. The Church is revolutionary, and it speaks out for morality.[8]

The repression ended in 1986 when a portion of the Philippine military and thousands of ordinary Filipinos in the streets, coupled with the U.S. government's reluctance to help Marcos and its de facto assistance to the rebels, drove the strongman into exile in Hawaii. It has been argued that this peaceful "people's power" revolution was the result of years of Catholic activism. In fact, the pivotal role of Cardinal Jaime Sin, the use of the Catholic station Radio Veritas to inspire thousand of people to take to the streets, and the media's publication of photographs of nuns kneeling in the path of tanks and rebel soldiers holding high the statue of the Virgin Mary solidified the impression that it was a Catholic rebellion. The church's role was weighty, so to some extent this perception was true.

The "miracle of EDSA," or the Epifanio de los Santos highway, formally the American-built Highway 54, upon which the people marched, established democracy once again in the country, but it also engendered a sinister side effect. With Marcos's power destroyed and with the country's power reverting to wealthy families of the pre-Marcos era, a period of confusion and uncertainty set in. During Corazon Aquino's presidency, there were a series of coup attempts, and the one in December 1989 was especially bloody. In the provinces, the New People's Army (NPA), the armed wing of the Philippine Communist Party, became even more active, especially once its leader, Jose Sison, had been released from prison. To assist the embattled Armed Forces of the Philippines, the Aquino government helped form anticommunist citizens groups.

The fundamentalist movement fit superbly into this post-Marcos confusion. In the years immediately after the dictator fell, the non-Catholic

Christian groups swarmed into the Philippines. In 1987 and 1988, twenty-four such groups registered within the country, doubling the monthly average during the years 1980–86. In 1988 there were 1,676 Christian groups in the Philippines, or nearly an increase of 1,400 since 1980. Many of these groups saw Catholicism as the root cause of the post-Marcos malaise. Brouwer, Gifford, and Rose relate that Eddie Villanueva, director of the influential Jesus Is Lord Fellowship and one-time political aspirant, stated that

> in 1986, God gave us the miracle of EDSA but look what our country-men have done. Instead of attributing the miracle to God, they have chosen to honor a so-called lady of peace and erected a statue and shrine to her, at the behest of the Catholic religious leaders, supported by our top government officials. This is pure and simple idolatry and because of it our whole nation suffers.[9]

The idea that fundamentalist groups have been used to counter social reform, especially the development of BCCs, is seen in the comments of Father Romeo Empestan, the one-time director of such communities in Bacolod on the troubled island of Negros. The BCCs are essentially Catholic human rights groups, attempting to empower the poor. At the center of the wild dynamics of government repression, vigilante groups, a communist insurgency, American interests, and rampant poverty, Empestan noted the following:

> When the church tried to speak about the rights of workers, little by little they [large plantation owners on Negros] questioned us . . . the landowners were defensive and they attacked the Church. . . . they said we [BCC priests] were causing trouble. So now they're trying to propa-gate counter religious movements. For example, the charismatic move-ment. A kind of religion that only touches on personal piety not social issues: "Praise the Lord" and such.
>
> It is an imported movement. Jimmy Swaggart is very active here, along with others whose names I do not know. They pick up Filipino lay leaders—giving them good maintenance [money], of course—and they go around recruiting. And last week our catechist told us that there

is some kind of foundation, this Jonathon Foundation, Inc., which is recruiting people, because if they get enrolled they will receive money from people who will write to them from abroad. And they say this is approved by the cardinal and by the diocese, but we know that it is not. Meaning to say, they are using all means to reinforce the kind of vertical religion, which is trying to cover up the main problem in the Philippines and in Negros. Vertical religion is myself and God, without touching any social realities.[10]

Thus, the national uncertainty, particularly in the provinces, during the 1980s and 1990s has, in fact, created a religious conflict. On the one hand, the Catholic Church and some mainstream Protestant denominations have been seen as communist-leaning radicals. On the other hand, the fundamentalist movement has closely allied itself with the Philippine military. Stridently anti-communist organizations such as the Alliance for Democracy and Morality, an association of more than a hundred groups that is allied with the International Baptist Church Ministries, which itself is the head of the nearly five hundred fundamentalist Baptist churches in the Philippines, have had direct ties to the AFP. Such connections have included the presentation of value formation courses for the AFP. These courses began in 1987 and, in the words of then-president Fidel Ramos, were intended to produce soldiers who were "God-centered." These courses also brought the support of the Kenneth Copeland Ministries, which helped distribute their publications to AFP officers attending seminars. Another fundamentalist organization, the Jesus Miracle Crusade International Ministry—an authoritarian charismatic group that encourages speaking in tongues and requires fasting—has held numerous anticommunist rallies, in effect, assisting in the military's propaganda campaigns. Perhaps the most recognizable American fundamentalist, the Moral Majority's late leader Rev. Jerry Falwell visited the Philippines in late 1985. There he gave support to fellow anticommunist President Marcos by saying the U.S. media was "unfair" in its treatment of the dictator and that he felt " a lot safer in Manila than New York or Washington." Falwell also said that if the communists ever gained control in the Philippines, "there will never be another election and neither the United States nor anybody else will ever, ever liberate the country."[11]

Today, the ongoing invasion of the U.S.-based fundamentalists is well defined, calculated, and forceful. The websites of numerous such groups serve as an example of the nature of the invasion. The purpose and mission of one group, the Joshua Project, a global plan by the U.S. Center for World Mission, follows. Please note that the term "unreached" peoples in the Philippines probably does not eliminate either Catholics or Muslims.

> Our Purpose . . . to spread a passion for the supremacy of God among all unreached peoples.
>
> Our Mission . . . to highlight the people groups of the world that have the least Christian presence in their midst and to encourage pioneer church-planting movements among every ethnic people group.
>
> Our Rationale . . . "This gospel of the Kingdom shall be preached in the whole world as a testimony to all the nations, and then the end will come."[12]

Another website by the Christian Light Foundation, a nondenominational "mission oriented organization whose purpose is to carry out the Great Commission around the globe," is equally forceful. Created in 1974 by a "group of born-again business men in Jacksonville, Florida," the foundation sets forth a mission statement that tells followers:

> to win the Philippines for Jesus Christ through whatever means the Holy Spirit leads us to: preach the gospel to the poor, assist churches and church planters with evangelism, and provide resources for evangelical Christians. . . . We believe in the absolute inerrancy of the Bible and are dedicated to spreading the Gospel throughout the world.[13]

The response of the Catholic Church to this incursion has been uncertain and, at least until now, somewhat ineffective. The church clearly recognizes the problem. In the early 1990s, Pope John Paul II stated that "[t]he sects have had great success and their work and influence . . . is significant and can become disastrous."[14] The pope and other church leaders have promoted a number of initiatives to counter the fundamentalist movement, some of which seem to have been taken from the pages of fundamentalist doctrine. One, the church needs to use more small communities of laypeople for its evangelization. Lay ministries, catechists, would be crucial. Two, a more mature use of the Bible as a source of prayer should be stressed. Three, the church needs to respond to the movement in terms of individual groups, because the groups are all different.

On a bright, sunlit morning at the Leyte Park Hotel, meanwhile, outside sat three enclosed jeepneys. The American missionaries were moving out, being driven to the airport, and then heading off to a landing in Davao. The assault would commence soon. Boxes were being loaded. The young troops waited patiently, gently laughing and quietly talking among themselves. Their battle was over here in Leyte. Perhaps a church had been planted. Whether it would grow in this heathen thorny thicket of Catholicism was not yet known.

7

THE BALICUATRO ISLANDS

TINAU

I began my investigation of some obscure events of MacArthur's liberation of the Philippines by taking a beautiful sail to the Balicuatro Islands. In 1945, with MacArthur already in Luzon, a small U.S.-Philippine force was sent to the islands to wipe out the Japanese garrison on Biri Island, the largest of the Balicuatros. It was a short, tough fight that has been given little attention in histories of the conflict. I was determined to find the battlefield and, hopefully, any eyewitnesses.

The *banca* (an outrigger) I sailed in chugged along, its engine groaning and missing but always true. Ten passengers were on board, all huddled under the canvas canopy away from the glaring sun. A few teachers were coming from a conference in Catarman on the mainland. There was an old lady who lovingly held a small dog. A couple of young men were laughing with the two boatmen, exchanging cigarettes, and joking in the Waray language. Everyone seemed to know each other. The sea rolled and threw foam onto the boat, but that was more pleasant than alarming. The banca's high prow pointed right out into the San Bernardino Strait, just off Samar's northwest coast.

Samar is a name that evokes various reactions. For many Manileños, the word implies a land of stark beauty whose people are provincial boors. Others remember the popular old song "Waray-Waray," in which the singer proudly states that he hails from Samar, but its lyrics are interpreted as comical bluster by non-Warays. The name Samar comes from the Waray *samad*, which means to wound or cut. This appellation seems fairly appropriate, given the island's history and people.[1]

The third largest in the Philippines, Samar is about five thousand square miles, or slightly larger than Connecticut or Jamaica, and is shaped sort of as a wedge with the wide edge on the north side. It was the first island Magellan sighted as he entered Philippine waters. Then, as today, it is a roughly hewn place. Its central area is both dense jungle (although the rampant illegal logging business has caused deforestation in some places) and rugged hills, crisscrossed by rivers. Looking at a map of the central island, one will see little in the way of roads or towns. The large vacant areas of the map suggest that many portions of the island have yet to be charted or maybe there is just not anything there. Surrounding the core of the island are lowland coastal areas, where most of the cities are situated and where the majority of the people live. Samar sits squarely in typhoon alley, and the vicious storms have ravaged both the people and the land for centuries. This is a poor island. The population's median age is seventeen, but there is little in the way of opportunity for young people here. Given these ingredients there is, not surprisingly, a strong communist presence, especially in the wild inner area.

Samar is perhaps best known for what happened in one of its small towns more than a century ago during the Philippine-American War. In 1898 Luzon-born Gen. Vicente Lukban, a follower of Aguinaldo's but one with a noticeable independent streak, had gone to Samar and appointed himself governor of the island. He also had a military command and was in charge of a sizable number of guerrilla troops, some of them fanatical religious cult members. Lukban took on the small American military presence in Leyte and Samar with some success. In 1901 the mayor of Balangiga, a remote town at the southern tip of the island, requested American soldiers to protect the town against pirates. The U.S. government in Manila, thinking that the good citizens were eager to be under American protection, quickly responded. Seventy-four U.S. troops arrived and quartered in the plaza underneath the picturesque, if crumbling, town church. What the troops did not know is that the mayor of Balangiga had advised Lukban he could set the Americans up in order to launch a surprise attack.[2]

For several months the people of Balangiga and the U.S. troops got along amicably. Friendships and romances formed. But instances of arrogance and poor decisions by the American commander, Capt. Thomas W. Connell, strained the relationship. The residents were simultaneously under tremendous pressure by Lukban's guerrilla forces not to fraternize with the enemy, which was an impossible task given the town's small size. One day in late September, troops noted with some surprise large numbers of women from nearby barrios entering the church while carrying small coffins. Sentries were told, or perhaps misunderstood the Waray explanation, that the coffins contained dead children, victims of cholera, from outlying areas. The sentries' natural reaction was not to inspect the boxes too closely. If the Americans had, according to traditional accounts, they might have noticed the coffins held bolos, not bodies, and that some of the mothers were men. It is unquestionable that weapons and men were hid in the church, but how they actually entered the church remains open to debate.

The next morning, by prearranged signal, the attack commenced. The church bells were used to call the guerrillas out of the church, where they had waited the night. At breakfast in the town square and, by one account, extremely hung over from attending a fiesta the night before, the Americans were caught unawares inside a mess tent. The attack was short and successful. Despite American bravery, thirty-eight were killed during the initial assault. The remaining thirty-six troops, nearly all of them wounded, made their way to bancas and set out to sea. Seven more died during this escape. Eventually, after suffering sniper fire and shark attacks, the survivors made their way to a U.S. outpost at Basey on Samar's western coast to tell their story. Three more died in the hospital, totaling forty-eight dead and making it the costliest engagement in the Philippine-American War. A few days later a contingent of the 11th Infantry, a group of Wyoming volunteers, returned to Balangiga, recovered the mutilated bodies of the slain Americans, burned Balangiga to the ground, and took the church bells as war booty.

When news of the attack reached the U.S. press, it was treated as nothing less than the Alamo or Little Big Horn. The chief U.S. military person in the Philippines, Maj. Gen. Adna Chaffee, Arthur MacArthur's successor, called for reprisals and ordered Brig. Gen. Jacob Smith to put down any resistance on Samar. Smith, in turn, directed Marine Maj. Littleton Waller to reduce Samar to a "howling wilderness," with no prisoners taken, and to kill all persons who were capable of bearing arms against the United States. When Waller asked at what age a person could be considered capable of bearing arms, Smith replied the age of ten and older.

Waller set out into infamy. In short order he and the Marines destroyed every village, including the foodstuffs, in their path. There is no proof, however, that they committed mass atrocities, as post–World War II Philippine nationalists have claimed. The Americans did not have an easy task: they were beset with poor supplies, horrible rain, and, not least, attacks by Filipino irregulars. Waller and company made it back to their base and soon uncovered a plot by local guerrillas to murder a Marine contingent. Waller, perhaps incoherent from a massive fever, ordered eleven Filipinos executed. This was followed out. A Philippine Constabulary outfit eventually captured Lukban as well. By the summer of 1902, the U.S. campaign on Samar was essentially over, but it entered the temple of American military lore. For years afterward, in U.S. Marine messes, members would stand if a Samar veteran entered.

Back in the United States, the news of the Balangiga massacre and its aftermath affected domestic politics. The press highlighted Smith's and Waller's morally suspect activities. Congress opened hearings, and supporters of the Philippine acquisition and the anti-expansionists went at it. Veterans' testimony revealed atrocities committed by U.S. troops. The public and Congress were aghast. Both Waller and Smith were eventually tried and acquitted. Their military careers were forever tarnished, but their soldiers held them up as heroes.

Two of the Balangiga church's bells eventually were placed in the Trophy Park at the F. E. Warren Air Force Base near Cheyenne, Wyoming, and third bell found itself at the 2nd Infantry Division's museum at Camp Red Cloud, Uijeongbu, South Korea. More importantly, they ended up at the nub of conflicting politics and interpretations. During the Fidel Ramos administration in the early 1990s, the Philippine government wanted them returned to Balangiga to commemorate the Philippine independence movement. U.S. veterans' groups have opposed this request, arguing that the bells honor American sacrifice. Some U.S. congressmen have urged sending the bells back to facilitate better relations with the Philippines. The Vatican weighed in, favoring a return; after all, the bells were the church's property. The bells, however, have remained in Wyoming and South Korea.

Like the bells, the battle itself and its historical interpretations have been at the nexus of differing ideas and ideologies. Nationalist groups in the Philippines have come to place Balangiga within the pantheon of the countrywide populist uprising under Aguinaldo. While it certainly occurred during his time, its connection to a central command or even philosophy is suspect. A recent study by Leyte native and Waray speaker Rolando O. Borrinaga suggests that the battle was quickly planned and carried out almost exclusively by Balangiga residents who were terrified by Lukban's guerrillas and angered by American arrogance. The Balangiga uprising was thus an isolated and perhaps unavoidable reaction to a difficult local situation. For a century the common U.S. narrative of the event has been that of a brave, nearly mythical defense given by U.S. troops against overwhelming odds, where Americans killed hundreds of the aggressors before being driven out to sea. Studies show that while they were outnumbered probably about six to one, American soldiers inflicted relatively few casualties on their attackers—anywhere from sixteen to fifty deaths.

I visited Balangiga but once, and I remember the drive more than I do the destination. I hired a small van and driver with an assistant in Catarman in Northern Samar and, armed with a map of the island and a brochure of the Balangiga, drove twelve hours down the west coast of Samar through places like Calbayog and Catbalogan and other smaller towns. The van did not have air-conditioning, and if it had shock absorbers when we started out, it did not when it returned. For long periods we traveled not on a road but on an interconnected series of ruts and holes. Numerous times the van had to come to a complete stop and then inch its way over a cavernous, water-filled split in the macadam.

We arrived in Balangiga late in the afternoon. The town plaza was nearly deserted. The pretty Spanish church standing right off the plaza was not the one U.S. soldiers saw in 1901, but it kept the original themes and was in the same place. The Balangiga memorial sat in the plaza. A circular affair ornamented with bright red flowers and a spiked rail fence, it produced a strange effect. The names of the Filipinos and Americans who died here were on its walls. The center of the memorial was a nearly life-size diorama featuring the U.S. soldiers sitting at their breakfast table and looking in astonishment at the Filipino figures, to the back and the left, who were waving bolos and charging through what appeared to be the door of the church. To the right was a short set of stairs, up which a Filipino climbed toward two Americans. I took this section to represent the U.S. barracks. Squarely in the diorama's center was the church's bell tower topped by two ornamental bells. The diorama's emotional and thematic consequence was curious in that the figures of importance here were the Americans, sitting stupidly with their mouths full. The mob of bolo-wielding Balangians seemed almost secondary, perhaps treacherous, and hardly the brave freedom fighters one would assume the designers wanted to portray.

We walked across the plaza and over to the municipal building, looking for the museum the brochure had mentioned. Inside, town business was being conducted. After some time we found a public relations official who informed us that the museum was only open in the month of September. It was June. She did graciously walk with us back to the memorial and explained how the battle occurred and how the Americans made their escape to the sea. When I queried her about the bells, she adamantly insisted that there would never be closure until the bells were back in Balangiga; they absolutely had to be returned. I looked up at the ceramic American soldiers, still with their mouths full, still waiting to die.

To prepare for our long drive home, we had dinner at a small cantina a block or so from the square. The people of all regions in the Philippines are slightly ethnocentric about their cuisine, so I waited until my Northern Samareño driver and his assistant finished complaining about the poor quality of the rice to ask what they thought about Balangiga. They seemed genuinely interested and asked a number of insightful questions about the event. Curious, I asked them what the schools in Samar, or at least the schools in Catarman, taught about the Battle of Balangiga. They told me this visit was the first time they had ever heard of it.

I was not thinking of Balangiga's bells or international relations, however, as the banca approached the island of Tinau—sometimes spelled Tingyao or Tingiao—after a forty-minute trip from San Jose. I was coming to explore the history of the islands' Japanese occupation during the war and their subsequent liberation by the United States. It had been nearly a decade since I had been here, and I had learned that Tinau had changed since I saw it last. Then, nearly on a dare from some expat friends in Makati, I had traveled down here, lured by the invitation from a family whose relatives I knew in Manila. Before I left Manila, an older American gave me two bits of advice. One, when offered *tuba*, the potent local drink, I would be impolite to refuse it, but I should take only a short snort because my intestines could not possibly handle a full glass the first time. I followed this advice. Second, he warned I would be going to an area with little social infrastructure and no police. It would be a place where no one would help me if things went wrong. I was to be polite, quiet, and, above all, generous. I followed this advice as well.

The banca pulled up to the landing site. It could have been a scene from a Joseph Conrad novel with a row of picturesque nipa houses set just back from the beautiful crystal-clear water, all under a brilliant blue sky. A set of concrete steps came down to the gently lapping ocean. Handsome, tan-skinned people in colorful clothes and with gleaming white teeth and indescribably friendly smiles were on the steps. Palm trees lined the white beach that stretched all the way down the coast.

It was low tide and the banca could not get to the steps, so we passengers had to go over the side into the foot-deep warm water and walk the final five yards together. Young men with bare torsos came out into the water and carried the women, including the old *lola* (grandmother) clutching her dog. Children, laughing and yelling, crowded to see what was being brought in from the mainland. Some jumped into the water, playing. Roosters crowed. It was a picture of warm, primal Pacific beauty and happiness. Yet below the beauty squatted a moral ambiguity that Conrad would find familiar. The walk from the pier to the barrio slowly revealed the island's odd secret. As was told to me by one observant resident, in this place there were no young women.

Tinau is one of a number of islands, referred to as the Balicuatro Islands, just off the coast of Northern Samar and directly east of Balicuatro Point. The largest island, Biri, is where the parish headquarters and post office are located. Others are San Pedro, San Juan, Talisay, and the tiny MacArthur

Island. Tinau is one of the more populated islands, with nearly all of its two thousand residents living in the barrio of San Antonio.

Walking the sandy streets of San Antonio, it became obvious that women between the ages of seventeen to about twenty-three or twenty-four just were not around. An island without young women—how was it possible? Yet the island's queer demographic situation was not highly unusual. Other places in the Philippines also seemingly have a tear in the community's fabric because approximately twenty-five hundred to three thousand Filipinos leave the country to work abroad every day, *every day*. It is also estimated that 8.5 million Filipinos send money to assist family members living back home. In 2004, overseas Filipino workers (OFWs) sent home $8.5 billion, or one-tenth of the country's gross domestic product. In 2005, that figure rose to more than $10.6 billion.[3] With so many people leaving their towns, however, chunks of communities disappear. The traditional cloth of Filipino communities may slowly be unraveling. It is just one of the effects of the diaspora.

This kind of phenomenon is not unknown in other countries, but it is rarely seen in such dramatic terms as in the Philippines. The reasons for this movement overseas are simple: in the provinces, as well as the larger cities, there is little in the way of professional opportunities, barely livable pay scales, and slight or no social security or insurance. But the exodus is not limited to the provincial poor or nearly poor. The professional brain drain has long been an anathema to the country, and it might be getting worse. For example, there is an alarming trend for Filipino doctors to switch to nursing in order to emigrate overseas. In 2004, the Philippine Medical Association estimates that 1,500 of its licensed doctors left the Philippines to fill nursing shortages worldwide, with many resettling in North America.[4]

Tinau has contributed mightily to the OFW experience in a rather unique way. Remittances to the Tinau community have largely come from the island's young women, who have followed a three-step process to success. First, they leave Tinau and become maids and nannies, but more often bar girls, usually in Angeles, in Pampanga Province, where the former U.S. military base at Clark Field essentially institutionalized prostitution and where a thriving international sex tourism trade now exists. Sometimes they go to Manila, where the go-go bars of Makati cater to foreign clientele. Some women get a flight to Japan, where they become "entertainers," the sanitized euphemism for prostitutes. Second, they begin to send money home to help their families. For some women, there is a third step: they marry one of their foreign customers, emigrate to his country, and are able to send even more cash back to the island. It must be emphasized that not all of Tinau's young women become bar girls. But the pressure for children to take care of their parents is extremely strong in the Philippines, and many do. Attempting to relieve their parents' financial condition, the girls of Tinau have unwittingly opened a number of cultural floodgates.

To fully comprehend the cultural changes that are taking place, it is imperative to understand what it traditionally has meant to be a young person on Tinau, which, it should be said, is similar to other parts of the Philippines. First, education on the island, and probably in all of Northern Samar, is abysmal. Both elementary and secondary schools are substandard by Philippine criteria. For example, as of this writing some teachers on Tinau did not pass their national certification exams. They are allowed to teach, however, because enforcement of the standards has been lax and, more importantly, Tinau needs living, breathing teachers. Instruction is supposed to be in English—the language of commerce, science, and law—to prepare students to be competitive in Manila and overseas, but English instruction is poor. The teachers are ill equipped to instruct students in the language, so they often teach in Waray, which is used nowhere else save Leyte and Samar. Again, as of this writing, without electricity, no student graduating from this school has ever done schoolwork on a computer or even on a typewriter. If a student does graduate from high school on Tinau and wants to go to college, usually the only possible school is the nearby University of Eastern Philippines, which is a secondary-grade institution at best and hardly in the same league as the Manila schools. In a head-to-head professional match, the Tinau student cannot possibly compete with an opposite number in Manila or Cebu or even Tacloban. The young people in San Antonio know all this.

Social services are available but sub par as well. San Antonio does not have a mayor, but it does have an elected *barangay*, or barrio, captain. There is no police force. A small health center on Tinau is run by a health official (not a doctor) who can administer basic necessities such as flu shots, bandages, and birth control pills. Unfortunately, the center is stocked through funds provided by local and provincial politicians. When supplies run out, they are not replaced until the month or so prior to an election, thereby allowing the politicians to crow about their largesse during a campaign speech. Consequently, there are usually no medical supplies in the medical center. Tinau does not have a dentist. There is a midwife, who is important because nearly all births on Tinau take place in the home. For any immediate health crisis, the patient needs to get on a banca, pray that the waves are not running high, and take the forty-minute trip to the hospital in Catarman. There is no undertaker here; thus, embalming is performed by morticians who come in from other places. After a body is prepared, the embalmers sail back to the mainland and usually dump the blood and embalming fluids into an area of the sea just off the island that supplies most of the barrio's fish. The San Antonians find this fact darkly amusing. No one on Tinau has insurance, and only the teachers and the few people who work in the small lighthouse have any kind of retirement funds. There is no vocational training or anything to prepare young people for a profession or a future.

Traditionally, what could a young person on Tinau expect out of his or her life? For the young man, it is pretty much what his papa has done: fishing, farming, maybe doing construction, and, if he has a banca, ferrying people back and forth from the mainland. Typically, the Tinau life will consist of marriage, children, and cockfights. He will carry a bolo most of his life. Drinking is heavy here, and not surprisingly given the complete lack of law enforcement, violence is high.

Like mother like daughter: after an early marriage, a woman will live her life in a constant cycle of childbirth and child rearing. If the family has a plot of land, she will probably help with the farmwork. If she can scrape enough money together, she might be able to open a sari-sari store from the front of her house. She will wear a duster. Much of her day will be spent physically trying to keep her house while exchanging tsmismis with the other women. Most of her time will be spent keeping her children free of the myriad maladies that seem to thrive on Tinau, particularly those transmitted by flies and mosquitoes. For relaxation she will probably gamble what little extra money she has on the local card games.

As it was it will be: people on Tinau face a life of hard work and virtually no escape from the social and physical ills poverty produces. There is, of course, overseas work. Well-paying positions as construction workers, drivers, maids, caregivers, sailors in the merchant marines, and so on exist all over the world, especially in the Middle East. If one takes note of the multitude of Arab-connected placement centers in Manila, one might assume that such positions are easy to obtain. In fact, they are, that is, if the applicant has the eighty-five thousand pesos (more than fifteen hundred dollars) to cover the placement "fee" the recruitment centers charge. Given that the annual income of a Tinau family is probably less than six hundred dollars, paying such a fee is usually well out of the question.

So there it is. The island's young people are poorly educated and trained in practically nothing. The government provides little of anything to anyone. The cycle of poverty is a legacy and a future that will go unbroken unless, of course, there is some way to break out of it.

America—the cycle can be quickly and decisively broken by going to America. Everyone works in America. Americans have dollars. Americans can buy anything because Americans are very rich. All of this news is wondrous, but how does one get to America? Then, perhaps miraculously, for a young woman, the secret of getting to America is revealed. The keeper of the secret is probably an older woman, maybe a mother or sister, maybe a cousin, maybe a neighbor. To get to America and the dollars necessary to support her parents, there is an interim place called Angeles. Angeles has bright lights, cool music, and handsome foreign men who are all very rich.

America via Angeles is indeed changing San Antonio and greatly. In fact, the people's physical appearance and, more importantly, their attitudes had changed so much since I first visited in 1996 that I hardly recognized it. I wanted to understand what was causing the dramatic metamorphosis. So late one afternoon I sat down with a municipality official, a man in his fifties who wanted to remain anonymous.[5] In his concrete house, drinking Sprites and hearing the sounds of a spirited basketball game on the school's court near the plaza, I asked how San Antonio had evolved over the past decade. The reply was immediate: "big changes" had taken place, which was fairly obvious. When I asked if these changes were an improvement, his answer was quick and resolute: "When I was growing up, when I was a little boy, the houses here were made of nipa. I think there was only three houses before made of wood and galvanized iron [for the roof]. Now there are many [made from] concrete."

Concrete is the all-important measure of development. On this island the consequence of concrete is almost impossible to describe. There are only two types of houses on Tinau: the older ones are *sawali* (woven bamboo) nipa huts with thatched roofs and the newer ones are made of concrete block with tin roofs. While the traditional nipa structures look picturesque and are superb for travel advertisements, they do not withstand typhoons. Concrete, of course, does much better, but it is also expensive. Since few people on Tinau can actually afford concrete with their normal incomes, outside assistance is almost mandatory. A concrete house not only means you are safer, you are on the upper social scale as well. It shows that you have money coming in from somewhere.

We sipped our Sprites. Clearly, San Antonio is developing. There is now concrete all around, and I saw very little when I came here years ago. What, I asked, has caused these changes, especially in the last ten years?

The official replied, "Well, one of the reasons is the coming of foreigners. [The people here] are well paid [because of the foreigners]. As I say, many families here, in this barangay, have uplifted their family condition. When the children get married to these foreigners [their lot improves] because of the large dollar."

After prefacing the question with as much *delicadeza* (finesse) as possible, I pointed out that certainly some of the women who marry the foreigners had also worked as bar girls in Angeles or Olongapo or Manila. That, in fact, the transformation found in San Antonio was due in part to the sex tourism industry. What did the townspeople think of that link? Did the parents actually know what their daughters did in Angeles? If they did, how could they wittingly send their daughters off to be prostitutes? He did not hesitate and answered clearly.

"Well, as I see, they [the families] just consider this to be normal. As I observe, most of our ladies just after they graduate from high school go to Angeles and Olongapo City looking for jobs.

"The parents are aware of this [the sex tourism business]. The parents, I believe, even permit the children to work in those places.

"There are people who don't like that, of course. There are still some. For me, I don't like it.

"But I don't say that all of them meet foreigner husbands by, shall we say, pick ups in Angeles and Olongapo. In fact, there are also some families here, their children, their daughters, get married that did not meet their husbands in those places."

This observation was absolutely true. There have been international marriages in this town that were not the result of paying a bar fine (the fee the bar charges a customer allowing him to take the girl out for the night) but rather the result of two people meeting and falling in love in traditional ways. But these instances I guessed to be in the minority.

What will happen in the future, I wondered. He said he doubted that the practice would stop anytime soon. The parish priest has for years delivered sermons on raising children the right way; asking people to be moral, responsible parents; and, in effect, begging parents not to send their daughters to Angeles. He is not having much influence. Against the almighty dollar, heaven cannot possibly win. The municipal official pragmatically discussed the inequities between families whose daughters married foreigners and those who did not: the disparities were financially wide and culturally important. A new class had already developed, and although he did not use the term "bourgeoisie," with all of its negative connotations, to describe this new group, he could have. Then he pointed out something I found remarkable: only until all families were "dollar earners," as he put it, could the whole town progress. In short, all the families must somehow be connected to the American dollar in order to have social equality. In this sense, I thought he was saying that all of the families had to send their daughters to the bars. We finished our Sprites and observed that there was no shortage of children on San Antonio's half dozen streets. The barrio had a future.

As I was leaving I happened to mention that I would be going to MacArthur Island to look for caves the Japanese had used during the war. He looked at me quizzically with a sudden interest that surprised me. He began to ask me questions: What did I know about the island? Did I know any foreigners there? Did I know what the foreigners were doing there? My honest answer to these questions was "nothing"; I had never been to MacArthur Island. The official had, however, certainly piqued my interest in going.

How is the newfound wealth changing the moral compass of Tinau's community? Here is one example. The day after I arrived I saw Ate (older sister or woman) Eva, as happy as a mother hen, clucking her way up and down San Antonio Street. And why should she not be happy? She has raised a bright young daughter who has now started to pay dividends. As Ate Eva tells it, and she does not hesitate to tell it, her daughter Anabel went up to Angeles a little more than a year ago, right after she graduated from high school and turned sixteen. An attractive girl, she easily found work as a dancer in a tourist bar, where she quickly met an American, who is thirty something and, as Ate Eva smiles, "very rich." The American paid the bar's near thousand-dollar fee to take Anabel's virginity and, after a whirlwind romance, convinced her to quit the bar and that kind of life and to have a new life, a good, clean one. He then began to support her with a monthly four-hundred-dollar allowance and promised to help her family as well. But he also had a job back in the States. So with assurances of his continued monthly support until they could get married, he left Anabel in her new Angeles apartment and went back to work in the States. He promised he would return.

Anabel is a sharp kid. Once her new American boyfriend was gone and her monthly allowance started to arrive regularly via Western Union, she quickly got her old job back at the bar and without telling her American boyfriend. There she soon met another American, who, quite smitten, offered to take Anabel out of the bar, to help her quit that kind of work, and to start a new life. He also promised to support her with a five-hundred-dollar monthly allowance and assistance to her family. She agreed, and he ended his vacation and went to his job back in the States, pledging to return. Now bringing in a monthly allowance of nine hundred dollars, Anabel moved back to Tinau. Her life was set, at least for a while. Her only worry was how to juggle her boyfriends' visits, but that should not be too daunting for a girl of her business acumen.

Ate Eva was just overjoyed telling this story. Two years ago she was just like her neighbors: she lived in a flimsy nipa house, she cooked her food with charcoal, and she had no running water. Today she has a concrete house—a mansion—with a generator that takes care of a refrigerator, a television, and a karaoke machine. Her stove is gas now. The family has a toilet. Anabel is going to college, studying to be a teacher. And she has a younger daughter, which means more dollars. Such promise, such goodness.

You see such promise and goodness as you walk up and down San Antonio Street. This avenue is really flattened sand but is kept quite clean. At regular intervals a dog lies in the sand, its territory recognized and guarded. Roosters continuously crow. As you walk you see several impressive structures that are visually at odds with the mongrels and chickens. One is the massive concrete house of the Soriano (a pseudonym) family. This house is sizable by anyone's standards. It has glass windows, large balconies, and tile decorations emblazoned on the concrete wall in front. From the back of the house one hears the chuga-chuga of two large generators. The Soriano family has hit the big time: two of their daughters went to Angeles to work in the bars, and both found husbands, one an American, one an Australian. Both men are apparently very rich. The daughters now live overseas, and their parents are comfortable, very comfortable, in fact. You can see Mama and Papa and a couple of brothers in their chairs in the street, just sitting out in front of the concrete house. The karaoke machine blasts from inside. They do this all day. They don't work. They don't have to work. They only have to get to the Western Union office on the mainland a couple of times a month and sign for the support checks. Now, thanks to the daughters, they also have their own boat to do that.

More and more of these so-called mansions are springing up all over San Antonio Street, and more families like the Soriano's are able to live the life of languor. In fact, in 2005 a quick and unscientific perusal of the barrio shows that out of the approximately 480 houses in San Antonio, 105 houses— all concrete—were built by families whose daughters had married foreigners and many within the past five years. That is nearly one-fourth of the barrio, and the number is growing at an astonishing rate.

But another group of people is here as well—those who do not live in concrete houses. You see them in their traditional, provincial-style nipa and thatch houses, which stand in distinct contrast with their neighbors' homes. These dark, smoky places use kerosene lamps and charcoal fires. The children man the rusty water pump that provides the only source of water for all of the family's needs. Usually the well and the outhouse are alarmingly close.

The social dichotomy that has mercurially divided Tinau over the past ten years is both striking and troubling. One is used to seeing such gut-wrenching disparities in Manila and other large cities, where squatters' shanties surround walled housing. But here in San Antonio a cultural chasm is isolating two groups of people who, maybe just a year ago, were at the same social level. Neighbors are now confronted by an intense greed and an almost insane concupiscence running through Tinau—dollar lust. It manifests itself in the craving for concrete and the hunger for a generator. When these things are finally acquired through a foreigner, a rearrangement of the social system occurs. People with nipa houses may find themselves not being invited to the parties thrown by the concrete crowd and perhaps may be shunned even by their own relatives. Children look at other children in derision, claiming that their family is better because they have an ate or cousin or someone "abroad." Other children gaze helplessly as they see their neighbors arriving from the mainland and carrying the large boxes containing the hand-me-down clothes and toys perhaps from their sister who lives in Michigan or Montana.

The dollar lust is so palpable here that one can almost smell it, and its fever is leading people down the path of the profane. Here is a story that shocks even the San Antonians. One family living on the far end of barrio had thirteen children. At least three of the daughters had worked in the bars of Angeles and Manila and had married and emigrated to America. During the late 1990s, as concrete replaced nipa, the family lived in one of the most prestigious houses in the barrio. Their youngest daughter, Mellie (a pseudonym), did things a bit differently. At fourteen she went up to Angeles and found a succession of foreign boyfriends, finally settling on an American to support her and her family. The man asked her to move back to San Antonio, away from the bar lights, until they were married. She did so but quickly found a boyfriend in San Antonio and got pregnant. Because the foreign fiancé was at work Stateside and would not immediately return, she was easily able to hide her pregnancy. Unfortunately, after giving birth in her family's concrete house, she became ill and had to be taken to the hospital in Catarman, where she tragically died. The parents were apparently fearful they would lose the weekly Western Union payment, even though their other daughters were sending money, so they became inventive. When the American man called, the parents told him Mellie was sick. Or Mellie was not there. Or Mellie had to go to Manila. After about six weeks the overwrought man left his job, caught a flight to the Philippines, made his way down to Tinau, and discovered that Mellie had been dead for nearly two months. Her parents had not only hid this from him, but they were also pocketing the support money. Neighbors say they could hear him screaming and breaking things inside the house before he left Tinau. It is doubtful he would return.

The town's fiesta provides a showcase for the cultural cleft on the island. The fiesta here is dedicated to San Antonio de Padua, the patron of the poor. Because there is no such thing as a local tax system, nearly all Philippine towns and barangays, including San Antonio, rely on the annual fiesta to raise private donations for the municipal coffers. The fiesta's high point is the dance in the plaza, where families are called to do a tango or a cha-cha and then place money in a hat. This money then supports public works in the town. San Antonians have been doing this dance for decades, and it is the major event on the social calendar.

But now even the fiesta is changing. Each year in increasing numbers, the girls who worked in the bars and married foreigners return to San Antonio for the fiesta. They come from such exotic locales as Alaska and Alabama, Melbourne and Yokohama. These women tell stories of their houses and appliances and of the huge sums of money they make working in fantastic places like Wal-Mart and JCPenney and the "pee-ex." Sometimes they bring their husbands, who stand around usually bemused or bewildered. Surrounded by adoring, fawning families and often by the local boyfriends, who will be introduced to the husbands as cousins or uncles, the women make themselves noticed. The women wear jewelry and laugh loudly. They dance and place wads of pesos in the hat, capturing the moment with the seemingly ever-present video camera. They are able to donate nearly incredible sums of money, for they are married to Americans or Australians or Japanese who are all very rich.

Outside the video camera's light is a mystified group of people, residents of San Antonio who have always come to the fiesta but who now cannot afford to compete with the families who have children abroad. One man drops a hundred-peso note—the amount he has always donated—into the hat and is chided by the man holding it. The collector says something like "C'mon, pare, so-and-so from California paid sixty-five thousand pesos just for the band! You only give one hundred?" Under the glare of the parvenu, it is a humiliating moment. His family has no dollars. Perhaps he does not have a daughter, or maybe he has been listening to the parish priest on Sunday morning. In any event he sits with his family at their table perplexed, amazed at how the town, and their lives, have been utterly changed by the women in the Guess jeans and the K-Mart necklaces.

How does one react to this moral ambiguity? One late night in the States I was watching Howard Stern, who commented that the Philippines was a place where the parents sold their children into prostitution. Stern's comments annoyed me (as well as countless Filipinos worldwide) for two reasons. First, it could be argued that in a limited way he was correct. Yes, some parents on Tinau and other places in the Philippines send their daughters off to work in the bars, hoping they will marry a foreigner and improve the family's condition. But it is only natural that people want to improve their lot in life. Further, it is not uncommon to find children attempting to comfort their parents and siblings. What annoyed me more about Stern's comment, however, was that he did not know the world in which these people live, a world in which their government and society do virtually nothing for them. Stern has not had to worry about his house blowing over in a typhoon or to contemplate spending his entire professional life staring at a carabao's rear end while working in a rice field. Morality aside, one could argue that these people, against great odds, have pulled themselves up by their own bootstraps and have made better lives for their families by marketing the only thing they had to sell.

But it would be impossible not to see the cupidity in Tinau and how the greed is clouding ethical acuity and deteriorating responsibility. At one time the people of Tinau, although poor, were hard working. Now, the dollar lust has dulled the people's perceptions of what is important and, for many, their ability to plan for the future. San Antonio did not have a drinking establishment until a couple of years ago; now there are three karaoke bars with, irony of ironies, bar girls imported from Leyte. Meanwhile, the medical center still lacks supplies. Despite the multitude of new concrete houses, the school is just as bad, leaving the students completely unprepared for their lives, save for working in a bar or signing a Western Union receipt form. The island is an agricultural delight and the waters around Tinau are stocked with everything from *lapu-lapu* (grouper) to lobster, but the entire island is abuzz with the news that a Jollibee fast-food place has opened up in Catarman.

Such demonstrations of poor planning, personal inertia, covetousness, and a near total reliance on others are common in OFW families, and they are certainly not limited to Tinau. On the contrary, they seem to be widespread across the islands. The effects of this near-total dependence on the OFW by the stay-behind families on future generations can only be guessed at.

The fiesta is over. The former bar girls have gone back abroad to Buffalo and Brisbane, and the barrio—its coffers overflowing—has returned to normal. I was standing beside a small nipa house. I could smell the dried fish cooking at the charcoal fire inside while outside a woman was squatting on the ground and doing the laundry in a plastic washtub. A couple of mangy, worm-skinny dogs were poking around. Tied up nearby was a gargantuan porker, a magnificently obese animal. An old man sitting in front of the house saw me look at the pig. The man told me his pig was a "hyper," meaning that it had been fed hormones, which made it grow faster and larger. It was much more valuable than a normal pig, which he called a "local." With a confident air he told me that he expected to get a super price when he sold it. I nodded in admiration, although later I found out that hypers are illegal because the meat is considered dangerous for human consumption.

We began to chat. I guessed his age to be around seventy, but he was probably somewhat younger. I asked him if he remembered the war. He said he was alive at the time but too young to remember anything; however, his parents and older siblings had told him stories about it. "What happened here on Tinau?" I asked. Waving his scrawny arm to accentuate his points and occasionally scratching his head, he told me about San Antonio's involvement in the great conflict.

During the war (he does not know what year) a contingent of Japanese soldiers came here from their camp on Biri. They rounded up all of the island's residents, including the children, and took them to the town's plaza, where I had today watched the boys play basketball. At the plaza the Japanese made the San Antonians kneel all day long in the sun. The people were humiliated. The Japanese kept asking the people where the guerrillas were. The people of San Antonio said nothing, probably because there were no guerrillas on Tinau. The Japanese eventually left. No one was hurt, but no one forgot, either.

When the war was nearly over, American GIs came to Tinau. I asked him about the American soldiers. He was told that they had handed out bread and American flags. "Americans are good people," he said matter-of-factly, without a hint of patronizing.

Later, after a wonderful dinner of fish and rice with my host family, I walked out of the house perhaps thirty feet and stood on the beach. I looked up into the night of a billion stars, seeing at least two shooters fly through the sky. Out over the water I could make out the Samar mainland. I glanced back up at the stars: the young girls of the barrio would be lying on their mats, dreaming of wonderful, rich foreigners who would make it so that their parents could sit out in front of a concrete mansion. And somewhere on the island, the parish priest just might be working on the Sunday sermon.

MACARTHUR ISLAND

The banca ride to MacArthur Island was about thirty minutes from Tinau. MacArthur Island, called Tampipi prior to the war, is so small it is not listed on most maps. I arrived again at low tide and, with rolled-up pants legs, walked like the old general the twenty yards in the bathwater-warm ocean. Once I was ashore it was immediately apparent that the little barrio on this island was much less developed than San Antonio. The small houses were of sawali nipa. The barrio had been constructed on something like a black marsh or backwater because some of the houses were on stilts. The heat was oppressive, and the flies were numerous and overwhelming.

Three guys from my adopted family in Tinau had accompanied me on the orders of their mother, who said I needed "bodyguards." We had lunch at their cousins' house. Sitting on a bamboo bench outside the house, some of the neighbors were swigging cheap Emperador brandy. One kind old soul with a toothless smile offered me a glass. I grinned a decline, patting my belly as if to say "too weak," which, considering the quality of the Emperador, was actually true. With flimsy masculinity, I went inside with the women.

There were about five women inside the house, plus countless children. Several of the kids stared at me in unabashed wonder, and I knew that I was probably the first white person they ever had in the house. The women were cooking over the charcoal stove. Like most nipa kitchens, this one was without a chimney or an opening for ventilation; consequently, the air was heavy with smoke. Filipino courtesy is mighty, and I sat down to a plate of boiled Pacific lobster, which is a small creature but quite tasty. A large plate of boiled *camotes* (sweet potatoes) was also placed on the table. Someone produced a bottle of mineral water, and I was thankful. MacArthur Island has no fresh water, save after a heavy rain. All potable water is brought in from the other islands.

After the meal I asked the friendly men from San Antonio, who were in their mid-twenties, to take me to the other side of the island. Supposedly, the Japanese had used caves there during the war. The women of the house instructed one young man from the family to go along as well. With a half gallon of bottled water, we set off for the small barrio called Cogon.

The hike proved interesting. The terrain was at first the same rather depressing and unattractive black, brackish marsh that surrounded the barrio. It gave way thankfully to a lush, green grassland. I found out that no one grows rice on MacArthur. In its place is the camote, a poor substitute. Then we went under the green canopy, and nearly at once we were in a bona fide jungle. The path was narrow but well worn and easy to follow.

For a good twenty minutes, we tramped along the path under the trees, sometimes climbing, sometimes nearly stumbling downhill. It was a fairly strenuous hike, made more so by the harsh heat. When we began the march, I had asked the guys how long it would take to reach Cogon, and they had said only about twenty minutes, no problem. As we trudged farther into the jungle, it occurred to me that in all likelihood not one of the four men had ever worn a wristwatch. With sweat pouring down my face, I chuckled at this notion. Time on this path was a loosely defined thing. As if on cue, our leader, the man from MacArthur, pulled off the path; we followed.

We rested. They squatted on their haunches, and I leaned against a tree, knowing full well how difficult it would be to stand again if I sat down. I studied my companions: all healthy, muscular young men, none was taller than five foot six. One of the San Antonio boys had been a successful amateur boxer, and he had not lost his physique. All wore T-shirts and baggy shorts. Flip-flops protected their feet, which were probably hardened enough not to need them. Because the guys from San Antonio were making a social call on their cousins, they did not bring their bolos, but the guide from MacArthur had his.

Bolos are usually ugly things. Forget the vision of a jewel-encrusted handle and a shining silver blade. Most bolos I have seen are handmade, crude, worn, and rusted, often with cracked handles. This kind of condition is not surprising: a bolo is the indispensable tool of the Visayans. It is used for doing farmwork, clearing land, and butchering. They have also been used for more deadly purposes. During the Philippine-American War, it was the Filipinos' chief and formidable weapon. The Balangiga massacre of U.S. troops was executed almost exclusively with bolos. In fact, as the guerrilla movement started in 1942, many Filipino troops were armed with bolos. When the U.S. 11th Airborne Division and the Philippine guerrillas rescued the Westerners from the Los Baños internment camp in 1945, some of the Filipinos rushed against the Japanese with only a bolo in hand. So while bolos may not be attractive pieces of cutlery, no one should doubt their sharpness.

The bolo that the MacArthur lad had was different. He unsheathed it as we rested, the guys chatting in Waray. It was a handsome bolo, and its blade seemed longer than most. It must have been new because there was no rust; it, in fact, gleamed. The handle was also different: it was curved, reminding me of the butt on a Colt revolver from the Old West. Could it be one of the talibong war bolos I read about in Vic Hurley's *Jungle Patrol?* Hurley was a young Chicago adventurer who tried to be a coconut farmer in Mindanao in the 1920s and, after failing miserably, wrote ripping good yarns and decent amateur histories of Americans in the prewar wilds of the islands. These stories often featured the intrepid American planter or constabulary officer with his loyal Filipino sidekick, braving the attacks of the bolomen deep inside Mindanao or the Visayas.

As I stood there admiring the blade and imagining myself as a Philippine constabulary officer circa 1904, our guide stepped out of his flip-flops, sheathed the bolo, and began to shimmy up a sizable palm tree. I had seen this feat done before on San Antonio, and it never failed to amaze me. Up he went, hugging the tree, using his arms and heels for locomotion, until he found his prey, which was disposed of quickly with the bolo. The coconut fell into the brush. Then coming back down just as quickly, he picked up the green coconut and took its top off with one quick chop.

As the guest, I was given the prize. The liquid at the top of a fresh coconut is called buko juice. It is absolutely thirst quenching, the sports drink of the tropics. Buko juice's taste is unique: with a little bit more consistency than water has, its fresh flavor enlivens the palate. But its effect might be situational. I remember once in an air-conditioned, posh Makati restaurant getting buko juice for dessert, and the waiter placed a clean coconut on the table with a dainty straw stuck in it. Here on MacArthur, with my shirt wringing wet, the odor of fetid jungle decay in my nostrils, and flies buzzing around my head, it tasted much better. I gulped heartily, taking more than my share, then passed the coconut around.

We started off again. Periodically we would hear the "kwahow, kwahow" of the large black bird native to Waray. It seemed to follow us as if it were monitoring our progress. I asked what the bird looked like, but we had a hard time spotting it. Finally, one of the guys pointed up to a high branch, and there it sat, large and shiny black, much like a raven or crow, but its curved, attractive head was something like a huge mockingbird's. I asked the guys what name the bird had, but they told me there was difficulty in translating the Waray.

The rest of the hike lasted about another twenty minutes. The path took us out from under the trees and back into a grassland. In some places the grass was nearly six feet high, encompassing us in a humid, green world navigable only by the path below our feet. But in other places the earth was blackened by a recent fire. When I asked the guide what had started the fire, he did not know, saying these fires just seemed to happen. As we walked through still-smoldering soil, the smoke stuck near the ground like a choking mist, and coupled with the blazing sun overhead, I could not help but ponder if I was in some Renaissance vision of hell. I declared to myself that MacArthur Island was not a nice place: it was terrifically hot, had no water or rice, and was now burning itself up. Ahead was a steep ridge, and one of the guys told me that Cogon was just over the top.

After a short but sharp climb, we entered the barrio of Cogon. At once I drew a contrast with the barrio of MacArthur and determined immediately Cogon was more attractive. Rather than houses on stilts over a fly-infested black marsh, the nipas here seemed well constructed and clean. Many of them had laundry on lines, adding color to the landscape. The official sounds of the provinces, barking dogs and crowing roosters, were in good form. Cogon even had a plaza. Granted, its pavement was cracked with grass shooting up between, but it was well swept. There was a basketball hoop set up on a post. The place even seemed cooler. I was starting to change my opinion of MacArthur when one of the boys tapped me and pointed. Off to my right was another white man. I would have been just as surprised if I had seen a yeti.

He was surely in his sixties, tall, tanned, and gray haired. Even at his age he seemed to be in good shape, and I instantly thought he was ex-military. I think he had been out doing something in his yard, which I noticed had vegetables and flowers planted in neat rows. It was a good guess he had lived there for some time. He had clearly gone native: shirtless, shorts, and flip-flops. After we shared a glance he gave me not quite a scowl and then ducked into the darkness of his concrete house.

The boys seemed somewhat confused. Why did the man and I not say hello? Why did we not talk? Why would two white men ignore each other? Was he an American? I told them I did not know what nationality he was, only that he probably did not like to talk to strangers. I realized that I did not understand why we did not acknowledge one another. But I did know that such shyness between Westerners happened frequently in these parts. Perhaps it was because Westerners were here to be away from others of their kind; perhaps it was out of some form of shared guilt.

We pushed though the barrio to the final destination, the rocks overlooking the beach. These were considerable formations, a solid twenty yards up over the sand. Spread before us the Pacific earned its name: the ocean was placid with barely a ripple of a wave washing ashore. Sounds from the barrio floated past and out to sea. The caves were supposedly below us. We sat down and rested, passing around the bottle of warm water.

One of the guys spoke pretty decent English. He told me that there were quite a few foreigners on MacArthur Island. Surprised, I asked where, and he pointed behind me and to the right. Sure enough, there was a row of concrete houses under swaying palms, all with brilliant ocean views. Unlike the brash, pretentious buildings on San Antonio, these were small, tasteful, and rather attractive. One was even painted in an artsy scheme that made it stand out in a smart, pleasing manner.

I remembered the odd interest the Tinau municipal official had in these foreigners, so I pressed the issue with my bodyguards. Who were these foreigners? What did they do here?

After some hesitation and a quick exchange of Waray among the guys, I was told they were surfers. I know very little about surfing, but looking out at an ocean as flat as board, I knew they were not hanging ten anywhere near this beach, at least not at this time of year. The guys muttered to themselves, and the English speaker offered some startling information.

"We think they are surfers. They tell people they are surfers, but we are not sure. They only come at certain months. We see them digging in the ocean."

"Digging in the ocean?" I asked. "For what?"

"People say something about the war. Something about a Japanese ship. But no one knows for sure what they do."

Now I understood people's interest in these foreigners. I looked out to what I thought to be shallow water. This was the San Bernardino Strait. Plenty of ships went down around Samar. But the air of secrecy smacked of yet another search for Yamashita's gold, the unrelenting myth of Japanese war booty buried somewhere in the islands. Perhaps it was something less understood, more insidious.

"Other people say they are just here for the girls."

"Explain this," I said, although I had a fair idea of what was coming. The San Antonio man continued.

"You see, people on this island are very stupid. Very stupid. The school here on MacArthur only goes up to third grade. The people here cannot read or write. The people here do not speak English. These white men come here and pay the parents for the girls. The girls are very young, fourteen, fifteen. But the girls go and live with them. The white men buy the parents concrete, so the parents are very happy."

"What do the girls think?" I asked.

He laughed. "Oh, the girls are very stupid. They are like the parents. They want to have babies with pointed noses like white people. Not flat ones like mine." He flattened his own nose with his finger, and the other guys laughed with him.

I wonder what we had here. A group of seasonal surfers? Prospectors? Perhaps a pod of pedophiles? I decided I really did not want to know, and we climbed down the rocks to the beach. At the base of the rock formation were indeed openings, and there were deep overhangs and indentures, but I doubted that they were used as caves. More than likely the Japanese dived into them to avoid detection from U.S. planes. We walked a short way down to the beach. On a rock was a painted sign: Welcome to Cogon.

The guys told me that there was another site where a Santo Niño, or statue of the child Jesus, looked out to the ocean. Many people believed the statue pointed to something underneath the water. I asked how far it was to the Santo Niño, and they said with little enthusiasm at least an hour's walk. Given that they told me Cogon was twenty minutes and it turned out to be nearly forty, I said, "Next time, *na lang* (okay)." The guys seemed happy. We headed back to the barrio.

As we walked past the row of the foreigners' concrete houses under those glorious palms, I saw a pretty Filipina, maybe sixteen years old, stare at me through a doorway. We passed back through Cogon and into the burned diabolical grassland.

BIRI ISLAND

Samar did not figure predominantly in either MacArthur's design for reconquest or the Japanese plan. The island was simply too inhospitable in terms of terrain to give it much strategic importance. Small-scale operations from November 1944 through February 1945 eradicated the inconsequential Japanese forces from the west coast of the island, ensuring the safety of the San Juanico Strait. Then in February MacArthur informed his staff that he wanted a short passage through the Visayan Islands to Luzon. To make this route possible, the San Bernardino Strait, the passageway between the northern tip of Samar and the Bicol Peninsula, would need to be cleared of the undersized enemy garrisons on several of the islands. Most notably they would have to eradicate the estimated hundred- to three-hundred-strong group on Biri Island ten miles off Samar's coast.[6]

On February 20, 1945, at dawn, the American Division with Philippine Army elements in support attacked. Four navy planes strafed and bombed suspected Japanese positions before the landings. At first, the attack was a near disaster. Approaching the island just south of its main barrio, also known as Biri, four American mechanized landing craft (LCMs) accompanied by four PT boats and one P-38 Lightning aircraft overhead attempted a landing. The unfortunate party first hit a reef offshore, and then while stationary, it was raked by intense machine-gun and mortar fire from the island. The U.S. forces took casualties but were aware enough to pull back off the reef and out of range. Three hours later, a 105mm howitzer battery landed on Macarite Island, just a couple hundred yards off the west coast of Biri. Here the beleaguered U.S. landing team was able to temporarily disembark. Meanwhile, Navy SBD Dauntless dive-bombers began to bomb and strafe enemy positions around the Biri barrio. As this was happening, a small U.S. advanced command post was set up on Biri south of the barrio.

The next day the U.S. force made its second attempt to take Biri. Setting off from Macarite at 7:30 a.m., U.S. forces were able to land on the west coast of Biri. There was no opposition. Near noon the Americal contingent was just south of the barrio when it met the Japanese. A harsh, daylong firefight erupted, gradually spilling into the town's streets. By 4:35 p.m., the barrio was taken, but approximately twenty Japanese soldiers were seen standing on top of an ammunition dump just north of the barrio, near an elementary school. The U.S. artillery on Macarite began firing. Suddenly, a flash and an incredible concussion took all the Japanese troops literally up in smoke. With the exception of a few encounters later that day and the next, the battle for Biri was over. The Japanese suffered seventy killed, its entire force, while the U.S. losses were five killed and fifty wounded. The San Bernardino Strait was secure.

I was excited about exploring such an unrecognized battlefield. The banca ride from Tinau to Biri took forty minutes, and just as my other voyages in the Balicuatros, it was marvelous. The sea was calm and blue. The sun was

hot, but I felt no effect underneath the boat's canvas canopy. To my left looking south was the northern coast of Samar, its green shoreline bolstered by the
rugged mountains behind it. To my right looking north was a series of small,
pleasant islands. Straight over the prow in the far distance was the outline of a
large, cloud-topped mountain, the active Bulusan Volcano in Sorsogon.

As we neared the southeastern tip of Biri, I noticed float-like objects
laid out in a pattern around a bamboo shanty that seemed, for no apparent
reason, to be sitting on the water. I asked the boatman what it was, and he
replied it was a pearl farm and that the people in the shanty were guards. He
went on to say that some rich Japanese businessman owned it. Furthermore,
the business was illegal—a foreign national could not own and run such a ven-
ture, but someone somehow "fixed it" so that it remained in operation.

We chugged up the west coast of Biri, entering the channel between
it and Macarite Island. The channel was perhaps a hundred yards wide at
its narrowest point. Both islands were cut from the same cloth: each had
a green central ridge that ran the length of the island and a narrow, flat
shoreline. Biri, to my right, was clearly the larger island, but there were other
telltale differences as well. On Macarite the shore was lined sporadically with
thatched sawali huts and wooden buildings. Biri had the same, but more often
appeared the enviable concrete and tin buildings, with roofs topped by shiny
metal water containers and satellite dishes. Clearly, there was some level of
affluence here.

The banca landed at a steep set of concrete steps at the Biri Barrio.
Towering over the steps and commanding attention from every angle was a
gleaming white statue nearly twenty feet high. The statue was of the island's
patron saint, St. Vincent Ferrer (1350–1419), a Spanish Dominican known for
his good looks, advanced oratorical skills, and his strong advocacy of penance.
Ferrer became famous in Barcelona when the city dwellers, suffering from
famine, waited desperately for the supply ships to arrive with corn. The saint,
in his daily sermon, said that the ships would come that day. They did, and the
city went wild in celebration. For decades Ferrer preached on the subjects of
sin, death, hell, and the need for penitence. According to sources at the time,
the effects of his sermons were remarkable: gambling, vice, and blasphemy
seemed to disappear wherever he went.[7]

Waiting for me underneath the statue was one of the municipality's officials, whom I assumed was in charge of tourism. Sitting on a spiffy red scooter, she was cheerful and in her forties. She immediately gave me a copy of the publication commemorating the 2005 Biri Fiesta in honor of St. Vincent Ferrer, as well as handful of tourist brochures. She asked me if I would distribute these back in America.

The fiesta publication's welcome statement was beguiling.

> Behold . . . BIRI ISLAND . . . amidst and blest with bountiful nature. The abode of cheerful, diligent, peace-loving and warmhearted people. . . .
>
> . . . be overwhelmed by its magnificent, unique, and marvelously set rock formations towering over the abundantly clear water . . . inviting. . . .
>
> . . . experience the awesome feeling of being near to God through these natural wonders as we the BIRIANONS welcome you all to join us in our thanksgiving to the Almighty as we celebrate the Feast Day of our Patron Saint, St. Vincent Ferrer.[8]

The history of Biri centered on the galleon trade. It seems the Spanish ships en route to Manila probably from Mexico would use the San Bernardino Strait. According to the fiesta publication, as a ship's captain would spy the island, he would order the decks to be swept, or "barren," in preparation for berthing at Capul Island on the other end of the strait. The word "Biri" grew out of this order to clean the decks.

The rest of the publication contained well wishes from presumably donors to the fiesta. Most came from people in Northern Samar, but quite a few were from outside the island: Honolulu; Gold Coast, Australia; East Aurora, New York; and Severn, Maryland. And one came from a well-known Makati film director, who mysteriously called Biri "The Island of No Return."

I complimented the official on the publication, and she graciously allowed me to keep it. She then whisked me off on a whirlwind tour of the barrio on foot. The first thing I noticed was that, unlike San Antonio or MacArthur, the streets were paved. Actually, they were half paved. One side of the street was concrete, which allowed for motorbikes to zoom along; the other, unpaved side was for pedestrian traffic. Neither riders nor walkers completely followed this plan. The second thing I noticed was that paved streets, even half-paved streets, absorb and throw off the heat and sun. My walking tour of Biri was one hot, bright experience. My guide knew this well, of course, and she walked underneath a blue Avon umbrella.

We stopped first at the St. Vincent parish church, a relatively new building that, as I was told, was constructed entirely by the people of Biri. It was a white, attractive church clearly inspired by traditional Spanish design, with the bell tower connected to the church but off to one side. This configuration is centuries old. In the event of an earthquake, if the tower tipped, it would not come crashing through the church roof. However, there had been a recent typhoon, a bad one, and the bell tower's roof had some sizable holes in it. My guide told me the church was being prepared for the upcoming fiesta, and indeed I saw frenetic activity going on both inside and around the structure. I was taken into a room just off the altar, where I met the parish priest, a pleasant man in his forties and dressed in a black T-shirt and khaki shorts. He spoke superb English. Our short conversation focused on how many Filipino priests had emigrated to America and how many more were needed.

Back out on Biri's hot, bright streets, we went to the municipal building, where in a courtyard the mayor sat in the shade, administering to several men holding folders and three-ring binders. My guide announced me as a visiting American writer and university professor, and the men immediately vacated their seats. It was somewhat embarrassing. The mayor and I chatted about such things as comparing the length of my plane flight to the Philippines, with that of his son's to the Middle East, where he works. Our polite but rather unfocused conversation continued until I asked him about the use of English in the schools. The mayor felt it was crucial that English be taught in schools. How else, he said with conviction, could his son have landed his job abroad? He declared most Filipinos realize the value of English instruction. I nodded.

The next stop was the important one—the Biri Elementary School, which was at the northern end of the barrio. Here was where the Japanese troops went up in smoke that day in February 1945. As we walked into the schoolyard at perhaps 10:00 a.m., the yard was full of children, some in uniforms and some not. I guessed it might have been recess. We went over to the school's main attraction: one large hole. My guide called it the lagoon. Its circumference was perhaps twenty yards, and at its deepest, it was at least ten feet down. The guide explained that it used to be larger, but erosion had set in. The outer areas were ringed with litter and garbage. At roughly the center of the hole was a small tree, and underneath it was a two-foot-tall concrete figure of a man. It was tilted, nearly ready to fall over. Its facial features had decayed to virtual nothingness, and one arm was missing. It wore something on its head that I took to be a helmet.

My guide assured me it was a statue of a Japanese soldier. I wondered whether its dilapidated condition was supposed to reflect the torn bodies of the Japanese. The children by now were squealing all around us, so to deflate their excitement at seeing an American, I lined them up and took a group picture. This strategy had worked well in other places, and it worked well here: they immediately drifted off.

I moved over to the ten-foot rectangular concrete marker that stood off to the side of the hole. Most of the slab held an insignia, "Veterans Federation of the Philippines," that was curled around a graphic of a sword, the Philippine stars, and what I took to be an olive branch. Below the sword appeared "R.A. . . ." and then nothing because a large chunk of concrete was missing. The actual dedication of the memorial read as follows: "This marker was the site of the Japanese imperial forces garrison. Japanese explosives were hit by the 105 mm mortar making this lagoon during the American invasion forces on Oct. 27, 1944."

I was nonplussed. Here was, in fact, the Japanese ammunition dump that historians Francis Cronin and Robert Smith described. Yes, it was hit by 105mm shells sent over from Macarite Island, but it happened on February 21, 1945. Who was wrong: the vaunted American writers or the people who lived here? I turned to my guide with this vexation but decided to let it lie.

My guide put her Avon umbrella back up (but I could not fit underneath it), and we left the school grounds. The street we walked down was adorned with blue banners strung from houses in preparation of the upcoming fiesta. Everything was very clean in spite of the chickens kept under their metal cages and the dogs lying fast asleep every twenty feet. We passed a truly impressive building, a large, teal-painted three-story concrete affair that held a sari-sari store on the ground level and living quarters on the upper two.

Giant flowerpots festooned the third story. Huge pillars rose up nearly to the roof. On the roof in each corner were emblems of anchors and other nautical devices. My guide saw my admiration and explained with a bright smile that this family's daughter had married an Australian.

Our final destination was the interview my guide had set up for me. I wanted to speak with someone who remembered the Battle of Biri. She took me to see Pedro (a pseudonym) and his wife. They lived in a small concrete and bamboo house. The living room was cool and dark, and staring at me from the walls I could make out a Santo Niño and the seemingly requisite portrait of the Virgin Mary. Pedro sat on a plastic chair, cane in hand, while his wife sat across the room, her bare feet tucked underneath her on the couch.

Pedro said he was born in 1927, and he was about fifteen years old when the Japanese first came to Biri. When they did arrive, 90 percent of the Biri barrio went to the farms or to caves in the rock formations. His family went off to nearby San Pedro Island. They feared the Japanese. He remembers that for two years nearly everything was done with *copra*, the dried husks of the coconut. They were used as fuel and to light the shack where his family lived. They traveled between places at low tide, always trying to avoid their occupiers. He shook his head. It was a hard life, and no one liked it.

When I asked how the Japanese treated the people here, Pedro's wife answered rather loudly that they would kill you if you did not bow to them. If you bowed, it was OK.

The Battle of Biri, as he described it, substantiated exactly the accounts I read: U.S. and Filipino troops arrived in February 1945. The fighting lasted a couple of days. The hole in the schoolyard was indeed caused by a shell fired from Macarite. Terrified of the fighting, people hid themselves the best they could. All of the Japanese on Biri were killed.

When it was over, a U.S. ship came, and the Americans distributed boxes of food and firearms. Pedro told me Filipinos here liked the Americans. The Americans helped the people, he said, not like the Japanese, whom he said everyone hated. He related that in 1953 he worked in Zamboanga unloading ships. When a Japanese ship arrived, he and others refused to work; they would not unload any Japanese ship. No, he would hate the Japanese until he died.

His wife added that when she was a teenager, an American soldier gave her a can of corned beef and other types of food, but if a Japanese were to have tried that, she would not have accepted it. No, definitely not, she said.

Pedro said their granddaughter married a Japanese man. The couple wanted to fly Pedro and his wife to Manila for a holiday, but they refused. The young people today, he said, do not understand what happened during the war. People today tolerate the Japanese only because of their money, he declared. From across the room, his wife grunted in agreement.

We chatted about the war, the history of Biri, and alternative names for the islands. Then he told me about Biri's famous *berbenota*, who has inhabited the island for several hundred years. The berbenota is an invisible giant who will help you if you are in trouble. In one celebrated story in 1996, a very poor mother on the north side of the island, distraught over her family's condition, called out one night to the berbenota to help her. The next day the regular supply ship from Masbate was sailing to Catarman with a cargo of foodstuffs, cigarettes, hardware, and other things to be sold in stores. Inexplicably, for the captain was well experienced in these waters, the ship went aground just off the Biri coast. The cheerful, diligent residents of Biri descended on the ship, ably assisted by people from probably all the surrounding islands, and within hours had relieved it of its cargo. Then they went to work on its machinery and then finally on its metal. In a short time the stricken ship was stripped clean, and the people of these parts had their bellies and wallets full. A photographer had snapped a picture of the event that ran in the newspapers, and people say in the background was a shadowy figure of a huge person smiling down on the ship—the berbenota.

Thanking Pedro and his wife, I took my leave. My guide had to depart as well, so I made my way back to the steps under the tall statue of St. Vincent Ferrer. As I waited for the guys to get the boat ready for our trip back to Tinau, I wondered if the good saint ever had the opportunity to chat with the berbenota, and if he had, what the topic of conversation was. Were these two on good terms? If so, did they discuss the foibles of particular Birianons? Was there any competition between them, perhaps with regard to job responsibilities? Did St. Vincent have any words to say to the berbenota after that shipwreck incident, perhaps telling the giant of his days in Barcelona?

The banca pulled away from the steep steps at the landing. The next day I would be leaving the Balicuatro Islands and, indeed, the Leyte-Samar region for Luzon. The boat slid through the clear water toward the Biri-Macarite channel. Looking back I saw the gleaming white statue of St. Vincent Ferrer, the patron saint of Biri, the man who was a strong advocate of penance.

PART 3
LUZON

8

THE LINGAYEN BEACHES

AND SOUTH

There was little doubt as to why MacArthur chose to invade Luzon at Lingayen. The area offered sheltered beaches and access to a well-developed highway and railroad system. Within relatively close proximity were the airfields at Clark Field and around the city of Angeles. Controlling Lingayen meant controlling the core of Luzon, the corridor into Manila. Manila, of course, was MacArthur's obsession. Without it his promise to return would not be fully realized. Without it he could not be redeemed.

Before MacArthur could land at Lingayen, he decided to take the island of Mindoro off the southern coast of Batangas and within proximity of Manila Bay. MacArthur wanted Mindoro, especially the southwestern portion, in order to control the sea routes into the Visayas Islands and to build air support for the operations in Luzon. The latter was particularly important because the army's attempts at airfield construction in Leyte were disappointing in the unsuitable terrain and climate. Consequently, MacArthur ordered Mindoro attacked before Lingayen.[1]

A small invasion force was put together in east Leyte and departed on December 12, 1944. It sailed south and then west, swinging around the southern tip of Negros. At that point the convoy was attacked by kamikazes. The USS *Nashville*, MacArthur's ship at Leyte, was hit and lost 113 men. More attacks and deaths followed until December 15 when the ships reached San Jose on Mindoro's southwestern coast. The force landed without any opposition and quickly took control of that part of the island. For the next several weeks, however, kamikazes attacked resupply convoys. But by the end of January 1945, the entire island was in the hands of U.S. forces, of which a total of sixteen died.

The importance of the Mindoro operation cannot be overstated. With the airfields established, the Fifth Air Force had three fighter groups, two medium bomber groups, and an assortment of other squadrons all ready to assist the fighting on Luzon. Heavy bombers came later. Without the airfields on Mindoro, MacArthur could not have moved on Luzon when he did.

MacArthur did not set foot on Mindoro until June 1945, when the fighting was well over. His convoy pulled out of Leyte in January 1945. The Lingayen invasion force steamed to Luzon in two parts. First, Adm. J. B. Oldendorf took 164 ships to prepare the gulf area for the amphibious forces that would follow. On board the battleship USS *California*, a veteran of Pearl Harbor, Oldendorf had the fleet rendezvous off Leyte on New Year's Day and start north.

Oldendorf's voyage to Lingayen on the west coast of Luzon was not an easy one. Almost from the outset enemy submarines, including midgets, attempted to torpedo the convoy. More dangerous were the aircraft based at Clark Field and its satellite airfields, Nichols Field in Manila, and other Japanese airstrips in Luzon. As the task force made its way through the Surigao Strait, around the southern tip of Negros, and up the west coast of Panay, the convoy was consistently attacked. As with the Mindoro-bound fleet, the results were often terrifying.

Many of the attacking planes were kamikazes, the almost mythical suicide squadrons that composed Japan's last throw of the dice. The kamikazes were the brainchild of Vice Adm. Takijiro Ohnishi, who was headquartered in the Bamban Hills in central Luzon. The pilots took off from fields in Luzon singing their anthem:

> *In serving on the seas, be a corpse saturated with water.*
> *In serving on the land, be a corpse covered with weeds.*
> *In serving in the sky, be a corpse that challenged the clouds.*
> *Let us all die close to the side of our sovereign.*[2]

Against this mind-set the U.S. fleet pushed northward. On the night of January 4, the escort carrier USS *Ommaney Bay* was hit by a twin-engine Japanese plane that crashed into the flight deck. Bombs penetrated the deck and exploded. Fires started that were impossible to extinguish. Intense heat and exploding ammunition prevented rescue attempts. An hour after the attack, the ship was abandoned. Oldendorf ordered the destroyer USS *Burns* to end it with a torpedo, and the *Ommaney Bay* went under with the loss of ninety-three hands.

The next day saw more kamikaze attacks, with some of the aircraft coming from the Mabalacat Airfield north of Angeles in Luzon. Approximately a hundred miles off of Corregidor, the USS *Louisville*, a heavy cruiser; the USS *Manila Bay*, a small carrier; and the HMAS *Australia* were badly hit and suffered loss of life but were able to carry on. More ships were also hit. But January 5 was only the beginning.

The fleet was now just west of Cape Bolinao, the thumb-shaped piece of land that forms the northwestern border of Lingayen Gulf. With its destination in sight, the task force was beginning to split into groups to start its operation, mostly bombardments and mine sweeping, a necessary prelude to the landings. After sunrise the kamikaze attacks began. The navy downed nearly all the planes and had little damage to the ships, but its luck did not hold. An attack at about noon on the battleship USS *New Mexico* caused the deaths of several high-ranking officers, as well as twenty-five sailors. The U.S. fleet experienced substantial loss of life. The USS *Columbia* lost thirteen men to a kamikaze. As night approached, more kamikazes arrived: the *Louisville* was hit so badly it had to retire from combat, and the *Australia* was hit again. That night a torpedo plane sent the destroyer USS *Hovey* to the bottom; forty-six men were lost.

The navy's leadership was surprised at the ferocity of the attacks. It had been assumed the kamikaze menace had largely ended at the Battle of Leyte Gulf. As January 6 drew to a close, the United States had lost one ship, eleven were damaged, and a rear admiral was dead. What the commanders did not know was that the kamikazes had shot their bolt. The next few days saw comparatively few attacks, partly because of the navy's raids over the Luzon airfields, especially at Clark, Bamban, and around Angeles.

On January 7, they entered Lingayen Gulf. Surveillance teams landed on Lingayen beaches and found no obstacles, save one mine, and only one ma-chine-gun emplacement that was quickly destroyed by naval fire. Everything seemed ready for the invasion until they faced another bout with the kami-kazes. That day the minesweeper USS *Palmer* was sunk with a loss of twenty-eight men.

The bombardment of Lingayen beaches began the next day, on the eighth. Ironically and fantastically, an American guerrilla leader, Lt. Col. Russell W. Volkmann, had found Japanese documents showing the Japanese under General Yamashita had moved their troops northeast into the moun-tains and planned to make a stand there instead of on the beach. In an attempt to save Filipino lives and property, Volkmann radioed MacArthur's command with this information, saying that there would not be any opposition on the beaches. There were, simply, no Japanese around. MacArthur's headquarters apparently ignored this information, because the navy never received word to cancel the bombardment. At 8:00 a.m., a procession of joyous Filipinos car-rying American flags were seen marching toward the beach to greet their lib-erators. Oldendorf sent a plane that dropped leaflets instructing them to clear the area. Then the shells of the huge naval guns began to rain down on the undefended towns. Lingayen, the capital of the province, was leveled. Quaint Binmaley with its grand cathedral was razed. The larger town of Dagupan suffered vast destruction. No Japanese were killed.

In the meantime, troops were preparing for the invasion. Task Force 79 brought the general from Leyte. MacArthur was aboard the cruiser *Boise*, and it steamed up to Lingayen several days after Oldendorf did. The *Boise* survived an unsuccessful attack by a midget submarine, and the convoy itself was at-tacked by kamikazes. Other than that the voyage was uneventful.

On January 8 the *Boise* and its fleet were off Manila Bay, with Bataan and Corregidor in plain sight. For the men watching the shoreline, it was a vision of defeat and potential revenge. For MacArthur, it was a vision of the deepest emotions: memories of love, youth, family, and failure. As MacArthur saw the sun bouncing off Luzon, he recorded that "at the sight of those never-to-be forgotten scenes of my family's past, I felt an indescribable sense of loss, of sorrow, of loneliness, and of solemn consecration."[3]

The *Boise* turned Cape Bolinao without significant incident and sailed into the Lingayen Gulf. The entire invasion fleet was assembled by the morning of January 9. The night before had been comfortable, and the morning brought a windless, partially overcast sky. At 7:00 a.m., the invasion bombardment began. Three kamikazes from Nichols Field near Manila attacked, one managed to hit the USS *Columbia* and kill twenty-four men. The *Australia* was hit by kamikazes for the fifth time since leaving Leyte.

For the soldiers on the transport ships, the scene before them would have been mysterious. If staring due south, they would have seen a mostly flat shoreline interrupted by the towns of Lingayen on their right center and San Fabian on the left. To the extreme left lay the dark green mountains of the southern tip of the Cordillera Central Range. To the extreme right stood the smaller wooded hills of the Bolinao Peninsula, the thumb of land they had just rounded. The soldiers had no idea how many Japanese were waiting for them. The predebarkation bombardments had created a beachhead of smoke and dust, punctuated by sporadic flames, but there was no indication of what was behind it. Were the Japanese hiding within the haze, perhaps entrenched in the hills and mountains, waiting to launch a banzai counterattack?

At 9:00 a.m., the invasion began. The first wave of landing craft started their forty-five-hundred-yard zigzag run to the beach. They encountered no real resistance. Small arms and a few artillery pieces, mostly in the San Fabian area, hardly even harassed the oncoming craft. U.S. troops came ashore at various beaches along the semicircle-shaped shoreline of Lingayen Gulf, which in peacetime was a superb swimming beach. As at Leyte, these beaches were color coded. White beaches 1, 2, and 3 were the most eastern, near the towns of Mabilao and San Fabian. Blue Beach was just east of Dagupan. The Yellow and Crimson beaches were west of Dagupan and just off the town of Binmaley. The Orange and Green landing areas, the most western, were near Lingayen and the important Japanese airfield.

Within the first few hours, all the important objectives were met. U.S. troops had marched through and held the towns of Lingayen and San Fabian. The airfield near the provincial capital was taken. Roads and bridges outside the towns were secured. A beachhead four miles deep and twenty in length had been established. Everywhere Filipinos poured onto the beaches and roads, surrounding the U.S. liberators with smiles and Old Glory.

MacArthur came back to Luzon at about 2:00 p.m., walking ashore just south of San Fabian. As at Leyte, he landed with much of his staff, including Lieutenant General Sutherland. And while his aquatic escapades were not planned in Leyte, they most certainly were deliberate in Lingayen. Apparently, the Seabees had hurriedly constructed a makeshift pier so that the general would not have to get wet. MacArthur would not have it. He waded through the surf and the cameras, onto the sand, and into a crowd of cheering Filipinos. The general then began to walk up and down the beach, stopping to talk with his men.

For the rest of the day, MacArthur conferred with his commanders. Late in the afternoon, he attempted to get to Dagupan, the largest city in the area, but found the only bridge into the city destroyed, so he spent that night on board the *Boise*. On January 13, with the bridge repaired, he moved his command to a home economics school in Dagupan. He then began walking the city's streets. The town was choked with soldiers and civilians waving the *V* sign. As MacArthur walked, people waved American flags, long hidden, and held their babies and children high to see the general. MacArthur, on the streets of Dagupan, was already an American legend.

One hundred and seventy thousand troops landed on Lingayen beaches over the next few days. Until January 26, MacArthur stayed in the Dagupan schoolhouse. During the day he would often be driven around the Lingayen area, inspecting the terrain and making plans for the drive on Manila. For these plans he would confer with what had become known as the Bataan Gang, men such as Sutherland and Brig. Gen. Charles Willoughby who had escaped to Australia with MacArthur. Two others were Lt. Gen. Robert Eichelberger, commander of the Eighth Army, and Lt. Gen. Walter Krueger, commander of the Sixth Army. These two commanders disliked each other with a passion, a situation MacArthur exploited continuously.

MacArthur had promised the Joint Chiefs of Staff that he would be able to take the area comprising the central plain of Luzon and extending down to Manila Bay within four to six weeks of landing at Lingayen. The seizure of the Clark Field complex near Angeles was an important aspect of the plan. The U.S. Army Air Forces needed to expand their facilities in order to carry out the expected heavy bombing raids on the Japanese homeland

and on Iwo Jima and Okinawa, as well as to thwart Japanese shipping in the area. Many of the airstrips at Clark were paved and thus immune to the rainy season that started in June. In taking Clark and the central plain, U.S. forces would also acquire control of two critical transportation arteries, Highway 3 and the Manila-Dagupan Railway, both of which ran directly into the capital city, Manila.

There have been numerous attempts to explain General MacArthur's obsession with taking Manila. One was strategic. A retaking of the capital city would not only avenge the loss of Bataan, it would also strike a severe blow to Japanese morale in the rest of the country. Manila was seen as the enemy's center of gravity, meaning that if Manila fell the rest of the Japanese defenses would cave in as well. Another reason was that the city sat on one of the world's finest harbors, which would prove invaluable for future advances on the Japanese homeland. It should be noted that these strategic assumptions were wrong: after Manila fell there was no perceptible drop in enemy morale, and even with the city in American hands, the Japanese fought tenaciously in other parts of the islands. The port city would prove useful but not critical to executing the rest of the war.

Humanitarian concerns provided another justification. MacArthur knew that thousands of Allied civilian internees and military prisoners were interned in Santo Tomas and Bilibid. MacArthur suspected that the Japanese might resort to mass executions, as they did in Puerto Princesa, Palawan. There in December 1944, as U.S. forces began to move north, the Japanese forced more than a hundred American prisoners of war (POWs) into an air raid shelter, doused them with gasoline, and set them alight with hand grenades. It was a widespread belief within the U.S. military that such a reaction was indeed possible in Manila.

A fourth explanation, and one given intense scrutiny, focused on the general's personal vanity. For MacArthur, Manila was the symbol of his return, and more importantly, it was his cherished prewar home. Until he could march through the city streets and reclaim his treasured belongings at the Manila Hotel, he would not have succeeded. The depth of this obsession is seen in the fact that on February 2, 1945, days before the actual battle for Manila would begin, MacArthur had already drawn up plans for his victory parade into the city. These plans included an itinerary of the route the general would take, the amount of troops to be on hand for the ceremony, the tunes the band would play, and so on in astonishingly minute detail. It would be the liberation of Paris in the Pacific.

Manila, as the focal point of the Luzon campaign, was to be taken from several directions. General Eichelberger would approach Manila from the south after landing in Batangas while General Krueger would come down Highway 3 from the north. Krueger's command caused MacArthur much consternation. The German-born general estimated that there were approximately 235,000 Japanese troops on Luzon, with many of them positioned on the army's left flank, and he guessed that Manila would be defended to the last. Because of these figures, his timetable for taking Manila was two to three weeks longer than what MacArthur wanted. Instead, MacArthur relied on other figures: he believed an estimated 153,000 Japanese were on Luzon, with many located south of the capital city, and that they would not defend Manila at all. Given this scenario, MacArthur believed Krueger would have little to fear as he went down Highway 3 and that he would easily be able to take and hold Manila.

Krueger's estimates were far more precise than MacArthur's. Despite the catastrophic loss of Leyte, the Japanese held formidable numbers in the Philippines. General Yamashita had roughly 255,000 troops on Luzon, but by then he had little air support. Moreover, his supplies and equipment could not easily get through the U.S.-dominated seas. His supplies were running low, and he had few vehicles to move them. Furthermore, U.S. air attacks coupled with Filipino guerrilla activities made transportation a nightmare. Given this scenario, Yamashita knew that he could not possibly defend Luzon. Instead, he opted to attempt a protracted delaying action.

Logically, the Japanese could only hold high ground. If Yamashita had opposed the landings at Lingayen, the U.S. naval guns would have butchered his troops. If he had any hope of defending Manila, he would have to attempt to stop the Americans somewhere north of the city, away from the plains of Pampanga and Bulacan, which were more suitable to the larger, highly maneuverable U.S. forces and where, without air support, his troops would be highly vulnerable. Under no circumstances did he want to entrap his men on

Bataan, hoping for reinforcements from the sea, which probably could not get through anyway. Consequently, he decided to divide his forces and place them in three mountainous strongholds. With Yamashita in direct command, 152,000 troops, named the Shobu Group, were sent into the mountains of northern Luzon and northeast of Lingayen. There, his troops would have excellent natural defenses and access to the rich Cagayan Valley, where they would be able to find food. A second force of 30,000 men, the Kembu Group, was positioned in the hills north of Angeles and around Clark Field, where they hoped to cut off Highway 3 and the railway line. A third group, the Shimbu, numbering 80,000 men who would be responsible for all of southern Luzon, was stationed mainly in Manila and the hills east and northeast of the city. Yamashita thought that a detachment of naval troops in Manila would destroy items of military importance and then leave the city.

The stage was set. MacArthur faced a split, poorly supplied enemy with little hope of reinforcement but with a fanatical desire to die for the emperor. Many of his own men were exhausted from the fighting on Leyte, but they were well equipped and confident. The wide, flat central plain of Luzon lay before MacArthur, and at its end was the city of Manila, his home.

PANGASINAN–WHITE BEACH

My push from Lingayen to Manila began at White Beach. I spent the first night at the Sierra Vista Resort, a splendid little find just east of White Beach in San Fabian. It was near the barrio of Nibaliw, which was close to the most northeastern of the main landing points. Right before dusk I went down to the beach to take in the air of the China Sea. Standing on the beach and looking to the east, I saw the mountains of La Union, which stretched up the length of Luzon. Imposing in their dark green shadow, I knew it was in these mountains that Yamashita had spread his forces in a futile attempt to stall the American drive. To the west was one long beach that curved eventually to Lingayen some thirty miles away. The sand at White Beach was not gray, brown, or green, and certainly not white. It was relatively free of garbage, a somewhat uncommon condition for Philippine beaches, but the odd rubber tubing, plastic bag, and wrapping paper from a variety of products washed up daily. Children played in the dark water while their fathers waded twenty yards into the sea, casting nets. Dogs cavorted. Directly behind the beach a line of nipa structures extended for miles. These were open-air affairs called sheds, and each had a sign out front. There was Potch's Shed, Irish and Ivey's Shed, and Janet's Store and Shed. The sheds were usually rented out to middle-class families on a day trip from Dagupan or other large cities. They had benches, and families came to sit in the shade and eat and drink to their hearts' content.

The next day I began the crawl. In the nipa-hut dining area, I ate my American breakfast of bacon and eggs with superbly brewed coffee while the security guard watched an action movie on TV. It is seemingly an unwritten law in Philippine restaurants, bars, and even buses that TVs and stereo systems must be turned up to full volume at all times, but especially at 6:45 a.m. As I sipped my coffee and contemplated the history I would encounter that day, I was treated to a soundtrack of gunfire, grenades, screams, punches, curses, and explosions, all at ear-splitting decibels. Somewhat embarrassed by the personal failings that prohibited me from enjoying this aubade, I meekly asked the waiter if I could watch the morning news. He gently acknowledged my discomfort. The security guard skulked away soon after the waiter flipped the channel to FOX News, and I finished breakfast considering the number of dead in the latest suicide bombing in Iraq.

I would tour the Lingayen beaches by trike, which I hired from the resort. My driver's name was Ernie, and he had a brand-new vehicle. A trike is a small motorcycle with a covered carriage welded on. Normally, I regarded trikes to be Satan's sidecars and trike drivers to be men physically mutated to absorb the spine-bending hurls over bumps, potholes, and curbs. Ernie and his trike, though, were something else. His machine was austerely handsome. It had none of the dazzling decorations—American eagles, the Chicago Bulls' emblem, the Virgin Mary, and so on—one often sees on the sidecar; rather, Ernie's had a simple pumpkin paint job and an ID number. The car's interior seemed larger than most because I could actually stretch my five-foot-ten frame comfortably. Most importantly, it had a padded ceiling, which meant that when we went over a bump I would not crack my skull. And Ernie did things I never saw other drivers do. When we went through the five-inch-deep flood of water at an intersection, he actually slowed to a crawl so that the water would not splash into the car. After a particularly bad bump, he would duck his head into the car and ask if I were OK.

We drove westward out of Nibaliw, planning to go to Lingayen first and then work our way back toward Dagupan and San Fabien. How different Pangasinan was from Samar! The landscape was sea-level flat. All the houses were concrete. A number of homes were huge and quite attractive; my favorite had a medieval Moorish tower in the front. Clearly there was money in Dagupan. Unlike in supine Samar, the people here seemed busy; they were doing things. Along the road were dozens of places where people were setting out the just-harvested bangus fish, the region's freshwater delicacy. Construction was under way. People were setting up their stalls to sell *bagoong* (fermented shrimp or fish paste), engaging in commerce and responsibility.

This is Ilocano country. Pangasinan is at the southern most point of Ilocano influence, although the Ilocanos were apparently not the original people of the area. Demographically, the Ilocanos stretch all the way up the western half of northern Luzon, up to Aparri. Ilocanos are renowned for their industry and frugality. In fact, Ilocanos were heavily recruited to work the Hawaiian sugar fields in the early part of the twentieth century, and today much of the Hawaiian Filipino community contains Ilocano bloodlines. After one look at Pangasinan, it was not difficult to understand how the group gained its reputation.

LINGAYEN

We arrived in the town of Lingayen after an hour's trike drive. Lingayen was on the western edge of the invasion. Ernie pulled up in front of the provincial capitol building. Although rather small, it was a beautiful edifice, sitting proudly within its provincial environment. Set in a decidedly neoclassical style and painted in something akin to old gold with white trim, the building was a lovely testament to the aspirations of an almost innocent America, an America so confident in its cultural righteousness that it graciously gave examples of it to other people. Gleaming white columns conveyed strength; ornate statues and flowerpots emanated beauty. The structure was clearly related to American state capitols, showing that its builders considered the Philippines as at least a reflection of America. On the front steps of the capitol building were two plaques. The left one dated the building to 1918 and listed Ralph Harrington Doane as its architect. The plaque on the right read: "Rebuilt with the aid of the people of the United States of America under the Philippine Rehabilitation Act of 1946."

The irony here is superb. The benevolent Americans built it so that they could impart classical grace and beauty to the Filipinos, then the heroic Americans destroyed it even though there were no enemy troops in the area, and later the generous Americans rebuilt it at their taxpayers' expense. I would see this pattern again.

As in Leyte, Doane worked his magic on me. The building's interior was wonderful, with interesting paintings and wooden door frames, large windows through which gorgeous sunlight streamed, and a shiny, solid floor that allowed the administrators' heels to click assuredly as they walked from office to office. The capitol was, without question, an American building, and it gave me a warm, comfortable feeling. In Doane's work, all seemed to reflect the typical bustle of a provincial administrative building. As I walked toward the rear of the building, I saw a man operating a copier machine, and I noted in passing that it was exactly the same type that my graduate school department had used in 1978.

I went out through the building and toward the beach, stopping at the small park between them. At first I was somewhat surprised. When I had been here last in 1992, the park consisted of a dilapidated old Japanese plane and, if my memory serves me right, an equally deteriorated American tank. Now, these retired tools of war had been reborn. An American tank, an M10, sat painted in a color scheme much like that of the Gulf War, pointing its barrel at a Japanese aircraft sitting directly across from it. The airplane (the same one I saw over a decade before) had its holes plugged up and sported new paint. It was identified as a Zero, but it appeared to be a two-seater, and I am not sure Zeros were designated as such. There was also a set of antiaircraft guns, as well a three-inch naval gun. Set into the ground was an ornate compass that indicated the direction of the U.S. landing, straight ahead.

I followed the compass. At the edge of the park was a brand-new memorial structure fashioned in a peculiar architectural style. It seemed to be something like a pagoda, and yet it was reminiscent of a Filipino traditional nipa house. It was an open-air construction, with seven or so stations that held photographs of the Lingayen operation. A poster announced the celebration of the event's fiftieth anniversary, but I was a few months late. At any rate, the material was interesting, the shade provided relief from the sun, and the huge, waving palm trees nearby all produced a pleasant effect. Through the palms and over a short wall, I could see the ocean.

Lingayen beach, or Orange Beach, was nearly deserted. A couple of kids wandered around, and a jeep full of teenagers cruised by on the flat sand. The view was hazy and insignificant. It was an uneventful place under a very hot sun. I tried to imagine the Old Man grandiosely stepping through the shallow water, his officers resolutely walking behind him, cameras whirring, enlisted men grinning, exuberant Filipinos waving American flags, and the shattered remains of the barrios burning. The sun above and the rap music from the circling jeep hamstrung my powers of imagination. I gave up without much resistance and started to walk back to the shade.

The coolness of the little grove off to the side of the memorial structure was lovely. At least a score of goats frolicked in the grass in the large field adjacent to the grove; the sound of their bells added to the delight of the shade. I stood and read the stone commemorative marker that faced the sea. Its steel plaque read: "On this beach, General Lloyd [sic] Wheaton landed his troops on 7 November 1899 to cut off the retreat of General Emilio Aguinaldo; and General of the Army Douglas MacArthur began his campaign on 9 January 1945 for the liberation of Luzon from the Japanese invaders."

I read it again and then again. There was an incredible undercurrent with the memorial statement. True enough, Wheaton did land here as part of tri-point attempt at pinning Aguinaldo down before he could escape into the mountains. And as will be discussed in the Angeles section, the U.S. endeavor was a large-scale failure: Aguinaldo would escape and elude American troops for over another year. That the plaque places Wheaton's essentially insignificant action before MacArthur's grand landing is difficult to understand. The mystery was not lost on Manila newspapers during the memorial's dedication. When MacArthur visited Lingayen in 1961, reporters demanded to know what he thought of the plaque. Ever the professional, the Old Man commented that Wheaton, who went on to serve under Arthur MacArthur, was one of his father's best officers. It was a clearly classy moment in an embarrassing situation.[4]

BINMALEY

For the past several weeks all had been astir after debris from an American World War II airplane had been found in Lingayen Gulf. A fisherman had pulled up part of an engine with its propeller, a gas mask, and pelvic bones of one of the crew. Some time later the rest of the wreckage was brought to the surface with compressors and the assistance of local fishermen. The debris was taken to the small town of Binmaley, situated between Lingayen and Dagupan. The story had made the Manila papers, and several history websites ran white hot trying to figure out where the machine had come from, what had happened to it, and the names of the fliers. On the way back from Lingayen, I asked Ernie to stop at the police station, where the newspapers had said the wreckage was on display.

The trike pulled up to the station. Two of Binmaley's finest were sitting on a bench in the shade having a *meriendia* (snack). I started looking for the airplane's remains, which were nowhere to be seen. We stood awkwardly in the sun for several moments. Finally, Ernie asked the police for some assistance, and one of them languidly pointed to what I had thought was a pile of trash.

Ernie and I walked over to it, and underneath some discarded plywood, which was apparently being used as protection, was an engine. The machine rested on the grass with its propeller bent underneath. It was mostly rusted, and other parts of it were clearly burned. With twisted pipes sticking out oddly from its block, it reminded me of a big, fat spider sitting on the ground. I suppose it could be argued that for being in the ocean for fifty years it was in good shape, but I found it in every manner possible unimpressive. People walked past without a glance; the policemen were eating and laughing. Ernie and I just looked at it.

I got Ernie to ask the police what had happened to the American's bones. According to the officers they had been taken inside and awaited identification. We could not see them. So I remained there, staring at the heap of metal. I began to muse over the pelvic bone. Could authorities identify it, and, if so, how could they reunite the remains with the man's family? Would it involve a DNA search that I would eventually watch on TV? I then imagined an old woman in a nursing home in someplace like western Indiana suddenly receiving the news that her long-dead brother's remains had been found. Such curious elation would there be. Photographs would be taken out of albums, and newspapers would reprint pictures of a bright-faced farm kid in a uniform. The old woman would give interviews to the local media. A gravesite volley would be performed by the town's American Legion. The recipient of this attention would most likely have been some young man in his twenties when he died, probably without issue and few to remember him now save for the sister in the nursing home. And now here he was, inside the Binmaley police station, probably in an envelope stuffed in a box.

I decided I wanted to leave, knowing that if I stared at the engine any longer I would become emotional. Ernie started up the trike, and I took one last look at the engine. I believe I whispered something like a prayer for the dead boy from Indiana or wherever, and then we were into the trike and off toward Dagupan. I had a noticeable lump in my throat. About a year later I discovered that historians had determined the engine was Japanese.

DAGUPAN

Dagupan is a delta town. It forms the midsection of the gulf's shoreline, and four rivers and their tributaries are included in the general area. The city is situated in a low, swampy place, and coupled with its nearness to the sea, it has been an ideal spot for fishermen and salt makers for centuries. The earliest settlers, whom many believe came from Indonesia, had a well-formed monarchy, their own religion, and a thriving trade in *bangus*, a cultivated freshwater fish, as well as in tuba and salt. The tradesmen of the area were expert boat makers. The Spanish came in 1583, and tax records show that there were at least a thousand families living in the city in 1590.[5]

A number of important changes occurred during the Spanish centuries-old reign. Perhaps the most important was the Ilocanos' migration in the mid-eighteenth century from the north to the gulf area as a result of the sailboat trade. The Ilocanos were quickly assimilated into the local culture. The Spanish were quick to see the quality of Dagupan ships, and a number of builders were sent to Spain to further their craft. For the next hundred years, Dagupan provided most of the oceangoing vessels in Luzon. In the mid-nineteenth century, the Chinese arrived, like the Ilocanos, attracted by the shipbuilding industry. Maybe the biggest development in the area was the Manila-Dagupan railway's construction in 1891 for it connected most of central and western Luzon's commerce. The gulf area had become modern.

I first visited Dagupan in 1991, and I thought it was the most boring place in the islands. It seemed hot and dark, noisy and disheveled. I remember not being able to find a good restaurant, and the whole town seemed to close down after 9:00 p.m., except for the nightclub right next to my hotel. It blasted out-of-date disco fare until 4:00 a.m. Remembering those initial impressions, I pulled into town in Ernie's trike.

The school that MacArthur once used as his headquarters sits on one of the main arteries in the center of Dagupan and across the street from the museum. I entered the museum first, and I asked the curator (I assume it was the curator for he seemed to be the only person in the building) if there was material on MacArthur. He led me to a room that held material that was not in use. Eventually, he produced two large and interesting framed black-and-white photographs of the general walking the city's streets. The curator was polite, although he revealed nothing about MacArthur or the photographs. He did mention, several times in fact, that if I wanted to buy any books (the subject of which was not disclosed) I could go to the shop downstairs.

Not wanting to spend time on a potentially fruitless book hunt, I walked out of the museum and through a nice little park, stopping to look at the locomotive from the old Manila-Dagupan railway. English contractors first developed the railway in the nineteenth century. During the Philippine-American War, it had served as a vital supply line for the invading U.S. forces. It was just as important during World War II, when it also served as a major supply route for both the Japanese and the Americans. The locomotive, old number 17, sat there in the middle of the park, protected by a yellow fence and accented by prewar lamplights. The engine was dull black and rust spotted, but even so it seemed to be in respectable shape. This train was part of the railway that hauled the prisoners from the Bataan death march to the camp at O'Donnell. But for some reason I did not consider that history; rather, I recalled stories some of the American old-timers had told me about taking the train up from Manila in the 1950s. That would have been a comfortable trip filled with images out of Hollywood: men in linen suits and silk ties with decent booze in their silver pocket flasks and beautiful mestiza women alongside them in the cars. They could take a scenic trip through the countryside, when a man could leave his wife in Manila and spend the weekend with his mistress in any of the hotels along the way. It was a time when Americans were beloved, a trip in the warm afterglow of MacArthur. Now it was noon, and the park was filled with children who took no notice of the engine or the foreigner among them.

The CELEX Pilot School students were very vocally on lunch break. Blue-and-white-uniformed primary school kids were at play all over the grounds. Inside the office I first met with one of the administrative personnel, a woman in her sixties. After bemusing me with questions about where I lived, my marital status, and my profession in the States, she took me to the principal's office. The middle-aged principal quickly tried to hide his lunch underneath his desk, and I tried to stop him by saying it was I who was intruding. Both embarrassed, we chatted, and I explained my project. He seemed to know what I wanted, and we started the tour.

Out we went from the office and into the schoolyard, passing a sign that read Speak English Only. None of the children in the yard seemed to have had the least bit of interest in the sign and did not abide by its command. We stopped as he presented the building that had been MacArthur's GHQ: a medium-sized, prewar Spanish wooden house, with the sliding shell windows that marked its architectural type. From the outside it looked well kept, wearing its age well. We walked up a worn flight of stairs and onto the second floor. In the shaded upstairs it was perfectly cool without air-conditioning, a tribute to its nineteenth-century designers. A child ran up to the principal, took his hand, and held it to his own forehead in the Filipino expression of respect.

A preschool class of about twenty children was in session. The principal nodded to the two women who were leading the class. He then said, "Class, we have a visitor from the United States. Please say hello."

In unison, twenty young heads turned to me and said, "Good morning, teacher!"

Presumably, this greeting was not the answer the principal wanted. He patiently tried it again, "Class, is this how we greet our guest? Let's try to say hello again."

After a moment of indecision, the class summoned up its collective will and with strengthened volume and conviction again greeted me: "Good morning, teacher!" The principal said something I did not quite get, and we moved on.

MacArthur had bivouacked on the second floor of the building, which by now was not in good shape. It needed a large-scale restoration: there were holes in every wall, the ceiling needed work, and paint was peeling everywhere. From behind us the administrative lady kept chirping about not having any funds. Who would help them with such restoration? The principal chipped in that even the U.S. ambassador had visited here some time ago and agreed that they needed funds to return the building to its 1945 splendor. If not, said the principal, all of the original wood and artifacts would soon be lost. I am neither an architect nor an art historian. I had to take them at their word that all of what I saw was "original." I looked around and did not see any artifacts whatsoever.

But I was wrong. They then took me to the most important room in the building. After listening to the principal's brief historical narrative, I stood outside the doorway, peering into the small, tiled, and rather shabby room. Both the principal and the assistant confirmed it was the real thing. I looked in awe.

There before me was MacArthur's bathtub.

I doubt that it was porcelain, but it was some type of ceramic, about a yard tall, with four claw feet on the floor and the old spoked taps. Here the general would have immersed himself, washing off the dirt and sweat, perhaps with his pipe clenched between his teeth and probably swearing softly at Krueger. I immediately raised my camera, for this was a shot of a lifetime. Inconceivably, inexplicably, my camera's shutter would not budge. Befuddled, I tried again and then again. Nothing. The shutter was stuck. My trusty Nikon had worked minutes before (and would work minutes after), but right now I was not going to get a picture. A strange sensation crept over me. It was as if the spirit of the Old Man himself had reached out from beyond and held tight the shutter, as if to say, "You will not violate the sanctity of my lavatory!"

Disappointed, I turned away, and with the tour over, we prepared to part company. The administrative lady kept wringing her hands behind me: What was going to happen here without the funds? How could such original artifacts be saved? Just what would happen to the bathtub? We chatted about a few financial avenues, including contacting the Filipino-American Memorial Endowment (FAME), the Filipino-American historical group down in Manila. At the top of the stairs, I asked if I could make a donation to the house. There seemed to be a stunned silence, almost indecision, and then acceptance. I gave them some money, walked down the stairs, and went to find Ernie.

BLUE BEACH AT BONUAN

After some difficulty, Ernie found Blue Beach, situated in Barrio Bonuan, between Dagupan and San Fabian. At Blue Beach there was not one but two MacArthur memorials. We parked the trike in a small park right in front of the beach. Overgrown grass surrounded the place, but the park itself was clean and maintained. At its center was a tall column topped by a painted statue of the general smoking his pipe. The statue was recognizable as MacArthur but just barely. At the square base of the column were a number of inscriptions. I Shall Return was written on a sword and a snake. On another side read The Defenders of Bataan and Corregidor, and on its opposite was something about the Filipino troops. Yet it seemed that some of the actual plaques had been ripped off the base. There was once a chain that ran around the column connecting yard-high poles, but it had been removed as well. I considered the fact that in the Philippines there is still a thriving market for scrap metal, an enterprise that began at the end of the war with people like Eddie Woolbright. It is doubtful that these pieces would ever return.

I walked back toward the barrio and the second memorial, which was so unobtrusive we would have missed it entirely if we were not confronted by a security guard. Oddly, the memorial sat behind a barbed-wire fence that actually defended some type of residential compound that was not in any way related to the memorial. The compound's security guard allowed me into the small enclosed area, and I had to walk through his guardhouse in order to reach the object. Happily, the chain that connected the shell-formed fence posts was still there. The plaque simply read:

On this shore, known as Blue Beach, Bonuan, Dagupan City, the first combat troops of the Sixth Army of the United States of America under the command of General Douglas MacArthur landed 9 January 1945 to liberate the island of Luzon thus fulfilling his promise to the Filipino people: "I shall return."

This memorial, just as the other one in Dagupan, gave me pause to consider the actual intent of such things. Why would one erect a memorial where no one could find it? Did at one time someone have a plan to rejuvenate the barrio with tourist dollars, and this memorial was its centerpiece? Were the condominiums' developers banking on the memorial to draw people to this obscure beach? The memorial offered no clues.

Ernie and I saddled up and headed back to the resort. It had been a long, successful day, thanks much to Ernie's abilities. He was the finest trike driver I had ever encountered.

9

THE MacARTHUR HIGHWAY

The trip from Dagupan to Manila began in a muddy, dark bus station. The bus I chose was an air-conditioned "special," as opposed to the spartan "ordinary," the latter having neither air-conditioning nor shock absorbers. My companions this weekday were people from all stations and walks of life: men with briefcases going to work, couples with large bags indicating a lengthy visit to somewhere, and women holding children, traveling perhaps to the next town.

The bus pulled out of the Dagupan station on a beautiful, hot morning that was punctuated by short, intense rainstorms. As we began to move southward, once again I was impressed by the attractive, even stately, houses. The Ilocano world was well kept and orderly. On the TV next to the driver, a Pinoy comedy was playing, and the passengers gently laughed and guffawed as Pangasinan slid past.

Traveling south, we went through Santa Barbara and into the larger city of Urdaneta. This city figured in the Japanese defense of the island. Anticipating the invasion, General Yamashita had stationed a tank division in Urdaneta a week before the Lingayen landing, and once the landing had commenced, he had ordered a counterattack on January 16. It was a halfhearted affair; Yamashita simply wanted to delay the Americans until more supplies could be moved north to the Shobu Group's redoubts. Not surprising, the U.S. forces decimated the Japanese attack. The next day in barrios just outside of Urdaneta, U.S. and Japanese forces fought a series of ferocious encounters that resulted in the loss of many Japanese tanks and most of the garrison. Five Americans died, and MacArthur's troops moved farther south unimpeded.

Urdaneta seemed like a no-nonsense sort of place. Similar to the other towns of the area, it appeared dominated by commerce and development. This city is the bagoong capital of the Philippines. The fermented shrimp or fish paste, with an incredible odor and delicious taste, is sold nearly on every street. Through the bus window I marveled at the stalls where the bagoong jars sat filled with the sickly pink delicacy, as well as the rows and rows of fish drying in the sun. The diaspora has influenced Urdaneta, too: at a red light in the center of town I noticed that the bus stop outside was donated by the Association of United Urdanetarians of Southern California.

The bus went on to Villasis. This town was anchored by a wonderful old clock in the city's center and a huge Purina plant just outside town. The bus passed many attractive, old-style Spanish tropical houses. There was much building in progress, including a number of planned communities. One large development wore the could-be-anywhere-in-America sign: The Heights of Wedgewood.

And so it went for hours on Highway 3 (or Route 3 in military histories), christened the MacArthur Highway in 1961, as I took a pleasant journey south through the central plain of Luzon. Out the window I saw sugar and rice fields, all very attractive. Carabao, the gentle work animal that has become a symbol of the Philippines, were in abundance, either pulling the plow or lying peacefully in the muddy water. I saw fishponds as well. The traffic was light, the sun was bright, and the bus was filled with quiet laughter.

Through small towns I would read the road signs. Evidently, Spain and the United States were still locked in some type of struggle because signs from both the Knights of Columbus and the Rotarians were everywhere. I also became interested in how the spelling of the road's name alternated with the towns I passed through. At one point it would be the McArthur Hi-way. At others it would be the M'Arthur Hi-way. And at still others it would be correctly spelled, MacArthur Highway. No matter.

This historical road reflects how fortunes change. In 1941 the Filipino and American forces fled south toward Manila and Bataan, chased by an enemy flushed with confidence. Three years later the Japanese were the ones being pushed down the road, pursued by a general who was intent on getting vengeance. Almost two decades after his defeat on Bataan, an eighty-year-old MacArthur came back to say his farewells.

His return in 1961 was nearly as momentous as the one in 1944. He landed in Manila on July 3 and received a tumultuous welcome. On July 6 he went to Lingayen, arriving in Dagupan by train. He wore his uniform when he visited the old school building that had been his headquarters. Then he dedicated the Lingayen memorial. On the return to Manila with a kilometer-long motorcade, he stopped briefly at Hacienda Luisita, my next destination. Along the way thousands choked the MacArthur Highway to see their savior. He passed through San Fernando, finally reaching Malacanang at 9:00 p.m. It had been a long day for an old man in weakened health.[1]

10
HACIENDA LUISITA AND
CAMP O'DONNELL

acArthur drove his officers hard, and the U.S. advance south toward Manila was rapid.[1] Using Routes 13 and 3, forces pushed
through towns like Paniqui and Carmen virtually unopposed. At
Moncada they took two hundred prisoners. On January 21 American soldiers
reached Tarlac, at the junction of the Manila Railroad and Routes 13 and
3, but it had been destroyed after being bombed repeatedly by the Japanese.
After it fell, Tarlac had become a key supply base for the Japanese; consequently, it had received extensive attention from U.S. bombers. There were
purportedly six thousand Japanese troops there. As these troops pulled back to
leave the city to the Americans, they began to torch it. When the U.S. forces
arrived, Tarlac was almost totally destroyed.

A number of important things happened here. Engineers put the
Manila-Dagupan railway into working order, giving, theoretically, the army
transportation straight into Manila. They set up general headquarters in a
huge sugar plantation known as Hacienda Luisita. Reconnaissance teams located Camp O'Donnell, the infamous prison that had held American and
Filipino soldiers after Bataan. The Japanese released the Filipinos shortly after
capture and had moved most of the U.S. prisoners to Japan and China; some
went to other camps in the Philippines. The Americans found and examined
the camp's dilapidated nipa structures and crude burial grounds.

MacArthur arrived in Tarlac on January 25 and stayed until March 4.
Once, driving down from Dagupan in an open jeep, he spied an old cannon

sunk into a concrete block by the side of the road. He had the driver stop the jeep, and he and his personal and staff doctor, Lt. Col. Roger Egeberg, got out. MacArthur proudly told Egeberg that at this spot forty-five years earlier his father's assistant was killed by a Filipino bullet. Egeberg, who might have believed that history was cyclic, hurriedly got back into the jeep.[2]

I got off the bus at the new Starbucks, which sat on the end of the Luisita Mall right off the highway in San Miguel. There, half a cup of the blend of the day later, I met Lino Dizon and his colleague and fellow instructor, Patrick, who doubled as our driver. Lino and Patrick were on the faculty at Tarlac State University's Center for Tarlaqueño Studies. Lino had agreed to show me around Hacienda Luisita. I could not have asked for a better guide.

We chatted as the cool trumpet of Chet Baker and other long-dead American jazz greats provided a backdrop. The coffee was good, and I was glad to be talking to someone from the state university system of the Philippines. My interaction with Filipino academics usually had been limited to those in Manila or, more often, to those in the United States. We talked about his research on the Thomasites, the American teachers who came to the Philippines at the start of the twentieth century. His interest in the teachers began years earlier with, of all things, an old ghost story.

Lino is from Concepcion, a town a few miles southeast of Tarlac and hometown of Senator Benigno "Ninoy" Aquino Jr. In Concepcion people told fantastic stories of an American ghost that haunted the town's school buildings. In the old American-built Gabaldon school (schoolhouses that were named after Hon. Isauro Gabaldon of Nueva Ecija, who sponsored the funding bill in 1907), the children said the spirit preferred to emerge in the Garden House, where the agriculture classes met, as well as the home economics building, where the girls learned the domestic arts. The specter appeared for decades, and it was simply called Mr. White. It is not recorded that he was a particularly evil apparition, only that he appeared to generations of students until the old American school buildings were destroyed. Then, it seemed, the ghost of Mr. White vanished.

The Mr. White of the schoolhouse was, some say, the apparition of a real person, a long-dead American teacher. Frank Russell White from Millburn, Illinois, arrived with other American educators in 1901.[3] At age twenty-six, he was the first American teacher sent to Tarlac Province, where he established the first municipal public school in 1902. Seven years later he became the colonial administration's director of education. His tenure was noted for his zeal in institutionalizing vocational or industrial education, today a somewhat controversial issue. White was an indefatigable worker, and he died at the age of thirty-eight, according to former governor-general W. Cameron Forbes, as a result of his labors.

A member of the Thomasites, White was part of a grand pedagogical experiment. Some called it a magnificent moral mission, others claimed it was of devious design.[4] Nearly one thousand Thomasites arrived in 1901. Two contingents actually landed in Manila before the ship that was their namesake, the SS *Thomas*, did. White arrived in this first landing. The Thomasites were usually young men and women, just out of college, highly idealistic, and filled with a strong dash of evangelical Christianity and a sense of adventure. Their job was to bring enlightenment to the Catholic natives via basic public education in English and math. They went out into the provincial schoolrooms with little equipment and with teacher's aides who were hardly more advanced than the students. The Filipinos' traditional hospitality made life more than bearable for many of the teachers, some of whom stayed in the islands long after their tenure was up and built strong bonds with the local community. For others, however, the harsh realities of the provinces created disillusion and depression, which often manifested itself in racial chauvinism. For all intents and purposes, they introduced America to the Filipinos. W. Cameron Forbes, who served as the U.S. governor of the Philippines from 1909 to 1913 and was energetically dedicated to the country's economic development, albeit with an elevated colonial attitude, described the American teachers in 1928.

> It was not only for his services in teaching the school curriculum that the American teacher was useful, in fact, seen with broader vision that was perhaps a small part of his contribution to the Filipino. The American teacher brought with him the American spirit. He was an apostle of progress. He gave the children a healthy outlook toward life; he explained to them the principles of hygiene and sanitation. He brought

with him the spirit of service. He inculcated into them a realization of the dignity of labor. And the children carried this spirit into the homes, where it made its impress upon the parents.[5]

Forbes's account of the Americans as apostles of progress may have been as idealistic as the teachers were. No one can deny that America made a concerted effort to bring public education to the Filipinos, and by its own standards it was highly successful. But White's motives and meaningfulness and that of other U.S. educators have often been debated during the postwar years.[6] As mentioned earlier, during the first two years of occupation, the military introduced American education with the objective of pacifying the Filipinos. MacArthur's father was a strong proponent of public education, considering it a military subject, and his predecessor, General Otis, actually picked out schoolbooks for the fledgling school system. This military-influenced pedagogy paid immediate dividends. As early as January 1900, the Schurman Commission recommended the establishment of secularized and free public schools, with instruction in English starting in the primary schools. Within a year schoolhouses began to spring up all over the country, and Filipino children began to learn their alphabets in English. In the first decade of the century, the Philippine Normal School (now College) was created to train teachers. Gifted Filipino students, the *pensionados*, went to the United States to study. A state university system was also established, and technical and agricultural schools spread across the islands. In fact, under the U.S. administration, especially in White's tenure, the curriculum strongly emphasized the mechanical trades, such as woodworking and agriculture for the boys and housekeeping for the girls. Mirroring the theoretical connection between sports and Christianity, athletics were stressed, especially baseball, basketball, track and field, and boxing. Thus, by the outbreak of World War II, the Philippines had a nonreligious educational system open to all classes of people that had produced a dramatic rise in literacy.

There is, of course, a counterargument. Many, if not most, postwar scholars, especially postcolonial writers, have insisted that education was used to Americanize the Filipino and to keep the elite class in power, all of which would lead to future favorable political and economic activities for the United

States and the Philippine ascendancy.[7] Free public education was designed to help suppress the violent independence movement and mold the Filipinos into a subservient colonial people.

It was true that during the early years of the colonial educational system the schools did provide a heavy dose of American culture, including U.S. history and American literature. Nationalist writers such as Renato Constantino say that this effort was to fix Filipino children with a sense of cultural envy and to make them think anything American was intrinsically better. Constantino offered that the pensionado system was designed only to bring the Filipino elite over to the American side because most of the people selected to go to the United States were from upper-class families. He asserts the system did nothing for anyone else. Its emphasis on practical and mechanical subjects for others was at the expense of academics, developing a nation of farmers, furniture makers, and basket weavers, and thus ensuring the place of the landed families. More importantly, through English-based instruction, the Americans could control the direction of the Filipino culture. English could confuse a Filipino's sense of history and connection to the past, and it could create a culture based on the conquerors' needs—in this case, a smooth colonial administration and a healthy market for American products.[8] In short, the Americans instituted an educational system to indoctrinate and control Filipinos, not enlighten them.

Compelling evidence shows that Constantino and other nationalists may have been, at least in part, right. The Filipinos' industrial training, which marked the first years of their American education, was inspired by Booker T. Washington's practical emphasis at Tuskegee.[9] In places like Tarlac, as in Alabama, industrial education allowed the white administrators to characterize themselves as benevolent guardians of a subordinate race while simultaneously shaping a compliant and productive people using the American archetypal myth of hard work. Fred W. Atkinson, the first general superintendent of the Educational Bureau, visited Washington at Tuskegee before setting sail for Manila. He apparently was quite impressed. Once in Manila he vigorously attempted to apply the Tuskegee industrial paradigm, saying that it could aid in the "training [of] some six to eight millions of tropical, indolent people for self-government."[10] The Filipinos, however, did not warm to industrial training, preferring to have an education that liberated them from manual labor rather than reinforce it. Atkinson's idea floundered for several years. White revived the concept, and it was emphatically applied for decades afterward.

The second issue, using English as the language of instruction, has haunted the American educational system in the Philippines since its inception and still stands at the crux of a controversy. In 1902, the rationale for its use in the schools was that since there were so many Filipino languages that not one could be chosen as a medium of instruction, one unifying language had to be used. Spanish had to be abandoned since most Filipinos were illiterate in the language. Knowledge of English, however, would emancipate lower-class Filipinos from their dependency on the Catholic Church and their upper-class patrons. Throughout the decades and despite the nationalists' heightened demands for using Pilipino (an artificial hybrid of several languages but predominantly Tagalog) in the classroom, the original logic essentially held sway: given the ninety languages spoken in the islands, given that English is the language of government and commerce, and given that Filipino students need a unifying method of instruction, English seemed the logical choice.

But in 1991 a report of the Congressional Commission on Education recommended that Pilipino should be the medium of instruction for basic education. Consequently, in that year and in 1998, initiatives were introduced to teach in Pilipino. By 2000, all subjects, save English and foreign languages, were taught in Pilipino. However, in 2003 President Gloria Macapagal-Arroyo promoted the return to an intensified use of English in school, suggesting that with so much earning potential for Filipino workers overseas, students need to keep their English skills. She issued Executive Order 210 to strengthen the use of English as the primary language of instruction at the secondary level in all public institutions. In 2006 the order was implemented, making English the primary language of instruction for English, mathematics, and science courses starting at grade 3 and the primary language of instruction at the secondary level in all public and private schools.

Arroyo's initiative has brought about numerous negative responses, especially from Filipino language departments in Manila universities, which contend that Pilipino should be used as the language of instruction, as well as from those nationalists who have always been opposed to teaching English. The argument is that Arroyo is simply bending to the lucrative OFW potential rather than serving the people's dire cultural needs. Indeed, they see English as being used to amplify the diaspora: with a better grasp of English, Filipinos are better equipped to leave the country.[11]

Such a statement is a new twist on the nationalists' long-standing attack on the language issue.[12] Typically, opponents of English-language instruction say it is associated with cultural imperialism. Its use as the language of instruction separates the Filipino people from their own culture, undermining traditional Filipino values. English distances government administrators, who must use English, from the people they are meant to serve. It further divides Philippine society because only those who can speak and write English rise to positions of power. Today, as it was when the Americans occupied the country, English is the language of the dominant elite. For nationalists, the struggle over English was and is a struggle over American hegemony.

The debate over English instruction may be of little consequence in the future, given the present status of Philippine education. In short, it is in a rapid state of decay. The government released statistics in 2004 that revealed some astonishing facts. Only six out of every thousand sixth graders are prepared to continue into high school. Two out of every thousand high school seniors are academically fit to enter college. Just nineteen out of every hundred teachers are competent to teach in English, the language of instruction. One student out of seven does not receive instruction in a classroom. One student out of five does not have a desk. One student out of three does not have a single textbook. Not surprisingly, the provinces represent the brunt of these sad figures.[13]

At the college level, the situation is just as bad. Only a few institutions can meet international standards, and these schools are reserved for the wealthy. Mostly owing to financial reasons, the dropout rate is 60 percent. More alarming is that graduates have a difficult time passing the country's licensing examinations. *The Chronicle of Higher Education* reported in 2001 that of every thousand students who enter Philippine colleges and universities, three hundred will graduate, only fifty will take the examinations, and only twenty will pass. While other Southeast Asian nations, particularly Malaysia and Singapore, are producing qualified engineers and information technology specialists, the Philippines is producing large amounts of students who must take jobs far below their supposed training, that is, if they get a job at all. In 2007 the Department of Labor and Employment reported that 39 percent of unemployed Filipinos are college graduates.[14]

There are some fairly obvious reasons for the dire condition of Philippine education. The poor performance of the Philippine economy and the growing population are the major contributors. While the number of students increase, the ability of the government to support a free, basic education has declined. Then there is the corruption in the Department of Education. An award-winning study by Yvonne T. Chua shows that corruption is endemic within the Philippine public education system at all levels.[15] In procuring school supplies, kickbacks, bribes, shady contracts, and general dirty dealing have resulted in a serious lack of desks and books. To be hired, a teacher expects to pay a bribe of anywhere from a goat to thousands of pesos to the school. Sometimes the bribe has bordered on the bizarre: in some places new teachers reportedly have had to clean the principal's house before they were given their teaching appointments. Other accusations against the public education system include the falsification of teaching credentials, the harassment of teachers by superiors, and the almost constant lack of school materials, leading parents to harangue for money for schools.

Another reason, perhaps the gravest, for the sad state of Philippine public education is the flight of qualified teachers for jobs overseas and particularly to America. Filipino educators, saddled with absurdly low salaries, poor classroom conditions, and the corruption-rife system, are leaving the country in droves. Indeed, U.S. school systems are recruiting them. In 2001 the Compton, California, school district (noted for its high student crime rate) offered fifty-eight teachers from Cebu jobs; all accepted. The Cebu example is common and widespread. The Philippine Overseas Employment Administration reported that over two thousand teachers went abroad between 1992 and 2002, with almost half of them going to the United States. It can be assumed that these teachers had the best credentials because strict U.S. recruitment standards demand that teachers meet a "highly qualified" status.[16] Furthermore, Filipino teachers must always compete against applicants from other English-speaking countries, so it stands to reason that the ones who leave the Philippines are the most English proficient.

The emigration of qualified teachers, particularly at the secondary level, has two glaring ramifications. The first is that the student-to-teacher ratio is widening. Now standing at greater than one to fifty per class, the ratio rises yearly because there are fewer teachers serving a growing, some say exploding, population. The second is that many of the teachers who remain in the Philippines are not the best and the brightest. In 2003, the self-assessment test for high school teachers revealed that only 19 percent of teachers in English, science, and mathematics earned a score of 75 percent in English proficiency. Given that English is now the language of instruction, one wonders how well students can compete.[17]

How the Philippine education system deals with these problems will be interesting to see. It is inconceivable that these difficulties will be solved anytime soon. As present-day recipients of the Thomasite experiment, Filipino students can only hope for some type of government intervention. Many, however, will be lining up at the overseas employment agencies that dot nearly all Philippine cities. A message is seemingly being sent to Filipino students: study English as best you can for there are many openings for truck drivers in Iraq and maids in Saudi Arabia.

✴ ✴ ✴

Lino Dizon and I left the Starbucks and began our tour of Hacienda Luisita. The road led past some large manufacturing buildings and straight into a vast sugarcane universe that chronicled significant points in the Philippine past. For me, I felt another moment of excitement when history and the present intersected, a strange but pleasant experience. Not only was I about to see another one of MacArthur's headquarters, I was also going to be walking in the footsteps of one of my favorite American writers, John Dos Passos. Actually, I had been already walking in his footsteps: Dos Passos, a war correspondent, had spent a short time in Tacloban and Lingayen after the invasion. In January 1945 he finally caught up with and interviewed MacArthur, as well as Willoughby and others, in the Hacienda Luisita headquarters. His description of the interview is sparse, barely two pages long. In it he describes how MacArthur was "remarkably slender and erect for his age" and how his skin was "surprisingly taut and smooth . . . [t]here's an air of breeding about him." Dos Passos seemed bedazzled by MacArthur's speech patterns: "[h]is sentences are long with carefully balanced clauses. He rarely pauses for an answer. . . . There is something disarming in the direct way his rather elaborate thoughts take shape in elaborate phrases."[18]

Dos Passos was also an accomplished painter, and his verbal landscape of life in San Miguel, the barrio outside of Hacienda Luisita, in his book *Tour of Duty*, was consistent with his lifelong interest in social equality and human rights. Essentially, Dos Passos used the same type of contrast and irony as in his fabulous trilogy, *U.S.A.*, to illustrate moral hypocrisy in its various forms. In describing Sam Miguel, he contrasts the "sickly looking people" and their town ravaged by war with the great sugar hacienda, which had manicured gardens protected by brick walls and swimming pools full of "tanned Americans diving and splashing and whooping." He also ironically describes the resurrection of the Manila-Dagupan railway. Told through an Australian soldier, Dos Passos's story pointedly questions if either the Americans or the Japanese did anything to advance the progress of the Filipinos.[19]

The contraposition Dos Passos drew then might be applied today. Hacienda Luisita, at the end of the nineteenth century, was totally uncultivated.[20] It owes its existence to the laborers who built the railroad. The huge Tabacalera company bought the land in the 1890s from the Spanish crown and used it to house settlers, mostly men who were clearing the land in order to lay the rails. In 1928 Tabacalera set up a sugar mill, and it showed an immediate profit. Profits continued to roll in until the mid-1950s, when labor unrest convinced Tabacalera to sell. Part of the more than ten thousand–hectare estate was sold to the government and then subdivided among the tenants. The larger part was sold to the Cojuangcos, a highly influential Chinese Filipino family, with the stipulation that the land would be distributed to the local farmers after ten years. In 1958 the estate was given to Ninoy Aquino, husband of Corazon Cojuangco, to manage. Through his determination and exerted effort, Aquino turned it into a profitable estate in which labor and management worked harmoniously. Aquino gave his workers free housing, education, and medical care. He left the manager's position in 1959 to run for office. When Aquino's archenemy Ferdinand Marcos became president, he filed a motion to distribute the land through the Agrarian Reform Program. Before this plan could be implemented, Aquino was assassinated, and his widow took control of the country. The Cojuangco-Aquino family then made plans to develop Luisita into residential communities, commercial centers, and a golf course. The farmers never received the land.

Today, Hacienda Luisita, which comprises eleven barrios and twenty-five thousand people over sixteen thousand acres, continues to be at the axis of labor and management issues.[21] On November 6, 2004, following years of fruitless negotiations, two labor unions representing the plantation employees struck after three hundred workers had been laid off. Ten days later violence erupted. At the picket line near the hacienda headquarters, the number of strikers had grown to about fifteen thousand people, including wives and children. Approximately one thousand members of the Philippine National Police drawn from other Central Luzon towns, as well as AFP soldiers from nearby Camp Aquino, first attempted to disperse the strikers with water cannons and tear gas. This tactic failed, and an hour later government forces fired live ammunition into the crowd. Seven strikers were killed, and more than a hundred were wounded. Police chased fleeing workers into their houses, and scores were arrested. The "massacre," as the Manila newspapers and leftist publications called it, resulted in Senate and congressional inquiries. The government said the workers were being led by Communists or communist sympathizers such as the people's organization Bagong Alyansang Makabayan (Bayan) and other progressive and trade union groups.

The incident in 2004 was only the latest in a long line of labor-government engagements, and it followed a tradition of agrarian unrest clashing with national politics in the area around Hacienda Luisita. The most famous of the peasant advocacy groups was the Hukbalahap.[22] Large landowners governed the majority of the land in the area, and for the peasant workers life was short and hard. Agrarian unrest had sporadically occurred in Central Luzon as far back as the early 1930s, but the laborers had consolidated and made gains during the years immediately before the war. When the Japanese took control, their hand was heavy, and underneath the shadow of mighty Mount Arayat, a resistance movement formed from the prewar labor activist groups throughout the region. Together they called themselves the Hukbo ng Bayan Laban sa mga Hapon, or Hukbalahaps, which translated to the People's Anti-Japanese Army. Led by communist intellectuals and Socialists-Nationalists, the Huks quickly formed an effective guerrilla group that harassed the Japanese, punished collaborators, and provided a semblance of authority and discipline in the area. They received widespread popular support. During the war, although there was friction, the Huks worked in close coordination with U.S. Army Forces Far East (USAFFE) guerrilla groups and helped American escapees and downed pilots. The Huks were very aggressive, and their methods were considered cruel. In early 1945 their numbers were close to ten thousand, and this figure would grow. As U.S. forces pushed into Tarlac and Pampanga, Huk guerrillas worked side by side with the Americans. U.S. officers complimented them for their assistance and dedication, noting that the Huks "fought the Japanese furiously and unceasingly" and that they were the "most effective resistance organization in Luzon."[23]

Immediately after liberation, however, the United States changed its view of the Huks. While other USAFFE-affiliated guerrilla groups were absorbed into the regular forces and allowed to keep their weapons, the Huks were ordered to disarm and disband. Some did, some took to the hills, and some were tricked into disarming through American promises of new weapons to replace any that were handed in but none were given. The USAFFE had numerous reasons for decapitating the Huks, but one of the most important was that early in the war the Huk leadership refused to cooperate with USAFFE commander Lt. Col. Claude Thorpe and his successors. Consequently, many in the U.S. command felt that the Huks could not be trusted. Moreover, the Huks' sizable support and following in the barrios and some of their leaders' clear communist connections led U.S. and Filipino strategists to view the Huks as agents of China or the Soviet Union. They questioned the Huks' long-term objectives. The terms "subversive" and "radical" started to appear in U.S. reports about the Huks. Their contributions to the war effort were minimized and even repudiated. To make matters worse, U.S. counterintelligence personnel gave local authority to figures who often represented the landlord class.

With the Japanese gone, the landlords of Central Luzon—many of whom had spent the war in the relative comfort of Manila—attempted to resume their nineteenth-century hacienda-style landlord-peasant relationship.

But the effects of the war and socio-agricultural developments had warped the traditional ties between the elite owners and their peasant workers. Tensions rose, and violence occurred between the two traditional classes. For the land-owners, the world had changed: where once the elite contended with a disar-ranged group of farmers, now in Pampanga, Tarlac, and Nueva Ecija, they had to deal with organized, seasoned, and, indeed, blooded soldier-activists. The vested families, with the backing of the newly created Manila govern-ment, which itself was awash in corruption and political chicanery, reacted rather predictably. Peasant meetings were outlawed. Anticommunist vigilante groups appeared. In August 1946 a leading leftist leader, Juan Feleo, was be-headed by unknown persons wearing uniforms. After talks between the Huks and the government broke down, Philippine troops were called in, and an active rebellion began in 1946. For the next five years Central Luzon, known in the Manila papers as "Huklandia," was witness to a murderous rampage of assassination, arrest, abuse, and imprisonment. The Huks, which now incorporated communist factions and called itself the Democratic Alliance, drew popular support and fought against the government troops extremely well. Huk cadres overran numerous towns in Central Luzon. Landlords fled, aghast, back to Manila; however, the troops of the new Philippine Republic used tanks and napalm, torture and threats. Repression was the order of the day, and the people of the Luzon plain felt that they were under martial law. Eventually, the government, especially under former World War II guerrilla and Minister of Defense Ramon Magsaysay, successfully used reform to pac-ify the Huks. Tired of fighting and living in the bush, the Huks watched as their revolution essentially died out in 1951. On February 17, 1954, the young Manila reporter Benigno Aquino interviewed Huk leader Luis Taruc. This meeting evolved into capitulation negotiations, and in May, Taruc surren-dered himself to the government, in essence ending the Huk organization.[24]

If asked why the revolution failed, the Huks of the time and many his-torians of today would blame the United States. Key to this argument was the arrival of Lt. Col. Edward Lansdale, a U.S. intelligence officer, who be-friended the charismatic Magsaysay. Under Lansdale's direction, the United States poured money into Magsaysay's social programs, which were imple-mented in the barrios. This effort severely undercut Huk authority. As Beijing fell to Mao Zedong and as allied forces fled in panic in Korea, U.S. paranoia peaked, and weapons poured into the Philippines. In 1946 the countries had signed the U.S.-Philippines Military Assistance Pact, which permitted the Joint United States Military Advisory Group (JUSMAG) to equip and train the Philippine military. President Manual Roxas signed the bases agreement, giving the United States control over Subic Bay and Clark Field, or 400,000 acres of prime real estate. At the time of the Huk uprising in 1950, the Philippine military was essentially under U.S. control, and a near complete dependence on U.S. assistance marked the Philippines' national defense posture for the next forty years.

The Huk rebellion has fallen into gentle obscurity, but the effects of the uprising are still being felt for both the United States and the Philippines at a number of levels. For the United States, the victory of the Lansdale plan in the Philippines was seen as a Cold War blueprint for defeating communism. The plan was relatively simple: find a respectable, friendly, and popular politician; support his social agenda and military operations; watch the people respond accordingly; and see communism wither on the vine. This plan, while effective in the Philippines, never worked again. The United States tried it in Vietnam a decade or so later, and it failed catastrophically. During George W. Bush's presidency, and apparently under the Obama administration, the government attempted a variation in chaotic Iraq and Afghanistan, but it seemed to fail there as well.

For the Philippines, the Huks' dissolution morphed into the Soviet-inspired Partido Komunista ng Pilipinas (Communist Party of the Philippines, or PKP), an ineffective, reserved cadre in late 1950s and 1960s that seemed content to rail against capitalism while quietly running gambling and prostitution operations in Pampanga. Reacting to this development, as well as to the wave of student unrest and the corruption of the Marcos government in the late 1960s, former English professor Jose Sison's group split from the PKP and formed the Communist Party of the Philippines (CPP). Over the next decade Sison organized the group into two bodies—the political wing, or the National Democratic Front (NDF), which served as an umbrella group for a number of radical organizations, and the armed wing, the New People's Army (NPA).

Beginning violent operations in the early 1970s, the NPA has fought the longest communist revolution in modern history.[25] The NPA has been more effective than the Huks because it has spread its cell-like operations over the entire country as opposed to the Huks' narrow affair in Central Luzon. Many of its strikes have been successful, and all have grabbed the media's attention. Barrios throughout the country are effectively in NPA control, but the group has never really approached the actual overthrow of the government, possibly because of Sison's strategy of fighting a protracted rural war à la Mao's example. There have been no significant gains in set battles. In fact, the bloodiest operation was the mid-1980s' purging of suspected informants in Mindanao. After hearing rumors that the government had penetrated the NPA and NDF with undercover operatives, the Mindanao Communists launched a pitiless investigation, code-named Operasyon Kampanyang Ahos (Cebuano for "repelling evil spirits with garlic"). Here, evidence suggests that hundreds of communist rank and file were liquidated by its own leadership in a fit paranoia.[26] It should be said, however, that while the NPA has not come close to taking down the government, the Philippine military has been equally unsuccessful in eliminating the NPA, despite assistance from the United States. Plagued with corruption, rotting equipment, unequal public support, and poor morale, the AFP stands scant chance of extirpating the NPA. Seemingly, it is a case of the ineffective against the incompetent.

The ineptitude of the conflicting forces is one reason the rebellion has lasted longer than thirty years. A deeply felt ideology and superb propaganda have also helped the CPP's cause. From its inception, the CPP and its associated groups have held firmly to a dogma that has not flinched in the face of remarkable world events. Its canon is found in a core narrative that continues to run through all CPP, leftist, and much nationalistic rhetoric, and the story almost entirely depends on America. Exemplified best by Jose Sison's 1971 exhortative primer, *Philippine Society and Revolution*, the narrative synthesizes philosophical elements of Mao and Philippine nationalist writers to present the following story. According to the Communists, the people of the Philippines for centuries were the rebellious subjects of feudal Spain. After defeating the Spanish in 1898, the people were hoodwinked by the land-hungry Americans. Despite a valiant but unsuccessful war of national liberation against genocidal America, the people became the unwanted subjects of imperial America and its henchmen, the Philippine bourgeoisie and landlord classes. This arrangement has not changed in a century, for the United States still controls the Philippine government and sustains the upper class, which exploits and controls the workers. Capitalism, the handmaiden of U.S. hegemony, creates corruption within the government and military, which in turn fosters fascism at the national and local levels.[27] Standing against the evil American triumvirate of imperialism, feudalism, and capitalism is the Philippine worker, the son of the Philippine-American War patriots and the Huks. Indeed, according to Sison, the Left's struggle is "a continuation and resumption of the Philippine revolution and the Filipino-American War."[28] In Sison's story the Filipino is described romantically, with the virtues of patriotism, a strong Asian identity (as opposed to a Western orientation), a populist conviction, and a nonelite background.

The creation of this mythic Filipino offers a bipolar impression of society where good and evil are clearly drawn. More importantly, it offers an implicit ultimatum: if you are not part of Sison's solution, you are part of the problem. It is remarkable how little this core narrative has changed over the years, especially when considering the context in which it was produced.

Americans might assume that anti-U.S. feeling is limited to left-wing radicals, but it is shared by many middle-age and younger Filipinos who are products of the nationalistic philosophy that has dominated Philippine education in the postwar years. This sentiment, moreover, has a good deal of merit. On July 4, 1946, the Filipinos celebrated their first independence day, at least their first from the United States, but it was tempered by disappointment. When the war ended, the Filipinos expected massive U.S. aid to rebuild their shattered country. After all, as the Filipinos saw it, they had stood by their Western colonialist masters and bore the brunt of the destruction. To their surprise, the aid they received was insignificant, especially when compared to that given to Europe and, to the Filipinos' disbelief, Japan. Further, to receive the postwar economic aid, the Philippine government had to comply with the International Monetary Fund's strict frugality program. Bell's Philippine Trade Act of 1946, which was tied to the assistance package, gave U.S. companies free access to the Philippines, but Philippine companies gained unrestricted access to American markets only as long as their products did not become significant competition to those of U.S. firms. This restriction reduced virtually all Philippine exports to the United States to those items that were not manufactured, thus essentially farm products. The Filipinos ultimately interpreted this act as a U.S. declaration that the Philippines was still a banana republic incapable of standing on its own two feet. Another provision of the bill gave parity to Americans with Filipinos with regard to ownership of Philippine natural resources, such as mines, without extending the same parity to Filipinos in the United States. It was, as many would later claim, a new form of colonialism—a neocolonialism that prolongs Philippine dependence without the cost or odor of colonial administration. Filipinos are cognizant of this unequal and exploitative relationship and still have a sensitive reaction to the United States that few Americans realize or even recognize.[29]

Of all the historical components that make up the Hacienda Luisita story, however, former president Corazon Aquino might be the most mystifying, at least to Americans.[30] Born Corazon Cojuangco, her father was Jose, the grandson of the Jose Cojuangco who had fled China's Fujian Province for Manila and then Tarlac, where he built an agricultural and banking empire and dynasty. Cory's father was a national politician, but he escaped the devastation of World War II and took his family to the United States in 1946. There, Cory went to Catholic high schools in Philadelphia and New York and then graduated from the affluent College of Mount Saint Vincent in New York. She was, by all accounts, a reserved, intelligent young woman of means and deeply devoted to her faith. After graduation she returned to the Philippines, and soon after married a local Tarlac man, Benigno "Ninoy" Aquino.

Her husband became a successful provincial governor, blending progressive ideas with traditional hardball politics. In 1967 he won a seat in the Senate, from which he continually harangued then-president Ferdinand Marcos. Unwilling to give up his office, Marcos declared martial law in 1972 and immediately arrested his political enemies, Aquino chief among them. For seven years Aquino sat in prison, becoming a world-renowned symbol of political resistance. In 1978 Marcos permitted Aquino to run for election, one that was clearly rigged in Marcos's favor. Two years later Aquino suffered a heart attack and was allowed to immigrate to America for surgery. He and his family lived in Boston, where he lectured at Harvard. Fearful he would lose influence by being out of the country, he decided to return to the Philippines in August 1983. Assassinated on the Manila airport's tarmac, he instantly achieved martyr status, and in the Catholic Philippines, some viewed his death as a religious phenomenon. Others saw him as part of the nationalist lineage, an extension of José Rizal. So potent was the public backlash to his assassination that strongman Marcos called for snap presidential elections in an attempt to placate the people and authenticate his regime.

Cory, with much doubt, ran for office in her husband's absence. She was in a difficult position. Marcos still wielded considerable if declining power, and more importantly, the country was a financial disaster. Her economic advisers told her that breaking up the monopolies and initiating land reform would go a long way to righting the rolling ship. Some suggested she should allow the farmers to be part owners of Hacienda Luisita, and she promised if elected she would use the hacienda as an example of true land reform.[31] She seemed uncertain about what to do regarding the U.S. bases at Subic Bay and Clark Field. While Aquino had signed her party's program for the bases' removal, she did not publicly call for their termination. She quickly lost the confidence of the Far Left when she did not acquiesce to their demands on land reform, the nationalization of banks, and the abrogation of the bases' treaty.

On Friday, February 7, 1986, the Philippines held its elections and its people held their breath.[32] The National Citizens' Movement for Free Elections (NAMFREL), an organization supported by the Catholic Church and various labor and civic groups, was charged with monitoring for election fraud. Immediately allegations of irregularities arose, and for the next forty-eight hours, accusations flew back and forth from both parties. The church seemed about to weigh in on Cory Aquino's side. The Reform the Armed Forces Movement (RAM), a romanticized underground group of military officers, publicly suggested fraud. That Sunday night thirty-eight of the computer technicians working at the government's vote-counting center walked out to protest alleged number manipulations. President Ronald Reagan, after a ridiculous statement about how fraud was occurring on both sides, offered to send envoy Philip Habib to help smooth out the problem. Later that week the European Parliament condemned the election as fraudulent.

Then one of the most spectacular political events of the century occurred. On February 22, a group of RAM officers aborted a planned revolt
against Marcos and took refuge at Camp Aguinaldo, a sprawling camp on
EDSA, Manila's main artery. The contingent of soldiers was led by Secretary
of Defense Juan Ponce Enrile and national police chief Gen. Fidel Ramos.
All were frightened, and they had need to be: Marcos commanded a force of
140,000; the mutineers had 300. Ponce Enrile and Ramos held a press conference saying that Marcos had stolen the election and that Aquino was the
lawful president. They announced their intentions to end the regime and their
willingness to die in the attempt. Now barricaded into two camps—Aguinaldo
and Crame, which faced each other across EDSA—Ponce Enrile and Ramos
waited for their former boss's reaction. Any betting person did not give them
much of a chance. Marcos had overwhelming power and had an irresistible
urge to stay in control. What could 300 do against a regime that had enjoyed
U.S. support for twenty years?

The answer came from the unlikely amalgam of the Catholic Church,
the Philippine military, thousands upon thousands of Manileños, and, to a
degree not exactly known, the United States. At 9:00 p.m. on February 23,
the archbishop, Cardinal Jaime Sin, went on Radio Veritas, the Catholic
channel, and appealed to Filipinos of goodwill to guard the rebels' camp.
By the next day a huge crowd of people had gathered outside Camp Crame,
where Ponce Enrile and Ramos had consolidated their command. Marcos
sent tanks up EDSA, but they never attacked. They were halted before nuns
holding rosaries. That night Marcos had Radio Veritas shut down, but a clandestine station, Radio Bandito, came on the air in support of the rebels.
Soldiers from all over the country began to join the rebel cause. The next
day, violence did erupt as rebel helicopters rocketed Malacañang Palace. To
his credit, Marcos refused to give the order to shoot into the crowds, despite
his loyal generals' pleas. On the twenty-fifth, Cory Aquino was inaugurated
as president, and the U.S. military flew Marcos and his family to the safety of
Clark Air Base (formerly Clark Field).

There have been different interpretations of this event. The most prev-
alent is also the most romantic: thousands of Filipinos took to the streets and
forced a dictator to abdicate and flee. Indeed, Manila's middle class did march

down EDSA and stood toe-to-toe against Marcos's tanks, and the entire world watched, wildly enthusiastic, as they emerged victorious. A second and nearly romantic view is that the disgruntled RAM officers, led by their patrons Ponce Enrile and Ramos, were patriots who sacrificed their careers and put their lives on the line for the good of the country. Without question, the People Power Revolution was a military coup and a nearly bloodless one at that. Both of these views are obviously correct, but there is a third perspective: the overthrow of Marcos was clearly assisted—some say staged—by the United States.

That the United States was involved in the overthrow is certain; but to what extent it was a U.S.-backed coup, as writer and activist Leonard Davis has claimed, is not clear. Beginning with the election campaign, when American public relations companies coached both candidates, U.S. participation was murky. Private Americans raised money for Aquino. The U.S. Embassy in Manila gave its advice on how to court U.S. public opinion.[33] NAMFREL was partly funded through U.S. aid, and Davis claims that RAM was directly supported by the Central Intelligence Agency (CIA). During the actual revolt, helicopters loyal to the Harvard alum Ponce Enrile and the West Point alum Ramos were allowed to refuel at Clark Air Base. U.S. eavesdropping passed on information to the rebels, and when Marcos troops destroyed a Radio Veritas transmitter, the CIA set up a backup system. The documented conversation in Washington between George Shultz, Caspar Weinberger, Philip Habib, Michael Armacost, and others show that the Reagan administration eventually favored deposing Marcos. Of course, the United States still flew Marcos out of the country and gave his family asylum in Hawaii.

If, in fact, the revolution was really only a staged coup, attempting to place the U.S.-friendly Aquino in office, then it is interesting to speculate if the United States actually received just compensation for its hard work. At best, the tenure of Aquino's presidency was fraught with inconsistencies.[34] Granted, no one could have lived up to the Joan of Arc image the media laid on her. The problems she faced were incredible; she knew it, as did everyone else. In fact, the March 10, 1986, cover of *Time*, which featured the fall of Marcos, ran with the title "Now for the hard part." Despite realizing the challenges she faced, people strongly expected that she would fix the country's economic and social ills or least begin to. There was a deep yearning in the

Philippines and throughout the world to see the nation prosper under her inspired hand.

For many Americans the lasting political image of the Philippines was the fall of Marcos and the ascendancy of Cory Aquino, but what happened next seems to float in the haze of memory. A series of contradictions occurred that nearly at once dashed the hopes of the country. Even though Aquino was clearly not a revolutionary personality, all expected her government to lead a reformation of the Philippines, eradicate the corrupt social and political systems, return to a stable economy, throw off its utter dependence on the United States, and end the violent communist and noncommunist activities. Rather, a restoration occurred. Many of the wealthy families, including Aquino's own, that did actually suffer under the Marcos regime were restored to the positions of power they had held in the mid-1960s. Her cabinet contained a wide array of characters who had all been against Marcos, but the cast included leftist-leaning human rights people, a variety of businessmen, and Marcos's former go-to man Ponce Enrile. This coalition broke down almost immediately, and neither her ability to mediate nor the ghost of her husband could hold it together. In 1988 the country's economic growth rate was 6 percent, but little of this advancement touched the poor. Poverty remained just as rife as it had before, spurred on by corruption and the lack of any land reform. Ever the peace-loving Catholic, she wanted to heal the nation by extending an olive branch to the Communists, and she began by releasing all political prisoners, including Jose Sison. An almost immediate increase of NPA attacks, however, showed the president the necessity of having a counterinsurgency plan. Quickly, she had the ear of her U.S.-backed military, and a major crackdown on the NPA ensued. Replete with the use of anticommunist vigilante groups, their evangelical fervor—and American-inspired Christian fundamentalism was indeed present—resulted in a human rights record worse than the Marcos regime's. Finally, within a year of Aquino assuming the presidency, many of her ardent supporters in the media were chastising her for the corruption they uncovered not only in her government but also within her own family. Her vast popular appeal nearly squandered, she survived a series of coup attempts during her presidency, and only the loyalty and professionalism of Ramos saved her.

The sad fact is that she did not implement any of the reforms promised in the 1986 election campaign. The economy went into a profound slump. Although Marcos was gone, his followers remained, and they consistently created political havoc. The restored elite also refused any type of meaningful land reform. Frustrated by an addled political system and angered by the government's inability to address their concerns, Filipinos demonstrated in the streets, sometimes violently. The coup de grace was the ongoing power failures in Manila in the late 1980s and early 1990s. Aquino did not heed the engineers' warnings and saw the capital city endure devastating brownouts, some occurring on a daily basis, which further inspired her enemies. Metaphorically, the lights were going out on her ability to govern. She did not seek reelection.

Aquino stayed on my mind as Lino, Patrick, and I meandered through the Luisita. Inside the air-conditioned car I could not feel the heat of the land, but I could somehow feel the presence of Aquino. She was, of course, this plantation's matriarch, and her aura extended over the expansive cane fields. It made me think of the hours I sat in front of the television in 1986 as the election neared and the revolt succeeded. I was living in Washington, D.C., which had a large anti-Marcos Filipino population, and I recalled the fervor of their meetings and demonstrations. Who could forget the sight of the nuns kneeling in front of the tank? Courage. Belief. For a brief moment, all of the hope and sweat paid off in one national paroxysm of joy, but now the situation was the same as before and even before that. The old pre-Marcos families still maintained control. Land ownership still went unreformed. Agrarian unrest still led to violence. The U.S.-backed military still wrestled with the unrest, with communism, with Muslim radicals, and among themselves. I then understood why Sison's communist narrative was so enduring: he never had to change it.

When we arrived at MacArthur's residence, we were immediately met by the guard. Unlike most of the security guards one meets in the Philippines, who are usually kids from the provinces or some bellied retiree carrying a stock-sawed rusty shotgun, this one had a distinct military presence. He was in his late thirties or early forties, in shape, in a pressed and creased uniform, and in possession of an M-16 rifle. The guard politely told us to wait, and we politely did so. He entered the house through the side entrance, surely the maid's, and returned a few minutes later with a somewhat embarrassed woman, I presumed the dame of the house. She was in her thirties, fair skinned, and quite attractive. In superb English she apologized, but her husband was not there and that she could not allow a tour without his permission. She seemed truly sorry, which made me feel quite ridiculous. Anyway, she continued, there really was not anything to see except the plaque out front. She then said it would be fine if I took some pictures.

We walked to the front of the house, which had a covered entranceway. Children's toys, including an astonishing number of plastic three-wheelers, covered the stone floor. At the side of the dark, ornately engraved mahogany front door was a historical marker that read:

> This building was used by General of the Army Douglas MacArthur commander-in-chief AFWESPAC [Army Forces Western Pacific] as his private quarters during the liberation of Luzon from the early part of February up to March 1945.
>
> With him at the time were President Sergio Osmeña of the Philippine Commonwealth and General Carlos P. Romulo as his personal aide. April, 6, 1965.

If the house was anything like it had been during the war, MacArthur had indeed lived well here in Tarlac. It was the original general manager's residence, done in the prewar Spanish style. It has been exquisitely maintained, right down to the polished horse's head atop the hitching posts. Plants and trees, many in pots, surrounded the entranceway. From the front door one looked out to a manicured lawn, decorative shrubs, and a stone birdbath. Different types of trees bordered the lawn. Altogether, it seemed a civil place to live, but I kept thinking about how Dos Passos would have described it in 1945.

A few minutes' drive brought us to MacArthur's actual headquarters. In contrast to the general's residence, it was a dull, one-story building that was still used for some type of military or security function. It was here that Dos Passos interviewed MacArthur and Willoughby. We were not allowed in this building either, but, once again, we were directed to a historical marker on an outside wall. It read, "This building was the headquarters of AFWESPAC during the liberation of Luzon from February up to March 1945 where General of the Army Douglas MacArthur directed the complete capitulation of the Japanese Imperial Army in the Philippines."

This claim is, of course, debatable. By the time MacArthur left Hacienda Luisita, the Japanese had not yet capitulated, completely or otherwise. But it seemed trite to deny the people of Hacienda Luisita bragging rights. We decided to move on to our last destination of the visit, the notorious Camp O'Donnell.

We drove out of Hacienda Luisita, past the military installation, and back onto the MacArthur Highway in the direction of the small town of Capas, fifteen miles south of Tarlac. Down a narrow back street we stopped at a compact, redbrick building. It is always somewhat surprising to see red brick in the Philippines, and I admired the economy of the building's traditional lines. Lino said it had once been a train station, and here the prisoners from the death march were unloaded after their twenty-five-mile train ride from San Fernando. The tracks were long since gone. Outside the building, near the wire fence where someone had hung the day's washing, was the first death march marker I had seen. Donated by individuals and organizations and set up by FAME, the markers run all the way from Mariveles in Bataan, the start of the march, to Camp O'Donnell. On the sides of each concrete obelisk is the depiction of two pathetic soldiers—one has fallen on all fours, crawling along; the other is bent over, about to collapse. Both figures wear the old prewar pie plate helmet. This particular marker was designated KM 106 of the march.

I tried to envision what it would have looked like when that old, small-gauge train pulled up in April 1942. South of here, in San Fernando, the American and Filipino prisoners were separated. Later, a hundred men were stuffed into each World War I–era, forty-by-eight-foot wooden and metal boxcar, and then doors were closed. The ride was a nightmare of indescribable heat, and the fetid air smelled of urine, vomit, and dysentery's effects. Occasionally, the Japanese would open the doors, and the prisoners would pass out the dead bodies, which were dumped along the tracks. Once, when the train stopped at Angeles and the doors were opened, Filipino civilians ran to the train and tried to throw food to the men. The guards beat them with clubs. When the train finally did arrive at the station in Capas, the men were ordered out and counted. Pacita Pestano-Jacinto described the event in her diary:

> I saw the baggage trains come in. They slid the sidings open and the prisoners tumbled out, gasping for breath, almost smothered by the stinking air in those close-packed wagons. I can't tell you how they looked. No words can describe the horror of it: the way the men clawed like dogs at food that people in their pity threw at them. They were guarded closely. No one could call out. A little rice, wrapped up, would scatter as it fell. The men, Filipinos and Americans alike, would fall of their knees and paw the dust for every little grain.
>
> They were made to stand in line before being herded toward the camp proper. They stood there, men released, as the Japanese said, from bondage, from fighting. But they were duped into a living hell. I saw only the beginning. I saw the sentries make free with murderous bamboo poles.[35]

After a short rest the men were ordered to form two columns, and they began their ill-fated march to Camp O'Donnell.

We were luckier and left Capas by car as the skies began to darken. We hoped we could see Camp O'Donnell before the rain started. Through farmlands we drove about eight miles down a two-lane road, passing the marked route of the death march. As we entered the grounds, I recalled what I thought when I first saw the POW camp in Andersonville, Georgia: the flat, empty landscape with its soothing, green pastoral tranquility gave no hint at all of the horror that once existed there. Even with the threatening clouds rolling in, I felt a sense of unaccountable serenity. Then I saw the giant obelisk.

The structure was overwhelming, but I was not sure in what sense. It was tall, perhaps sixty to seventy yards high; dark gray in color; and topped by a sharply pointed cone. There seemed to be some type of ornamentation at the top, but it was difficult to see it in the now falling rain. As we approached, it reminded me of a rocket ship from some 1950s' B-movie that had somehow comically landed here on the Luzon plain. We parked and walked to the memorial, which had a stone pavement underneath and a black concrete wall around it. This, I was told, was the Capas National Shrine. The tower's three segments apparently represented the Filipino, American, and Japanese people. On the wall that encircled the obelisk were the names of the Filipino and American soldiers who died here. As we silently read the names, the rain began to fall harder.

In 1942 O'Donnell was a nearly built camp that had been housing Filipino army training units.[36] After U.S. forces surrendered, the Japanese command decided to use it to hold the thousands of American and Filipino soldiers coming out of Bataan first and then Corregidor. It made a perfect prison. The entire camp area was surrounded by a flat field covered in cogongrass. A high barbed-wire fence was constructed with wooden guard and gun towers at intervals. Inside the wire were nipa-roofed structures that were used as barracks. Many were not yet complete when the prisoners arrived.

Life inside the camp was so gruesome that it has passed into legend. The men had come into the camp half-starved and exhausted, and many suffered from dysentery, malaria, and other serious maladies. No real medical facilities were available here. Wormy rice was the common meal, which was sometimes augmented by a small portion of camote. As the U.S. forces retreated, they attempted to destroy the camp's water supply; therefore, when the prisoners were marched inside, only two water pumps were working. For cooking, prisoners had to use muddy stream water that POWs transported two miles back to camp in oil barrels carried on bamboo poles. The area was fly infested, which was exacerbated by the latrines and the graves. The burial details at O'Donnell had a difficult task. The Americans died at a rate of about forty to fifty men a day; the Filipinos, about a hundred a day. As soon as a grave was dug, water seeped into it, pushing up the bodies. It was not uncommon for members of the burial details to die during their work and be thrown into the hole as well.

Numerous primary narratives document conditions in the camp. One of the best comes not from a prisoner but a Filipino administrator who had gone to O'Donnell attempting to find his son, a soldier. Dr. Victor Buencamino wrote:

The concentration camp at Capaz [Capas] for Filipino and American war prisoners looks like a graveyard. Only there are no tombs and mausoleums and headstones. Instead, there are thousands of walking corpses, breathing skeletons, lying, sitting, crawling, shuffling aimlessly in a bare, treeless, sun-scorched, desert-like area. Capaz is the bivouac of the living dead.

Everywhere suffering humanity walked, squatted, slept, died. There was a cold chill in my heart as I beheld the gruesome sights wrought by the war: a blind officer begging for water to quench his thirst; a young soldier pale and yellow with malaria, shivering on the sand; an old colonel with a blackened leg begging for medicine; an Igorot private shouting deliriously; hundreds of youths with tattered, bloodstained rags clamoring for food to appease their hunger; an officer on a crutch wandering pointlessly; thousands of dust begrimed, mud-stained, bony, skeletal, emaciated, sunken-eyed youths fighting for the slow drops of trickling water from a single faucet; hundreds lying simply on the ground waiting for eternal sleep; a rigid corpse with a smile on his face.[37]

Despite its short existence, the number of deaths in O'Donnell was staggering. While exact figures are unobtainable, there could have been as many as twenty-five thousand Filipino and fifteen hundred American dead by June 1942, the first forty days of the camp's existence. By then, Filipino prisoners had been released, and the American prisoners had been transferred in small groups to Cabanatuan and other places. Many POWs eventually were shipped to camps in Japan, Korea, and Manchuria, where their suffering continued. After the summer of 1942 some Americans, mostly the sick ones who could not be transported, remained at O'Donnell. Some men were organized into work details that helped build the airfields around Bamban and Angeles. Eventually, all Americans were removed from the camp, and it became a rehabilitation center for the Filipino soldiers.

We next drove over to the wall memorial for the Americans. We walked through a small park while the rain fell fiercely, whacking and bending the fabric of our one and only umbrella. The memorial held a centerpiece, titled Battling Bastards of Bataan, that was decorated with plaques of the Philippine and American flags. The monument was built in 2000 by the organization The Battling Bastards of Bataan, named after the moniker the American and Filipino troops gave themselves in 1942. Next to this wall is the memorial to the Filipino dead. We saw thousands of names carved in stone in a rainy green field.

The Americans' memorial also had a white concrete cross, whose base was engraved with the words "In memory of the American Dead; O'Donnell War Personnel Enclosure 1942, Omnia Pro Patria." All for country. This cross, apparently, is the second one erected here. The original was removed and taken to the Andersonville National Prisoner of War Museum in Georgia, where it serves to remind Americans of what happened at Camp O'Donnell.[38]

The rain ended abruptly, in tropical fashion. We took a few moments to consider our surroundings a final time and looked at the green, flat land spiked by the tall, dark tower. As we drove away, I saw two re-created nipa-roofed guard towers. Again I thought of Andersonville, which also had a replica of its sentry boxes. Like that Civil War prison, which can be found miles off of a minor road in rural Georgia, this Philippine ground, far from the highway, is a monument to the dead and those who suffered. Both stand for the incredible inhumanity that one person or one group of people can inflict on another. These places are less war memorials than they are testimonies to incarceration. Clearly, both should be seen less as a necrology and more as a warning. On the day I saw O'Donnell, however, Lino, Patrick, and I were its only visitors—just us, the rain, and the names on the walls.

The sun was shining as Lino and Patrick dropped me off at the McDonald's along the section of the MacArthur Highway that cut through Capas. I would be able to catch a southbound bus here. In typical Filipino fashion they offered to stay and keep me company until a bus arrived, but I would not have it. The McDonald's sat aside an oddly concocted intersection where traffic had to do a switchback in order to access the highway. I stood outside, writing in my journal and waiting for the bus, enveloped in the tang of french fries and diesel exhaust from the scores of Isuzu jeepneys and buses that plied their trade. I heard the occasional "Hey, Joe!" yelled from a bus, and, rather inexplicably, a peace sign would flash from some passerby.

As I watched the traffic, I thought of how well Hacienda Luisita and Camp O'Donnell illustrate the American experience here and of how

America is perceived today. Hacienda Luisita, with its tradition of conflict between the rich and the poor, between the landlord and the worker, between the exploiter and the exploited, stands as a dubious memorial to U.S. pragmatism. America always backed the side from which it could benefit, and if that side should comprise the incredibly few families that controlled the social system, then true democracy and basic morality would just have to be accommodated in the best way possible. The hacienda also exemplifies the general American ignorance of Philippine history. Looking at the breadth of the twentieth century, it seems hard to believe that the United States ever had anything but some type of domination of the islands in mind. This position is obvious during the colonial and commonwealth periods and later as well. The United States did indeed liberate the Filipinos from the Japanese, but after the war, it immediately reestablished the elite landowners and helped crush a bona fide if communistic movement for land and labor reform. Similarly, former president Aquino, whose tenure was marked by uncertainty and human rights abuses, also oversaw a return of the conservative, elite status quo of the pre-Marcos era and her country's persistent reliance on the United States. Hacienda Luisita, on whose land she once lived, continues to have workers' blood spilled on it. Its sugarcane testifies to American hypocrisy, even duplicity. In terms of a memorial to questionable U.S. political choices, the plantation is absolutely appropriate.

Opposing this view is Camp O'Donnell. On that sad turf, thousands of Filipinos and Americans suffered together, and they did it, especially the Filipinos, for their ideals. So many men paid the ultimate sacrifice that the motto "All for country" is indeed fitting. What Filipino or American could not feel an intense pride in his country when looking at the honored names on the wall? All melodrama aside, it is quite true that the shared anguish of what transpired at O'Donnell has ordained the two peoples as brothers. But judging by the amount of people we saw at the shrine that day, it remains to be seen how much longer that brotherhood will be remembered.

11

THE HILLS OF BAMBAN

On January 22, 1945, U.S. forward troops had reached Capas. With only minimal opposition, the American forces cleared the small barrios around Capas and moved south on Highway 3. They took Bamban Airfield with no resistance at all. However, the town of Bamban in Tarlac Province, as well as the surrounding hills, was polluted with Japanese troops, and the Americans had to clean the area if they wanted to secure nearby Clark Field, then and today the finest airstrip in the country. Over the next week, an intense mountain fight raged, resulting in what would become known as the Battle of the Bamban Hills.[1]

The cities of Tarlac and Angeles and the surrounding environs sit in the midsection of Luzon's central plain, or more commonly referred to as the nation's rice bin. It is a lowland country, barely a few feet above sea level, and stretches from the Lingayen area down to the outskirts of Manila. It is bordered to the west by the high Zambales Mountains and to the east by the higher Cordilleras, with an average width between the two mountain ranges at about forty miles. The plain is dramatically punctuated by Mount Arayat, a 3,350-foot extinct volcano whose cone dominates the landscape from Tarlac to San Fernando. The Pampanga River flows through these lowlands, as do several others, and often floods in wet weather. The plain is sutured by the Manila-Dagupan railway and Highway 3, both of which cross the Bamban River.

The Bamban Hills, part of the Zambales range, are just south of Tarlac and west and northwest of Angeles. The hills rise to heights of six hundred to a thousand feet and form a series of parallel ridges that touch the city of Bamban to the north and Clark Field to the south. Between the ridges flow the Bamban River and lesser streams, some unnamed and only existing in the rainy season. For the Japanese, the hills were a critical element in defending the lowlands and ultimately Manila. Capitalizing on prewar, American-built runways, the Japanese established a huge complex of aircraft installations that ran the fifteen miles from Bamban to Clark Field. Fifteen separate landing strips, both paved and unpaved, ran down both sides of Highway 3, with fields and facilities located in Bamban, Mabalacat, Angeles, Porac, and Clark Field. If these airfields were protected and if the highway and the railroad tracks were blocked, the Americans' push to Manila would be hazardous indeed. From these fields the Japanese would harass MacArthur's invasion force, with often tragic consequences.

The protection of these airfields centered on the Bamban Hills to the west. From these dominating heights, the Japanese gun emplacements had a clear view of Highway 3 and the railroad line. Japanese gunners could easily control the landing strips. The Japanese forces of the Kembu Group had dug tunnels and utilized caves throughout the hills, awaiting the American army's eventual appearance. Despite being low on supplies, the Kembu Group was well established in the mountains, making it a formidable opponent.

U.S. intelligence officials knew, of course, of the Kembu Group and had estimated the total strength of the Japanese presence in the Clark Field area, which included the hills, to be between four thousand and eight thousand men. In reality, the troops under Gen. Osamu Tsukada were approximately thirty thousand strong; however, his command was a bricolage of army, navy, auxiliary, and service personnel, with its top-shelf troops numbering probably no more than five thousand men. Both the men's health and morale were not strong. Indeed, many of Tsukada's troops were Korean, Formosan, and Okinawan labor personnel, and these soldiers were easily given to estrangement and apathy. In terms of weaponry, the group was lightly armed, having relatively few heavy pieces. It did have a high number of automatic weapons and often employed armaments stripped from destroyed aircraft in the region.

Out of the three Japanese commands under Yamashita, Kembu was the weakest. With such a force, Tsukada knew he could not defeat the Americans, but he could possibly control the highway and the railway. Even with such an inadequate deployment, he had something of great value the Americans did not—namely, very high ground. His position could never be taken by bombardment. Only by sending infantry up its steep and sometimes naked slopes could the hills of Bamban be wrestled into American hands.

The job of pushing the Japanese off the Bamban Hills was awarded to Maj. Gen. Oscar Griswold and the 40th Division. On January 20, twenty-four B-24 Liberator bombers had saturated the hills with heavy ordinance. On January 23, artillery and tanks also began to shell the Japanese positions. The next day the U.S. forces began the attack at noon, opting to strike first at two of the most northern Japanese positions—Hill 500 and Lafe Hill. Both were steep-sided rocks, with little in the way of vegetation the attackers could use as cover. As in so many other Pacific encounters, the Japanese were hidden in caves and tunnels and used their cover effectively. U.S. M7 and M10 tanks were called in and positioned at the bottom of the slopes, firing upward and into the caves. Despite the terrain and the Japanese fire, Lafe Hill was taken before nightfall; however, Hill 500 offered tremendous resistance. It was not until January 25 that the mount fell to the Americans. The two ridges had cost the Americans fifteen dead, but they had cost the Japanese three hundred.

With these two points taken, the 40th Division began the slow, arduous process of driving south toward Clark Field and Fort Stotsenburg. Each ridge that was secured was done so in virtually the same way. As soon as U.S. troops moved into an exposed position on some slope, Japanese machine guns and mortars would pin the Americans in place, whereby U.S. artillery support would be called in. The GIs would hunker in their positions until the friendly shells began to fall on the Japanese, and then they would charge forward as far as they could until they were pinned down again or, in many cases, ran over the Japanese position. This *danse macabre* occurred continuously over the next few days. Although the railway and the highway from Bamban south to Mabalacat were in American hands, Griswold came to the obvious conclusion that the drive south would take much longer than expected.

Yet other events were more promising. On January 26, the 145th Infantry captured the eastern part of Clark Field. The next day the 145th marched into the city of Angeles, habituated now by Filipino guerrillas.

Ironically, the taking of Angeles and Clark Field while the 40th Division was still engaged with the Kembu Group presented some difficult questions. MacArthur was adamant about moving on Manila as soon as possible, and General Krueger, the overall commander, was feeling MacArthur's wrath. A free U.S. unit, the 37th Division, could be used to drive south to the capital, but in doing so its vulnerable rear position might be attacked by an element of the Kembu Group. If the 37th were to assist the 40th in the hills, the drive to Manila would be delayed.

Krueger and Griswold reached a type of strategic compromise. For a couple of days, the 37th would assist the 40th in pushing the Japanese back farther into the mountains, thereby allowing engineering units to begin rebuilding Clark Field. At the same time, a portion of the 37th would drive south and capture the city of San Fernando, which also was a vital railway and highway juncture.

It all worked according to plan. On January 28, the 40th began the attack on two crucial points—Storm King Mountain and Snake Hill. In horrific fighting, replete with banzai counterattacks, the Americans captured the hills, although mopping-up operations in the hills lasted longer than a week. On January 29, a reshuffled U.S. force attacked the Kembu Group once more. At both northern and southern ends of the hills, the Americans pressed the fight. Heavy fighting occurred within Fort Stotsenburg in the western part of the Clark Field complex, and the Japanese counterattacked with tanks. By now, Japanese opposition had become fanatical, and gains could only be measured in yards per day. Outcrops with such names as Stout Hill and Top of the World became important parts of a strategic lexicon.

One mountain point—named Sikuaku by the resident Aetas, Hill 1700 by the Americans, and Fujiyama by the Japanese—became particularly important. The hill has steep sides leading to its knife-like peak. Up the sides, the force of three thousand Japanese marines and engineers had fortified caves for its defense. The Americans had fought their way up Snake Hill and now had come to the Aetas' Burog, or Hill 1500, which connected with Hill 1700. On February 25 at 9:15 a.m., the attack on Hill 1700 began. Heavy artillery and tank fire were brought to bear on the defenders, especially on their caves. The barrage was so heavy that the mountain was completely concealed by dust.

Using this cover, U.S. forces climbed and fought their way up the mountain from several different sides. Before 10:00 a.m., Americans were standing on its peak, with Old Glory planted in the debris. There were 343 Japanese dead, with the rest escaping west deep into the Zambales Mountains.

In the end, all the hills were taken. About 150 U.S. soldiers were killed, and perhaps 2,500 Japanese died. The Kembu Group was not destroyed. Tsukada and his men were still in the area, but they posed little immediate threat to Clark Field or Highway 3 and the railway. Indeed, by the end of February, U.S. forces had long been in Manila, albeit after fighting one of the most ferocious battles of the war.

✳ ✳ ✳

The town of Bamban today is a city of approximately forty thousand people. It is a dusty, quiet-looking place, stuck midway between the far more prominent cities of Tarlac and Angeles, but one of its locals has figured prominently in the history of the nation. During the Philippine-American War, after his defeats outside Manila, Emilio Aguinaldo briefly set up his national capital at Bamban before setting up his capital in the town of Tarlac. A few months later, Filipino forces set up a defensive line along the Paruao River, just south of Bamban. In the autumn of 1899, American and Filipino troops clashed in such places as Mabalacat, Magalang, and at the Paruao River. During the world war, the city was heavily damaged. The area thus is of national historical significance.[2]

I toured Bamban and its celebrated hills with Rhonie Dela Cruz, president and founder of the Bamban Historical Society. Some people in Manila's FAME suggested that I contact Rhonie, saying he was a dedicated young man with a zeal for the past. With Rhonie was his friend Billy; another member of the society, who would serve as today's volunteer driver; and Lino Dizon, who had come down from Tarlac to join us. Cramped into a small truck, we made a day of it in this rough terrain. I could not have asked for a better group to accompany me. These energetic young men and professional historian all had an intense knowledge of the area and its history.

Rhonie was interesting and engaging. In his thirties, he was a businessman from a local family and passionate about preserving his hometown's history. His specialty is understanding the role Bamban played in World War II.

He even visited Japan to acquire research on the occupation of the area. With a couple of friends, he launched the society in 1999 to plant and maintain historical markers in the Bamban area, nearly all of them related to the war. They also established a museum and plan to retrieve artifacts from the numerous tunnels that honeycomb the surrounding hills.

Our first stop was in Barrio San Nicolas. During the ride I got a quick background on Bamban and its recent history. In the 1930s sugar was the main crop of the surrounding towns, creating a rich industrial area. A huge Chinese community was connected to the industry. When the sugar market collapsed in the 1960s, so did the area's economy. Many residents immigrated to the United States, particularly former Philippine military men and especially those from the vaunted Philippine Scouts. The OFW phenomenon has also taken many persons out of the area. Today, sugar is a minor product, and as with so many other parts of the country, overseas remittances form a critical aspect of the economy.

When the world war broke out, the area was still a player on the world's sugar market, and the major operator in the area was the Central Luzon Milling Company. The main refinery was the Sugar Central, which two American brothers had built in the late 1920s.[3] In December 1941 the complex served as a headquarters for Maj. Gen. Jonathan Wainwright, who moved up from Fort Stotsenburg. Wainwright and his staff stayed at the mansion house, which had tiled bathrooms and hot running water.[4] After the fall of the Philippines, the dreaded Japanese Kempeitai used the Sugar Central as its headquarters. The complex's mansion house, clubhouse, and various other structures that were once used by company executives became places of torture. Civilians, American and Filipino soldiers-turned-guerrillas, and Huks were taken to the Sugar Central, usually in retaliation for anti-Japanese activities. Particularly feared was the swimming pool, where a person was given the "water cure," in which the Japanese forced large amounts of water into a person. Nothing is left of the Central today.

As a gap occurred in the narration, I suddenly focused on the part about the two American brothers. Years earlier I had known a wonderful man, now deceased, named Earl Hornbostel. I corresponded with him for quite some time and continue to correspond with his daughter in the States. Hornbostel, an American, had grown up in Manila and was interned by the Japanese in Santo Tomas. Later he was moved to Muntinlupa, where he was scheduled for execution but was rescued the day before by U.S. troops. I remembered him telling me of the Fassoth brothers from Hawaii. He told me about how the people of Bamban respected them and how they helped Americans who escaped from the death march. Without looking for it, a delightful memory was stirred, and I was happy to make a connection between Hornbostel, a Manila-based American old-timer, and the Bamban Society.[5]

William and Martin Fassoth were twin brothers, sons of a sugar plantation owner on Maui. William came to the Philippines in 1913 to manage a sugar mill for an American company. In 1919 he took a long-term lease on 1,450 acres of land in Tarlac Province, and it became the core of his business. Martin joined his brother in 1923. They were successful planters and businessmen, and life was good.

The war changed everything. When the Japanese arrived, the Fassoths' entire crop was ruined, and the Japanese and Filipino sympathizers looted and destroyed their house and the barrio in which it was located. When a second home was demolished in a bombing raid, the two brothers plus William's wife and son decided to go to ground deep in the Pinatubo area. Here, they were joined by several other families fleeing the Japanese. In the spring of 1942, a Filipino planter and close friend helped the Fassoths establish a camp for American and Filipino guerrillas near the town of Dinalupihan. With the help of local residents, many of whom were Aetas, the middle-aged brothers saved many lives by offering nourishment and protection within the camp. By 1943, however, the Japanese had discovered the camp and captured the Fassoths. William's wife, Catalina, and his son, Vernon, eluded capture and aided escapees until the war's end. The twins were imprisoned but survived the war. Afterward, William, Martin, and Catalina received the Medal of Freedom.[6]

I was still roused by the Hornbostel connection and the Fassoth story when we made our first stop at the former grounds of the Old Municipal Hall of San Nicolas in Bamban. Rhonie took me to the society's marker. Its headline proclaimed that we were standing at the site of the first Japanese Kempeitai execution in Bamban, dated February 1942. On that spot, four men who had been brought down from San Jose, Nueva Ecija, were blind-folded and made to stand in a single file along a trench that was used as an air raid shelter. The townspeople were summoned to the place. A Kempeitai named Tamura proclaimed the men were guerrillas and took out his pistol. The four men from Nueva Ecija were each shot in the back of the head and pushed into the trench. Later they were covered over.

Others here also suffered under the Kempeitai. The marker listed eight names of men who had been executed for being guerrillas. It also pro-vided more names of those who were arrested and subsequently vanished. The marker could not possibly mention all of the atrocities. The Kempeitai's torture of suspected guerrillas in La Paz and Mabalacat; the seventeen sus-pects who were taken to Camp O'Donnell in August 1943 and never heard from again; the beheading of the Filipino guide who mislead Japanese troops searching for an American guerrilla; the rounding up of seventy men from Barrio Bangcu, the subsequent beatings, and the forced kneeling in the town plaza for two days; the 150 men who were marched from barrios around Bamban to the Sugar Central, where they were beaten and tortured—the whole area, it seemed, was drenched in blood.[7]

The Bamban Airfield was next.[8] The V-shaped strip itself is no longer there, and the site is now partially occupied by cane fields and an elementary school about a mile outside of Bamban town proper. We alighted from the truck, and Billy produced a laptop. Setting it on a stump, we watched a short movie on MacArthur's return. The society had set up a historical marker here: this one featured a superb narrative and photos of Japanese planes, as well as a picture of MacArthur at Bamban supposedly pointing off to the action in the hills to the west. MacArthur had come down from Tarlac on January 23 to inspect the just-captured field.

The airfield had been a thorn in the side of U.S. forces, and American pilots flew numerous sorties to knock it out. By October 1944, Bamban Airfield had become a collecting point of various army and navy air groups. Japanese aircraft, including many kamikazes, took off from Bamban to at-tack U.S. forces in Leyte, ships heading for Lingayen, and the troops that had landed at Lingayen. The U.S. command realized the importance of Bamban and the other airfields in the Angeles area and began sending carrier-based

Loyal soldiers and released residents at Oakwood mutiny.
(Photo by Joseph P. McCallus)

Military vehicle of loyal troops at Oakwood mutiny.
(Photo by Joseph P. McCallus)

Street scene, Tinau Island. (Photo by Joseph P. McCallus)

The capitol building at Lingayen. (Photo by Joseph P. McCallus)

The Price house, Tacloban; tower not shown. (Photo by Joseph P. McCallus)

The Price house, Paco.
(Photo by Joseph P. McCallus)

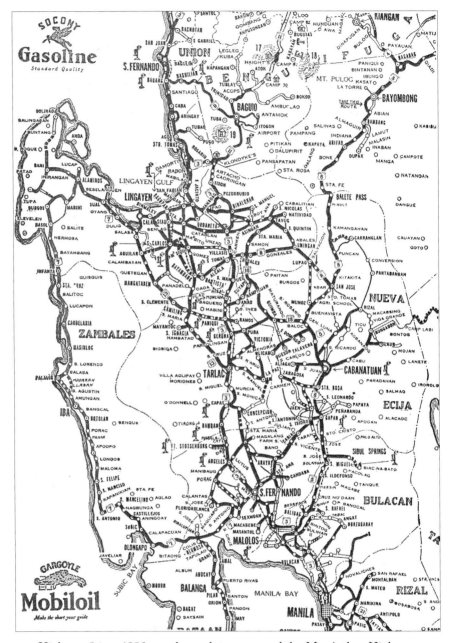

Highway 3 in a 1930s roadmap; later renamed the MacArthur Highway.
(From the collection of Benito Legarda Jr.)

The Capas train station and death march marker. (Photo by Joseph P. McCallus)

Memorial at Camp O'Donnell. (Photo by Joseph P. McCallus)

The San Fernando train station and death march marker. (Photo by Joseph P. McCallus)

MacArthur's headquarters and residence, Dagupan.
(Photo by Joseph P. McCallus)

Plaza Nuestra Señora de Guia, Ermita. (Photo by Joseph P. McCallus)

The Department of Tourism building, Manila. (Photo by Joseph P. McCallus)

Battery Hearn, Corregidor. (Photo by Joseph P. McCallus)

Pasig River, south bank, Manila. (Photo by Joseph P. McCallus)

The Manila American Cemetery. (Photo by Joseph P. McCallus)

planes on strikes in the area almost daily. A number of large-scale air battles occurred over Bamban in October and November 1944.

Ensign Robert Lee Clary, flying a Grumman F6F-5 Hellcat off the USS *Monterey*, was involved in one such battle.[9] The *Monterey* was a light aircraft carrier, busy sending planes into Central Luzon to attack targets around the Clark Field area. Clary was a veteran flyer, having seen action over the Marianas, Taiwan, and the Philippines. He probably would have been familiar with the terrain of Central Luzon and, just as so many pilots before him, used Mount Arayat as a signpost for navigation.

On the morning of November 5, 1944, Clary and his fellow fliers assaulted airfields in Tarlac and the Clark Field area, including the airfield at Bamban. At Bamban, the Japanese flew up to meet them. A sharp engagement ensued, with the Americans knocking down fourteen Japanese planes and destroying sixteen more on the ground. Clary was seen shooting down one aircraft, but he never made it back to the *Monterey*. His plane was probably hit from one of the many antiaircraft batteries near Bamban.

Scores of civilians as well as the Kempeitai also watched the dogfights. The commanding officer, the cruel and much-feared Lieutenant Yamaguchi, saw Clary's Hellcat come down in a field just outside of Barrio Culabasa. Immediately, Japanese soldiers in a truck drove to the crash site, with local residents running behind them. The soldiers kept the locals from approaching the plane, but they were only twenty-five yards away and close enough to see what happened next. The aircraft was burning, but the cockpit was untouched. Lieutenant Yamaguchi walked up to Ensign Clary, who some say was still alive; pulled his revolver; and fired three times. Yamaguchi then ordered his soldiers to pour gasoline over the cockpit, and Yamaguchi threw in the match. Everything burned to ashes.

After the Japanese returned to their garrison, some of the Bamban locals recovered what remained of Robert Lee Clary and buried him. After the war, his grave was found and registered. Yamaguchi was indicted for the deaths of civilians, local guerrillas, and Ensign Clary. The Bamban Historical Society plans to install a marker in his memory.

Our touring party took a short breather and sat in the schoolyard. We began to chat about the school and about the future of education in the

Philippines. This public school seemed typical of the institutions in poor barrios: no walls, no lights, broken desks. It had nothing that could pass for adequate pedagogical tools, nothing that would permit the students to compete
against the kids in Manila, and nothing that would allow them to get out of
this barrio. I was told in no uncertain terms how in this school, as in other
public provincial schools, the principal and teachers made money on the side,
essentially extorting funds from the parents. I offered that I had heard the
same thing in Samar. Everyone seemed to sigh, and for a fraction of a second
I saw in my mind the ghost of Mr. White, angry and frustrated, flying through
these fields. Then we squeezed back into the truck.

I had no map and at first tried to keep a mental record of our direction. As we twisted up and down the mountain road, my attempt soon became
fruitless. On the slope of a steep knoll, we stopped at an attractive memorial to
the Japanese troops who died in these hills. More specifically, it was built for a
Japanese officer, Vice Admiral Ohnishi, the officer who formed the first official
kamikaze group at Mabalacat Field in October 1944.[10] Given its surroundings, the memorial supplied a remarkable contrast. Set inside a white walled
garden, it was flanked by several Shinto shrines. An oblong tower standing more than six feet high had Japanese characters painted above an altar
that contained incense and small cups and featured a plaque in English and
Japanese, dedicating the memorial. Below the altar were painted two flags—
one Japanese, one Philippine—but between them was painted the red octopus
flag of the Japanese warlords with Japanese characters on it. Rhonie told me
that the memorial was dedicated in 2001, and since then many Japanese veterans and family members have come here to offer sake and prayer. Apparently
it is well known in Japan. Indeed, the society claims that a certain Makino-san,
a wealthy businessman and son of a Japanese pilot who was shot down over
Bamban, comes to the shrine yearly to offer prayers for his father. Makino-san
says he saw his father in a dream, and he told him to come to Bamban.

The shrine was impeccably clean and peaceful, with nothing to even
hint at debasement; there was no graffiti here. It made me wonder about how
the Filipinos remembered the Japanese. I spoke to the party members about
the Japanese and asked what they thought about them. Their responses were
quiet and measured. While there was no anger in anyone's words, nor was

there any admiration; rather, they expressed a historian's objectivity that I found gratifying. They also had a sense of thankfulness to the people in Japan who assisted the society in the creation of the shrine and perhaps even a tinge of friendship. Veterans gave Rhonie much help when he visited Japan, and I thought of how awkward that trip must have been for all concerned.

An old man appeared from seemingly nowhere. He was the caretaker of the place. The society members knew him well, and we followed him toward a small hole in the side of the hill. It was one of the entrances to a Japanese tunnel complex that was about three hundred meters long and was essentially the remains of a Japanese communications encampment. The narrow path to the entrance was guarded by a string of rusty barbed wire. The hole itself was rather small and completely surrounded by a thick, brilliant green vegetation. It was protected from intruders by a locked iron grill, for which our caretaker produced the key. We bowed low under the archway and made our way into the tunnel. Inside the air was surprisingly fresh and cool. A wire with light bulbs, which the society had installed, ran throughout the tunnel. The bright light revealed a barren place. I suppose I was expecting skeletons, or at least an old Japanese canteen, but there was nothing but clean dirt floors and walls. The old man led us through it. He knew the place well; indeed, it was where he actually lived. He mentioned that as a boy he would marvel at the tunnel and at the Japanese activity he saw around it.

Ohnishi had commanded the tunnel's operations, and it had served as the headquarters of the First Air Fleet, a conglomeration of Japanese naval planes and pilots from different outfits. Their headquarters were situated on two small hills that the Japanese called *Asahiyma* (Morning Sun). The communications tunnel was in the western one. At any one time fifty troops would be working in the tunnel, attempting to coordinate the activities of Japanese forces in the Philippines, Taiwan, and the headquarters in Japan. Much code work was done in here. The men would sleep outside the tunnels in the nipa huts that had been constructed in the area.

During the day Ohnishi walked the hills of Bamban, viewing the activities at the other airfields. Sometimes he walked down to the Sugar Central to bathe in the swimming pool and torture center. At other times he climbed the mount of what is now called Grotto of Our Lady of Lourdes. In the evening he returned to camp, where he and his troops doubtlessly spent quiet, beautiful nights in the mountains and waited for the Americans' approach and the possibility of death. Eventually, he vacated the hills. Ordered back to Taiwan, he left the communications complex on January 9, 1945.

It was difficult to balance the serenity of these hills with the thought of the kamikazes. Just as with the green fields of Camp O'Donnell, the lush hillsides here held hideous secrets. I tried to imagine Ohnishi giving orders for young men to commit suicide. Not heroes but victims, they received the ceremonial cup of sake before their final takeoff from the Bamban Airfield. Their last dive ended usually as splintered shards floating in the Pacific or, if lucky, as a burning wreck on an American ship. In the newsreels the public only sees the screaming end to the flight; but here is where it began, in the quiet green hills.

We thought we heard digging. According to Rhonie, everyone searches for gold in the Bamban Hills, even the former governor. As with the unconquerable myth of Yamashita's gold, many believe that the Japanese military stashed war booty in the tunnels and caves of these hills. Any reasonable sort of person would conclude that this rumor is nonsense, but it persists. More interesting is what type of historical artifacts could be recovered from the tunnels. Most of the tunnels the Japanese built were blown shut and buried by the Americans, entombing anyone and anything left inside. I asked Rhonie if the society had a metal detector, and he sadly admitted it did not. What a treasure trove of history could be up in these hills, I thought. I considered all the human remains that could be sent back to Japan to grateful families and what a Japanese rifle in superb condition would get on the market. I saw myself as being part of a TV special or interviewed by the media. Yes, I began thinking of just how I could get myself a metal detector for there was gold in these hills.

We continued on the tour and arrived at Hill 500. The Americans nicknamed it Stout Hill, the Japanese called it the Morning Sun, and it is known today as Grotto of Our Lady of Lourdes. I had seen this place many times from the bus window as I traveled the MacArthur Highway up north. An imposing, beautiful place, it is a dark green outcrop that spires high into the air somewhat like a shovel blade. At the summit are three crosses, and Filipinos climb the innumerable steps from the base to the top as a penitential pilgrimage. It is the Philippine version of Ireland's Croagh Patrick.

The truck pulled up to the base of the hill. The nearby stairway, concrete and broken into several layers, ran almost vertically up the hill. It had railings to help one journey up to forgiveness and redemption. On one side were small wooden posts that I took to be stations of the cross. At intervals were little shacks—each really just a piece or two of tin buttressed by some bamboo—outside of which the day's washing was drying. At the very top of the steps, I could just make out a small ceremonial structure painted sky blue and white, and given the colors, I took it to be the shrine to Our Lady. I weighed the number of stairs against the number of my sins and decided that I need not see the top.

Adjacent to the steps was a different shrine, one dedicated to the 40th Division in 1945. Rhonie unlocked a gate, and we entered a concrete courtyard. Over our heads residents peered at us from their hillside homes. At the far end of the empty yard stood three of the society's markers. The central marker told the entire Bamban story, featuring the Fighting 40th, the bearded American guerrillas, and the tiny, trusty Aeta. Another marker showed the planting of the U.S. flag on Hill 1700. The third marker was a landscape photograph of Stout Hill. On top of the central marker's concrete base was affixed a nearly life-size bronze statue of a U.S. soldier holding an M1 rifle. Luckily for him, four poles held up a tin roof, keeping him out of the sun. His face was strong, and he stared directly at the sari-sari store that served cold beer about thirty yards away. To the side of the markers were two tall flagpoles, and Rhonie proudly explained that we stood at the only nonofficial place where the Philippine and American flags flew together. I looked up and noted that the flags were at equal height. Turning I looked over the panorama before us. Centered in front of us was the Bamban Bridge, where in 1942 heroic Filipino forces fought toe-to-toe with the Japanese forces coming down from Lingayen. Beyond the bridge were the flat fields of Pampanga, and dominating them all, in the background, was the shadow of mighty Arayat.

As we left the courtyard, Rhonie locked the gate behind us. I took one last look at the bronze soldier and up the steps and considered the logic of this place. Here was hallowed soil, where Americans, Japanese, and Filipinos all slaughtered each other. Today, these grounds are presided over by Our Lady, who watches everything under Arayat—the two waving flags, the lonely bronze

soldier, the people in the shacks, and the cars on the MacArthur Highway—
from her splendid perch atop the penitential stairway.

Minutes after we departed from the grotto area, I once again lost my
bearings. We needed to cross a stream maybe a foot deep, I believe, in what
was called the Sacobia Valley. I guessed it was the Marimla River, but I was not
sure. Sugarcane rose all around, nearly blocking out the rest of the world. We
were apparently at a ford, and there was heavy trike traffic here on both sides.
We watched intrepid drivers plunging their machines through the muddy water, splashing, sometimes stalling, and happily yelling things to each other. As
we waited our turn to cross, someone in the truck began telling a story of how
the U.S. military tested the M16 in these hills before sending it off to Vietnam.
He claimed the Americans used the Aetas as target practice, saying they mis-
took them for monkeys in the trees. Everyone in the truck seemed to chuckle
at this comment. I had no idea if it were true, and I was not sure if they were
joking. In any event I felt too uncomfortable to laugh.

The truck easily crossed the stream, to the cheers of the trike population, but as I saw the water splash onto the hood I remembered crossing similar
streams in Pampanga and Zambales in 1992. They were bad times in Central
Luzon. Pinatubo had erupted the year before, and a choking dust still lingered
in the air. The *lahar* (liquefied mud and volcanic debris) had caused incredible
destruction down through the land and significantly altered the landscape. To
this day I offer pictures of a destroyed hotel near Angeles, with its swimming
pool lifted out of the ground and cracked in half, as evidence to the force of
lahar. During those immediate years after the eruption, at seemingly every
bridge—many of which were quickly reconstructed as shaky, one-lane con-
traptions—there was an interminable wait. Sometimes it would take an hour
for the drivers of opposing traffic to negotiate and allow a crossing. As late as
2002 I can remember that while taking a jeepney to Porac, we traveled over
a flat area that had once been farms. All the other passengers wore handker-
chiefs over their faces to protect them from the clouds of lahar dust. I did not,
and for an hour my eyes stung and my throat ached because of my ignorance.

Our road took us up again, winding higher and higher into the confusing green mountain world. As we wound our way along the narrow, unpaved,
and often one-lane mountain road, we were surprised when we nearly collided

with a late-model Mercedes-Benz occupied by four Koreans. We laughed and said they were looking for gold. In reality, my companions told me, they were probably land speculators. I thought, why here?

A minute or so later we arrived at a small group of houses. It was probably too small to be considered a village, but it was certainly organized well enough to be considered a community. This area was Sitio Burog. Rhonie had the truck stopped, and we piled out to take in the view. We were on what was called Hill 1500 and standing at the edge of a steep bluff. Before us was a range of hills that sat like a series of green shades, at once awesome, at once soothing. In this sublime masterpiece Rhonie identified a number of peaks— Storm King, Snake Hill, and others—and related the different military strategies and activities of each place.

While Rhonie was pointing out the topography, I occasionally looked back at the houses nearby. The roofs were either tin or thatched, and the houses were mostly rattan and good-looking weaves at that. A number had picket-type fences in front of them, with the day's laundry lending color to the properties. Telephone poles ran alongside the road and then off somewhere I could not imagine. This place seemed clean, quiet, and relaxed and indistinguishable from virtually anyplace else in the islands. Except for the residents who were immediately distinguishable from other Filipinos. These were Aetas, or as they are sometimes referred to, Negritoes. This area was ancestral Aeta land, and the small people milled around. Dogs barked. We heard the sounds of recorded music and happy children. Rhonie pointed to where Maj. John McSevney was killed. As roosters crowed, I listened to Rhonie telling me about finding Japanese bones in the area, but my mind was more on the Aeta. In fact, my skin was tingling at the thought of being in an Aeta village.

The Aeta are perhaps the earliest inhabitants of the Philippines.[11] One theory is that they are descendants from the original tribe that crossed the land bridges from mainland Asia thirty thousand years ago. I have heard them referred to as "real" or "original" Filipinos. With dark complexions, kinky hair, flat noses, and short statures—the men are about five feet tall and the women are shorter—the Aeta are usually looked down upon by other Filipinos and often ridiculed for their appearance. They have largely resisted the call of the

Catholic Church and are animists. For centuries the Aeta of Zambales have also believed in a supreme deity and worshiped Apo Namalyari, whose home is Mount Pinatubo. There are six major clans of Aeta, and their ancestral lands are all in Central Luzon: Tarlac, Pampanga, Nueva Ecija, Bataan, and the Pinatubo region.

One member of our party compared the Aeta to Native Americans. At least in terms of an outsider's perception, perhaps that was an accurate observation. The men are formidable hunters, expert with a bow, and the women are accomplished weavers. Most Filipinos believe the Aeta have highly developed senses of smell and direction. Traditionally, the Aeta practiced decorative disfigurements, including body scarring and the chipping of teeth. All of these ingredients make the Aeta an almost mythical group of people in the Filipinos' eyes, but that does not stop the Filipinos from making snide remarks about their skin color or their hair.

Throughout history the Aeta have shown a fierce resistance to change but have exhibited a cultural flexibility as well. Despite having much of their land seized when the United States set up the Subic Bay and Clark Field complexes, the Aeta got along quite well with the Americans. During World War II, many Aeta became guerrillas and fought the Japanese. For example, in 1942 Lt. Henry Clay Conner, a Fort Stotsenburg officer, fled into the Zambales Mountains and helped form the 155th Provisional Guerrilla Battalion.[12] Conner was able to use three thousand Aetas against the Japanese, employing them as scouts, guides, and packers. Today, there are still Aetas who receive Philippine veteran's pensions because of their own, their father's, or their grandfather's service during the war. After the war, and especially during the Vietnam War, the Aeta were known to work with U.S. military personnel in jungle training exercises around Subic Bay. In fact, after the base shut down, Aetas often worked as tour guides.

When Pinatubo erupted, it is not known exactly how many Aeta were killed, but it was surely in the hundreds. Just as devastating to these people was their displacement. After the eruption, the people were gathered into various evacuation shelters and resettlement camps throughout Central Luzon, stripped of their ability to continue their traditional life. Many groups in the Philippines, most notably the mainstream churches, banded together and assisted in their resettlement. In these camps the Aeta came into contact with extensive Western influence. The traditional Aeta wardrobe, which consisted pretty much of just a G-string, was replaced by shorts, T-shirts, and sandals. The people's traditional herbal cures gave way to the free hospitalization and medicine the government provided. Perhaps most alarming is that rather than return to the time-honored work in the forests or fields, many young Aeta today are working as laborers. Some still live in the Zambales area, serving as guides and survival instructors in the tourist industry, but others have taken a different route: begging on city streets, as I had seen near Tarlac. Paradoxically, this exposure to the outside world has not decreased their numbers. Fifteen years after Pinatubo, the population of Aeta in Central Luzon has doubled to nearly 100,000.[13]

Despite the assistance they received after the eruption and despite their increased population, the future of the group is entirely uncertain.[14] When the United States pulled its forces out of the Philippines in 1991–92, the Aetas were eager to reclaim their ancestral lands. The ownership of the land, however, was taken over by the Philippine government under the auspices of the Bases Conversion and Development Act of 1992. A Bases Conversion and Development Authority was created, which in turn established the Clark Special Economic Zone. An executive order then created the Clark Development Corporation (CDC), a part-private, part-government body tasked to turn the former Clark Air Base area into a world-class airport and an industrial, commercial, and residential center. This economic plan essentially put an end to Aeta dreams of reclaiming much of their ancestral homes, and it has engendered more misery. In 1998, in Capas, Tarlac, the CDC and a German corporation initiated a waste disposal project near an Aeta resettlement camp on former Aeta land. In Sitio Burog, Bamban, the CDC has plans to convert an Aeta village into a fruit plantation. Nearby, the CDC has scheduled a tourist road to Pinatubo through Sitio San Martin, another Aeta village. In 2005, two Aeta leaders voiced their opposition to the expansion of mining operations in Aeta lands in Zambales, Bataan, and Pampanga; they were abducted and murdered.

The traditional Aeta world is not only being challenged from land speculators, mining operations, and blue jeans. Because they are a displaced people, because they are animists, probably because their population seems to be growing, and, most importantly, because they live in the 10/40 window, the Aeta are natural marks for American evangelical missionaries. The Mission to Unreached Peoples—a Seattle-based group that sends missionaries to such godless countries as Poland, Hungary, and India—has set up for the Aeta a Bible training center, a children's home, and a "school [that] especially targets Aeta children for education and evangelism."[15] In November 2001, the Church of the Nazarene, a Pentecostal movement, was established in an Aeta community of thirty-seven families. The evangelist group hopes to build a water project to "draw people to the Church."

As we crowded around Rhonie and listened, I happened to notice that a couple of young Aeta men had silently come up and stood beside us. They seemed to be listening intently, but I doubt that their English allowed them to understand much of Rhonie's lecture. Periodically their eyes shot to mine and then back at Rhonie. One of the society members noticed and whispered to me, "They think you are up here looking for gold."

After contemplating Hill 1500, most of which was blasted away in the fighting, we left the village and pushed up toward Hill 1700. The one-lane road quickly became more narrow. Vegetation continually brushed the sides of the truck. In some spots I could not see a road at all, and Billy the driver seemed to suicidally send the truck into a wall of leaves. At all times the truck and its occupants were absorbing bumps, most of them jarring. I told the crew I wanted the hill to be renamed the Kidney Breaker. At one point we saw an Aeta man who was nearly covered by the large bunch of bananas he was carrying on his back. The truck stopped, and he and Rhonie had a laugh-filled conversation. They were clearly on good terms.

Perhaps twenty minutes later the truck stopped at a small clearing. It was the end of the line. We got out, and maybe two hundred yards ahead was Hill 1700. Rugged, gnarly, sheathed in a totally green coat, save for the one area of sheer dark rocks, it commanded the landscape. There was not a single tree on the whole mountain; instead, it was covered in soft-looking, high grass from base to peak. It would take a great deal of strength to climb that hill, and I could not comprehend how one could do it while being fired at by an enemy.

We were not going to attempt it, thankfully. From here the magnificent green panorama that we saw from the Aeta village presented itself again, only this time through a much wider lens. On the ground close by, I noticed several strange small structures, perhaps three feet high, made of dried leaves with tin roofs held down by tree limbs. Curious, I asked Rhonie about them and found out they were Aeta sheds used in the harvesting of bananas and other fruits. These grounds were clearly those of the tribal people.

Rhonie told the story of his climb up Hill 1700.[16] In February 2004 he and two other members of the society decided to commemorate the flag raising of the battle of the hills' final encounter. Loaded with cameras, they embarked on the arduous northern approach, which even the American troops had decided to abandon because of its scale. The society members were able to find a tunnel entrance and foxholes, but most everything was covered in Pinatubo ash and then sealed over with vegetation. The summit was only about fifty square yards. Late on a cloudy afternoon, they planted the American flag on it. He said when the flag went in the ground the sun came out, and Old Glory waved for fifteen minutes. Then they said a prayer for the Americans, for the Filipinos, and for the Japanese and came back down the mountain.

We did not stay very long. It was getting late in the day, and we had covered quite a few miles. As my tour of the Bamban Hills ended, I looked back at the summit. As I looked up at the green rock, I did not see U.S. troops charging up its dangerous slopes. I saw instead young Filipino men standing under the Stars and Stripes, saying a prayer.

12

ANGELES CITY AND CLARK FIELD

The bus station at Dau, the gateway into the nearby city of Angeles, has always delivered a shock to my senses. When I left the air-conditioned bus and stepped onto the pavement, I was immediately smacked by the heat, the diesel exhaust, and the charcoal smoke from the nearby food vendors. That day, as all days, it was crowded. Because so many foreigners pass through here, and have been doing so for years and years, people are not surprised to see a white or black face. Indeed, they welcome the foreigner. Young boys doggedly begged for money as they migrated to each incoming bus, quietly cursing those who would not give, while trike drivers patiently waited outside the terminal, hoping to charge unimaginable rates to their helpless Western customers for the short trip into Angeles. There was a quiet resignation here. The boys, the drivers, and usually even the foreigners have all engaged in this exercise countless times before.

Angeles is an ineffable place, an *olla podrida* (hodgepodge) of evolution, conflict, cooperation, and exploitation. Under the shadow of Mount Arayat to the east and the foothills of Mount Pinatubo to the west, Angeles sits snugly wrapped in its harlequin-painted past, knowing full well that its reputation is a lightning rod for divergent thoughts. It is a place of peculiar contrasts: Angeles is at once the center of the fiercely independent Kapampagan culture, but nowhere else in the islands is the American influence so tied to the population.

In the late eighteenth century, the Spanish settled the city and named it Kuliat after the many vines growing in the area. It was initially a barrio of San Fernando, twenty miles away. In the mid-nineteenth century, it became an independent city and was renamed Angeles after the Los Angeles Custodios, or the Holy Guardian Angels. The angels have guarded it well, for throughout its history it has remained a center for the sugar, rice, and fishery industries that surround it.[1]

The Americans first came to Angeles in 1898. The Philippine-American War had broken out earlier that year. During the first months, the U.S. forces routed a brave but poorly equipped and ineptly led Filipino army out of the Manila area. The Filipino forces regrouped fifty miles north in Pampanga, and their commander-president, Emilio Aguinaldo, set up his government in Angeles and celebrated the nation's first anniversary there on June 12, 1899. The chief U.S. commander, Gen. Elwell Otis, wanted to finish off the Filipinos during the summer. Bolstered with an influx of fresh troops, Otis devised a scheme to annihilate Aguinaldo and his forces. Otis knew that he had the power to defeat his adversary in set battles, but he was concerned that Aguinaldo would retreat into the Luzon mountains and organize a guerrilla offensive. Wishing to avoid a partisan quagmire, Otis designed a complex three-pronged strategy. As discussed in chapter 4, Maj. Gen. Henry Lawton was to travel up the Rio Grande River first north and then west to the Lingayen Gulf, flanking and containing Aguinaldo's escape route into the mountain ranges of north and Central Luzon; and Gen. Loyd Wheaton was to land forces on the Lingayen coast and obstruct roads heading north along the coast. Gen. Arthur MacArthur's troops were to travel northwest up the Angeles-Dagupan railway to push Aguinaldo into the pocket created by Lawton and Wheaton, squeezing him to death and ending all thoughts of Philippine independence.

It was a sophisticated plan, and in order for it to succeed, Otis needed a large amount of supplies brought up from Manila. The only way to do that quickly was via the railway. The Manila-Dagupan rail line—the very same line that the Japanese would die to protect a half century later—was anchored by the critical San Fernando–Angeles link. Angeles was to become the operation's supply hub, equipping both the Lawton and MacArthur detachments. The Filipino forces knew the importance of the San Fernando–Angeles link, and for three days in August 1899 fought the American troops in bloody engagements.

When the city of Angeles fell to U.S. forces, their engineering crews began the arduous work of repairing the damaged rail line.

Ultimately, the Otis plan did not work. Aguinaldo escaped into the mountains unscathed and, from there, directed his army for more than a year. A guerrilla conflict did break out in various parts of the country, with horrendous effects on the civilian population. But Otis's plan did signal the beginning of a long relationship between the city of Angeles and the U.S. military. In 1902 the 5th Cavalry Regiment established a camp six miles northwest of Angeles that was eventually named Fort Stotsenburg, after the U.S. colonel who fell at Quinqua (now Plaridel, Bulacan) the year before. By 1908 the post had spread over 150,000 acres, making it the second largest U.S. army camp anywhere. It is well to remember that during the period between the Spanish-American War and the First World War, the Philippines served as the chief training ground for the U.S. military, and Camp Stotsenburg was the most important camp in the islands.

In 1919 the newly formed U.S. Air Service began its operations in the Far East. A group of airmen constructed a crude landing strip one mile east of Camp Stotsenburg's parade ground. A year later it was officially named Clark Field, after Maj. Harold M. Clark, a pilot killed in an accident in the Panama Canal Zone. At the time it was the only U.S. air base west of Hawaii. Throughout the 1920s, the airfield grew and housed the 3rd Pursuit Squadron. In 1924, during a visit by the legendary Gen. Billy Mitchell, former president Aguinaldo was given flying lessons. In the 1930s the field became the home of the 28th Bomb Squadron, and just before World War II, it helped train a fledgling Philippine air force.[2]

Throughout the prewar years, and, in fact, throughout the Vietnam era, interactions between Americans stationed at Stotsenburg and Clark and the Filipinos in Angeles tended to be slight in volume and usually reinforced colonial stereotypes. To the American officers and their families, the Filipinos made superb, cheap servants. To the enlisted men, their cultural interactions often involved a local prostitute. As Charles Willeford describes in his prewar memoir, the U.S. Army did everything it could to institutionalize prostitution in Angeles, a practice that would essentially continue after the war, and would lay the groundwork for the islands' current, booming sex trade. It should be

noted, however, that a significant number of military men married local wom-
en, and during that time neither the army nor American society accepted
interracial families.[3]

The history of Clark is punctuated by several disasters, both man-made
and natural. The first of these occurred on December 8, 1941. Despite weeks'
worth of war preparations, despite knowing the attack on Pearl Harbor had
occurred nine hours before, and despite adequate early warning of a Japanese
invasion from a radar installation at Iba in Zambales, U.S. forces suffered
heavy losses at Clark Field on the first day of the war. Fifty-five Americans
were killed, more than a hundred were wounded, and many of the P-40 fighters and nearly all of the B-17 bombers of the Clark Field command were
destroyed. So ineffectual was the U.S. defense that the Japanese pilots, flying
back to their base in Formosa, wondered if the Americans had actually heard
that they were at war. By noon on December 8, U.S. offensive and defensive
air capabilities were nearly eliminated, as well as any real chance of successfully thwarting a Japanese invasion.

The debacle at Clark created a controversy that exists to this day. In an
attempt to pin responsibility on one of the three officers involved with planning
the nation's defense—namely, MacArthur, his chief of staff Sutherland, and
the commander of the U.S. Far East Air Force (USFEAF), Maj. Gen. Lewis
Brereton—inquests were held. Two conflicting scenarios emerged. First, did
Sutherland, with MacArthur's knowledge, order Brereton to move the entire
number of B-17s to the Del Monte Airfield in northern Mindanao? If this
were the case, then Brereton was completely derelict in his duty; the planes
would have been safe from the Japanese if he had followed Sutherland's orders
and moved them. Conversely, did Brereton, as he claimed, ask MacArthur
and Sutherland for permission to bomb the Japanese base in Formosa hours
after hearing about Pearl Harbor? If his assertion is true, and if he was denied
permission, as he also claimed, then MacArthur and Sutherland share responsibility for the planes being on the ground at the time of attack. The matter
will probably never be resolved because much of the evidence was either never
committed to paper or is now destroyed.[4]

The Japanese used Clark Field to attack U.S. forces sailing from Leyte
and Mindoro, with horrifying and casualty-causing results, but ultimately to

little avail. The areas around Clark and Fort Stotsenburg saw harsh combat as MacArthur's troops made their run to Manila. Despite a spirited defense, the Japanese did not hinder the U.S. advance.

Shortly after the war the Clark Field and Fort Stotsenburg were combined to form Clark Air Base. In 1949 responsibility for the station was transferred from the U.S. Army Air Corps to the U.S. Air Force. In the ensuing years, a somewhat backward, backwater installation was transformed into a huge, urbanized complex that featured numerous logistical and entertainment facilities, including what is reputed to be one of the best golf courses in Asia. In 1964 the air force completed work on the Regional Medical Center, a two-hundred-bed hospital that was considered quite progressive at the time. During the Vietnam War, the medical center was used extensively, and Clark itself was employed as a staging base for operations.

The relationship between the base and the city, similar to the relationship between the Philippines and the United States, became strained in the late 1960s. In 1968 a number of attacks on U.S. personnel by Filipinos caused the then-base commander to establish a curfew for servicemen. The Angeles city officials responded by declaring their town off-limits to Americans. Recriminations were followed by demonstrations by cadres of Filipino nationalists. Eventually, things were ironed out, but it was not the end of anti-base sentiment.

The U.S. bases at Angeles and Olongapo have always been controversial. In 1947 the Military Bases Agreement had provided the United States with a ninety-nine-year lease on the bases, much to the chagrin of many Philippine nationalists. The Rusk-Ramos Agreement in 1966 fixed the lease expiration date at 1991. In 1979 nearly 90 percent of Clark's 131,000 acres was returned to Philippine control. Clark was redesignated as a Philippine military base, but the United States was promised (and received) unhampered use of the facilities. These changes notwithstanding, the bases provided people from all points of the political spectrum ammunition for a passionate and often hyperbolic debate.

No one used the bases issue more skillfully than President Marcos. Throughout his twenty-two-year tenure, he publicly postured for two disparate audiences. For Filipino nationalists, he acknowledged the bases were an unwanted but perhaps necessary affront to Philippine sovereignty. As a third-world leader, he pledged to stand up to the United States, thus gaining more neutrality and respect for the Philippines. For the United States, Marcos positioned himself as a loyal ally and a strident anticommunist, agreeing that the bases were a critical component for the mutual defense of both countries. Beneath the masquerade was the simple fact that Marcos wanted money out of the United States. In the mid-1970s, at the height of his power, he contacted Washington, saying he needed "rent or a guaranteed level of military assistance."[5] The United States does not pay rent for any of its overseas installations, but it does dole out assistance. With the Philippines, it took the form of training and weaponry, as well as financial aid; however, it is theorized that much of this aid went directly into the bank accounts of Marcos and his cronies. Whether the succession of U.S. presidents suspected Marcos of enriching himself is not known, but the U.S. government turned a blind eye to him.

In the end, it was the Marcos regime that, perhaps ironically, hastened the bases' closure. The period from 1972, when he declared martial law, to his overthrow in 1986 saw the most concentrated anti-bases activity. Nearly all of it was tied to the anti-Marcos movement both in the Philippines and the United States. Particularly in the United States, where anti-Marcos coalitions were not fettered by the strongman's goons, the anti-bases plank was a large part of the opposition's propaganda platform. The coalitions were often formed by diverse groups, usually leftist in orientation. While Marcos claimed that his opposition consisted of communist-led or -inspired groups, a quick survey shows that this assertion was hardly true. For example, in the early 1980s, the U.S.-based Campaign Against Military Intervention in the Philippines consisted of such anti-Marcos groups as the Church Coalition for Human Rights in the Philippines, Clergy and Laity Concerned, Filipino Lawyers' Committee for Human Rights, and other similar organizations, many of which had strong ties to the Catholic, Mennonite, and Methodist churches. The Philadelphia-based Friends of the Filipino People drew in many American intellectuals, including Daniel Boone Schirmer. Other groups, such as the Philippine Solidarity Network and the Coalition Against the Marcos Dictatorship, were a miscellany of human rights activists, students, and professionals. Political refugees from the Philippines, often members of the elite class that Marcos overthrew, were sprinkled throughout all these groups. For example, the Movement for a

Free Philippines, perhaps the least left leaning of the groups, was led by Raul Manglapus, a prominent postwar politician in exile.

Communist groups also played in the anti-bases symphony. As the U.S.-based anti-Marcos groups, in the Philippines the CPP and its affiliated organizations, such as the National Democratic Front and the labor group Kilusang Mayo Uno (May First Labor Movement), made anti-bases appeals a major component of their propaganda. In publications such as the CPP's *Ang Bayan* and the NDF's *Liberation*, as well as the writing of leader Jose Sison, the bases were seen as the major source of Philippine dependency on the United States. In fact, the combination of the bases and the excesses of the Marcos regime made for an incredibly powerful rhetorical instrument.

The metaphorical entreaties both the anti-Marcos groups and the Communists used were primarily the same. Simply constructed here, the political argument went that because the bases existed for the mutual defense of both nations and because there had been no credible external threat to the Philippines since the end of World War II, the bases only served U.S. objectives. Given that the bases housed large numbers of personnel and equipment, possibly some of it nuclear, Clark and the Subic Bay installation served as magnets for nuclear attack. The bases violated Philippine sovereignty because by training the Philippine military in counterinsurgency programs, they invited U.S. intervention in internal Philippine affairs. It was a form of repression of the Filipino people. Up until 1986 the argument also emphasized that the bases kept Marcos in power through an infusion of financial aid. Finally, the bases acted as a springboard for U.S. intervention in other nations, making the Philippines an accomplice to America's imperialist ventures.

The anti-base groups made a strong social argument as well. Anti-Marcos groups claimed that servicemen's crimes against the civilians near the bases went unpunished. Filipino employees working at the bases were paid only one-eighth of the salary of U.S. workers. Prostitution was rampant in both Angeles and Olongapo. The bases fostered illegal activities such as smuggling post exchange (PX) commodities, drug trafficking, gambling and protection rackets, and all types of civic corruption. Given the large amount of U.S. money pouring in, the bases cultivated political and judicial corruption.

Logically, the anti-bases arguments were often effective. They often reinforced the dialectics with emotional components. A typical example of such propaganda appeared in an April 1983 issue of the CPP's *Ang Bayan*.

> There are glaring signs that US imperialism grossly violated Philippine sovereignty as it maintains its bases here. For one thing, US military personnel who commit crimes in the Philippines get off the hook quite easily, like the US sailor who was meted only one year in prison for repeatedly raping a number of young girls in Olongapo City. For another, the US marines who burned down six houses of peasants in Bataan last March have not been punished at all. Not the least to be forgotten are the 40 Filipinos who were killed in the bases from 1947 to 1977, some of whom were gunned down by American sentries who claimed to have mistaken them for wild boars.[6]

Messages such as this one were produced for more than two decades, but ultimately they were only partially successful in closing the bases. In September 1991, after a rancorous, emotional debate, the Philippine Senate voted to reject the proposed bases agreement that would have extended the life of the Clark and Subic installations. The debate had pitted pro-American senators against nationalist politicians, with each side representing long-standing currents in Philippine thought. It was a furious dispute, ripping Philippine public opinion neatly in halves. For years afterward the Left and nationalists would claim an overwhelming anti-American popular mandate; in reality, the treaty's rejection passed by one vote. In 1992 the last U.S. vessel, the USS *Belleau Wood*, sailed out of Subic Bay, ending an era.

The base closure discussions had been co-opted by Mount Pinatubo, which in June 1991 began a series of eruptions. On June 7 came the first magmatic eruption, and on the twelfth came a series of explosions that reached its climax on June 15. On that day Typhoon Yunya struck, and the combination of the volcanic ash and the storm reduced Central Luzon to wet, choking darkness. The Pinatubo eruption was ten times stronger than that of Mount St. Helens in 1980, and (disputably) eight hundred people were killed, many crushed under collapsed roofs. Fifty thousand square miles, mostly the provinces of Zambales, Pampanga, and Tarlac, were buried under inches of ash, and ash was recorded throughout all the islands and as far away as Malaysia. Rivers of lahar began to pour off the mountain and down into the flatlands, destroying fields and infrastructure. Problems with lahar continued for a decade, particularly during the rainy seasons. The eruption's effects on the affected area's population and economy were shocking.

Twenty-five miles away from the summit of Pinatubo, Angeles and Clark were in the heart of the cataclysm. Many but not all of the city's people were evacuated before the eruption. The base was evacuated and closed to all but security personnel by June 10. The installation suffered heavy damage. After months of analysis and consideration, the Stars and Stripes were removed from the base in November of that year, ending nearly a century of U.S.-Angeles union. The city and its American benefactor were now formally divorced.

What has replaced the base has been a work in progress. In 1992 the Philippine government passed legislation to convert Clark into a civilian enterprise to promote economic and social development. A year later the Clark Special Economic Zone was created, and it was supposed to work with its counterpart over in Subic. Roughly the size of Singapore, with its ready-made airport and infrastructure, Clark was envisioned as an industrial hub and aviation center. Recovering rapidly from Pinatubo, it became a duty-free zone in the mid-1990s, and shoppers from Manila travel to Angeles to purchase products made in America and Europe. Hotels and a casino were built. The Mimosa Leisure Estate is scheduled to be a world-class recreation center. A superb golf course, once the private domain of U.S. officers, is now open to all who can afford it. Today the complex is known as Clark Freeport, and it claims to employ twice as many workers as did the air force base.[7] Clark Field has been renamed the Diosdado Macapagal International Airport, after the former president.

Shadowing this development, however, has been the ongoing toxic waste controversy. During the near century the U.S. military used the Clark area (as well as Subic Bay), a wide variety of toxins found their way into the soil and water supply. These included solvents, heavy metals, asbestos, and pesticides. Government Accountability Office studies, as well as those by the Department of Defense, the World Health Organization, and private environmental companies, have all substantiated the existence of such poisons. Their effects, especially on the children living in these areas, have been doleful: hundreds of cases of abnormal births, kidney disease, impaired intelligence, and other toxic conditions have been reported since 1992.

As the poisons continue their work, both the U.S. and Philippine governments have shown no willingness to act. The U.S. government claims that it was not contractually bound to return the base areas to their original condition. A succession of Philippine administrations have raised the issue and then quietly let it go away. Environmental nongovernmental organizations (NGOs) have attempted to hold the United States accountable for pollution in the Clark-Subic areas and throughout the world but have achieved little. Given such inconsequence, a relic of the American period here might be a sick and dying Filipino child.[8]

While the U.S. government's presence is receding from the area, Americana lingers with the Americans who once served there. It is estimated that seven thousand Americans live in the Angeles area, the great majority of these former serviceman. With a lifeline strung by a monthly retirement check from the States, these men, ages forty to ninety, exist in a curious cultural enclave that deserves serious sociological scholarship. The community is held together by its organizations, such as the American Legion, the Veterans of Foreign Wars, and the Retiree Activities Office (RAO). The RAO is especially important: a self-funded group, it assists military retirees with immigration problems, taxes, and medical concerns.[9]

Another method of keeping the American memory alive in Angeles is through the Internet. Websites dedicated to the Clark experience focus on a variety of topics and include histories of the base, many photographs, and personal recollections. Although to many, Clark will always be a manifestation of American imperialism, it would be impossible not to see life here with the families, high school, athletics, and cars all as an absolutely normal and simple extension of an American town in the islands. Perhaps the most interesting, and certainly the most poignant, part of the websites are the message boards. Here one sees posts from Americans looking for anyone who remembers their parents, from Filipinos attempting to find their fathers, and from former servicemen trying to find old buddies or girlfriends.

One post came from a crew chief who was stationed at Clark at the end of the 1980s. Outside the gates a streetwise Filipino orphan named Bonk would always be there to guide him home after a rough night in the Angeles bars. The boy would make sure "that locals would stay away from me at an opportunistic situation [to mug him] [and] I remember him arguing with a guy that I was 'His' American . . . [i]t seemed whenever I needed eyes, he was there, like a ghost he would appear out of the dark grab my hand and at the least pull me toward the right direction till we made it to the main gate." Emotionally, the American regrets that he was too young to consider adopting the boy and plaintively wonders what became of him after Pinatubo. His post begs for any information about the former street waif. There were no replies to his message.[10]

THE PARADE GROUND

The Parade Ground at the old Fort Stotsenburg has always delighted me. It is a simple, large field, peaceful and stimulating, nestled between the high hills of the Bamban Range and the giant airstrips. The field is surrounded by old and impressive trees, whose species' names are identified on the small plaques hammered into them. Beyond the grounds were the buildings that now make up the Clark enterprise: stores, restaurants, housing, and, to the immediate east, a wonderful museum dedicated to the history of this place.

A museum is necessary, for much has happened here. Looking out over the field, I thought of the stories I had read and how these acres encapsulated the waves and events of the twentieth century. Stories of how before the war the U.S. Army cavalry officers would have their polo matches and afterward retire to cocktails and dinner in white jackets, their wives in long dresses, and Filipino servants at their beck and call. That life was ingloriously swept away by the Japanese, who planted crops in the field and rounded up and incarcerated Filipino women in nearby Angeles as sex slaves, the infamous "comfort women." Like a vengeful god, MacArthur arrived in 1945 as fire and smoke billowed from the battles raging in the mountains around the Parade Ground. Then a return to a peaceful existence of U.S. Air Force families playing baseball on the field, until it was covered by Pinatubo's ash.

I began to walk the perimeter of the field, using the sidewalk and reading the names of the trees. At roughly the midpoint of the south side, a type of gateway led into a narrow road that dissected the field in half. The gateway was constructed of two white concrete posts with the name of the fort painted in black letters, perhaps six feet high, on each side of the road and was flanked by two large monuments. The posts had a story themselves. The actual location for the two white pillars used to be on what was called Bong Highway, now M. L. Quezon Avenue. When the Japanese took control of the area, they used the posts as fill for one of the nearby runways. Incredibly, the posts were unearthed by accident in 1965 and found to be intact. They were moved here to serve as an entranceway to the old field.

The gate's two monuments were recently made statues that commemorated the Philippine-American War. To the right of the road was a trio of American soldiers on horseback, carrying rifles and a flag. Curiously, their heads were turned over their left shoulders to the south, toward Angeles. The figures seemed timid and uncertain. They were looking away from what faced them on the left side of road. There, a large cannon surrounded by five Filipino soldiers was pointed at the Americans. One soldier was depicted as loading ammunition while another was seen pointing toward the hapless cavalrymen. Between them the narrow road went through the vacant field, leading to the rash of hotels, golf courses, casinos—all sitting above possibly poisoned ground—and the future of this place.

GARFIELD'S LAST STAND

Garfield's Last Stand is a corner bar with a huge curved window that commands a view of the intersection between Fields Avenue and a rubble- and rubbish-paved side street whose name even its residents probably do not know. The window is Mylar coated, so that passersby see only their reflections as they look in while the occupants inside indulge in snug voyeurism. The bar's air-conditioning works quietly and efficiently. Unlike most of the Fields Avenue venues, no megabass Euro-club music booms here. Although there is music, it is on so low that no one is listening. Likewise, the muted television is on, but no one is watching. Instead, it is the patrons' conversations that are important in Garfield's.

This simple place is a U.S. Special Forces bar. Its high wooden tables are kept clean. The floor is swept. The wall decor is not exceptionally garish. Perhaps most eye-catching is its collection of soldiers' photos neatly pinned to the bulletin board on the wall. Most of these photos seem to be thirty years old; some are perhaps older. There is a black-and-white photo of a young sailor. Another picture, clearly of the Vietnam era, is of a beret-topped Special Forces soldier jauntily holding an M16 and sporting an absolutely splendid Clark Gable mustache. Others are of soldiers in various uniforms, some holding drinks, some holding girls. All of these pictures are of young men.

The five customers that day at Garfield's sat around one of the tall tables attended to by the staff, young women in modest attire: white blouses, Texas string ties, and plain skirts. The women were quiet and unassuming, hustling nothing and no one, simply supplying drinks when needed, then returning to their own table to resume their conversation in a provincial dialect. The drinks today for the five customers were rum and Cokes, Manhattans, and bourbon on the rocks. No beer. These were not beer men.

They were in their late fifties or early sixties. Undoubtedly strong, energetic men in their youth, they sat now with red and flaccid faces, a gray beard here, and a speckled but still splendid Clark Gable mustache there. Shorts and sandals were the uniform these days. The T-shirts only accentuated the remarkable bellies nearly all of them sported. Their loud, American-accented voices at times cracked after decades of smoke and drink.

In the cool air and mildly diffused light, the drinks glistened in their glasses as the young faces and impressive uniforms stared down from the wall, all providing a strange sense of serenity. These men were at ease here, and listening to their conversation, one would get the impression that they looked back on their lives with a sure sense of accomplishment. In fact, their conversation today, and probably most days, was a history lesson, a tutorial on the triumphs of U.S. Special Operations Forces in Asia and around the world—in Vietnam, in the Philippines, in the Middle East. Who better to give the lecture than the cream of America's military?

But there were both philosophy and religion here as well. A small notice on the wall reads, "I don't have a drinking problem. I drink. I get drunk. I fall down. No problem." Another: "No one is ugly at 2 am," while still another declaratively stated, "I love Johnny Cash." On one pillar hangs a plaque inscribed with so-called ten commandments, including, "Thou shalt remember that a bar fine [a tryst with a prostitute] is cheaper than alimony" and "Thou shalt remember in the Philippines thou art a walking ATM [automatic teller machine]." Directly across from it, on another pillar, was a Special Forces calendar. At the bottom of the page was a note to remember the Nick Rowe memorial.

It is a near-forgotten name from near-forgotten circumstances. James "Nick" Rowe was an American champion and a Special Forces legend.[11] A West Point graduate from Texas, he went to Vietnam with the Special Forces in 1963. That year, while serving as an adviser to South Vietnamese irregulars in the Mekong Delta, he was captured by the Viet Cong and spent the next five years and two months as a prisoner, confined mostly to a bamboo cage. Sickness, torture, and failed escape attempts marked his detention. His captors named him "Mr. Trouble."

But in December 1968 he did escape. On New Year's Eve Rowe saw an unexpected flight of U.S. helicopters coming over the treetops. He impulsively knocked down his guards and ran to a clearance where the choppers saw him, wearing the black prisoner pajamas that closely resembled the Viet Cong's uniforms. After a moment of indecision (some thought he was the enemy), the U.S. force picked him up. Rowe was one of only thirty-four Americans to escape captivity during the entire war. During his five years of imprisonment, he had been promoted from a lieutenant to a major.

With freedom came the evolution of the man. Back in his hometown of McAllen, Texas, there were parades in his honor, and he gave speeches in football stadiums. But Rowe was more than just a returned Vietnam hero; he was a renaissance man, a soldier-poet, perhaps a Sir Philip Sidney wearing a green beret. A warrior he certainly was, but he was also a writer and a teacher. His prison diary, which he originally wrote in German, Spanish, Chinese, and his own code to mislead his captors, was published in 1971 as *Five Years to Freedom*. In 1977 he both coauthored the novel *The Washington Connection* with Robin Moore and Lew Perdue and published his first novel, *The Judas Squad*.

He is also remembered for his pedagogical contributions to the Special Forces. In 1971 he published the *Southeast Asia Survival Journal*, which he wrote for the U.S. Air Force. After being recalled to active duty in 1981, he designed the Survival, Evasion, Resistance, and Escape (SERE) training course at the U.S. Army Special Forces School at Fort Bragg, North Carolina. This course is still considered to be the most important advanced training in the Special Operations Forces' field. Taught at the John F. Kennedy Special Warfare Center and School, SERE trains soldiers to avoid capture and, if caught, to survive and return home with honor.

Now Lieutenant Colonel Rowe, he was assigned to the Philippines in 1987 as the chief of the army division of the Joint U.S. Military Advisory Group, the counterinsurgency program fighting the communist New People's Army.[12] Rowe set up his own intelligence network, which became immediately successful. At that time, the NPA was in a state of convulsion: suspecting government infiltration, it was hysterically assassinating large numbers of its own cadres. Rowe and his special agents, in conjunction with the CIA, was indeed involved with the successful penetration of the NPA. But the mission's success came with perhaps predicable consequences. In early 1989 he wrote to Washington that there would be major terrorist acts in the Philippines and that he himself was targeted for assassination. He sent his Bible and his green beret home to his wife.

In Quezon City, on April 21, 1989, Rowe was returning to the U.S. Embassy. As one story puts it (and there are several), the air-conditioning in the chauffeured limousine was broken, and Rowe and the driver had cracked the bulletproof windows to ease the stifling heat. As they waited in traffic, a small white car pulled alongside. The hooded NPA cadres inside opened fire with an M16 and a .45-caliber pistol. Rowe, unarmed, died instantly.

The National Democratic Front, the communist umbrella group, crowed about the colonel's death. *Liberation*, the voice of the NDF, reported that "New People's Army guerrillas punished" Rowe. The NPA released a statement: "The death of Colonel Rowe signifies the firm commitment as the revolutionary forces to continue military actions against US personnel, as these are manifestations of the arrogant trampling of US imperialism on the people's independence and sovereignty."[13]

Rowe was buried in Arlington National Cemetery. His gravestone reads, "Killed by terrorists." His murderers were captured and imprisoned. One was released in 2005, much to the State Department's chagrin.

Twenty years later there are stll questions regarding his murder. The most compelling is, how did the NPA know Rowe's travel plans? Because he constantly altered his routes, presumably only U.S. Embassy personnel had knowledge of his daily activities, and that observation raised interesting concerns. Further, why was Rowe unarmed if he knew he was on the NPA hit list? What about the mysterious theory about a Vietnamese communist officer working with the NPA to kill Rowe, presumably to seek vengeance on his escape decades earlier? It is doubtful that any of these questions will ever be satisfactorily answered.

Rowe's assassination was part of the awkward evolution of U.S.-Philippine military relations since the fall of Marcos, a relationship that has, in many ways, defined the Philippine nation and marked its national identity. The Mutual Defense Treaty of 1951 made the Philippines exclusively dependent on the United States for its external security. This secure relationship existed for forty years. But the years between 1990 and 1995 saw major changes in the U.S.-Philippine connection. As discussed in chapter 11, the Philippine Senate's narrow decision in 1991 to abolish the bases agreement led to the U.S. military's withdrawal from the country. The Pinatubo eruption and the closing of the U.S. bases sent shock waves throughout the Pacific Rim, whose governments were comfortable living underneath or at least close to the American military umbrella. With the bases gone and with the Chinese becoming more assertive in the international arena, Southeast Asian nations became edgy, while the United States had to rethink its position in Asia. This reevaluation brought America back to the islands.

For several years after the U.S. withdrawal, Filipinos, especially the Left and the nationalists, rollicked in the fact that for the first time in several centuries there were no foreign troops on the archipelago. A palatable well-being, not quite euphoria, gripped the public: America, their old conqueror-benefactor-liberator-oppressor, had left. The nation was finally on its own. In 1995, however, a tense dispute between China, Vietnam, and the Philippines over the ownership of the Spratly Islands in the oil-rich South China Sea rocked the region. The Philippine government under President Fidel Ramos shivered in its newly won military independence. Ramos decided to invite U.S. forces back on a limited basis. The vehicle to do this was the Visiting Forces

Agreement (VFA), a negotiated concord designed to increase U.S. presence in the area. During its introduction in 1998, through its passage in the Philippine Senate, and its implementation the next year, the VFA created an uproar in the Philippines, similar to those during the bases debate just a few years before. The turbulence continues today.

At first glance, there is nothing remarkable about the agreement. The VFA's intent was to strengthen security in the Pacific area, to allow U.S. forces to visit the Philippines, to define the treatment of U.S. troops while on Philippine soil, to reaffirm the Mutual Defense Treaty, and to promote the countries' common security interests. In practice, its chief aim was to allow U.S. ships into Philippine ports and to permit U.S. and Philippine troops to train together. Both countries felt that it was in their national interests to have combined military maneuvers on Philippine soil. The United States has similar VFA-type relationships with other countries that engendered little or no resentment from the local population. But the Philippines was once an American colony, and resistance to the VFA has been intense.

In general, today's opposition to the VFA has centered on a number of issues that existed when the bases were still in operation. One is the fear of nuclear weapons. The United States has a policy of neither confirming nor denying that its ships or planes carry nuclear weapons, and the Filipinos felt that the VFA would provide the United States an opportunity to put such devices on Philippine soil. Second, some worried that by allowing the Americans to work with and train Philippine troops, the VFA would actually be serving as an instrument of human rights abuse; indeed, as noted earlier, the United States played a crucial support role in developing anticommunist civilian militias that terrified the provinces. Perhaps most galling, however, was the sovereignty issues. The VFA gives immunity from Philippine prosecution to U.S. personnel who commit crimes while on duty. It also allows U.S. troops to travel in the Philippines without passports or driver's licenses. For many, then, it was as if the bases had reopened.

The hostility to the VFA and to the ensuing combined military exercises has been vocal and widespread. Predictably, the Philippine Left has been in the vanguard of the dissidence. Much of the anti-VFA rhetoric echoes the major tenets commonly found in their earlier propaganda. For example, since the treaty's inception the CPP has issued statements saying the VFA was to be used to preposition U.S. troops in its client states without incurring the costs of keeping bases and was thus an instrument to restructure its global imperialist ambitions. Moreover, the CPP said the VFA was designed to allow the United States to conduct "wars of aggression against other countries, especially those in the Asia-Pacific region opposed to US hyper power hegemony." GABRIELA, a "legal wimmin's organization which opposes imperialism, feudalism, and bureaucrat capitalism," argued the VFA was unneeded given that the Philippines has no external enemies and that a U.\$. presence would only attract aggressors. Furthermore, American soldiers in the Philippines would only result in the exploitation of Philippine women by fostering prostitution. The League of Filipino Students issued a statement asking "all patriotic and progressive forces to unite against the VFA. Let us expose the pro-imperialist character of this regime which allows the intensified foreign domination over the country. Death to Imperialism!"[14] As the century ended, a coalition of leftist groups calling itself the Junk the VFA Movement began to protest the Balikatan Exercises, or the "shoulder-to-shoulder" maneuvers by the U.S. and Philippine armed forces.

Not all opposition to the VFA has come from the Far Left. In fact, a major opponent of the treaty has been the Catholic Church. In 1998 the Catholic Bishop's Conference of the Philippines (CBCP) began an anti-VFA signature campaign, as well as the reading of VFA pastoral statements during or after masses. A CBCP spokesperson called the VFA "one-sided as it was made between a master and a lackey," and the bishops expressed strong concern over treaty provisions that would allow possible nuclear weapons in the country and give the U.S. military the right to exercise jurisdiction over its servicemen.[15] The Ecumenical Bishops Forum, a coalition of Catholic and mainstream Protestant denominations, produced a statement that read in part that the VFA "is an evil spirit" that would bring "untold destruction."[16]

From the perspective of both the Philippine and U.S. governments, the arrangement could not be understood without accounting for the threat of terrorism in the country, a component VFA opponents rarely discuss.[17] Terrorism, revolution, and the potential for social collapse have shaded the country for nearly forty years and longer if one counts the Huk movement of the early 1950s. As described earlier, the CPP, through the NPA, has overseen a communist insurgency since 1969. Reaching its zenith in the mid-1980s, the party saw its power diminish greatly, although not completely, after its disastrous boycott of the 1986 election and the rise of the anticommunist groups designed and promoted by the CIA and the U.S. military. The NPA still operates in most of the country's provinces, but its numbers are nowhere near the high-water mark of the late Marcos years. In 2002 President Bush had the CPP and its NPA placed on the U.S. list of terrorist groups, and it has pressured the government of the Netherlands to revoke the visa of the party's leader in exile, Jose Sison. In 2005 the European Union placed the CPP and the NPA on its list of terrorist groups. These measures seem to have substantially curbed the organization's ability to carry out effective operations.

With the communist threat in relative, but perhaps temporary, decline, the greatest terrorist threat in the Philippines comes from the various Muslim extremists. The Muslim insurgency is multifarious and includes at least three major groups and one smaller organization, all with different characters and agendas yet all with common ideological elements. Perhaps the most notorious is the Abu Sayyaf Group (Bearer of the Sword), a fierce band of Islamist extremists with a proclivity for kidnapping. Operating out of western Mindanao and the Sulu islands, it gained fame in 2001 when it kidnapped a group of tourists, including two American missionaries. One of the Americans was killed in a rescue attempt by the military in 2002, but another American tourist had been beheaded. The group has ties to al Qaeda: reportedly Abu Sayyaf provided support for Ramzi Yousef, the al Qaeda operative convicted of bombing the World Trade Center in 1993.

Extensive pressure by the U.S.-supported Philippine military effectively weakened the Abu Sayyaf in Basilan and the Sulu Islands in 2001, but the group rebuilt. Under the leadership of Khadaffy Janjalani, Abu Sayyaf temporarily abandoned its penchant for kidnappings and turned to urban terror. In 2004 it claimed responsibility (along with the Rajah Solaiman Islamic Movement) for the bombing of a SuperFerry vessel in Manila Bay, which killed more than one hundred people. Three simultaneous bombings in three different cities in 2005 demonstrated that Abu Sayyaf had high levels of technical and organizational competence.

The United States was quick to move against the Abu Sayyaf after 9/11. In 2002 it consigned thirteen hundred troops to work with the AFP on Basilan Island. Three years later it worked again with the AFP on operations in western Mindanao. One of the primary objectives of the combined work has been to destroy Abu Sayyaf training grounds and to kill or capture Janjalani and other leaders. Furthermore, the U.S.-Philippine maneuvers have trained police officers and conducted civil affairs and humanitarian efforts in Abu Sayyaf's areas of operations.

The Americans' presence seems to be having some effect. The Philippine and U.S. governments enjoyed a tremendous public relations bonanza in January 2007 when DNA testing by the Federal Bureau of Investigation (FBI) confirmed that a body found by the AFP was that of Khadaffy Janjalani. Janjalani once had a bounty of $5 million on his head and had been on the FBI's Most Wanted Terrorists List since 2001. He was assumed killed in September 2006 in a clash with government soldiers stationed in Jolo. The battle was part of Operation Ultimatum, which began in August 2006. A second Abu Sayyaf commander, Abu Solaiman, was also slain in Jolo while fighting with the AFP in January 2007. In June 2007 the Philippine media carried pictures of U.S. Ambassador Kristie Kenney hugging Muslim women in Sulu after awarding $10 million to informants who tipped the government as to the whereabouts of Janjalani and Solaiman.[18] While these losses surely have had a devastating effect on the terrorist group's morale, it is doubtful that the Abu Sayyaf will be eradicated anytime soon. Rather, the group will exist, at least for a moment, as a low-level security threat but one capable of quickly expanding. Events in 2008 and 2009—shootouts, kidnappings, beheadings—demonstrate that the group has rebounded well.

Another Islamist extremist group is Jeemah Islamiyah (Islamic Organization), a pan-Southeast Asian group whose exact size and makeup are murky. It gained world attention by killing more than two hundred people in the 2002 bombing of a Bali nightclub. It has also claimed responsibility for suicide and car bombings in Indonesia. In the Philippines, a series of bombings in Manila in December 2000 killed twenty-two people. Fathur Rahman al-Ghozi, leader of a Filipino cell of Jeemah Islamiyah, confessed to the bombings and was later convicted and imprisoned on explosives charges.

He escaped from prison and died after a shootout with police. The extent of Jeemah Islamiyah's presence and influence among Philippine Muslims is uncertain, but it does exist.

Perhaps the most chilling is the mysterious Rajah Solaiman Islamic Movement (RSIM). While nearly all the Muslim extremists are from the Mindanao area, the RSIM comprises northern Filipinos who are mostly Muslim converts from Christianity. The RSIM call themselves reverts for they maintain that Filipinos were Muslims until colonized by the Spanish. The importance of the RSIM is that it can strike Manila and other large Luzon cities. Philippine officials uncovered a planned bombing in Manila in 2004, and the RSIM helped carry out the horrific ferryboat bombing. In 2005 it bombed a Makati commuter bus, killing several passengers. Significantly, the group has worked together with the Abu Sayyaf Group and the two large Muslim independence groups—the Moro National Liberation Front (MNLF) and the Moro Islamic Liberation Front (MILF).

Philippine administrations have been dealing with the MNLF and MILF, which have led the Muslim insurrection since the Marcos administration, often with some degree of success. In 1996 the MNLF signed a peace treaty with the government that gave four provinces in Mindanao limited autonomy. Since then, the MILF took over the leading role in the insurrection, advocating a complete break with the Manila government and an independent Muslim state in Mindanao. It has worked closely with the Abu Sayyaf Group and the Jeemah Islamiyah, providing training and organizational support to both groups. The Arroyo government has entered into peace negotiations with the MILF, but Washington and many in Manila have doubted the sincerity of the MILF leadership. In 2007, in an attempt to free kidnapped Italian priest Giancarlo Rossi, fourteen Filipino Marines were killed (ten beheaded) by alleged splinter groups of the MILF and the Abu Sayyaf Group on Basilan Island. While Father Rossi was eventually freed, trust in the MILF may have been permanently destroyed.

The effectiveness of Philippine counterterrorism efforts against the Muslim insurgency is at least in part to the Balikatan operations, or the practical application of the VFA. The World Trade Center attack led the Bush administration to cast a severe eye toward the Abu Sayyaf Group's connection to al Qaeda. President Arroyo quickly allowed the United States to send troops to help train the AFP in antiterrorist methods. Other measures followed. The military logistics and support agreement was signed in November 2002, allowing the United States to store matériel in the Philippines for use throughout the region. Earlier that year Special Operations personnel, part of a thirteen-hundred-man-strong contingent, trained and advised the AFP. The U.S. military took a strictly non-combat role because the Philippine Constitution forbade the use of foreign troops on its soil. U.S. soldiers, by agreement, took orders from Filipino officers and could not, unless attacked, use any type of force.

The relatively passive nature of U.S. Special Forces paid dividends. On Basilan Island, the Abu Sayyaf Group's stronghold and where the Balikatan Exercises were held, insurgent ranks fell drastically. But continued Abu Sayyaf Group bombings and operations on Jolo Island led the U.S. and Philippine governments to develop a more aggressive plan. In early 2003 U.S. Special Operations Forces were scheduled to integrate with AFP platoons, with substantial U.S. Navy support positioned offshore. Thus, the Americans would not be restrained to a passive role; rather, the U.S. forces, including AH-1 Cobra helicopters and AV-8B Harrier jets, could be requested by AFP commanders.

The Philippine public's reaction to the plan was illustrative of the ironic position in which President Arroyo, as well as other Philippine presidents, have found themselves. Pragmatic people saw the advantage of using U.S. assistance to eradicate the terrorists. But leftist and nationalist politicians, as well as many media writers, admonished the Arroyo government for planning to use foreign troops in a combat role on Philippine land. Muslim leaders worried that there would be anti-American repercussions. The plan was scrapped, and the rules of engagement for U.S. troops were rethought. It would not be until 2005 that the Balikatan maneuvers would resume, with, once again, American troops assuming a passive role. The irony here is noteworthy: the country has been faced with a long-standing, cancerous insurgency, marked by despicable acts of terrorism, that the AFP has not been able to destroy. The United States, the legal military partner of the Philippines, has shown the willingness and the ability to help the AFP defeat the insurgency. Both the Arroyo and Bush governments were prevented in destroying the insurgency because of Philippine political and emotional sentiments that abhor any U.S. role in the country's affairs.

Philippine popular culture clearly strains under the inability to come to terms with its past or future relationships with the United States. Perhaps nothing represents this conflict better than the Subic rape case and its connection to the VFA. On November 3, 2005, a twenty-two-year-old Filipina filed a complaint in Olongapo City (the once raunchy navy town that sits on Subic Bay) against six U.S. Marines from the USS *Essex*, which was then visiting the Philippines. The servicemen were on liberty after taking part in the 2005 Balikatan counterterrorism maneuvers. The complainant claimed that she had met the soldiers that night in a bar frequented by U.S. servicemen, spent the night dancing with them, and later, while intoxicated, was gang-raped by the six Americans inside a van. The U.S. Embassy promised full cooperation, and the Philippine government promised an impartial investigation.[19]

The case quickly became an imbroglio. The driver of the van—the only witness to the event—retracted his initial sworn statement that a rape did occur; he claimed the police forced him to make such a statement. The woman's mother went on television to ask for justice for her daughter. The servicemen were placed under the custody of the U.S. Embassy, as per the statutes of the VFA concerning off-duty personnel. This act caused pandemonium. GABRIELA, the radical women's group with ties to communist organizations, called for President Arroyo to seek Philippine jurisdiction and cancel the joint Philippine-U.S. military operations. Other leftist groups followed suit, and soon anti-American demonstrations were being held outside the Olongapo City Hall.

In December 2005 rape charges were filed against four of the Marines—the other two had proved they were not at the scene—and the Filipino van driver was charged as a coconspirator. The next month the Philippine secretary of foreign affairs claimed the Philippines should take actual custody of the four accused. Although the driver of the van had all charges against him dropped, the four Marines were formally arrested. The U.S. government immediately invoked paragraph 6 of the VFA and retained custody. More anti-American demonstrations by militant groups followed.

Throughout 2006 the affair became even more chaotic, pitting leftist forces against the United States and the Arroyo government. The alleged victim, who used the court-appointed pseudonym "Nicole" and who was, it was revealed, dating another American serviceman when the alleged event occurred, went on television to deny she worked in the sex trade. Furthermore, she publicly called on the court to imprison her rapists for life. The case was moved out of Olongapo and into Makati. One day before the scheduled arraignment, known leftist personalities joined the panel of Nicole's private prosecutors: former vice president Teofisto Guingona, former senator Rene Saguisag, and former University of the Philippines College of Law dean Pacifico Agabin. Their feelings toward the U.S. military could not have been clearer: both Guingona and Saguisag had voted against renewing the U.S. bases' leases in 1991, and Guingona had voted against the VFA in 1999. The prosecution unsuccessfully attempted to have paragraph 6 of the VFA, which allowed the accused to remain in U.S. custody, declared unconstitutional. Adding fuel to the fire, Senator Joker Arroyo, the leftist anti-Marcos and anti-American luminary, called the U.S. soldiers "sex terrorists."[20]

The trial began on June 2. Witnesses said they saw Nicole drinking heavily and dancing with the Americans in the bar. Two of the bar's bouncers saw Nicole, apparently very intoxicated, riding on the back of one of the Marines and being put inside the van. Sometime later, witnesses said they saw Nicole, with her pants pulled down, being carried out of the van and dumped on the pavement. Two policemen discovered and comforted her, but at no time did she claim to the officers that she had been raped. Then she went back into the bar. She would not claim rape for several more days. One of the Marines, Lance Cpl. Daniel Smith, who was twenty years old at the time of the alleged crime, claimed that he did have consensual sex with "an Asian female" inside the van as his buddies cheered him on. Meanwhile, the sanctity of the courtroom evaporated, if it ever really existed, as various persons involved in the case gave interviews to the media: Nicole; one of the accused, Staff Sgt. Chad Carpentier; and the van driver. Climatically, Nicole took the stand and identified Smith as her rapist.

As the trial continued, leftist groups, Nicole, and her mother exerted pressure on the court and the government. Through television appearances, editorials, and websites, as well as public demonstrations, they called for the replacement of the government prosecutors, who, in their view, were not doing enough to convict the accused. Several groups formed the Justice for

Nicole, Justice for Our Nation Coalition, which began to protest against the government. On November 1, 2006, one year to the day after the alleged rape, Nicole, now a national figure, led a rally at Subic. The next day police in Manila had to violently disperse a similar demonstration held by the League of Filipino Students, a major element of the leftist coalition. Nicole began to meet with legislators, accusing the court of incompetence.

In early December 2006, on national television, the court found Corporal Smith guilty of rape, with Judge Benjamin Pozon calling the act "bestial . . . chilling, naked sadism." As the verdict was read, activists in the courtroom chanted, "Jail him! Jail him!" Smith was subsequently sentenced to forty years in prison. The three other Marines were acquitted. The judges ordered that Smith be confined in the Manila jail before his appeal was heard, which was in direct violation of the U.S. interpretation of the VFA's terms. He was also ordered to pay Nicole 100,000 pesos ($2,000, and the average annual wage in the Philippines is $800) in compensatory and moral damages.

Accustomed to seeing justice prejudiced by political and emotional considerations, many Filipinos initially felt sympathy for Smith. Some wondered at how Nicole could first claim she was raped by six soldiers, then four, then one. If Smith was actually guilty and if the three other Marines were cheering him on as a rape occurred as claimed, they would need to be convicted as coconspirators; but they were released. The prosecution also prohibited the van's driver, the only other witness to the event, from testifying. The fact that all parties were admittedly drunk, that Nicole's evidence against Smith was completely uncorroborated, and that the three other Marines in the van testified that the sex was consensual, all gave some Filipinos pause. They wondered if a forty-year sentence, which was far above what is normally given to Filipinos for rape offensives, was deserved. Suspicions were rife that Smith had become a sacrificial lamb offered to the Left, a victim of the divided attitudes Filipinos have of the U.S. military presence.

Despite some Filipinos' initial sympathy, the verdict, the first time an American soldier was convicted of a crime since the early 1990s and the first since the establishment of the VFA, was seen as a landmark victory for women's rights and Philippine nationalism. After the decision was read, GABRIELA quickly issued the following statement: "True justice for Nicole can only be achieved with the abrogation of the US-RP Visiting Forces Agreement. Justice cannot be complete if the threat against Filipino women and children represented by the VFA and US military intervention is not removed."[21]

Surprisingly, GABRIELA almost got its wish. The United States reacted with uncustomary spitefulness to the verdict. On December 22 Adm. William J. Fallon announced that the United States would cancel the huge, annual binational Balikatan Exercises, as well as aid and reconstruction programs, until he felt sure that U.S. servicemen's rights were protected. The Philippine government publicly agreed with the U.S. position that Smith should remain in the custody of the U.S. Embassy and, quietly and without a court order, moved Smith to the embassy, further infuriating the Philippine Left. After the diplomatic dust settled, the Balikatan Exercises resumed without fanfare in March 2007, but no war games were held; rather, U.S. and Philippine troops built roads and schoolhouses in Jolo, the impoverished bastion of the Abu Sayyaf Group.[22]

Ultimately, it seemed that both the U.S. and Philippine governments played into the hands of the leftist and nationalist sentiments.[23] The trial and the Americans' refusal to hand over the convicted prisoner to Philippine authorities rekindled the flame of anti-Americanism, which has not burned as brightly since the 1960s, when U.S. soldiers shot and killed several Filipinos who were trespassing on military soil. For some, the "ugly American" had returned; for others, he had never left. Rina Jimenez-David, a normally levelheaded columnist writing for the *Philippine Daily Inquirer*, a nationalist and anti-American newspaper, said this about the trial:

> We did have our "Nicole-moment." That day when the Philippine Senate voted to reject the RP-US bases agreement. But even that resounding victory for the nationalist cause would ultimately be eroded by the VFA and the continuing presence of the American military on our soil. Which just goes to show that when Americans want to f—k with you, they'll f—k you any which way.[24]

Jimenez-David's comments are typical of the existing attitudes toward the United States in some segments of Philippine society. For certain, the VFA will continue to stoke anti-American feelings in the future. Happily, however, the case of Corporal Smith was resolved. In March 2009 Nicole publicly recanted her testimony, allowing Smith to leave his confinement in the U.S. Embassy. Nicole was given a U.S. visa and quickly emigrated.

The trial, however, sparked a renewed U.S. public relations effort. In July 2007 the USS *Peleliu* was involved in a project called Pacific Partnership and provided medical missions to areas in Cotabato, Tawi-Tawi, and Jolo, all with marked Muslim insurgent activities. In Bicol, volunteers from the *Peleliu* built thirty-five homes to complement the $5 million dollars in relief money that had been sent to the region after it had been hit with two devastating typhoons. Simultaneously, Ambassador Kristie Kenney doled out U.S. aid in high-profile events. In early July newspapers profiled Kenney inspecting U.S. Agency for International Development (USAID) projects in Central Mindanao and addressing the Women's Forum on Poverty Reduction. For her efforts the Filipinos conferred upon Ambassador Kenney the traditional Moro title of *babay-a-pinadtaya sa Kutawato* (adored and respected darling of Cotabato City). All this activity has caused not a few Filipinos to wonder aloud what the U.S. intentions are in the region and what the Americans will do to achieve them.[25]

FIELDS AVENUE

There is a long street that runs from the MacArthur Highway several miles along the south side of Clark. Collectively, the street is known as Fields Avenue, although at one point it is called Don Juico Street and at another it is Perimeter Road. This street is renowned in certain circles because it is ground zero for sexual tourism. It is a place where usually middle-class, middle-aged men from all over the Americas, Europe, Australia, and Japan come to meet poor young girls from all over the Philippine provinces. On Fields Avenue the lonely encounter the desperate.

As in Thailand, prostitution in Angeles owes much, perhaps everything, to the U.S. military. The trade began with the first U.S. camps at the beginning of the twentieth century. During the 1930s the army essentially regulated the brothels near the base by providing medical checkups for both the women and their American customers, an arrangement that continued until the pullout in 1991. Prostitution exploded, however, during the Vietnam War, when Angeles became an R & R destination for soldiers and airmen. In the 1980s prostitution reached its peak, with hundreds of bars and clubs lining Fields Avenue and adjacent streets in Barrio Balibago. The paroxysm caused varied reactions with the local population. Some Filipinos saw it as a distasteful necessity that assisted poor families. Many capitalized on the economic opportunities and the influx of dollars. Others made it part of a political platform.

The U.S. military's presence in Angeles and nearby Olongapo and the resulting prostitution were central points in nationalist and communist propaganda. Most of NDF's and GABRIELA's discussions concerning the bases in the 1980s referenced the U.S. involvement in sanctioning the oldest profession. Despite often hyperbolic claims, their arguments were usually sound: the U.S. military did institutionalize prostitution here, and it was an affront to Philippine national sensitivity and led to the degradation of women. After Pinatubo had all but destroyed Olongapo, seriously damaged Angeles, and hastened the U.S. military's withdrawal, the bars and clubs nearly disappeared.

What happened next is quite interesting. Slowly during the mid-1990s, the clubs resurrected, but this time they catered to sporting gentlemen from all over the world. Fields Avenue quickly reclaimed its place on the world's sex trade stage. Now the street was crowded not with young GI Joes but fortysomething bankers from Brisbane and accountants from Osaka. Remarkably, the Philippine Left remained relatively mute about the resurgence of the flesh trade in Angeles. It seemed that as long as there were no American soldiers involved the women could still practice their craft with foreigners.

Even though the U.S. military is gone from Fields Avenue, its memory remains. The street is characteristically clogged with jeepneys, and their routes, painted on each vehicle, remind passengers of the entrances to the former giant base: Friendship Gate, Checkpoint, and Main Gate. Coming down Fields Avenue, one will pass the American Hotel and the American Legion. Even the clubs' names echo America: the Roadhouse, the Alaska Club, Midnight Rodeo, and, perhaps the oldest bar on the street, the DMZ (demilitarized zone). One can actually see former U.S. military men ambling up and down the street, their bellies bouncing and sheathed pool cues in hand. But it is their philosophy that owes most to the U.S. military—that is, the instilled attitude of outright exclusiveness of being a superior foreign man in a subservient foreign land.

At about 8:00 p.m., the street comes alive. From out of hotels and the backs of jeepneys, hopping from trikes or rented vans, men will converge on the street. They represent all mankind: Germans in dark shirts; Americans in jeans; polite Japanese, who travel in groups of three or four; Australians easily recognizable in their uniforms of sleeveless T-shirts, shorts, and sandals; and Koreans, the latest arrivals, looking slightly unsure of themselves. In the early evening some will already have a teenage girl on their arm; most will not yet. All these men will have paid a considerable sum of money to walk on this cracked macadam street, where the tropical humidity fuses with neon and exhaust and alcohol and music; they are in this artificial Eden looking for a redemption of their own definition. Absolution can be found in any one of the clubs that line the street all the way down to the MacArthur Highway.

Prostitution is illegal in the Philippines. In Angeles, however, sex is available for money, and the modus operandi is the bar fine. The transaction happens much like this: in any given club a man sees a girl, decides he likes her, and buys her a drink. If the customer wants the girl, and if the girl is willing, the man will contact the *mamasan* (the older female who manages the girls) to pay the bar fine. Officially, the bar fine simply pays the establishment so the girl can leave before the end of her work shift. If the girl does leave with the customer, what happens next is entirely up to both parties. The girl does get a cut of the bar fine, but if she wants more money, she must rely on a tip, or gift, from the customer. It is at this juncture where the obvious occurs.

Foreigners own and operate the bars for the pleasure of foreigners in a system set up for the benefit of one group largely at the expense of another. Rarely are Filipino men seen in the bars. These places do not practice segregation; rather, most local men cannot afford the Western prices for either the beer or the girls. So the Filipinos either do not frequent the bars or have been subjugated into positions of servitude, perhaps as bartenders or dishwashers, while the Filipinas are in positions of carnal convenience. In these places the foreign man can sit in smug superiority, knowing he has men to serve him and women to please him. It was surely like this when the Americans ran Angeles just twenty years ago. Looking further back, the Fields Avenue adventure certainly must be related to the one felt by the Americans sitting in the Manila Hotel or the Army and Navy Club in the 1920s. True, the glasses of champagne served on linen tablecloths have been replaced by bottles of San Miguel over Formica, but the basic concept is still there: foreign men exert their will here, carving out a place of their own in a land that is not theirs.

Fields Avenue is perhaps one of the last frontiers of colonialism, a boozy, nocturnal relic of the great American experiment a century before. But the culture changes when the foreigner leaves the neon sanctity of the club and ventures farther away from Fields. Several blocks down past Checkpoint, connecting with Fields Avenue and running nearly parallel to the MacArthur Highway, is a narrow street with a rather schizophrenic atmosphere. On the right side walking toward the highway, one sees a row of apartment houses, all connected, mostly quiet and dark, and seemingly unused and vacant. On the left side is a newly built series of cantinas and karaoke bars, loud, confused, and bright, where young people sit on plastic chairs, eating and drinking. The night air is heavy from the charcoal fires. One hears laughter and singing. It is a warm, comfortable place. There are no foreigners here.

The row of "karaokes" used to be located a block up on Fields Avenue, right across the street from all of the bars. They were ramshackle then, just poorly lit tin shacks sitting on a dirt lot. The sight of these loud and slightly onerous-looking structures conflicted with the sparkling grandeur of the foreign-owned emporiums, such as the Bunny Ranch, Brown Sugar, and Camelot, on the other side of the street. Apparently, the city decided everyone would be better served if these shacks were torn down and their customers moved to newer shacks out of the tourists' sight. Now the old karaokes have been replaced by a long structure resembling a strip mall, housing the new sing-a-longs and a string of small stores selling cell phones, cell phone parts, and cell phone cards.

I stopped in at Tessie's karaoke stall. Like the others, it is a Visayan place; the row of stalls here might contain families from Cebu or Negros or Bicol. Immigrants within their own country, these Visayan people have scrimped and saved and now own little places here in Pampanga. Sitting comfortably in a chair on the sidewalk amid the shockingly wide and bright smiles of the young people, I listened to a girl belt out the old warhorse "Torn Between Two Lovers" on the machine. In front of me was the black wall of apartments, a strange nothingness blocking my view of the lights of Fields Avenue.

I looked at the young people here at Tessie's. Many were certainly from the same barrio, and some were surely related. These kids grew up together, were classmates, and knew everyone else's families. They were having a splendid time with their Red Horse malt beer and plates of noodles or rice. And why not have a good time? Dollars were coming in from their sisters or cousins or girlfriends or wives who were just a street away, frenetically trying to sell themselves to a foreigner. If everyone here was not so happy, I might have thought the situation a bit odd.

THE VETERANS OF FOREIGN WARS POST

Post 2485 is the largest Veterans of Foreign Wars (VFW) post in Asia.[26] It sits on a street just behind Fields Avenue, housed in an attractive faux stucco complex, right next to the Clarkview Christian Center. The center is run by the Church of God, which, as its inscription says, is a ministry to the military. In fact, the post sponsors the center. I noticed in the entranceway, right off the reserved parking spaces for the post commander and his deputy, several large plaques announcing this post's community achievement awards for the past several years.

Once inside, the Pampangan morning heat and dust immediately gave way to air-conditioned comfort and clean floors. The decor followed a U.S. military theme, not surprisingly. In the bar hung an inspirational print of two eagle portraits side by side against a background of the American and the Philippine flags. Its title declared, "These colors don't run." Nearby was a stirring print of the battleship USS *Missouri* at the USS *Arizona* Memorial in Pearl Harbor, with a caption that impassionedly read, "The beginning and the end" and "guarding her sister." Between the two prints was a photo-plaque commemorating the employee of the month, an attractive young Filipina named Tina.

It was exactly 7:00 a.m. The waitress, in a modest beige suit, brought the menu, and I enjoyed reading the breakfast fare. Entrees were of rank or designation: the Commander in Chief (steak and eggs), the Private (a stack of pancakes), and the Filipino Scout (a dish with rice instead of hash browns). A civilian, I opted for the American Patriot (straight-up sausage and eggs). As I waited for breakfast, I remembered the old post building that had been right around the corner. It was a much smaller affair, ramshackle in comparison to the new building, and for some unexplained reason it was a homier place and unpretentious to a fault. Perhaps my discomfort with the new VFW was because of the rather emphatic conversation taking place at the table behind me.

Two middle-aged American men, clearly post members and apparently employees of the bar and restaurant, were bickering about the post commander. He commands respect, said one man; he needs to earn respect, countered the other. The squabbling, which was much too loud for a public place, continued. They went on about relationships with the staff. One of them said you cannot get too close to the Filipino staff or they will start to ask for favors; the other man heartily agreed. I glanced up at Tina's photo on the wall. Then they went back to the topic of the commander and then his wife. Both men cannot tolerate her: she meddles, she complains. Their discussion was punctuated by the metallic snaps of Zippo lighters.

By 7:30 a.m. the bar was almost filled. It was a racially mixed crowd. The men, middle-aged retirees save for the one or two elderly, sat with their coffee and cigarettes. All wore T-shirts or a light jersey with the post symbol on it. Everyone had on short pants and either sneakers or flip-flops. I noted that one retiree wore his hair in a ponytail, and another had an honest-to-God mullet. There was much laughing and smoking and coughing as cable news showed the latest round of Palestinian violence. Two Filipinos, somewhat younger and dressed for a day at the office, walked in and sat down at the bar. They were obviously on friendly terms with the retirees. Above the coughing, I heard one retiree ask the Filipinos about all of the new call centers "on base," an anachronistic reference given that the "base" had not existed for fifteen years.

Tim (a pseudonym) arrived shortly thereafter. A large-boned man with a pronounced belly, he was perhaps fifty years old or a little older. His round, fleshy face was flushed, and the areas around his eyes were swollen, giving him a swinish appearance. Just as the other post members that morning, he wore clothing—shorts and a T-shirt—that reflected his rank, although, unlike some of his comrades, he was not slovenly. Tim shared his thoughts with me that morning on being a military retiree in the Philippines.[27]

He had been a navy man, twenty years in, most of it spent in Japan or on board a ship. He had enjoyed Japan, picked up some of the lingo, and loved the food. When his service was up, the navy gave him a free plane ticket to anyplace he wanted to call home. Tim chose the Philippines rather than his hometown back in Washington State.

"The Philippines is the number one destination for all military retirees," he said,"outside of the States, of course. People just want to come here."

Tim took out a short, black cigarette holder and affixed a cheap local brand cigarette to it. Given his attire and the surroundings, using the holder made him look slightly ridiculous.

He continued, "I'd been here before a couple of times. I liked it OK. When I came here in '95 after I retired I figured I would stay for a month at most and then go back to the States. I had some pretty decent experience in the navy, and I got a community college degree, so I figured I could get a job pretty easy back home.

"But I just kept staying. It went to six months. Then I said I would leave after nine. And that turned into a year and a half. It was too easy. It's an easy life here. The money was enough to get by. Nobody here is rich, but nobody starves. Then in '97 the Asian [stock market] crash changed everything. In just a couple of weeks the peso went from 25 to one [dollar] to forty-five to one. Then fifty. Then fifty-five. My retirement check just doubled, almost over-night. I could live twice as well. Why go back there?"

We chatted. I did not ask if he had ever been back home since retiring or if he had any family; I sensed that it was not the sensitive thing to do. He did say that every year he had to leave the Philippines for at least twenty-four hours to keep his visa legal. He goes for a week or so to Thailand, he said, and most of the retirees do the same. Its beer, food, and girls are all better. The people seem friendlier, too, but, unlike the Filipinos, they have poor English skills. "That is a major problem," he said.

I asked, "So what is life like here as a military retiree?"

Tim shrugged and became contemplative. "In a way Angeles is no dif-ferent than anyplace else. People [the retirees] have their own set of friends, or they raise a family. Everyone has their own hangouts. I used to be on a pool team. You pretty much have to play pool or darts in the bars here to have a social life. So in a way it is just like anyplace in the States."

Tim told me he occasionally manages a bar down on Fields Avenue, a substitute when the regular managers have to leave for a while. He cannot do it all the time though. "You are expected," he confided, "to drink with the customers. That is part of the job. The bar gives you a job and you give the bar part of your liver. And that's not an exaggeration."

Then I asked about the level of alcoholism among retirees. "Probably high, real high," he said, diverting his eyes to different parts of the room. I attempted to change the subject by saying that many people back home would envy the retiree community here. After all, it seemed that the men here were doing exactly what they wanted to be doing, and that was enviable.

Tim responded quickly: "Well, what else can these guys do? Look, I spent twenty years living outside of the States. So did all of these guys, more even for some. We spent all that time being in the military, some of us on a ship, being away from the States, being taken care of, like. And living here in Angeles is just like that. We are taken care of. There is nothing we cannot have. We have the RAO that we can go to. Our medical needs are looked after. There are damn good Filipino doctors around here, and a good hospital. There is our own cemetery. So we are all taken care of. If we stay here we will always be taken care of."

After a short pause, I remarked that what struck me as odd was the age factor. Looking around, most of the retirees were in their forties and fifties. I told Tim that was awfully young to stop being a productive person.

"Not actually true," he said. "Some of the vets here work. Some have their own sort of business, but it is tricky because the Philippine government gives you a lot of shit. You cannot have a job a Filipino could do. Well, what the hell does that mean? What can't a Filipino do? Some of the guys work in the bars as managers, like I do. Others do other things. But you really can keep busy if you join a pool or dart league. There are fantastic pool leagues here. Most of the guys do that."

We talked about the changes that have come to Angeles since the closing of the base. Tim seemed well up on this subject, quickly explaining how direct flights into Clark from places like Singapore and Hong Kong are going to completely make over Angeles. He seemed to have numbers at his grasp. For instance, three thousand more beds are needed immediately if a commercial plane is diverted to Clark and the passengers must stay the night. "Three thousand immediately," he emphasized. "Hotels are being built, big, pricey hotels. Then there are all the condos springing up. Rents are rising dramatically." He told me his former residence, a two-bedroom townhouse in Sta. Maria (a nearby neighborhood) went for 10,000 pesos a month (roughly $200) in 2000, and that was high then. Now the same place is going for 24,000 (about $530). He had to move, he said, and he was not happy about it. The military retirees, he stressed, all on fixed incomes, are very vulnerable, and any amount of inflation is serious.

"Part of the problem," he said, "is the Koreans. They're taking the place over. They're into everything. They're driving prices through the roof. They can take a direct flight from Seoul into Clark. They come for the golf, which is cheap, at least for them, not for anybody else . . . Well, maybe for the Japanese, too. They come to drink, for the girls . . . They can gamble here, which they can't do in Korea."

I interrupted Tim and asked, "How did that make the Koreans different from any of the other nationalities that come to Angeles?" Apparently, I hit a nerve. Tim became animated.

"Because they're coming here in large numbers and staying. They're putting up their own businesses. And these businesses, like all the Korean restaurants you're starting to see, well, these are for other Koreans not Filipinos . . . or us. And here's another thing. If you'll notice, they say they are all here to learn English in Filipino schools. You know why? Because in Korea every man must do two years of military service. And it's not marching around once a month with a toy gun or anything. This is two years in uniform up at the DMZ or someplace. But there's a loophole. If you're a university student and you're overseas, you're exempt. That's why you see so many young Korean guys here."

"So many of the Koreans are essentially draft dodgers," I offered, having no idea if anything he said was true. Tim nodded excitedly.

"While we pay taxes to keep them safe! [Tim uses an explicative to describe Koreans in general.] They come here and they set up a mafia. Read the papers. All of the drug dealing is done by Korean gangs. They are building housing developments for themselves. Do you think they'll allow us or

Filipinos in? Hell, no! It's Korean only. Everyone else, keep out! They're buying up the clubs here [in Angeles]. They abuse the girls. Ask any of the girls in the clubs, and they'll tell you they don't want to work for a Koreano. They just abuse the girls. They are just a low-class people, just factory workers and shipyard workers and the such who come here to blow their money and ruin this place while they are doing it. Just a low-class bunch of people."

Over Tim's right shoulder, Tina, employee of the month, smiled down at me from her photo-plaque as Tim stuck another cigarette into his black holder.

13

SAN FERNANDO TO MANILA

It was late morning at the Clarkton Hotel. I was about to find a jeepney and travel to San Fernando. The hotel's restaurant was half filled with tourists from the West and girls who worked down the street. The hotel staff was preparing for lunch. In the adjacent Olympic-size pool, an elderly Japanese man was doing backstroke laps. I watched with admiration as he flawlessly touched the concrete coping and twisted back in the other direction. I found his effortless swimming relaxing, Zen-like. I mused that he would have been too young to have fought in World War II, but he was certainly old enough to remember it.

The Clarkton sits at the upper end of Fields Avenue, officially Don Juico Avenue, and has since the 1970s, when it was built basically for the U.S. Air Force. It has changed ownership numerous times since then and is now under German management. Sitting there I tried to remember when I first saw the hotel in 1992, when Pinatubo's ash still covered roofs and yards. The restaurant was much simpler then. Abutting the restaurant, the hotel's bar sat under a ceiling but essentially had only one wall, giving it little protection from people splashing in the pool just ten feet away. If the wind blew the wrong way during a rainstorm, the patrons simply had to evacuate it. Because of the open walls, it was not air-conditioned; fans slowly turned overhead, reminding me of an Oriental bar from a golden-age Hollywood movie. On the one wall were pictures of U.S. fighter planes and plaques of gratitude from such organizations as the VFW and the American Legion. At one end of the room was a pool table. The bar itself was wooden and beaten. Australian accents were heard more often, but not substantially more, than American ones. One heard tales from an Aussie gold prospector who had worked in Papua New Guinea or from the New Zealander shrimp boat skipper or perhaps from the old American pilot.

Over the years, the German management has made some changes. Today, the bar area has been closed in by a glass wall that still allows you to gaze at the swimmers but within an air-conditioned cocoon. Prints of German soccer matches and large posters of the Bavarian forest and Continental beers have replaced the pictures of American fighter planes. The pool table has been removed; now it is an alcove known as the "Kaffee Kulture," where one can sit at small tables and drink small cups of coffee served with Swiss cookies. The bar has been radically redesigned. Its former horseshoe is now something like a *V*, an odd, angular structure that makes it awkward to carry on a conversation at the closed end and impossible at the open end. Everything has been painted a curious pale yellow. Now the men you see speak to each other or on their cell phones in German. Computers are everywhere: an entire row behind the bar, some on the side of the bar, and more near the Kaffee Kulture.

Looking at the bar from my seat in the restaurant, I thought of 1992. I thought of the pool table and the American posters, but mostly about the men I had met there, all of whom are now dead. Their stories, some of which seemed almost half true, would never be heard again. An era, I said to myself, had surely passed.

Somewhat awash in this weltschmerz, I picked up my bags and headed out, riding a jeepney down Fields, past the large American cemetery. At noon I caught a San Fernando–bound jeepney, determined to make my run into Manila as close as possible to the route the troops took in 1945. Save for an open jeep, no vehicle could serve this purpose better than the jeepney. The Angeles jeepney terminal was relatively new, replacing one that had been essentially an open space of mud and tire ruts. This new station, unlike its predecessor, was clean and organized with fresh concrete and macadam, canopied shelters, and security guards all around. There used to be a collection of sheds around here, and the air was usually thick with charcoal smoke and the smell of food cooking. The sheds have been replaced by tidy, antiseptic-looking Chowking and

Jollibee fast-food joints. One thing has remained the same—the appearance of the vehicles. The jeepneys have endured as living examples of the postwar years with horses as hood ornaments; names like Rollie, Rambo, or perhaps the Fernandez Family; and such painted adornments as American flags, American eagles, zodiac signs, and the Virgin Mary.

I was very disappointed that the jeepney's front passenger seat was taken. It meant that I had to climb in the back and huddle with the masses, which would make it difficult for me to consider the landscape during the forty-minute trip.

On this day I rode down the MacArthur Highway with several middle-aged women who looked as if they were returning to the office from lunch; a mother and her ten-year-old son; a gaggle of school girls in uniforms; and a couple of young men talking to each other. Both of the facing benches were filled. Sitting hip to hip, shoulder to shoulder, we all exchanged glances at least once, but we mostly averted our eyes. Except for myself and the young boy, everyone at one time or another had their cell phones out, texting away. Texting is a Philippine obsession, as it has become worldwide. I marveled at the dexterity of their thumbs as messages flew out from the humble jeepney to the world over.

Ten minutes out of Angeles, it began to pour. The passengers nonchalantly unraveled the plastic curtains that hung over the side of the compartment. It was surprising how close and warm it became with the air now mostly cut off and how odor became instantly amplified. I attempted to calculate my location by factoring on Mount Arayat, but the rain and the faded plastic curtains made this task impossible. All I could see were outlines of jeepneys and other vehicles splashing through the rain, so I spent the trip staring at my feet. A mile or so outside of San Fernando, the deluge abruptly stopped, and the sun burst through the clouds, hot and strong. Earlier I had asked the driver to let me off as close to the train station as possible, and roughly in the center of town, I hopped out.

San Fernando, the capital of Pampanga, is a large, bustling city of about 220,000 people located nearly in the middle of the province. Because it is the major agricultural processing center of Central Luzon and because it has a substantial number of manufacturing plants, the town always seems in a galvanic fit of activity. Despite the wealth of car dealerships and fast-food joints, it is an old place, boasting an eighteenth-century church among numerous nineteenth-century structures. For the past century, it has stood at the epicenter of Pampangan events. During the Philippine-American War, it was heavily damaged, and U.S. troops were at one time quartered there. At that time one of its residents, Pedro Abad Santos, a revolutionary leader under Gen. Maximino Hizon, himself a San Fernandan, was captured by the Americans and sentenced to a lengthy prison term. His family hired an American lawyer, millionaire-mining-magnate-to-be John Hausserman, who secured a pardon for him. Abad Santos became a Marxist, studied in Moscow, and in 1932 started the first Philippine Communist Party, the Socialist Party of the Philippines. He would eventually join the Huks. In World War II, the Japanese occupied his town, but no fighting occurred. The war would, however, provide San Fernando with historical notoriety because of its train station.[1]

I did not know how to find the San Fernando train station, but the directions from a few friendly residents sent me down a narrow street in what seemed to be a typical middle-class neighborhood. The houses, built very close together, were attractive. Most had security bars on all doors and windows. Women stood outside a sari-sari store retelling the events of the morning. High school students were peddling their bikes back to school after lunch with book bags strapped to their backs. I could smell food, and I realized that my morose reverie at the Clarkton Hotel and the ensuing jeepney ride had caused me to skip lunch.

Large sections of the street were essentially underwater. As I sloshed through the unavoidable ponds, I noted the persons calmly walking by in their flip-flops, and I realized the absurdity of wearing shoes in the tropics. I stopped in front of a small white building where a large rock painted rust red stood, surrounded by shiny metal posts connected by a chain. A plaque from the National Historical Commission dated 1967 was attached to the rock. The plaque had a Tagalog passage on top with the English translation below it. The English read:

> At this railway station of San Fernando, the Filipino and American prisoners of war who had been marched all the way from Bataan to

Pampanga, in one of the ghastliest forced marches in history, were loaded like cattle on boxcars, where, because every compartment was packed to the limit, many suffocated or were crushed to death during the trip to Capas.

An old man hastily came out from the building and introduced himself as being connected with the historical commission. His English was superb, and he rather hurriedly told me the story of the redbrick building across the street, the infamous San Fernando train station. I thanked him, figuring I had interrupted something going on inside, and he went back, I suspect happily, into the house.

I walked across the street, navigating the patches of water, to the old, long redbrick building. It was apparent that this once-important building was now in poor shape. All of the windowpanes were gone. Some were replaced by concrete blocks, and others were just left open. Tin sheets enclosed the doorways. As I got closer to the building, I saw that the bricks were crumbling, and the concrete slabs that were probably used to shore up weak spots were crumbling as well. Fixed to the side of the building was a marker from the National Historical Commission dated 2004. It was entirely in Tagalog, and my dubious translating came up with the following:

> Railroad Station of San Fernando
> Built in 1892 as part of the Manila-Dagupan Manila Railroad Company, here José Rizal stopped when he visited San Fernando. Also in this station, in April 1942, soldiers were put in the train that was part of the Death March and taken to Camp O'Donnell, Capas, Tarlac, to be put in prison.

Going to an open window at the side of the building, I peered into the station. It was surprisingly narrow and completely vacant, save for some old cement bags filled with refuse. An odor of dampness and decay hung in the air. The opaque light was poor, and it gave a rather ghostly impression. In such a light I could envision Dr. José Rizal, dapper and handsome, walking through the station in the late 1800s to meet townsmen. He would shortly be shot in the back by a Spanish firing squad, a victim of patriotism and politics. I could also visualize Japanese soldiers with swords and rifles—brutal, frightening men, some maniacal—enforcing the will of a small man in Tokyo, whose people called him a god. All around me would have been thousands of Filipino and American prisoners, dazed, defeated, and defenseless, waiting for a train that would take them to the horrors of O'Donnell. They had been abandoned to their fate by the square-jawed strategic planners in Washington.

Abandonment seemed to be the theme here. Just as the soldiers had been abandoned by their government, the train station had been abandoned by its owners. It was all quite depressing, and I wanted to be away from the disintegrating old building. At least at O'Donnell there was greenery and a sense of serenity; however, at this place, there was just rot. Walking back down the street and in front of the station, I stopped at the death march marker KM 102. On the two sides facing away from the street and toward the building were written two inscriptions:

In memory of Cpl. LaPrade D. Brown 192 Tank Battalion
Died March 29, 1943 in Bilibid Prison, Manila
Sponsored by Alberta M. Clayton, his sister, and Maywood Bataan Day
Org. Maywood Illinois USA

In memory of the young men of Maywood who passed through the portals of the San Fernando Rail Station—most never to return to their homes and families—and who endured unspeakable atrocities in the course of service to their country.

The 192nd Tank Battalion was a National Guard unit that was formed in 1940. Company B of that unit was from Maywood. When the men arrived in the Philippines in November 1941, they were stationed at Fort Stotsenburg. After Pearl Harbor, part of the battalion engaged Japanese tanks at Lingayen; it would be the first time in history that a U.S. tank fought an enemy tank. As U.S. forces fell back into Bataan, the 192nd was the last unit in before the bridges were blown up. On April 9 they were ordered to destroy their tanks, and they surrendered. The men were subsequently marched to San Fernando and then on to O'Donnell. A few who lived out the war in Cabanatuan were rescued by U.S. Rangers in 1945, and their story appeared in a rather forgettable movie called *The Great Raid*. Some died in the Japanese transport ships torpedoed and bombed by U.S. forces. Most, however, ended the war in Japan working as slaves in factories or mines.

Only 268 of the 598 men of the battalion made it back to the States, and only 43 of the 89 men of Company B. Those who returned to Maywood, Illinois, may have been surprised at what their families had been doing. When the Maywood residents first heard that Bataan and then the Philippines had fallen, family members banded together to collect money to buy supplies for the American prisoners. The group expanded and became known as the American Bataan Clan (ABC). On September 12, 1942, with the Maywood soldiers' whereabouts still unknown, the ABC held the first Bataan Day Parade to raise funds to send care packages to the POWs. Eventually the ABC changed its name to the Maywood Bataan Day Organization. Every year but one ever since, the parade has been held in Maywood on the second Sunday in September.[2]

I tried to visualize the main parade route in Maywood on a sunny September Sunday. The usual images of a parade in small-town America appeared: the equestrian club, majorettes in front of the high school band, floats, and the vintage cars with local dignitaries in them. But I kept losing the vision to a perplexing question: why have the parade at all? The surviving men came home, resumed their lives, and now certainly nearly all are dead. The people of Maywood have grown up with other wars and other soldiers. Surely the San Fernando obelisk dedicated to the 192nd satisfied the collective need to remember their sons and husbands who did not make it back. But every year they march down that Illinois street, marking what had happened right where I stood in the lowlands of Pampanga.

A pedicab splashed through the water, and the driver and the passenger glanced at me curiously as I stood at the obelisk. I wondered if they knew where Maywood was or what Cpl. LaPrade D. Brown did here. I considered how odd it was that a man's name would be here forever among strangers in front of a dilapidated train station. Odder still was that people in his hometown held an annual parade in honor of a place most would never see and of soldiers most would never know. It was then I thought that perhaps abandonment was not the theme of this place after all. I walked back up the street, dodging the flooded areas and taking in the aroma of Pampangan cuisine. The sun had become furious.

To accurately follow MacArthur into Manila, I needed to continue down the MacArthur Highway. This route meant taking another jeepney, for most buses now use the modern expressway. I could have rented a car, but I told myself I wanted to enter Manila as MacArthur had, in a jeep.

My dedication to historical accuracy proved to be ridiculous. Out of San Fernando I again found myself hunched in the back of a jeepney, seeing nothing but my own feet and those around me. I had particularly wanted to see Calumpit and the Bagbag Bridge, a site of intense fighting during the Philippine-American War. I did not see that bridge, nor was I cognizant of passing over the bridge that figured during the Second World War. In fact, I am not sure I went through Calumpit. Indeed, at times I was not certain I was on the MacArthur Highway. All my attention was on my feet and avoiding knocking my head against the metal handrail above me. At Malolos I hopped out to see the church where Aguinaldo proclaimed the Philippine nation's independence and signed the Constitution. Unfortunately, the interior was under large-scale renovation, and my memory of this historic city was limited to a meal at a giant two-story McDonald's near the church.

I jumped into another jeepney, and once again I could not get a front seat. The post–San Fernando leg of the trip had become disastrous. From the back of the jeepney, I saw little but my fellow passengers and other passing jeepneys along the two-lane MacArthur Highway. Sometimes I noted a bridge or a church, but mostly I saw a series of little shops, often dedicated to the galvanizing trade. Towns such as Bocaue, Valenzuela, Malabon all slid by as we entered the congested introduction to the behemoth Metro Manila.

I got off the final jeepney at Calookan, at a place called Monumento. Frankly, my body ached, particularly my back and neck, and I made solemn vows about not taking more long-distance jeepney rides. But I was in Manila. Specifically, I was north of the Pasig River in a spot that typified the postwar city, with its crowds of people, polluted air, and dirty concrete. Manila had long since lost its romantic American tourist moniker of Pearl of the Orient. Virtually everything is different in Manila now.

PART 4
MANILA

14

THE WAR YEARS

anila's street names are all changed, of course, or at least many of them are. There is something Orwellian about this alteration, as if changing the names means that eventually no one will know what happened on these streets. History will be erased. Culture will be warped. The clouding of history is already evident in this place. For example, visitors would not know that the vast majority of this historic city's buildings were built after March 1945. Few outsiders would know that in this city, at one time perhaps the most progressive in Asia, occurred one of the most horrendous events of the twentieth century. Here Japanese and U.S. forces met on February 3, 1945, and did battle for twenty-nine consecutive days, with nearly a million civilians caught between them. More than a hundred thousand noncombatants perished in what some called the carnival of death.

Manila is an old city. It was first settled by Muslims centuries before the Spanish. These settlers traded with the Chinese and other area peoples. The local population was the Tagalog group, who gave the city its name: *may* (there is) and *nilad*, the name of a type of shrub that grew in the area, primarily along the Pasig River, which intersects the area. The Spanish came in 1570 and, after defeating the Tagalog leader Rajah Solaiman in 1571, established a fort and a colony.[1]

For the next three hundred years, the Spanish dominated the city. They converted the Tagalogs to Catholicism and built exquisite churches. They also established a central government in Manila. The culture and the arts blossomed. Despite some disruptions—several Chinese revolts and the 1762–64 occupation by British forces—Manila flourished as part of the galleon trade, an important stopover point for Spanish ships on their way to Acapulco, Mexico.

But at the end of the nineteenth century, an independence movement evolved and took shape in Luzon, particularly in the Manila area. The group, known as the Katipunan, grew until an open rebellion broke out in 1896. The fighting was intense but not decisive. Then came the Spanish-American War and, with it, Commodore Dewey and his fleet. The Spanish surrendered to the Americans, not the Filipinos, and thus began the Philippine-American War.

When the Americans arrived in the city in 1898, they found a confused, frightened population. It did not take long, however, for the U.S. administration to ease the Manileños' apprehension. As previously discussed, public schools were immediately established. The Manila charter was rewritten in 1901, and city leaders—save for the mayor—were now elected. U.S. engineers established two breakwaters in Manila Bay, creating an enclosed harbor, and the administration built a new set of wharves, cargo containers, and other implements of shipping. Before, ships had to unload their cargoes onto barges; now, they could unload directly onshore, making Manila one of the finest ports in Asia. The Americans also introduced a new building material—concrete reinforced with steel—which proved a successful combination against typhoons. Sanitation became a priority. After the Bureau of Health was established, the first sewer system was constructed; small pox vaccines were given; cholera, the scourge of Manila, was wiped out; and the Philippine General Hospital was built. The city's first freshwater system was established through the building of the Novaliches Dam and the Balara Filters. Electric streetcars began to run. The Manila Fire Department, the nation's first, was formed.[2]

The American empire controlled Manila and the country after defeating the regular Philippine forces in 1900 and through the 1920s. Its empire in Manila featured a number of architectural projects. One was the grand architectural tribute to neoclassicism begun by designers such as Daniel Burnham, William Parsons, and Ralph Harrington Doane. Having already served on the McMillan Commission to realize Pierre L'Enfant's plan for the Mall in Washington, D.C., and having designed New York's Flatiron Building,

Burnham arrived in the Philippines in the early 1900s and planned a magnificent thirty-acre park that would house the Philippine government and other buildings. He designed and built or had built the Legislative, the Finance, and the Agricultural buildings, all of which are in the Beaux-Arts style and neo-classic in temperament. His successor, William Parsons, designed the Manila Hotel, the Philippine General Hospital, the Elks Club, and the Army and Navy Club. Four great bridges were built across the Pasig, while four great city avenues intersected the city. Such grandiose classicism was seemingly appropriate, said Manila writer Nick Joaquin, because Filipinos and Americans alike felt like they were Romans founding a new republic.[3]

But the empire had a dark side—segregation. Although Filipinos and Americans mixed freely in many social situations and, in fact, far more openly than people of different races did in many parts of the United States, there were certain circumstances in which enforced separation did exist. American social establishments, such as the Elks and the Army and Navy clubs, would not allow Filipino members. The course at the Manila Golf Club was also off-limits to Filipinos. Officially, there were color lines in all of the cabarets, meaning that the dining room and the dance floor were divided into two sections, with the white people usually toward the front and the Filipinos to the rear. Most observed this arrangement. By the 1930s, however, many Filipino and American leaders became infuriated and actively rallied against the practice.

Despite the segregation and the formation of trade policies that tied Philippine independence to American markets, many Filipinos still see the American half century as a sort of golden age, much to the nationalists' chagrin. With commonwealth status created in 1934 and with independence promised for 1946, the era was one of order and discipline, of modest but secure economic gains, and of ideas of freedom and self-governance.

The golden age ended abruptly on December 8, 1941. After landing at Lingayen and other places in the islands, the Japanese drove quickly and decisively through Luzon. MacArthur decided to activate Plan Orange and withdraw all troops to the Bataan Peninsula. Manila was declared an open city, much to the shock of its residents, who assumed the Americans were invincible and would protect them. The retreating U.S. troops destroyed as much strategic hardware as they could, then opened the food storehouses to the civilians. For several days the people held their breath, thinking only of the horror stories they had heard about the Japanese massacre in Nanjing, China. On January 3, 1942, Manileños awoke to the sight of Japanese troops on their streets. The occupation had begun.

Life under the Japanese was at first quite odd. After the fall of Corregidor in May 1942, the Japanese had no real military concerns in the islands. They had no need to intimidate the population, so they turned their attention to reeducation. Filipinos had lived under Spanish religious and intellectual influence for more than three hundred years, and they had enjoyed American culture and education for the last forty years. Through an immense and sustained propaganda drive, the Japanese attempted to wash these effects from the people, especially in Manila, the heart of Western authority in the Philippines. The propaganda corps consisted of media specialists: newspapermen, radio and movie personnel, novelists, and poets. Most interesting, clergymen of both Catholic and Protestant denominations were also part of the corps. These soldiers' task was to wipe away the stains of Europe and America and replace them with the Asian ideals of hard work, honesty, prudence, and frugality.[4]

Initially, quite a few Manileños were receptive to the Japanese propaganda, especially those who shared a pronounced disappointment and disillusionment with the United States. They knew MacArthur had run to Australia, Bataan had fallen, and there was no relief in sight. In May, the sight of thousands of bedraggled American POWs from the Corregidor garrison being marched through the Manila streets on their way to prison shattered much of whatever remaining confidence the people had in their colonial benefactor. Afterward, Manila returned to a relatively normal state: newspapers began to publish, radio was back on the air, and the schools reopened. All of the occupiers' propaganda activities fostered a distinctly pro-Japanese and anti-American line among the populace. To demonstrate that there were strong commonalities between the two cultures, churches began to hold services with Japanese clergy officiating.

But these efforts were not completely successful. According to Marcial P. Lichauco in May 1942:

The Japanese Propaganda Office began exhibiting in all the theatres today a moving picture film showing the raid on Pearl Harbor. It is very well staged and the scenes are most impressive. . . . Throughout it all there is a running comment to the effect that America's Pacific Fleet has been crushed in the course of one sudden assault by the Sons of Nippon and that the supposed invincibility of the white man is nothing but a myth the Japanese have destroyed. The picture ends with an appeal to the people of Asia to rally around the Japanese who will protect them against further encroachments by the people of the white race. It is very good propaganda but the entire film, I am happy to report, was witnessed by a large Filipino audience in absolute silence.[5]

Political reorganization came next. The Japanese found and installed a puppet regime under President José P. Laurel. The new government's role was to aid the Japanese military administration in its historic task to return Asia to the Asians. A new constitution was formed, and a new National Assembly was elected. Independence was declared on October 14, 1943. Later, a pro-Japan group led by old veterans of the revolution and the Philippine-American War formed the Makabayan Katipunan Ng Mga Pilipino (Alliance of Philippine Patriots), or Makapili. This dreaded organization's members operated as spies and guerrillas for the Japanese.

The Japanese had driven out the Westerner and had granted, at least on paper, independence for the nation, but they never won the people's respect. This resistance was due in no small measure to cultural conflict. Although the Japanese asserted that they had returned the Filipinos to their Asian inheritance, they demanded a strict obedience, and public humiliation was commonplace. These degradations began at the onset of the occupation and continued throughout. When asked what they remember about the occupation, Manileños will invariably talk about how they were made to bow in front of a Japanese sentry or how they received or saw someone else receive a slap in the face from a soldier. The city's residents anxiously lived with the threat of potential Japanese violence. Such fear is demonstrated in the diary of Dr. Victor Buencamino, the head of the National Rice and Corn Corporation.

Some sentries are odious, like the one in Santa Mesa, who is a mean looking fellow. A man bowed before him, holding a cigar. He slapped the man, got the cigar and burned the man's face with it. Saw another naked woman tied to a post. She was a mestiza. Street urchins were giggling.

My Japanese neighbors are singing. They have a drinking party. There is no sunshine without shadow. Now I am in the shadow.

Fortunately, I have not been the subject of abuse. Still no slaps, no insults. I wonder what I will do if I were slapped.[6]

As the occupation wore on, guerrilla activity increased, and the Japanese became progressively more paranoid. After guerrilla attacks in the Manila area, Yamashita ordered the Kempeitai, assisted by the Makapili, to go through the city neighborhoods where the guerrillas were thought to be living. When a neighborhood was suspected of harboring guerrillas or their sympathizers, they cordoned off the area and called it the *zona*. All residents were made to walk in front of a person, usually a Filipino, who wore a sack over his head with eye slits. It thus came to be known as the "secret eye." If the secret eye identified a person as being a suspect, that resident would be taken away. Often, the destination was Fort Santiago and its torture chambers. Too often, the person never returned. One Manila resident recorded the following in 1942:

There is an old prison in the Walled City. It dates back to the first years of the Spanish reign in the Philippines. Its thick walls, slimy with lichen and moss, hold secrets of torture on the rack from the hands of the Spanish inquisition. When America came, its dungeons were sealed and forgotten.

Now, it is alive again. Fort Santiago. People don't say its name aloud. They whisper it. Its hateful cells lie in wait for new victims.[7]

The decline of Manila during the war's last two years owed everything to Japanese mismanagement, which was particularly apparent with the city's food supply. As early as the end of 1942, Japanese poor planning and inflexible policies created massive inflation and a thriving black market. Their attempt to have a central rice distribution system failed miserably. The Japanese had minted occupation money, which by then was worthless. People sold their personal possessions for food. All Manileños felt the pangs of hunger, and malnutrition was a fact of life. By the end of 1944, electric power and running water had all but ended in Manila. There were no streetcars. Indeed, there were no more carriages for the horses had long been eaten. Enterprising persons would go into the provinces to buy dogs, take them back to Manila, and sell them for food. Looting was widespread: gangs of men forced their way into homes and carted away anything they could sell, including pianos, refrigerators, and furniture. The threat of disease was high. Because of inflation, even death became a luxury, with many people renting coffins to bury their family members. They were the fortunate ones.[8]

In a February 1995 address to the Rotary Club of Makati, Edgar Krohn Jr., a Filipino of German heritage and a survivor of the Battle of Manila, recalled the state of the city before the arrival of the U.S. forces:

By January, 1945, people were dying of starvation in the streets and in as much as there were no longer any facilities to remove the bodies, they were merely covered with newspapers and if not picked up after a few days by push-carts operated by the city hall, the bodies were left to decompose where they were. Many of these starving people would sit around the public markets waiting for the vendors to throw away some rotting vegetables which they would fight over. . . .

Numerous checkpoints were established within the city and everyone passing by was thoroughly searched [by the Japanese]. The residents walked in fear as very often soldiers would cordon off an area, load a certain number of men onto trucks and drive them off for forced labor or some defensive fortification. Many of these men were never seen again. We waited for deliverance. . . .

There are some people and many of them born after the end of the war, who say that the allied forces could very well have by-passed the Philippines and have invaded Formosa instead. My question to them is: could we have lasted another seven months under such intolerable conditions? I ask those who were in Manila at the time if we could have lasted. I think not.[9]

For the Japanese, the strategic stage for final victory began in May 1944. Convinced that they would face a climatic confrontation with the U.S. forces in the Philippines, the Japanese concocted the Sho Plan, which saw the defeat of the Americans on the land, on the sea, and in the air. But that plan was destroyed after the battles of Leyte and Leyte Gulf and the overwhelming defeat of the Japanese forces. Yamashita rethought the Philippine situation and opted for a protected delaying action, allowing the Japanese homeland more time to prepare for an invasion and possibly even making the Philippines a bargaining chip at a peace-negotiating table. In Yamashita's view, Manila was not a crucial part of the defensive plan; in fact, it was more of a liability than a strength.

The Japanese defense of Manila is a testament to a confused military hierarchy and to flat-out insubordination. Yamashita, as described earlier, had chosen to defend only the high grounds of northern Luzon, the Bamban Hills around Clark Field, and the mountains east of Manila. He decided not to defend the city in any meaningful way for several reasons: Manila had a large number (approximately one million) of civilians; many of its buildings were constructed of flammable materials, and possible fires could threaten his own forces; and the city was perfectly flat, making it difficult to defend. But Yamashita had problems in deciding just what to do with Manila. His first preference was to move all troops out of Manila and declare it an open city, as MacArthur had done three years earlier. This option proved impossible because Yamashita did not have the political authority to declare it as such, and none was forthcoming from Tokyo. Furthermore, he had large stocks of military supplies in Manila but few vehicles and little gasoline to move them to the mountains. In December 1944, Yamashita drew up plans to begin a tactical withdrawal from the city, taking as much as he could with him and planning to destroy the rest.

He instituted the plan in January 1945. By the end of the month, less than two thousand men of the army detachment remained. Yamashita himself left the city and went to Baguio in the mountains, assuming the balance of the troops would follow as planned. Operational control of the remaining naval detachment in the city was handed over to the army's Lt. Gen. Shizuo Yokoyama. Yokoyama had been lead to believe that four thousand of these naval troops would be responsible for destroying bridges and evacuating as much equipment and supplies as possible before February 20, the projected date of the U.S. forces' arrival. To Yokoyama's astonishment, he learned that instead of having fewer troops in Manila, as he had ordered, the naval command was actually increasing its force: in January the Japanese navy had sent an additional four thousand troops into Manila, bringing the combined services total to more than sixteen thousand men still in the city.

Yokoyama immediately conferred with navy officers, who ignored the orders to evacuate and demanded that Manila be defended to the last man. They felt that the city provided a natural fortress from which they could inflict incredible casualties, and probably because they were naval personnel, they simply did not want to retreat into the mountains. The naval commander in Manila, Rear Adm. Sanji Iwabuchi, did not feel compelled to follow Yokoyama's directives until completing his naval orders, which were, essentially, to defend the city. Yokoyama knew he could not countermand Iwabuchi's orders; thus, he eventually and uneasily yielded to them. Yamashita did not comprehend Yokoyama's submission to Iwabuchi until mid-February, halfway through the battle. One could argue that by that time Iwabuchi may have lost control of at least some of his forces. Thus one could also assert that Iwabuchi and his men were a rogue element, outside the pale of Japanese overall command.

Iwabuchi saw, correctly, that the U.S. force would probably attack from the north and the south. Accordingly, he established a northern perimeter that stretched from Intramuros east-southeast to the Paco area. A second force was set up to defend the central area from Nielson Field in Makati north to Ermita. But Iwabuchi mistakenly thought that the brunt of the attack would come from the south, and he deployed his best artillery to defend Paranaque, Pasay, and Nichols Field.

Such confused military planning coupled with the flawed command structure created a chaotic situation for the Japanese, which helped foster their paranoiac activities. Another factor was the change in Japanese attitude toward Filipinos. By the end of 1944, the Japanese ended all pretenses of being the great Asian liberators of the Philippines. Indeed, Filipinos were now cast as the enemy. A December 1944 prescription from the naval defense force in Manila said:

> When Filipinos are to be killed, they must be gathered into one place and disposed of with the consideration that ammunition and manpower must not be used in excess. Because the disposal of dead bodies is a troublesome task they should be gathered into houses which are scheduled to be burned or demolished. They should also be thrown into the river.[10]

By the beginning of the Battle of Manila, the orders simply read, "Kill all humans not Japanese." This directive was, in effect, a version of the infamous *senko-seisaku* (kill all, burn all, destroy all) system the Japanese used in Manchuria. Moreover, Manila was not the only location in the Philippines where such orders were apparently given. During February 1945, large-scale civilian massacres occurred in various places in Batangas and Laguna provinces.

The players in this carnival of death were all now ready: a vainglorious American general and his devoted soldiers, an uncontrollable Japanese admiral and his trapped men, and, caught between all of them, a million innocent civilians. Neither the city of Manila nor the American era would survive.

15

SANTO TOMAS

In January, shortly after MacArthur landed on Lingayen, his headquarters picked up information that General Yamashita was beginning to evacuate Manila. MacArthur was seemingly convinced that Manila would be declared an open city, and he ordered General Krueger southward to take the city. Krueger sensed a Japanese trap with Manila as the bait, and he proceeded with caution, which irritated MacArthur.[1]

On January 31, MacArthur visited the 1st Cavalry headquarters at Guimba, on the Tarlac–Nueva Ecija border, nearly fifty miles southeast of San Fabian. There he ordered Maj. Gen. Vernon D. Mudge, the division commander, "Get to Manila! Go around the Japs, bounce off the Japs, save your men, but get to Manila! Free the internees at Santo Tomas. Take Malacanang Palace and the Legislative Building." These thrilling words unintentionally and unavoidably destroyed the city.

Mudge put together three "flying columns," or motorized, high-speed battle groups. They began at Guimba at midnight on February 1, made it to Cabanatuan with little or no opposition, and down Highway 5 to Plaridel, Bulacan. At this point, where Highway 5 intersects with Highway 3, the 37th Division met with stiff Japanese resistance. The 1st Cavalry waited until the heavy infantry extirpated the opposition and reopened the highway, and then raced straight into Manila. It was late in the day on February 3.

The flying columns attacked their three objectives. They easily took Malacanang Palace because its Filipino defenders saluted the Americans instead of firing at them. The Legislative Building was different. As the cavalry moved through northern Manila, attempting to reach the Quezon Bridge and cross the Pasig River, Japanese troops barricaded into Far Eastern University ambushed the men. The fighting was so fierce that this detachment of U.S. troops was ordered to withdraw and converge with the one waiting to liberate the Westerners interned at the University of Santo Tomas.

The story of the Santo Tomas internees is both emotional and highly documented. When the Japanese set up their administration at the beginning of January 1942, they had more than five thousand foreign nationals, mostly Americans but with substantial numbers of British and other Allied peoples, on their hands. All Germans and Italians were quickly released, but the rest began a long incarceration. At first, the civilians were taken with military prisoners to Bilibid, a wagon wheel–shaped prison built by the Spanish. It soon overflowed. On January 5 the University of Santo Tomas (UST), with its high walls, large buildings, and open yard, began to receive truckloads of scared and confused civilians, whose lives would be irrevocably changed.[2]

The school's full title is the Pontifical and Royal University of Santo Tomas, the Catholic University of the Philippines. It uses "Pontifical" because of its relation to Rome and "Royal" because its administration and students volunteered to fight the British in the eighteenth century. Dedicated to St. Thomas Aquinas, Santo Tomas is the oldest existing university in Asia and, in terms of student population in one campus, the largest Catholic university in the world. It was founded in 1611 inside the walls of Intramuros, but because of a growing student population, the campus was moved to the present site in Sampaloc in 1927. Among its illustrious alumni are José Rizal, who attended Santo Tomas in 1882; former president Manuel Quezon, who graduated from its law school; and the brilliant young paralytic, Apolinarino Mabini, who was considered the "brains" of the Philippine revolution.

Life in Santo Tomas, after the initial fear and confusion of incarceration, settled into a routine. Most people were quartered in the Main Building, the Education Building, and the gym, but if one had the money and wanted to escape the crowds, the Japanese allowed a certain amount of shanties to be built on the grounds outside. In typical Western fashion, the internees quickly organized. Multiple committees were formed to run the camp. A Central

Committee was appointed by the Japanese, but elected committees were formed for medical, educational, sanitary, and public safety concerns. There was an internee police force and a jail. A school was set up. Even a newsletter was published and circulated. The camp began to function as a city.

As with any social structure, there were divisions. Although the majority of internees were American, many other nationalities were interned as well. People naturally tended to group along national lines. Wealth also played a part. The shanties, whose open-air construction and distance from the closeness of the dormitories were coveted, could only be built by those who could afford the materials, or the affluent. The Japanese provided meals, but they were in an increasingly short supply. From the beginning and almost to the end, those who could afford it could also augment their diet by purchasing food from Filipino vendors who visited the camp. One of the biggest divisions was, quite simply, that some people had more to eat than other people.

Hunger constantly affected the internees. A typical description comes from Emily Van Sickle, who remembers January 1945 this way:

> Misery from hunger was a sight too harrowing to describe. Children—and sometimes adults—dug in garbage cans outside the Japanese kitchen for whatever partially edible stuff they might retrieve, while Japanese soldiers looked on and laughed; very funny to observe Anglo-Saxons raiding the refuse. Occasionally a "magnanimous" soldier would give some child a banana or a piece of candy.
>
> Long since vanished were the once numerous pigeons that used to nest in some ledges on the main building; enticed with bits of corn, they had been snared and eaten by internees made crafty by hunger. Dogs and cats disappeared every day, the strays first, then personal pets.
>
> There were hundreds of men and women . . . whose flesh was drawn taut over ribs and backbone, resembling the hide of starved dogs. Knees, knuckles, elbows protruded in gnarled and swollen knots, while weakened muscles stood out like cords with the slightest movement. Arms and leg bones were scarcely hidden by their parchment-thin covering of skin. And the children—it made one's heart ache to see the skinny limbs and pot bellies that resulted from an inadequate diet.[3]

In September 1944 the first air raids on Manila began, offering proof to the internees that they had not been forgotten. The internees waited eagerly for liberation as the U.S. air strikes became commonplace. People heard through the grapevine about the landings at Leyte, and rumors were rife that they would be freed shortly. But emancipation did not come at Christmas. Through January the situation only became worse. For some, despair set in.

At dusk on February 3 it began. A group of U.S. planes flew low over the campus, and one pilot threw out a case for a pair of pilot's goggles. Inside the case was a note: "Roll out the barrel, Christmas will be either today or tomorrow." The cryptic message went through the camp like wildfire. Just before 9:00 p.m. the internees heard in the distance a low rumble, which they took to be a bombing run. But they did not see any planes or hear any explosions. The rumble only got louder, shaking the ground, and then flares lit up the night sky. Small arms fire was heard. The prisoners huddled together in the darkness of the Main Building, wondering what was happening. The Japanese troops had all gone into the Education Building next door.

Suddenly there was a crash. The main gate went down, and in rolled a column of Sherman tanks, led by one with "Battlin' Basic" written on its side and another with "Georgia Peach." Their searchlights scanned the yard, and infantrymen walked behind them. The internees streamed out of the Main Building, delirious, oblivious to the fact that a Japanese garrison was still present on the grounds. They surrounded the troopers, screaming, cheering, pulling men out of tanks, and carrying them on their emaciated shoulders. Suddenly, amid the prisoners was Lieutenant Abiko, a cruel and despised Japanese executive officer. He attempted to pull a grenade from underneath his shirt and take as many with him as he could; a GI shot first. Abiko, still alive, was dragged to the medical clinic in the Main Building. On the way he was spat upon, kicked, and slashed at by internees with kitchen knives. Women burned him with cigarettes. He died shortly after the doctor tended to his wounds. At the bottom of the stairway inside the Main Building, both internees and soldiers sang "God Bless America," "America," and then "The Star-Spangled Banner." After thirty-seven months of captivity, they were free.

One of the flying columns had arrived. The cavalry had saved the day. While the sight of the troops drove the internees to hysteria, the condition of the internees also greatly affected the U.S. soldiers. Cpl. Leon D'Angelo wrote,

> Oh God, the parents were all skin and bones. The kids were a little bet-
> ter cause the parents had given them their food. But it broke your heart
> to see these people so hungry. One lady offered me a diamond ring for
> some coffee. I went back to the truck for the coffee and handed it to
> her. She held out the ring and I told her, "Lady, there's no way in the
> world—we're not here to hurt you, we're here to help you."
>
> This little girl of about 7 years old, asked me to take her to her Mama.
> So we got through the crowd, to the stairs and up to the second floor.
> Two women were sitting there and one was the little girl's Mama. They
> were twin sisters, married to twin brothers, both Army Lieutenants, sup-
> posedly in Bilibid.
>
> I wasn't ready for this, they were so thin and weak, they could hardly
> stand up. But they did. All they could say was "God bless you, you all
> have come." We sat and talked for a while then I gave them the last k-
> ration I had and left.[4]

For two more days all was in limbo. While the freed civilians feasted on K rations and Hershey bars, sixty-five Japanese had taken several hundred internee hostages, men and boys, in the Education Building alongside the Main Building. Negotiations continued until the morning of February 5. Finally, an agreement was reached: the Japanese soldiers, keeping one side-arm, were allowed to vacate the building and walk off the campus to the Sampaloc Rotunda and their own lines. At 7:00 a.m., the remaining Japanese contingent at Santo Tomas marched out, escorted by U.S. troops. At the pre-arranged point at Sampaloc, U.S. and Japanese troops saluted each other, and the Americans went back to Santo Tomas. Unfortunately for the Japanese, the lines had changed, and they marched right into a bewildered group of U.S. troops who promptly killed the Japanese commander and most of his men.

The morning of February 7, General MacArthur visited Santo Tomas. Despite his visit being preceded by Japanese shelling, an honor guard was formed. When MacArthur arrived, accompanied by a phalanx of high-ranking officers and newspapermen, pandemonium broke loose. The internees began screaming and crowding him, with men weeping and women holding up their children so he could touch them. Staying an hour and a half, he shook hands with the grateful internees and then left, deeply touched by the incident. He was off to Bilibid Prison to find the remnants of his Bataan command and more civilians.

After MacArthur left Santo Tomas, the shelling began in earnest. Eva Anna Nixon reported:

> On Wednesday, February 7, the whole camp was stunned by the holo-caust of real war. . . . We had awakened that morning to happy news. The Army food supplies were arriving. The menu for supper went up: corned beef hash, green beans, fruit cocktail. . . . Little did we dream that morning as we watched the shells fall out in front of the main building many of us would die that day. I stood in the lunch line with the intelligent lawyer, Mr. McFie, and we discussed the future of the Philippines and China. A few hours later he was dying with his brains blown out.[5]

The shelling would continue for days, killing and wounding Americans and other Westerners who had thought they were safe. Outside the walls of Santo Tomas, Filipinos were dying by the tens of thousands.

✳ ✳ ✳

The University of Santo Tomas is still very much a city university, its square gate enclosing grounds that are bordered by highly trafficked streets. Just as in 1942, today's UST is dominated by the imposing Main Building, which sits directly in the middle of the square campus. Three stories of dark gray concrete dominate from all angles: its regular twentieth-century lines broken by Greek ornamentation, religious statues, decorative palm trees, and a crucifix-topped, Art Deco tower. On a deck above the main doorway is the *tria haec* (these three)—statues of Faith, Hope, and Charity—clustered around a giant clock.

I approached the main doorway, signing in and glancing up at the metal plaque dedicated by the American Association of the Philippines in February

1954. It read, "Through these portals passed up to ten thousand Americans and other nationals of the free world who were interned within these walls by the Japanese military. Suffering great physical privation and national humiliation from January 4, 1942, until liberated February 3, 1945, by the American forces under General Douglas MacArthur."

The security guard was very helpful when I asked him where I could find information on the war. He pointed me in the direction of the public relations office, and I went inside the building. I immediately felt that I was in an old prestigious college. The foyer was magnificent, with huge murals of religious scenes and Catholic history on the walls. The floor was stone. All door arches and frames were of dark wood. A wide central stairway with huge wooden banisters rubbed smooth by age was commanded by a bust of Aquinas, staring somewhat sternly down at the students from his perch on the landing. The schedule seemed to be between classes, and the stairway and halls were choked with young people, normal college kids on a normal weekday at school. It would have been in this area that the starving, rapturous internees sang "God Bless America" with their liberators, as the body of the dying Japanese officer was dragged before them.

In the public relations office all was in turmoil. The 70th University Athletic Association of the Philippines (UAAP) basketball season was beginning that week, and the staff was trying to bundle a commemorative publication for distribution. Stacks of these glossy publications covered every available space. UST was the defending league champion, and I glanced through the slick, thick-papered piece as I waited for the director to see me. She did, and after an exchange of cards, I was pointed to the museum on the second floor. Up past the nose of Aquinas I went to the oldest museum in the nation.

The receptionist collected my thirty pesos, and when I told her my interest in the internment camp, she politely told me to look around while the assistants set up the World War II exhibit. Somewhat perplexed at why they would set up a dismantled exhibit just for me, I spent some time meandering around the natural history collection and its selection of stuffed wildlife. Here was the flying fox from Samar, a giant crocodile, a number of eagles, and a fruit bat. All of the prizes looked as though they were from 1941 at the least. I knew that during the war the Japanese allowed some internees to catalogue various parts of the collection, and I wondered if caring for these confined specimens gave the prisoners any type of empathy.

Two men arrived with large cardboard poster boards from a storage room and placed them against the wall. When they finished I was told that this was the internee exhibit. There were eight boards, all five feet high and about three feet wide, arranged chronologically by topic. They contained the Santo Tomas internee story preceded by a background on World War II. Virtually all of it was general knowledge, but there were some photographs I had never seen, particularly of the starkly emaciated prisoners. I spent the most time with the last two boards, which contained a list of the internees. I found the name of Merv Simpson's stepfather, John McFie, and his wife, Merv's mother. Here was my old friend, Earl Hornbostel. The major chronicler of the event, A. V. H. Hartendorp, was there as well. I searched in vain, however, for Walter Scott Price's name. Why was it omitted? I assumed that it was because he was transferred to Los Baños, but he had been a prisoner here, and I found its absence somewhat disconcerting.

Outside again and on the grounds, I held a copy of a map drawn by an internee. Things have changed, of course. At some point the Education Building received a facelift and became the UST Hospital. An impressive statue of Bishop Miguel de Benavides, who donated his personal library to help found the institution in 1605, now stands facing down the lane toward España Street where a row of internee huts once existed. The yard's shanty plots, which once precariously held the lives of hundreds of inmates who comically named them Glamourville, Out Yonder, the Southwest Territory, Shantytown, and Froggy Bottom, were now being put to better use as classroom and faculty buildings. The long open corridor where Battlin' Basic and Georgia Peach rolled up was still there, and a row of acacia trees still runs from the bishop's statue to the front gate. Surely they were the same trees that provided shade to the prisoners.

The Santo Tomas rescue, combined with the taking of nearby Bilibid Prison, was one of the shining moments in U.S. military history, and it was particularly gratifying for MacArthur. But the story is not without its detractors. Some Filipinos scoff at the notion of the United States saving the lives of several thousand Westerners but ultimately causing the deaths of a hundred thousand Manileños. Some wonder why the Americans seemed to stop fighting after taking the campus, allowing the Japanese to regroup and begin their horrifying slaughter. These emotional questions have sober answers: MacArthur had every right to save U.S. citizens he thought were in danger of execution, and the flying columns were not designed to attack Manila but to take just three objectives. One incident, however, is not so easily explained. On February 6, the day *before* he made his way into Manila and visited Santo Tomas, MacArthur proclaimed the following:

> At 6:30 this morning, Manila had fallen. . . . The fall of Manila was the end of one great phase of the Pacific struggle and set the stage for another. . . . We are well on our way but Japan itself is our final goal. With Australia saved, the Philippines liberated, and the ultimate redemption of the East Indies and Malaya made a certainty, our motto becomes: "on to Tokyo."[6]

But MacArthur was mistaken. In fact, to some he was criminally negligent. He must have at least suspected that there were thousands of well-armed, deeply entrenched Japanese troops still in the city, and that hundreds of thousands of Manileños were trapped behind their lines. Manila had not fallen. The battle, and the horror of Manila, was just beginning.

16
ERMITA

O ver the Pasig River south of Santo Tomas and just below the walled
city of Intramuros lies Ermita. This *arrabal* (township) was named
after the Catholic hermitage that was built here in the sixteenth century. Today, as during the war, it sits neatly next to Roxas Boulevard (formerly
Dewey) and the bay, with T. M. Kalaw (formerly San Luis) to the north, Taft
Avenue to the east, and Pedro Gil Street (formerly Herran) to the south.

Ermita is noteworthy in that it was, and to some degree still is, a melt-
ing pot of cultures. Here lived the old Spanish families like the Cuadras, the
Barbazas, and, perhaps most prominent, the Guerreros. But Ermita also became the favorite residential area of the Americans during the early colonial
period. Indeed, amid the sprawling acacia trees and the cool breeze coming off
the bay, Ermita evolved into a small American enclave. Many of the Americans
were managers of Manila operations and government workers, and some were
military personnel. When the bay was reclaimed and after Dewey Boulevard
was constructed, Americans quickly saw the value of seaside real estate and
began investing in the area. American social establishments, such as the Elks
and the Army and Navy clubs, sprang up by 1910. Protestant, Methodist,
Episcopalian, Presbyterian, and Baptist churches were built in the township.
The U.S.-inspired and U.S.-funded University of the Philippines (UP) was constructed near the Spanish-built Ateneo de Manila, and student dormitories
were abundant. High-rise apartment buildings were built, as were hotels. The
area was refined and progressive. It was a good place to live.[1]

Such ambience lasted only to January 1942, when the Americans and most other Westerners were rounded up and taken away. The area's atmosphere changed completely in February 1945. For during the second and third weeks of that month, this entire section of the city became a living hell.

Even though Ermita was the most devastated of all Manila districts, I wanted to see if anything remained of the prewar town. More importantly, I was looking for the remains of American architecture, specifically the works of Daniel Burnham and William Parsons. I began my walk, however, not looking for the high neoclassic designs of great American architects, but for a house of a long-dead expatriate. I started my walk in a place called Paco.

Paco abuts Ermita on the east. The word "paco" may come from a fern that grows in the area, but this association is not certain. At the onset of the war, Paco was mostly a working-class area, although the section that bordered Ermita was wealthy. Here, residents were a mixture of successful Filipino professionals, old Spanish families, Americans, and Europeans. The family of Elpidio Quirino, the future president, lived on Colorado Street (now Felipe Agoncillo). The Spanish Consulate was on the same street. Close by lived Walter Scott Price, the American "transportation king" from Leyte, who was at the time wallowing in the Los Baños prison camp. At the corner of Colorado and California streets was his Manila mansion, where he and his wife entertained the papal legate and the archbishop of Manila, as well as many others.

Just as its sibling in Tacloban did, the Manila Price house figured historically during the war. It, too, had its garden violated for building bomb shelters. Here, however, the L-shaped shelters were constructed by and for the residents, not for Japanese officers. For months, neighbors in the area had gone to the Price compound when there was a U.S. air raid. In February, as the U.S. shelling began in Manila, it became even more popular. The Japanese had decided to attempt a retreat back into Ermita and, after torching Paco's commercial center and many of its houses, set up gun positions on street corners. They planned to kill civilians as they fled their burning homes. This dual U.S.-Japanese threat caused a large number of people to flee and seek safety in the Price house and the shelter, both of which were somewhat protected by an eight-foot wall. The residence was only two streets away from the Philippine General Hospital, and during ferocious American artillery attacks, those who were denied shelter in the hospital also found the compound. On February 10, approximately two hundred people were inside the Price residence and its yard.[2]

All morning the terrified neighbors of the area cowered in the shelter and within the house. The shelling was terrific. At 1:00 p.m., a group of Japanese soldiers entered the grounds and set up a machine gun facing a huddle of people on the driveway near the California Street gate. Several of the refugees pleaded with the Japanese that there were only women and children on the grounds, and after some consideration, the soldiers dismantled the gun and left. The U.S. shelling continued. At 4:00 p.m., the Japanese returned and ordered all people out of the house, and those crouching in the yard were ordered toward the garage, which was in the back of the house. As the people began to move, the Japanese opened up with automatic and rifle fire. They threw hand grenades into the shelter. Then they went body to body bayoneting anyone who moved.

Leticia Sta. Maria Rinongbayan was a child when her family sought shelter at the Price residence. She remembered:

> We (my brother [Carlos, 13], sister [Zenaida, 12], and a cousin Mario) were waiting with other people on the lawn/patio. Somehow my sister and I got separated from Carlos after the shooting. I saw him and Mario already dead. [Then] A Japanese soldier was on top of the wall fence and he was shooting at everyone laying on the lawn. My sister covered me with her body. She was shot. I was covered by her blood.[3]

Three hours later a second squad of Japanese entered the compound through the Colorado Street gate. The survivors from the earlier massacre had assembled in a bunch inside the compound alongside the California Street wall. They were discovered and shot against the wall. Then the Japanese soldiers went inside the house, where they found alcohol. They began to party, drinking, singing, and clapping their hands to old schoolboy and military songs, accompanied by the groans of the dying civilians outside in the yard. It is thought that most of the estimated two hundred people who went to the Price residence that day were murdered.

The area around Taft Avenue over to Felipe Agoncillo Street has changed dramatically since Simeona and Walter Scott Price threw their parties. It is no longer a quiet, urbane neighborhood for the upper-middle and upper classes. Rather, it is now a heavily congested area, with innumerable jeepneys and buses plying their trade, congesting the air with exhaust fumes and blaring horns.

I was eager to find the Price house, but I quickly saw that identifying where it stood would be difficult. Not only had the street names changed, so had the address numbers. The Price residence had been 534; now all the addresses carried four digits, and nothing in the area began with a five. My only bit of evidence was that the compound had stood on the corner of California and Colorado, and thus I knew that there were four possible points where it could have been. Now, at one corner, was a pool hall. A second corner featured a tall concrete wall that surrounded a parking lot and was adorned with posters of political candidates and a statue of Mary accompanied by a sign that asked all pedestrians to "always pray the rosary." On the third corner was a nondescript building that housed pawnshops and other small businesses. The fourth, nearly hidden behind an eight-foot concrete wall and the verdure of large trees, was a stately two-story house. Behind it towered a tall glass office building with the mysterious word "Yakult" at its top.

From across Escoda Street I pondered the house. Yes, this place was or had been a private home, and its owner was surely wealthy. But there would have been other wealthy private homes in this area during the war; in fact, all four corners probably held such houses. I considered the details of the house, which did not suggest anything in particular, save for a relatively recent paint job. It was a large but not ostentatious building, built out of stone and concrete with a high wall surrounding it. The wooden frames around the windows gave it an almost Tudor appearance. But it did have a large gate on the Escoda Street side, and I could see a smaller gate on the Felipe Agoncillo Street side. This was exactly how survivors of the massacre described the layout of the house. My rising excitement was tempered by the sign on the outside wall, which held the painted slogan, "Yakult Everyday! Everyday ok! Sigurado ka tiyan!" (You can be sure!) What did it mean?

I walked across the street and approached the smaller gate on the Felipe

Agoncillo driveway. There was a security guard station, and the guard holding a shotgun told me to register. I did, telling another shotgun-toting guard that I was an American professor writing a book on World War II and was looking for the Walter Scott Price house. Was this it? This guard said, "For a while, sir," and called someone. The head of security came and politely asked me what I wanted. I repeated my credentials and my questions. I knew from historical evidence that the Price house stood on the corner of California and Colorado, and that was right here.

He shook his head. No, he assured me, the Japanese destroyed all the houses around here during the war. The house here was built after the war, maybe in the 1950s. His body language suggested I should leave.

I was disappointed. But peering through the gate I saw, unmistakably, a porte cochère at the front of the house. A porte cochère was usually not built on a house since the demise of the carriage, which occurred before the 1950s. I pressed the director, asking if there was anyone inside the house who could help me. Minutes passed as I appealed to the security director further, knowing this man had a job to do and that I was not making his day any easier. I was sure I was right, or at least I was sure I wanted to be proved wrong. Finally exasperated, the man, whose good heart showed, gently took me by the arm and out into Agoncillo Street.

"I cannot answer your questions," he said apologetically. "I do not know the answers. But see that house down the street on the right? That is the former owner of the house. Talk to him."

I thanked him, we shook hands, and I walked down the street. The house that I came to was old, wooden, and in rough shape. An elderly man was sitting on the porch, smoking a cigarette and reading the newspaper. The porch was at least eight feet high, and I could only see his head, but I got his attention and asked him if he was the owner of this house. I received another disappointing answer: no, the owner was in the States. Looking up, I then asked him who the owner was of the big house down the street and told him I was an American university professor writing a book on the war.

The man leaned out over the porch banister and considered me. He had close-cropped silver hair, and I noticed he had but a single tooth in his mouth, and that one did not have much time left. "Do you mean that house?"

he said in fine English, pointing to from whence I came. "That is Mr. Price's house. But he is dead a long time."

Elated, I thanked him and, with squared shoulders, strode back down Agoncillo Street to the Price house. I politely told the security director of my discovery and said I wanted to take pictures of the house. He said he would have to get permission. After several phone calls and a fifteen-minute wait, I was taken inside the gate, through a hallway of the house, and then into a modern building connected to the house by a walkway. I was to see one of the directors of the Yakult Company, Mr. Go (a pseudonym).

Mr. Go was a Chinoy, a Filipino of Chinese ancestry, in his thirties. His office was trendy, immaculate, and visually punctuated by the crucifix and statue of the Holy Family on his desk. After a perfunctory greeting and after his secretary placed a tray of the company's product, biogenic milk, on the desk between us, I asked him point blank: "Is this the Walter Scott Price house?"

"Yes, it is," he said without reservation. He went on to say that the house was approximately 80 percent original, although changes were made by Yakult and two previous owners. I later found out that the one of the house's reincarnations was that of a brothel masquerading as a hotel, and afterward it became the Manila Club, home of the British Association in Manila.[4] I was welcome to take pictures of the outside of the house but not the interior. I promised I would abide by this instruction and thanked him.

I discussed my research for a few moments, telling Mr. Go of the details of the massacre that happened here more than sixty years ago. His features remained firm, and I had no way of knowing if he was already aware he worked over an area where hundreds of innocents were murdered. As we shook hands at my parting, he said quite thoughtfully, "Do you know the irony here? Yakult is a Japanese company."

The galvanic disclosure made me flinch. I thanked him again and left, telling him I could find my way out. Once back inside the original house, I paused to consider the fine masonry and an exquisite doorway with its curved wooden lattice windows. Walter Scott Price and Simeona would have walked through these halls. Some of their children would have grown up here. Their grandchildren would have played inside this house. I took some photographs.

Outside I met the security director, and now we were old friends. I related to him about the L-shaped air raid shelter in the garden, how the Japanese came in through the gates, and the chronology of the massacre in the shelter and the garage. We looked around. There was no more garden, only concrete busy with Yakult trucks and sport utility vehicles and scooters on a working day. There was no garage, although the director seemed to think it would have been built against the Escoda Street wall. I silently disagreed, thinking instead it was behind the house, where the Yakult addition now stood. We were standing where the California Street driveway would have been, and the director excitedly pointed out that the large gate was original. We walked over to it. Yes, the steel gate, elegantly simple, could have well been the one the Japanese pushed open that February afternoon, hauling in the machine gun. It would have been from this spot that they let loose on the terrified people. I turned and faced the house: it would have been an easy slaughter.

In looking up at the house, I thought again of Walter Scott Price and how odd it was that both of his houses were connected to the war. As he lay wasting away in Los Baños, first the Japanese and then MacArthur slept in his Leyte bed, both having chased his wife and children out of the property. Near the time of his rescue, his Manila home became a refuge and then a killing field for his friends and neighbors. During the few days of life he had after Los Baños, did his children tell him of the houses? Did they tell him of the horrors here in Manila?

Waving good-bye to the smiling security director, I made my way out of the Agoncillo gate and turned the corner to walk down Escoda. The street was named for Josefa Llanes Escoda, truly one of the finest women in Philippine history. Educated at the University of the Philippines and later at Columbia University, her résumé of civic work is astonishing: she helped develop the Philippine Red Cross, establishing chapters around the country; she founded the Girls Scouts of the Philippines, Boys Town of the Philippines, and the Federation of Women's Clubs of the Philippines; she worked to improve conditions in prisons; and she was a tireless advocate of women's issues. During the war, she and her husband provided food, medicine, and other supplies to Filipino and American prisoners in the camps. Under suspicion of being a guerrilla, her husband was arrested in late 1944 and sent to Fort Santiago, where he would eventually be executed. She refused to leave his side and was imprisoned herself. Early in January 1945, she was seen being removed from Fort Santiago and taken to a building on the campus of Far Eastern University. There, it is assumed she was executed. Her body was never found.

Escoda Street offered a stroll through pure, old postwar Manila, an experience one does not find in shimmering, global Makati. The hot air was a miasma of diesel exhaust and humidity. Along the sidewalks of dark, dirty, broken concrete, people in makeshift stalls fried banana sticks in palm oil. Vendors competing shoulder to shoulder supplied pirated DVDs of the latest movies. The Metro Rail Transit (MRT) ran above Taft Avenue, one of the few remaining American street names. The train's rumble added to the sweltering cacophony. As I passed underneath the tracks and near one of the concrete pylons, the odor of urine was overpowering.

On Taft Avenue, in front of the Philippine General Hospital and the UP medical compound, I saw students and office workers, jeepney passengers and children, all naturally oblivious to the ghosts that surely must be walking these streets. Sixty years ago this street would have been a thoroughfare of terror. The berserk Japanese troops shot anyone who ventured out, especially those trying to escape their burning houses. From across the Pasig River and from areas east of the city, U.S. artillery fire destroyed entire blocks, and the residents were often caught underneath their destroyed homes. Frantically, people tried to make their way to the largest, perhaps safest, structure in the area, the American-designed Philippine General Hospital.

Some made it safely, others did not. Some witnessed events that surely would haunt them forever. On February 12, a Spanish thirteen-year-old, Luis Esteban, joined a group of neighbors who had banded together and attempted the exodus from Pennsylvania Avenue to the hospital, a walk of just a few blocks. As U.S. shells wailed down around them, they were stopped by Japanese troops. The group that Esteban was with became temporarily divided. People panicked and began screaming. He looked back at the others of his group.

> Screams were also coming from one of the [neighbor's] maids, a young
> girl in her late teens. From where we were crouching across the road we

could see several Japanese soldiers pin her down while the others took turn raping her. The poor girl was raped repeatedly, after which they put an end to her young life by sticking a bayonet in her and ripping her stomach open.[5]

Esteban made it to the Philippine General Hospital, which became a sanctum for the Ermita-Paco survivors. As U.S. forces continued its shelling, refugee numbers had swollen to seven thousand. The Japanese had emplaced sandbags and machine guns at the hospital's entrance and at street corners surrounding the large complex; however, no troops were actually stationed within the hospital walls. For days the U.S. forces would not operate against the hospital, owing to the tradition of medical sanctuary. On February 12, however, the planners assumed it was occupied by the Japanese and lifted the artillery restrictions. Now those refugees inside the compound who had escaped the personal insanity of the Japanese had to contend with the impersonal horror of an American bombardment.

Within the buildings, patients, families, neighbors, and complete strangers huddled together in the corridors and wards under the harrowing whine of artillery shells. Some were sick, some were wounded, all were terrified. Doctors, nurses, interns, and orderlies tried to attend to both the patients and the asylum seekers, a Herculean endeavor given the circumstances. There was no electricity, and at night only candles provided light. There was no food save for what the refugees were able to carry through the Japanese lines. There was no water, and the smoke of burning buildings only further parched already dried mouths and throats. An artesian well on the grounds undoubtedly saved the lives of some suffering inside, but reaching it also took lives: refugees had to dash out of the building and through the flying shrapnel and sniper fire to fill their containers at the pump. And there was another nightmare: Japanese soldiers snuck into the building during the night and snatched women, whose raped and mutilated bodies would be found on the grounds in the light of day.

The shelling of the hospital grounds continued for three days as the casualties inside the hospital mounted. It was especially heavy on February 14, when the United States used immense portions of high explosives and white phosphorus shells. The next day, American infantrymen were just across Taft Avenue at the front of the hospital, stalled, and taking causalities from the last remaining Japanese artillery pieces in pillboxes and sandbag emplacements. Tanks were called in, and the ensuing duels between the two forces resulted in the hospital buildings incurring even more hits.

The Japanese fought desperately, and it was not until February 17 that U.S. troops were on the grounds, taking hospital and university buildings after bitter hand-to-hand fighting. That day, the Americans finally made it into the hospital proper, with patients and refugees, who had endured a week of U.S. bombardment, screaming in delight at the sight of GIs walking through the wards. Young Luis Esteban remembered:

> The first one [American] we saw was down on one knee, carbine at the ready. We mobbed him, hugging and kissing him in joy. A few feet behind him was another G.I. We mobbed him, too. And the third and the fourth. We couldn't contain ourselves. The poor soldiers realised that there were snipers about and they were trying to quiet us down. It was hopeless. The snipers didn't worry us. We were with the Americans! We were liberated![6]

The fact that U.S. shelling was seen by the people as a method of liberation seems extraordinary now. At its end, the battle for the Philippine General Hospital cost 150 civilian dead, with perhaps a thousand wounded. But there were other losses as well. Half of the physical plant was razed, and nearly all the equipment and supplies were lost. The clinical histories of thousands of patients spanning a thirty-four-year service were destroyed.

Today the Philippine General Hospital sits very much as it did in 1945, a cream-colored handsome structure that immediately impresses. Commissioned in 1907 and finished in 1910, the building was the product of William Parsons, whose modern American design deferred to Spanish influences, or what in America was called the California school. The extensive two-story hospital was built of reinforced concrete and featured high, broad archways that introduced corridors, wings, and courtyards. With its red-tiled roof and numerous flanking palm trees, the building would not appear out of place in Los Angeles or San Diego. During the prewar years, it was considered state of the art, equipped with the most up-to-date medical facilities, and today it is still considered a progressive medical center.[7]

The hospital's mission statement calls it the haven for the underprivileged. Walking into the compound from Taft Avenue, I found it to be the case. Immediately Taft's noise barrage seemed to stop, and the air smelled cleaner. In a large, open-air building were people—many elderly, all clearly disadvantaged—waiting, I presumed, for treatment. On these grounds, it was impossible not to feel a sense of nobility. It was refreshing. The state of Philippine medicine, so damaged by the flight of highly trained personnel to overseas destinations, is also hampered by the belief many Filipinos hold that if you do not have money you will not be treated. Not here. The poor congregated in numbers to this lovely center of kindness, so bright with hope.

I walked to the wide main entrance. At the doorway I stood to ponder three or more historical plaques. One I had seen before. It read, "Rebuilt with the aid of the people of the United States of America under the Philippine Rehabilitation Act of 1946." Again, the Americans built it, they destroyed it, and they rebuilt it. I turned to the other wall and read a plaque commemorating those who died here in 1945. I raised my camera to photograph it.

A tall woman wearing some type of identification badge came suddenly from inside the building and said in a loud voice, "No cameras here, please! No taking pictures!"

I was surprised, both at the tone of her voice and the notion that I was in the wrong. Perhaps she thought I was some type of paparazzi hoping to snap a photo of a celebrity coming into the institution. I pointed to the wall and said I only wanted to photograph the plaques.

"No picture taking! No! Please leave at once!"

Intimidated by her harsh demeanor, I walked embarrassed over the sunlit grounds and past the poor people in the waiting shed. They seemed to look at me curiously. With one last glance at the hospital, I turned and went back out to the street.

I was going to travel west into deep Ermita, the real Manila, deep into time, deep into the visions of such men as Daniel Burnham and William Parsons, and deep into the suffering of thousands of innocent people. I wanted to explore something that did not exist any longer. Back onto Taft, I then turned down Pedro Gil Street (named after the pre- and postwar physician, journalist, and legislator), passing the large classical designs of the UP medical buildings. I pushed into the heart of Ermita, across Mabini, a street named for the revolutionary leader, Apolonio Mabini. Then one block over to M. H. del Pilar, where I turned and walked north. Del Pilar was named for another revolutionary hero, Marcelo Hilario del Pilar, one of the early founders of the Propaganda Movement, which formed the heart of the revolution against Spain.

Both Mabini and del Pilar streets sit just behind Roxas Boulevard and the seafront, and were once the nucleus of Manila's red-light district. In the early 1990s the mayor drove out all of the foreign bar owners, who pimped thousands of young provincial girls to Western tourists. For years afterward, the Mabini–del Pilar area tried to pass itself off as an upscale antique district but never succeeded. Now, the old ways seem to be making a comeback. The businesses on del Pilar had a definite Western influence: here was a Dutch bar and restaurant, an Australian pub, and several bars that were clearly designed for sexual tourists of all nationalities. There were even a number of store signs in Arabic. The bright international flavor is somewhat misleading, though. M. H. del Pilar is a narrow, dark street, with broken sidewalks, tin sidings, bad odors, and poor people.

I came to the T-shaped intersection of Arquiza and del Pilar. The Ermita church was to my right, set back from the street, quiet and unassuming. As with nearly all churches in the islands, it boasts a storied past. In May 1571 a party of Miquel Lopez de Legaspi's company wandered into the area and saw natives adoring a wooden statue placed in a tree. The Spaniards decided it was the Virgin Mary, perhaps lost by one of Magellan's men years earlier, and gave it the name Nuestra Señora de Guia (Our Lady of Guidance). On that spot a small Spanish hermitage was built, hence the name Ermita. From the hermitage a succession of eight churches were built, all later destroyed in one way or another. In front of me was the ninth church, a simple white affair succeeding the gorgeous 135-year-old edition blown away in February 1945.

That day was the first time I ventured inside, although I had stood in front of it on many occasions. Despite its plain exterior, the inside was beautiful: on the ceilings were murals, perhaps twelve in all, of traditional Christian scenes, mostly of the Passion. The church was silent and empty except for myself and a young woman kneeling in the first pew near the altar. I stood off to one side, not wanting to disturb her in prayer. Presently, she blessed herself, stood up, and walked to the entrance at the rear of the church.

Near the doorway were two statues, and she visited both. The first was a Santo Niño, the child Jesus, standing with hands in prayer and wrapped in a luxuriously intricate woven gown. His hair, made probably from abaca, was auburn and curled way down the statue's back. On the folded hands someone had strung garlands of *sampaguitas*, the fragrant white flowers of a species of jasmine that are popular here. The second larger statue was of Christ carrying the cross and bent almost on one knee. Like the Santo Niño, he was immaculately dressed, here in a long red gown, with curly black hair made of Manila hemp flowing down past his shoulders. The girl stood in front of this statue as well for a few moments and then suddenly stuck her hand underneath the gown for just a moment. She bowed her head, removed her hand, and left the church.

Now alone, I wondered what had brought her here at mid-morning on a weekday. I was also curious as to why she stuck her hand underneath the gown. Going over to the statue, I gently lifted the heavy material to find a perfectly formed foot of Christ.

I left the church and returned to the street. Standing in front of the church on M. H. del Pilar, I looked west toward the seafront. A little park there ran from M. H. del Pilar over to Roxas Boulevard, right in front of the U.S. Embassy. Named Plaza Nuestra Señora de Guia, it used to be known as Plaza Fergusson, after Arthur W. Fergusson, an American executive secretary throughout the imperial period. His knowledge of Spanish allowed him to be a translator at the 1898 Treaty of Paris, the confab that gave the islands to the United States. As an interpreter in Manila, he worked successfully with both Americans and Filipinos, and thus he became one of the most popular officials of his era. His bust once stood in the plaza, but it resides now on the embassy grounds, having been replaced by a postmodern angular bronze work of the park's patroness. At one time the park was probably a nice place, but at least for a decade, strange, disenfranchised persons have inhabited it. Drug users, pimps, beggars, and the mentally unstable seemed to congregate here in the plaza, whose western boundary looks to the hope of America while its eastern boundary to the guidance of Our Lady.

On February 9, 1945, this little park formed the epicenter of evil. Late in the afternoon that day, Japanese troops began to knock on the doors of homes and businesses in the then-up-scale neighborhood. Many of the residents were from established families and expatriates who, for various reasons, were not interned at Santo Tomas. The Japanese told them to gather in the park. Perhaps fifteen hundred to two thousand persons packed under the trees, uncertain as to the Japanese intentions. Then the Japanese went through the crowd, identifying and separating the young women and teenage girls. As many as four hundred females were taken away. The men, older women, and children were taken to the Manila Hotel and to apartment buildings in the area.[8]

The young women were put into groups of about twenty-five. From Plaza Fergusson they were taken to nearby apartment buildings, such as the Miramar and the Alhambra, while some were ordered around the corner to the Bay View Hotel, then one of the most fashionable hotels in Manila. At the Bay View, a few women were put into hotel rooms, but most were ordered to the main dining room. The women were Filipinos, Chinese, and Caucasians of mostly European nationalities. Unknown to the women at the time was that the Japanese had set up these places as *joro* houses (forced brothels) so that their soldiers could slake their lust after coming off the firing line.

The tales told of the next few days in the Bay View are horrific. Girls just into their teens were raped repeatedly, some more than fifteen times. Often, the girls would have just been taken from their sisters or mothers. Many of the girls were slapped and beaten. Some were gang-raped. A few were mutilated. The girls would then be taken back to the dining room or other locations, where they were ordered to wait and be chosen again. They also related a racial element: the Japanese seemed to favor the fair-skinned girls, apparently to satisfy feelings of hatred and superiority.

The testimony of Pacita Tapia, a Filipina, was recorded in 1945. It serves to illustrate the atrocity of the Bay View Hotel.

All night long that first night, small groups of Japanese —two or three at a time—would come into the room every few minutes and would select girls after examining them by flashlights, and even though the girls attempted to get away from them and although the girls pleaded, begged, and cried out and struggled, the Japanese would finally, by strength, grasp and drag the girls out of the room. They would take the girls one or two at a time and the girls would not return for intervals ranging from a few minutes up to maybe three-quarters of an hour. In one or two places when the girls resisted, I remember the Japanese would point their knives or bayonets at their stomachs and the girls were so paralyzed with fear they could resist no further.[9]

A number of women were released the next day. For some, however, the rapes would continue until February 12, when the Bay View Hotel caught fire, allowing the women to dash to safety.

For a moment I considered the narrow park and its twisted place in history from the front of the church. I looked back at the church and remembered reading the account by Wilfrido Maria Guerrero, whose family had lived next to the plaza. He saw that the "Ermita Church was filled with civilian refugees from houses torched by the Japanese. Soldiers headed towards the church [and] started shooting the people fleeing from it." He saw how the "Japanese systemically burned the church," how "fire reached the choir loft, then the steeple and the belfry," and how the "belfry gave way and the bell crashed down without a whimper."[10]

Then I crossed M. H. del Pilar and walked past the busy Wendy's and down the plaza toward Roxas Boulevard and the U.S. Embassy. I was in uneasy air. Men sidled up to me and quietly asked if I would like to purchase one of the "real" Rolex watches in their hands. Hands reached out and demanded pesos. Others held out a wad of pesos, telling me I would get a good deal if I exchanged my dollars with them. People wanted me to buy various types of tourist trinkets. There were tourists to be had. On the opposite side of the plaza was Club Edo, a Japanese KTV (karaoke television) bar, where tired businessmen from Tokyo could relax with poor girls from the provinces. On my side of the plaza was the Swagman Hotel, an Ermita postwar landmark of sorts, where one could see middle-aged and elderly Australian and American men entering and leaving arm in arm with young Filipinas.

At Roxas I turned right and walked up the block, past the Bayview Park Hotel, which was built over the ruins of the sinister original and painted a noisome shade of fleshy pink. From the corner of United Nations Avenue and Roxas, I could see exactly the four shoreline points the U.S. forces had to take before they could move on Intramuros: the U.S. Embassy, the former Army and Navy Club and the Elks Club, the open space of the Luneta, and the Manila Hotel.

To my left across the street was the embassy. The attractive building was almost completely shaded by trees. On the sidewalk out front was the long line of Filipino supplicants, eyes wide with hope for visas and hands full with large envelopes and folders to substantiate their claims of entrance. Every morning there was a queue here; it would begin just after midnight and last most of the day. This building was now largely rebuilt. The original was the U.S. high commissioner's residence during the colonial period and became the home of General Homma in 1942. It then became the Japanese Embassy in 1943 and thus the objective of the U.S. 12th Calvary on February 20, 1945.

The U.S. Army attacked the residence from across Dewey Boulevard, and after a two-hour fight, it became theirs. The fight then spilled over to the two American clubs close by. Here, despite the use of tanks, the combat became intimate. Hand grenades were thrown at close quarters. Soldiers fought room to room. The Army and Navy Club's building was particularly hard hit as land mines and barrels of oil burned the fabulous woodwork and destroyed the roof. Although sharp, the engagement ended quickly; many of the Japanese had withdrawn during the night to positions closer to Intramuros.

To see the two historic buildings, I had to cross the wide Roxas, a somewhat daunting task given the morning traffic. Then I walked down South Boulevard and saw the top of the Manila Hotel peaking over the park's trees adjacent to the Rizal Avenue Extension on my right and the old club buildings on my left. Down the street I could see the bay. The street was lightly populated, with only a few joggers and people on their way to work. It seemed to be rather tranquil.

At the bay, I saw the vision that captivated Daniel Burnham, who thought in 1905 that the harborside boulevard should be used to its maximum potential. In doing so, he meant to house and entertain the continually growing influx of Americans in Manila. He called for three buildings to realize this potential: the Army and Navy Club as a social club for the military, the Elks Club for the American military and expatriates, and the Manila Hotel for the Americans living in or visiting the city. Burnham would turn the actual design of these buildings to other Americans, including William Parsons.

Today's Army and Navy Club, at least from the street, is a dignified white structure, nearly hidden by beautiful palms and acacia trees, and guarded by a well-carved wrought iron fence. The original was a spacious H-shaped affair that was, obviously, meant for military personnel, officers, and their families. The club had a reputation of being among the best of its type in the world, with excellent food, a superb staff, and a swimming pool. It also boasted a bowling ally, tennis and squash courts, and a huge officer's bar. It was the hub of Manila's military social life, exemplified by the radio broadcast of the annual Army-Navy football game, *the* event of the 1930s. During its heyday, MacArthur and many other important U.S. officials frequented the club's swank American environment, but it was off-limits to all but highly placed Filipinos, save, of course, for the waiters. After the war, it survived as an incorporated club, but it fell on hard times after the 1960s. The city took it over in the early 1980s, and for a while it housed the city architect's office until the crumbling building forced its occupants out. Afterward, the once-grand structure was used as a manufacturing place for the city's Christmas lanterns. The building decayed further, nearly to the point of no return. Then the city took action. It was resurrected as the Museo de Manila, but after a grand opening, it quickly closed its doors. As of now, a newly formed Manila heritage group will try and refurbish the once-mighty colonial building.

Such decay and uncertainty have not been the case with its next-door neighbor, the former Elks Club. While the Army and Navy Club has seen times of degrading use and vacancy, the Elks Club eventually became the Museo Pambata (Children's Museum). Daily, busloads of youngsters enter the doors that once housed a whites-only, men-only private club. Just as the Army and Navy Club, this building was also painted white, but multicolored banners near the windows gave it a festive appearance, one that children would appreciate. On the outside wall of the Museo Pambata is a National Historical Institute plaque that identifies the building as the Elks Club, notes that Parsons was the designer, and offers kudos to him in its description that he was someone who loved the Philippines and donated his time from the heart. The marker also identifies the building's other roles as the Museum of Philippine Art, the headquarters of the Overseas Press Club, and now the children's museum.

In many ways this building might be the most historically important American artifact. It formed the center of American society in the early period, and without it the community may not have jelled the way it did. During the first few years of occupation, many Americans did not own private houses, and the club became a meeting place for businessmen and former soldiers with their families. Its patriotic theme clearly indicated that it catered to the ex-military men whose sentiment was against Philippine independence. These audacious men really founded the American Philippines, and the club was their fulcrum. Now, more than a century later, the fire-breathing soldiers of '99 have been replaced by curious Filipino children, who are doubtlessly ecstatic to be out of the classroom.

Leaving these twin testaments to Burnham and Parson's colonial fantasies, I made my way northwest on Roxas. Down the street, I could see the Manila Hotel. In front of me was Rizal Park, the long green expanse commonly known as the Luneta, synonymous with lunette, or half moon. This national park is dedicated to the memory of José Rizal, who was executed here, along with other Filipinos deemed a threat to the Spanish rule. Only a few years later, Burnham saw the U-shaped 148 acres as the centerpiece for his government center and designed his quintet of government buildings in a crescent at one end. As noted earlier, only three were ever finished.

Standing with the hotel to one side and the park's monument to Rizal in front of me, it was easy to envision the horrible dynamics of a February day in 1945. The park is dominated by the Rizal monument, a beautiful granite and bronze affair that holds the hero's remains and is guarded continuously by soldiers. As with other Manila landmarks, this one, too, has strong associations with the world war. Here, at the foot of the monument, survivors who had been chased out of the Elks Club clustered and shivered in fear. A larger group that had just recently fled the Manila Hotel also made its way to the

Luneta. This latter group had been part of a contingent of anywhere from two thousand to five thousand people detained in the Manila Hotel and of a sizable number of women who had been sequestered there and raped at will by Japanese troops coming off the battle line. On the night of February 18, with U.S. troops making their way up Dewey Boulevard, Japanese soldiers went through the hotel annex collecting pieces of furniture and anything else combustible they could find. In the basement, they built a bonfire and lit it. Something in the cellar exploded, and the building shuddered. Flames began to race out of the basement windows and upward into the hotel, where the civilians were being kept. Many jumped out of the windows. Some survived and made their way to the nearby Luneta and the sanctuary of the Rizal monument. There were men and women of all nationalities, many of them former residents of the area around Plaza Fergusson. At the foot of the Rizal monument, where the remains of the patriot rested, they huddled, exhausted. There they informed each other of those people who had survived, or did not survive, the rape of Ermita.

On February 22 MacArthur returned to his old home at the hotel. It was an odd episode in the battle. MacArthur naturally enough was curious to see what had remained of his home and possessions during the three-plus years the Japanese had occupied Manila. He had reason to believe that most of his personal belongings, including a vast library, were still there. The U.S. attack started on February 21, with tanks and artillery blasting away at the fortified positions around and inside the hotel. Although the shelling continued into the next day, MacArthur stood on the Luneta, under the fire of Japanese machine guns, watching the fight. Horrified, he saw the penthouse, his home, burst into flames. Remarkably, MacArthur then joined the infantry assault team as the men fought floor to floor, landing to landing, until they reached the penthouse. Stepping over the Japanese commander's body, MacArthur saw that all was lost. His possessions were smoking remains.

As Richard Connaughton, John Pimlott, and Duncan Anderson observed, MacArthur's actions at the Manila Hotel were extraordinary. Why would a five-star general assist in an infantry assault? In doing so, was his attention diverted from other and more important aspects of the battle? Did his obsession with his personal furnishings muddle his judgment? What was it about the Manila Hotel that would turn a sixty-five-year-old general into essentially a squad leader?[11]

Whatever captivated MacArthur, there is something extraordinary about the hotel, even today. I had stayed in the Manila Hotel before, and I remembered it vividly. At first I was apprehensive about my stay because I had read and heard complaints about the place: it was like an old lady who had lost both her charm and beauty, she could hardly compete with the newer Makati queens such as the Peninsula and the InterContinental, and her new Chinese owner was nicknamed Cheap Charlie from Chinatown because he refused to make the required renovations. If, in fact, the hotel had fallen on hard times, it would have been difficult to imagine her in her heyday, for I thought it was a lovely place. The lobby was inspiring with its plush sofas, towering indoor palms, fantastic chandeliers, rows of Doric columns, polished marble floors, and carved, dark wooden ceiling. It was everything a five-star tropical hotel should be and, given the ghosts that certainly inhabit it, perhaps more.

Walking over to the concierge, I asked if it would be possible to see the MacArthur Suite. No, I was told, it was under renovation. Something in her voice told me it was a stock response, and although disappointed, I did not press the matter. Instead, I sat in the voluptuous lobby, enjoying the old lady and her wrappings.

The hotel was part of Burnham's vision of Manila, and the hotel itself was designed by Parsons and built in 1912. Parson's hand is clearly seen in its breezy California style, and it is obvious that the hotel and the Philippine General Hospital are cousins. The hotel also bears resemblance to the two clubs just down the street that Parsons also designed. Indeed, for many years, it was a whites-only establishment, serving the higher echelons of American and European travelers during the first part of the century.

Now back outside I thought of Burnham's neo-Hellenic vision of Manila while looking down the length of the Luneta. During the first hundred or so feet of my stroll, I considered the early accounts I had read of this place. One hundred or so years earlier this area would have been the entertainment heart of the city. Nearly in the shadow of the old Spanish walls of Intramuros, ladies and gentlemen of all nationalities would have promenaded around the park, either sitting in their carriages or walking, and listened to the band perform. Soldiers and sailors would have played their games, including baseball and rugby. All would have watched the spectacular sunset over Manila Bay, and after the band had launched into "The Star-Spangled Banner," Old Glory would come down for the night.

Today much of the park's entertainment is live, as it is still a major destination for family gatherings and excursions. There are re-creations of traditional Filipino wooden houses, and art exhibits are common. The Luneta features an observatory, an open-air theater, restaurants, and a number of kiosks devoted to a variety of services. At one end of the park is an orchidarium, and it has Chinese and Japanese gardens. But as I ambled down the wide walkway, I noted the various inconsistencies that seemingly always cropped up in Manila. While there was great beauty here—architecture, memorials, flowers, greenery, and colorful Philippine flags all wrapped up in an exquisite historical atmosphere—it was tempered with a slight anxiety. Aside from the few tourists I saw that weekday morning, most of the people here seemed to be in difficult straits. I discerned that at least some of them were homeless and probably slept under the nearby foliage. I felt a sense of apprehension here, a vague feeling of being uncomfortable. Perhaps it was just me. Only moments before, I had seen a young girl guide through the street a horribly burned old man who was disfigured beyond belief. Together they made their way from car to car stopped helplessly at the red light, the man holding out his hand for donations.

My walk up the Luneta ended at Agrifina Circle, now the Teodoro Valenica Circle, renamed after the Marcos-era journalist who championed the preservation of this area of Manila. The circle offers a fascinating mix of culture and history. Walking counterclockwise, I first approached the Department of Tourism building, formally the Department of Agriculture building, which is striking in its classical form.

I climbed the wide steps. Looking out over the Luneta, I remembered Nick Joaquin's words of a Philippine-American Roman republic. Here it was—a grand building for a grand idea. The building's neoclassical lines and white concrete immediately reminded me that the whole area was a reflection of the Mall in Washington, D.C. In fact, this style of architecture was once called Potomac Greek in reference to its obvious inspiration. As I reached the top of the steps, I saw the plaque on the wall: "Rebuilt with the aid of the people of the United States of America Under the Philippine Rehabilitation Act of 1946." Like a mantra, the idea had followed me from Leyte to Lingayen and down the MacArthur Highway: the Americans built it, the Americans destroyed it, the Americans rebuilt it.

Across the circle was the former Department of Finance building, which is now the National Museum of the Filipino People. It appeared to be the twin of the tourism building. Behind it was the former legislative building, now home to the National Museum of the Philippines, the third of Burnham's designs. Between the two American buildings stood a round, colorful, and well-kept plaza. In its center, facing west to the sea, was a tall statue of Lapu-Lapu, the Visayan chieftain who slew Magellan and thus became immortalized as the first national hero. He stood in his loincloth and feathers, his hands resting on his giant bolo, and silently looked at the Rizal monument and the sea beyond. History, at least in these islands, is a crush of improbables. Here, a heathen warrior celebrated by Catholic Filipinos for killing a Spanish Catholic evangelical was placed directly between two Greek-inspired, American colonial era buildings that were once destroyed by U.S. artillery while fighting the Japanese.

In February 1945, the weeklong battle for three government buildings was difficult. These three- and four-story structures, all with basements, were made of reinforced concrete and perfectly suited for defense. It was estimated that each of the buildings housed as many as three hundred Japanese troops, who had effectively positioned machine guns in sandbagged emplacements and barricades. They turned doors and windows into gun turrets. The area around the buildings was a killing zone.

Not surprisingly, the U.S. command decided to reduce the buildings and their defenders as much as possible before sending in the infantry. The attack began on February 24, with U.S. forces using howitzers, heavy mortars, and tanks against the trio. The barrage continued for two days, and then a contingent of U.S. troops entered the Legislative Department building. They were thrown out an hour later. In the afternoon an attack was made on the Agriculture Department building, but it was repulsed as well. The battle continued in this manner for several more days, with the Japanese defenders fighting maniacally.

Flamethrowers became the chief U.S. weapon, as by now the fighting was in corridors and basements. On the February 28, the legislative building fell, and the agriculture building was taken on March 1. The finance building was the last to fall. This episode was somewhat unusual in that a number of Japanese actually surrendered. But most did not, and the Battle of Manila lasted for three more days. On March 3, with its destruction, all organized Japanese resistance in Manila ended.

Nearly a week before, on February 27, however, General MacArthur had gone to Malacanang Palace and participated in the ceremony that restored the commonwealth government. After President Osmeña made a brief address, MacArthur stood to speak. Something seemed different with the Old Man. He spoke slowly, unsurely, pausing often. In part, his words spoke of Japanese guilt and vindication for Bataan.

> More than three years have elapsed—years of bitterness, struggle and sacrifice—since I withdrew our forces and installations from this beautiful city that, open and undefended . . . [it might] be spared the violence of military ravage. The enemy would not have it so and much that I sought to preserve has been unnecessarily destroyed by its desperate action. . . .
>
> Then we were but a small force struggling to stem the advance of overpowering hordes. . . . That struggle was not in vain! . . . My country has kept the faith!
>
> Your country thus is again at liberty to pursue its destiny to an honored position in the family of free nations. Your capital city, cruelly punished though it may be, has remained its rightful place—the Citadel of Democracy in the East. Your indomitable—[12]

At this point his voice finally broke, his emotions cracked, and he stopped. Resuming after a few moments, he led the audience in the Lord's Prayer. But he had shown his hand. Just a few days before, he had watched a lifetime of treasure burn at the Manila Hotel. His beloved city, where he had spent much of his life and where he planned to retire, was in ashes. His Philippines, his home, his personal north star—all was gone. He was without a compass.

17

CORREGIDOR

As Manila lay dying, another battle was taking place close by—the second epic Battle of Corregidor, at the mouth of Manila Bay. At its conclusion, the United States would have complete mastery of the Manila region, and MacArthur would have yet another photo event to add to his album of redemption.

Few other words are associated more often with MacArthur than those of Corregidor Island. The island itself is in the shape of a tadpole, with its head to the China Sea and its tail facing Manila. It is four miles long and a half mile at the widest point. The head of the island is its highest elevation at 538 feet. Corregidor is one of five islands at the mouth of the bay; the others are much smaller, being little more than boulders cropping up out of the ocean. The island has no fresh water; it has always relied on supplies from nearby Mariveles on Bataan and from towns in Cavite. The Spanish developed the island as a maritime installation in the early nineteenth century. At that time, the authorities used the island to stop ships entering the bay in order to check their transit and cargo papers. The name Corregidor is said to come from this practice of an alderman "correcting" the papers.[1]

The United States was quick to use the island for its own military purposes. It first used the island as a hospital area during the Philippine-American War. An army post, named Fort Mills after Gen. Samuel Meyers Mills, a recent army chief of artillery, was built in 1908. For the next thirty-odd years, it would be heavily fortified and thus nicknamed America's Rock of Gibraltar.

By 1932 the Malinta Tunnel—a huge labyrinth of storage, communication, and medical facilities dug into the rock—had been completed. By December 1941, Corregidor held twenty-three artillery batteries and several detachments of American and Filipino troops. It was perhaps America's most advanced fortress.

Prior to the war, troops viewed an assignment to Corregidor as a dream detail. It was an idyllic place, where the offshore breezes made it relatively cool and clean. There was a small barrio where soldiers could have their uniforms cleaned and repaired. Schools were established for the children of both U.S. and Philippine armed forces. The island had an ice plant, a movie theater, and a nine-hole golf course. There were tennis courts and a bowling alley. Baseball was played fervently between units. Officers and enlisted men had clubs and their own beaches. Fishing was a favorite pastime. Families were here together, and children grew up on the "Rock." For the bachelors, the entertainment of Manila was just a short boat ride away.

It was clear that when war broke out, the island would be crucial in the defense of the Philippines. Corregidor entered the war when MacArthur and Quezon arrived with their families on Christmas Eve 1941. The first, and most say the heaviest, Japanese bombing occurred on December 29, with almost daily bombings thereafter. There was no air support for the trapped persons there. While Carlos Romulo valiantly broadcast the Voice of Freedom from inside Malinta, and the Filipino and American forces bravely battled their attackers, without reinforcements Corregidor's defense was unrealizable from the beginning. After receiving orders from Roosevelt, MacArthur, his family, and members of his staff escaped aboard PT boats in the early morning hours of March 12, 1942. Quezon had left three weeks earlier. The bombing continued.

The Japanese invaded. After incredible fighting, the Rock fell silent on May 6, and General Wainwright surrendered a force of almost sixteen thousand men and women. The Japanese kept these people on the island for two weeks as hostages while Wainwright did his best to convince other forces in the Philippines to lay down their arms. During this time, they also buried the dead. On May 24 the soldiers, now separated by nationality, were taken to Manila. Their Japanese captors marched the Americans through the streets of Manila on a Sunday, a day when Manileños were typically out on a stroll. The Japanese had hoped this humiliation would end the notion of Western invincibility, but it backfired. As the defeated men tramped by, so many Filipinos offered food and water to the prisoners that the Japanese guards had to force the crowds back. Both U.S. and Philippine personnel first were taken to Bilibid Prison in Manila. The Americans were transported up to Cabanatuan and eventually to abhorrent circumstances in Formosa, Manchuria, and Japan.

Some of the Americans, ironically, found themselves once again on Corregidor. After its fall in 1942, the Japanese lost interest in the island; indeed, they doubted they would need to fight in the Philippines again. They kept a squad of about five hundred POWs, some of whom had served there before, to clean up and restore the batteries. The POWs worked slowly, and little of the restoration was actually accomplished. Their captors did not seem to care. Few Japanese troops were stationed there. Not until late summer 1944 did the Japanese command even begin to rethink its Corregidor defenses. When the United States returned to Manila, only five thousand Japanese were on the island.

The reconquest of Corregidor took nearly six weeks. From late January through early February 1945, U.S. bomber aircraft—B-24 Liberators, B-25 Mitchells, and A-20 Havocs—pulverized the island. From the sea came cruisers, destroyers, and mine sweepers. Japanese guns hidden in the cliffs managed to sink a sweeper and damage some destroyers, but they were eventually taken out by naval fire. On February 16, a combined airborne group known as the Rock Force led the invasion. Commanded by Col. George M. Jones, the men landed on Topside, the head of the island, and easily overran its defenders. Most Japanese retreated to the tunnels, and many took their own lives with explosives. Others used banzai charges into U.S. lines. All was futile. By March 2, 4,500 Japanese and 197 Americans had died. MacArthur came back to Corregidor that day. On the parade ground Colonel Jones saluted and said, "Sir, I present you the fortress Corregidor."

✳ ✳ ✳

I was visiting Corregidor for the third time. It was the Fourth of July. The tour group boarded the boat near Manila's Cultural Center, and inside the air-conditioned craft, short documentaries about Corregidor and the war were played. It was a full boat. More than half the passengers were Filipinos, although I detected several had American accents. There were a number of Japanese men on board (who slept through the war movies), but I saw no Japanese women. A traditionally dressed Indian mother sat with her teenage son. The rest seemed to be from the States or Australia. A group of five Americans was more conspicuous than the others because one young man wore a T-shirt with the San Miguel beer logo modified to read Peace Corps Philippines.

We left the dock at about 7:00 a.m. The bay was calm. I sat on the port side so I could get a good view of the Cavite coast, where Commodore Dewey defeated the Spanish fleet in 1898. I tried to imagine Dewey's flagship, the USS *Olympia*, leading the small U.S. squadron back and forth and pummeling the antiquated Spanish ships. Many contemporary historians, who see the naval engagement as some ridiculous spectacle of overbearing U.S. military might, have skewered the story of Dewey at Manila Bay. True, Dewey's ships were more modern, and true, the actual battle was one-sided. But it is conveniently forgotten that when Dewey sailed to Manila out from Hong Kong Harbor, British sailors saluted the squadron, fully expecting the Spanish to rout the U.S. Navy, which had not fought a battle since the Civil War. As Dewey approached the fortified island of Corregidor, intelligence reports told him the channel was mined and that the guns of the island were deadly. Disregarding these reports he sailed past Corregidor at night almost undetected, until a smokestack from the USS *McCulloch* belched fire. Alerted, signal rockets went up from Corregidor, and the fleet was fired on from nearby El Fraile Island. As sunlight began to shine down on the bay, the batteries from Fort San Antonio Abad in Malate opened up with little effect. Then the Spanish fleet and batteries on Sangley Point began to fire. Calmly, Dewey sailed back and forth in formation, and the Spanish fleet was destroyed by noon. The American colonial era in the Philippines had begun.

After about an hour's trip on the tour boat, Corregidor appeared, compact and lovely. Dense green foliage cloaked its steep sides, and passengers commented on the black cave openings that were near the waterline. We landed not far from the dock where MacArthur, his family, and friends had boarded the PT boats and escaped. Once out of the hydrofoil, the passengers were split into groups of English and Japanese speakers and boarded buses that were remodeled to resemble vintage trolley cars. On my bus were both Filipinos and Americans, with a single Australian sitting next to me. The tour guide at the front of the bus, Rollie (a pseudonym), used a microphone. He was seventy-one years old and had grown up on Corregidor.

Our bus chugged up a steep incline toward Topside, and Rollie began to tell us stories. Things were much different now than when the United States retook the Rock. For one thing, then it really was a rock. By the time the Japanese and United States had stopped shelling the island, the vegetation was gone, the island denuded. After the war, airplanes flew over the island and dropped seeds. Now it was lush, with a wide variety of birds inhabiting the trees. We also saw monkeys and monitor lizards; the latter, Rollie informed us, tastes like chicken. He also confided to us that he had seen three ghosts on the island, each one of whom was an American soldier. Rollie was also kind enough to offer to autograph Alfonso Aluit's book on the history of Corregidor, which was for sale at the front of the bus. What Mr. Aluit would think of this arrangement was anybody's guess.

The first of the ruins we visited was Middleside Barracks, a rambling catastrophe that once housed both U.S. and Philippine enlisted men, although the two forces were segregated. Rollie explained that the reason for this segregation was that American troops preferred bacon and eggs for breakfast while the Filipinos wanted dried fish. The Americans on the bus, all white people, managed weedy smiles.

We then stopped at Battery Way. This mortar pit had four huge guns sticking up like green metallic thumbs. Along with the walls around the pit, they were pockmarked with shell and shrapnel holes. It was in this pit that the last big gun of Corregidor was fired. Its commander, Maj. William "Wild Bill" Massello Jr., himself seriously wounded, had the telephone ripped from the wall so that he would not receive the order to surrender. From a stretcher he lay pulling the lanyard of the last usable twelve-inch mortar. Finally, on the morning of May 6 with Japanese troops on the island and after eleven consecutive hours of firing, the old mortar's breechlock froze. The guns of Corregidor fell silent.

We visited a series of batteries next. Remarkable in its size, Battery

Hearn is where the twelve-inch seacoast gun still points to the sea. Then we saw Battery Grubbs, which had a dubious history. Here two massive ten-inch model 1895 guns were mounted on disappearing carriages. One was almost immediately knocked out of commission by Japanese shells while the other never really worked. The battery itself was abandoned. It was still interesting to walk around the ruins of the emplacement with its rusted metal and shell-holed walls and to look at the nearly century-old American architecture.

The high point of the afternoon was seeing the Malinta Tunnel. As we pulled up in front of the metal doors, Rollie called our attention to a small building with restrooms off to our side. This is important, Rollie maintained, for it was in the men's room five years earlier that Rollie saw his third ghost. Our guide then switched to Tagalog and said something about the GI ghost being gay.

We disembarked and stood in front of the closed door. It was a dramatic moment. Rollie first told us that the word "malinta" means many leeches, which sent a shiver down several tourists' spines. He then told us emphatically that while we could take photos in the tunnel, videos were absolutely prohibited. Rollie did not say why. Furthermore, he warned, the air would be hot and stale, and visitors would be brought outside if they felt sick. Also, those who were claustrophobic, he cautioned, should not go in. Finally, Rollie held up his hand.

"Remember," he said slowly, intently looking at all of our faces, "the most important rule about walking through this tunnel . . . do not fart!"

With that command ringing in our ears, Rollie motioned, and the massive doors swung ominously open. We walked into what felt like a subway for there were trolley tracks running down the center. The air did change and become stale, but it was not as hot as some feared. We had all paid extra for the light and sound show, which began within a few minutes. Stopping at "laterals," or the tunnels that went off laterally from the main passageway, we would gaze at mannequins dressed in period garb while a soundtrack of explosions played. Sometimes the mannequins would talk to each other or to us, as did the one dressed as Manuel Quezon. Here was the handiwork of FAME Philippines. While its effort with the death march markers was impressive, this restoration of the tunnel and the show was a magnificent creation.

The short show in Malinta was over, as was the tour itself. As the bus drove back to the dock, Rollie asked if anyone knew what day it was. Someone offered Wednesday, but Rollie quickly countered, "No! It's the Fourth of July! To all Americans, happy birthday!"

The Fourth of July is an odd day in the Philippines. Officially, it is Philippine-American Friendship Day, an event that goes largely unnoticed. However, from 1946 to 1964, Philippine Independence Day was also celebrated on July 4, after that day in 1946 when the United States signed into law the Republic of the Philippines. In 1962 President Diosdado Macapagal, President Arroyo's father, began proceedings to move the country's independence day to June 12, the day in 1898 when Emilio Aguinaldo proclaimed the country's freedom from colonial dominance. Macapagal wrote that an independence day is when a country comes together as one in a common struggle and announces its natural sovereignty. Besides, July 4 was already taken. The date that the Republic of the Philippines was established—October 14, 1943—was never even considered.

Some Filipinos have questioned Macapagal's historical interpretation of the 1898 event. Although Aguinaldo did, in fact, throw off the yoke of Spanish supremacy (with assistance from Commodore Dewey), Filipinos were immediately harnessed to the plow of American colonialism and remained there for almost fifty years. Some have felt that it was only on July 4, 1946, that the people could truly say they were independent. Furthermore, not everyone agrees that the Philippines was a united country in 1898. Many Visayans see the fighting in 1898 as a Tagalog war of independence and June 12 as another example of their ethnic authority.

We all parted company at the dock in the early afternoon. Most of the visitors (and Rollie) went back to Manila, but I went to the Corregidor Inn. As an overnight guest, I had access to some exclusive activities. After a short rest I met the rest of the small party of other overnighters, all middle-aged Filipinos and an American teacher from Brownsville, Texas, with his Filipina wife.

Our first activity was a tour of the island's hospital and nearby morgue. Unlike the ruins we saw during the day tour, we were allowed to enter these buildings. The structures seemed to be standing by the force of sheer will. Walls and columns were crumbling, exposing the metal bars used to reinforce the concrete, and they stuck out in a twisted and sometimes dangerous fashion. There was no roof, and trees were growing on every floor. Debris of all types littered the place. Curiously, however, we all noticed graffiti that read, "Ankbar lived here," or another that made reference to Allah.

The guide explained the graffiti. In the 1960s, President Marcos ill advisedly laid claim to the region known as Sabah in Malaysia. It was rumored that he had concocted a plan to invade that part of Malaysia to justify the claim and even recruited a number of Muslim Special Forces personnel from Mindanao. At that time, Corregidor had not yet been well restored, and tourism was light; so secrecy could be kept on the island. The soldiers were quartered and trained here in the hospital area. The recruits, however, soon realized that they were being trained to kill fellow Muslims, and furthermore, they were not being paid. A mutiny was planned and put into play. It was discovered, and the military systematically murdered all of the Muslims, dumping their bodies at sea. One survived to testify. The graffiti we saw was from these Muslim victims.

Or so went the story, which has taken its place within the corpus of Marcosian legend. There was, in fact, a group of mostly Muslim Special Forces trainees on the island in February 1968. During Senate committee hearings, the military did admit to shooting three "mutineers" among the trainees, after testimony was heard from the young soldier who had escaped. However, twenty-three trainees were never located, and foul play in their disappearance has always been suspected. Looking at the scribbling on the walls, I am sure each person in the group thought exactly the same thing I did: yes, that notice could have been written in 1968 or even last week.[2]

We were also able to take the Malinta Tunnel tour again, this time at night. This opportunity in itself made the trip a major event. We were a party of ten, and we were given hard hats and flashlights. I asked if I could bring a video camera, and the guides laughed at a seemingly inside joke and said, "Sure." The night was perfectly black, and off we went into the tunnel. Two young men were our guides: one kept in front as our narrator, one kept behind as our shepherd. The air was fusty and warm. Unlike the day tour, we were taken into the laterals off the main passageway. For nearly an hour we explored these dark subterranean warrens, some of which were large and wonderfully hewn, while others were rubble strewn and dangerous looking. At one point we were shown bones. Looking at them under a flashlight, I could not tell if they were American or Japanese. Or from a large dog. Whatever they were, they reinforced the notion of ghosts in the tunnel. When we made it back to the entrance, everyone's shirt was wringing wet, and two of the Filipinas talked about hearing the sound of marching boots.

The two guides, who had also been the waiters at the inn after the Malinta night tour, were tough taskmasters. They had us up at 5:00 a.m. for the sunrise at the Pacific War Memorial on Topside. It was too cloudy for a decent solar spectacle, but the presence of five eagles soaring low while hunting the mountain made up for it. By 5:45 a.m., we were in a Japanese tunnel. Unlike the exquisitely engineered Malinta Tunnel or even the tunnel I saw in Bamban, this one was a shabby affair. It was just a long hole hacked out of rock. At one point we had to climb thirty feet straight up a narrow shaft with the assistance of a rope, then twelve more yards with a bamboo ladder. Out through a small opening, we were off to breakfast by 6:30 a.m.

At mid-morning, the primal sound of the surf crashing down at the beach had called me. One of the inn's employees told me to go to the south beach, as it had less garbage than the one in the north. I followed this advice, mentally noting that it was or at least was near Black Beach, where U.S. amphibious forces landed in 1945. I walked down the hill, past the Jonathan Wainwright Park, and to the beach. Once there I wondered how the other beach could possibly be worse. The sand here was covered in every type of garbage known to man: bottles, plastics, shoes, and an entire variety of discarded items both degradable and not. This pollution was sad but not unusual. Corregidor was typical of perhaps most Philippine beach resorts, where the staff did their best to keep everything clean, but because people in other places decided to use the water as their own dump, the resorts suffered. In the case of Corregidor, the people in the poorer parts of Manila without sanitation threw things into the many *esteros* (estuaries) or the Pasig, which in turn emptied into the bay, and thus washed up on this beach.

Keeping my shoes on, I tiptoed over the garbage-sand to a point where I could almost safely go barefoot. Here, all things considered, the beach was quite nice. The surf was fairly high and thoroughly inviting, and after kicking off my boat shoes, I strode into the tide, telling myself not to worry about what I could not see. The water was warm, and I stood thigh deep gazing out over blue-gray water and to the high green hillsides all around me. Birds were swooping down off the hills with calls that were completely foreign to me. I was totally alone, and it was enjoyable. Suddenly I felt something soft wrap around my knee. As the surf subsided, I discovered a pair of men's boxer shorts attached to my leg, and I saw clearly why its owner had thrown them away. Shaking my leg violently, I made my way back to the beach and up to the inn. My boat would be leaving soon.

When MacArthur came to Corregidor on March 2, 1945, he gave a short but memorable statement standing on the parade ground. The ruins of his earlier command lay around him, but the flagpole, made from a mast of a Spanish ship Dewey had destroyed, still stood. MacArthur gave orders for the flag to be raised and not to let an enemy pull it down again. This time he did not choke on tears. But even as he spoke, there was fighting in Manila.

18

INTRAMUROS

The Battle of Manila would end in Intramuros. Both sides knew that that it would, and both sides knew the outcome was never in doubt. As MacArthur watched the engagement from the top of the Insular Life Building at the foot of the Jones Bridge, perhaps the zenith of Japanese barbarity was occurring in the Walled City of Intramuros below him.

Intramuros is one of the most historically important places in Asia. Its history is essentially the history of Manila. Built on a Muslim stronghold of Rajah Solaiman, it was captured by the officers of Spaniard Miguel Lopez de Legaspi in 1571, the year it was proclaimed a city of Spain. For nearly four centuries, it would survive numerous attacks by Chinese pirates, earthquakes, and an eighteenth-century British invasion. It would barely survive the Japanese and the Americans.[1]

The Walled City was constructed where the Pasig River empties into Manila Bay. From the time of Legaspi until the arrival of Commodore Dewey, it was the guardian of Spanish culture in the islands. In fact, until the Americans arrived, Filipinos of non-Spanish descent were prohibited from living there. The U.S. colonial administration made other modifications. During the Spanish era, Intramuros was surrounded by moats, but the Americans filled them in for sanitary reasons. They also developed the nearby port area, thereby cutting the city off from the seafront. Part of the original wall was torn down to make way for wharves and warehouses. In an effort to make traffic in and outside the city flow better, gaps were cut into the walls. In some physical respects, Intramuros became a modern city.

But for the most part, the city changed little after the U.S. superintendents took over. During the day one would still see university students carrying their books to Letran College and mid-level bureaucrats hurrying to their offices at the Ayuntamiento Building. Walking down the Calle Real in the 1920s, the smell of Spanish cooking and the sound of the Spanish language, which was still the medium of instruction in Intramuros schools, would fill the air. Spanish culture would be reflected in the many Catholic fiestas, processions, and feast day celebrations that marked the liturgical calendar. It was still a Spanish city, not because there was an overabundance of Spaniards living there, but because the Americans pretty much left it the way they found it—a largely medieval city dominated by religion.

In 1941 there were seven churches in Intramuros. The anchor was the giant Manila Cathedral. But there was also San Augustin, with its celebrated statue of the Virgin Mary and many works of art; the Recollect Church of San Nicolas de Tolentino with its early eighteenth-century artifacts; the relatively modern (1889) Jesuit church of San Ignacio; the San Francisco and the Venerable Orden Tercera; and the Capuchin Church of Lourdes. Some considered the Dominican church, Santo Domingo, to be the finest church of prewar Manila. It was a two-steepled Gothic Revival, with doors that were engraved works of art, an elaborate interior, and a huge library. Moreover, it held a much-revered image of the Nuesta Señora del Rosario, or de La Naval de Manila (Our Lady of the Rosary), named in gratitude for the Virgin Mary's help in the Spanish victories over the Dutch in the seventeenth century. In December 1941, it was bombed beyond salvation by the Japanese, becoming one of the first architectural casualties of the war. In fact, only San Augustin survived the war; all others were destroyed either in 1941 or 1945.

It is doubtful that MacArthur's generals spent much time considering the cultural worth of Intramuros. In fairness to them, they had other pressing concerns. A siege of the city would have allowed the Japanese to possibly resupply themselves and, worse, given them more time to murder the civilians inside. Ending the drama quickly was the Americans' only choice, and the military planners were faced with the improbable task of having to attack a strong medieval fortress head-on. The Japanese had fortified the wall, which was twenty feet thick at the higher portions and up to forty feet thick at its base. Tunnels and chambers inside the walls were used as gun emplacements. More importantly, given the Japanese mind-set in this endgame, the Japanese could not escape and would surely fight to their deaths.

Because there were pockets of enemy troops in the three huge government buildings just south of Intramuros, U.S. planners decided that the best approach would be from the north, where a jointure in the wall near the Government Mint provided the easiest access into the city. Furthermore, this area was lightly defended. Even so, MacArthur's subordinates were terrified of taking heavy casualties. The U.S. commanders planning the attack—from Maj. Gen. Robert S. Beightler through Major General Griswold up to Lieutenant General Krueger—requested air support to help the attacking American forces. MacArthur denied the request, saying that launching air strikes within a friendly city was "unthinkable" and would "result beyond question in the death of thousands of innocent civilians."[2] In place of air support, the army amassed more than 140 artillery pieces, including tanks, tank destroyers, large howitzers, and mortars.

On February 22, the artillerymen, mostly to the east of the Walled City, prepared for the massive bombardment scheduled for the next day. As night fell, they pinpointed areas of the wall that they wanted to demolish. In high buildings, observation posts were armed with machine guns. Men from the 129th Infantry waited near the boats they would take over the Pasig River; they must have known that if the bombardment was not successful they would be easy targets on the river. The other infantry spear, the 145th, waited behind the post office to the northeast. The men would have to dash over exposed flat land to the walls of Intramuros, and they, too, would be totally exposed.

The attack began at 7:30 a.m. on the twenty-third. The artillery bombardment lasted for one hour, centering on the walls near the Government Mint and to the east between the Quezon and Parian gates. It was considered the most intense, coordinated bombardment of the Luzon campaign. Those defenders who were still alive were in shock. The infantry assault came from two directions—from behind the general post office and through the northeastern wall, and from the small assault boats from across the Pasig River and through the gap near the Government Mint. Within a half hour, both forces had joined up without suffering a casualty. Suddenly, as they closed in on the Fort Santiago area, they encountered three thousand civilians the Japanese had been holding hostage in the San Augustin Church and the Delmonico Hotel. This cunning tactic worked. The Americans had to scramble to get the mostly women and children out of way. These were evacuated through the Quezon gate, across the river, and to safety. The attack faltered.

These civilians were the last residents of the area. By this time, most of the men of Intramuros had been systematically murdered. The atrocities here, as elsewhere, resulted to some degree from the Japanese hysteria about Filipino fifth-column work; but as in the other parts of the city, much of the human carnage must be attributed to the soldiers' base bestiality. There is simply no alternative explanation for some of the Japanese barbarism. For example, the Japanese dragged the male medical staff members of the San Juan de Dios Hospital out of their shelter at the Santa Rosa College, took them to the charred hulk of the Santo Domingo Church, and bayoneted them to death. The Japanese then went inside the ruined church and murdered any priest or nun they could find. Soon afterward, the thirty-seven Spanish priests of San Augustin Church, plus perhaps ninety other men, were taken to a shelter near the Manila Cathedral, where the former Palacio del Gobernador (Governor General's Palace) once stood. The building's foundation comprised massive granite blocks, and the Japanese had converted this building into an air raid shelter. They forced the men into the shelter and fired blindly, point blank, into the packed room. They left, threw grenades into the airholes, and then covered up the airholes with dirt. As the men attempted to clamber out, the laughing Japanese fired at them. When U.S. personnel uncovered the shelter, there were two survivors among the more than a hundred rotting corpses.

The Americans had little trouble in a now mostly destroyed Intramuros. By the end of February 25, Fort Santiago and the city's southwest corner—places where the Japanese had held out—were in U.S. hands. That day the U.S. forces also seized the adjacent port area, where Rear Admiral Iwabuchi and his staff committed suicide the next morning. The only remaining Japanese were ensconced in the large government buildings for the Legislative, Finance, and Agricultural departments—all the neoclassic cadavers of Daniel

Burnham's Philippine republic designs—that were situated just to the south-east of Intramuros. As discussed in chapter 16, the Americans attacked building by building, first with heavy artillery, then with flamethrowers, and then in some cases in vicious close-quarter fighting with the fervent defenders. By March 1, all three buildings were rubble, and the United States ruled Manila.

* * *

Where the 129th Infantry landed on the Pasig's south bank is now a brick-tiled open space that abuts a small park. I stood on the tiles at the river's edge and looked north across the river at such places as San Nicolas and Binondo. On that side, the riverscape seemed to alternate between newer, cleaner high-rise buildings and older, squat gray structures. A few of the latter could have gone back to the war, but I could not tell. Upriver was the venerable and rebuilt Jones Bridge, low and unassuming, and behind it was the gleaming rebuilt post office. Down river in the distance were huge red-orange cranes of the port area. The river itself was a peculiar shade of black, broken intermittently by pieces of garbage bobbing up and then disappearing. The Pasig River smelled like what it was—a wide, rolling open sewer.

I marveled at how the U.S. troops could have made it across the open river in the daylight. They were surely open targets. The photographs of the event show grim-faced GIs landing on a point quite near where I stood. They had to climb over the seawall that once stood nearby, determined to go into the city and end the horror. According to Richard Connaughton, John Pimlott, and Duncan Anderson's *The Battle for Manila*, the first living souls the troops ran into upon entering the city were two nuns carrying children in their arms, and the soldiers were amazed at how anyone could have survived the 155mm howitzer blasts. Somehow the nuns and children had survived, and the soldiers quickly ushered them through to safety.

Children were laughing near me in the small park. These were squatter families, poor and with little hope, living within the stench of the dead river. Their laundry was drying on the park benches, and they were cooking their lunches on small open fires near an attractive statue of Manuel Quezon, who was looking contemplatively southwest into the city. There was the frank spectacle of a naked body standing nearby in the park. Although this area seemed to be a memorial park because a polished slab said something about

Philippine-Mexican friendship, this place was not conducive to reflection, at least not peaceful reflection.

The loss of property and culture coupled with the influx of poverty marked Intramuros for decades after the war. Bulldozers came and cleared the debris, leaving desolated areas. The Sunken Gardens, part of the city's former moat, became a garbage dump. Sections of the wall were actually quarried for building stones. Streets and plazas became parking lots and storage areas. Squatters, who according to Nick Joaquin were mostly Waray, moved in and stayed in large numbers well into the 1960s. The once-splendid Spanish city became poor in nature and Visayan in character.

The story has a relatively happy ending. In the 1960s individuals began to fund restoration projects. Small assignments, such as rebuilding parts of Fort Santiago, came first. The enterprise gained momentum, and in 1979 the government created the Intramuros Administration to oversea the Walled City's full restoration and protection. To a large extent, the administration has been successful, for today the area has been rebuilt and gentrified, making it Manila's top tourist destination. Some of the planned restoration projects have yet to materialize, however, such as the rebuilding of the grand Ayuntamiento Building near the Manila Cathedral. And then there is the question of commercialization.

It was high noon, and I was in an area called the Puerta de Isabel, after the nineteenth-century Spanish queen known for her indiscreet affairs and abdication in 1868. I saw a Starbucks inside a gray concrete structure nearby. Taking the brew of the day (Yukon Gold) and an *ensaymada* (a small cake) for lunch, I sat inside the Starbucks at a large window. The interior of the place was made out of mortar and stone; curved in the shape of a tunnel, nearly womb-like; and decorated, of course, in recognizable Starbuck chic, pastel colors and art. Paul McCartney's music was on the sound system. I asked one of the young workers if this building was actually part of the Walled City, and he replied that it was. In fact, this chamber had been part of the wall itself. I was rocked: Starbucks had literally penetrated, impregnated, and become one with one of the most important historical artifacts in Asia. The company had already accomplished the same at China's Great Wall and Forbidden City. Now it had pulled it off here.

Outside, the patio was full of university students. It seemed to be a happy, artsy crowd of fashionable, chatty people. Given the cross-table conversations, it was obvious many knew each other. As I finished my ensaymada, a man in flip-flops and carrying a large canvas bag approached two young women sitting at one of the patio tables. After a short exchange he knelt down, took a huge, yellow workman's high-intensity lamp from his bag, and placed it on the table. After some dialogue and a minute or so, he reached into the bag and pulled out a pair of military binoculars. They looked to be a foot long, camouflaged, and outfitted with serious devices that I could not identify. The two women eagerly tried out the glasses, giggling and surely discussing how best these could be used. I saw the one woman shake her head no, and the binoculars were laid on the table with the lamp. The man then reached in again and extracted a box with a picture of an electric hair clipper and its accessories. This item elicited profound interest from the two women. I got up and left, not knowing if this innovative agent of capitalism made his sale.

Leaving the patio area, I turned the nearby corner through the open metal, spike-topped gates and proceeded down Magallanes Drive. I was walking on the inside of the wall, which ran the length of the street and beyond. As with Starbucks, other establishments had been built into the wall's chambers. In this magnificent centuries-old structure, the pride of imperial Spain, there was the Lampara Seafood Grill, the Le Dans Café, the Lets Get It On Piano Bar and Restaurant, and the Ivy G Salon and Spa. Moving farther down the street, I realized why the Starbucks crowd seemed to be all university students: I was right next to Letran College.

The Colegio de San Juan de Letran is a small college that dates back to 1630. It was started as a school for orphaned and destitute boys of Spanish descent. During the war, the Japanese used its buildings as billets. As I walked the narrow street, I saw that the area around the inner campus was impressively maintained, and its freshly painted buildings reflected the Spanish design. On one of the campus buildings a sign displayed the school mascot, a medieval knight on a rearing charger, with the cross on his shield and a flowing banner on his spear. Most of the sign was taken up by this declaration: "This is an English speaking campus." A medieval soldier in a postwar city embracing a twentieth-century language—it is doubtful that anything could more perfectly illustrate the Philippine culture's struggle between its past European and American masters.

I walked down the Calle de Beaterio and then back over to the Gen. Luna Street (formerly the Calle Real) alongside the mighty Manila Cathedral, whose first incarnation of bamboo and nipa was built in 1581. The present church is actually the sixth to stand on the site. Four were destroyed by fires and earthquakes and the fifth by U.S. artillery. I went inside, where it was quite dark, save for the lights on the altar. The church was not full, but a substantial number of people were sitting quietly at 12:45 p.m. on a weekday. They were of all types: the elderly, mothers, teenagers, and even the three young men whom I noticed outside acting like *braggadocios*. Over the loudspeaker the rosary was being said in English.

At the corner of Gen. Luna Street, there was a historical sign in front of the cathedral acknowledging the Palacio del Gobernador and the murdered civilians in 1945. Over the ghastly air raid shelter, a civil administration building has been erected. Its security guards wore replicas of uniforms from Aguinaldo's 1898 army. I walked straight down Luna and into Fort Santiago, perhaps the nation's most historic landmark.

Fort Santiago sits in the northwest corner of Intramuros, jutting up against the mouth of the Pasig River. It is named after Santiago de Vera, a late sixteenth-century Spanish governor who added the moat and stone breastworks onto a site previously developed by Muslim settlers. Despite its dark reputation today, it was a bright, colorful place. After paying a fifty-peso entrance fee and after kindly denying the four different offers of a horse-drawn carriage tour of the fort, I strolled down the grounds. I first passed the Visitors Center area, which housed a series of coffee and souvenir shops. These were in the womb-like tunnels that Starbucks had found, called a *baluartillo* (supply chamber). I remembered the uproar from Manila writers and historians when these shops were given license to operate within the fort. With cultural integrity versus open commercialism, it was hardly a fair fight.

Immediately past the souvenir shops were two structures that sat side by side, east to west. The first was the Baluartillo de San Francisco Javier, the other the Reducto de San Francisco Javier. I walked through the chamber that ran underneath the baluartillo and emerged at a grassy divide. Before me was the reducto, which now housed a chapel. From inside, altar candles flickered in the darkness. At the door of the chapel were two portraits: on the left was Jesus Christ and to the right the Virgin Mary. The son looked rather serious, the mother rather sad. Perhaps it was because the grassy divide that fronted the chapel was now part of a golf course. A series of signs to the left and within twenty feet of the portraits held such commandments as "Let faster players through," "No non-golfers allowed on the course," and "Observe golf etiquete [*sic*]."

The redbrick sidewalk carried me past the ruins of the American barracks, where U.S. troops were quartered for decades before the war. Outside the building were several rather impressive Spanish-era cannons that have been excavated, and to the right of that was the Galeria de los Presidentes de la Republica Pilipina, a series of presidential portraits done in metal. To the right of that and back against the wall of the fort was a small old memorial called the Fort Santiago Honor Roll. It listed the names of persons who had suffered within these walls during the war. I was somewhat surprised to see there were perhaps 150 names. Surely there had been many, many more victims than that incarcerated here. Why were these names chosen? Why were others omitted? In the front of the pockmarked building, sitting on a plastic chair in the shade of a balcony, was a security guard in his 1898 uniform. His hat was on a nearby table, and his legs were stretched out on another chair. Even though he was wearing designer sunglasses, he was obviously fast asleep. Why not? What could he possibly be guarding—the relics of American empire?

The most recognizable part of the fort is the main gate, a highly decorative wooden relief and sculpture. It is not the original, which was destroyed by U.S. forces, but it is a good copy. The relief commemorates the patron saint of Spain, James, the Slayer of Moors (Santiago Matamoros). The gate sits just behind the dark moat full of lily pads. It was quite picturesque.

Once inside the gate, all was well manicured and inviting. One of the fort's main attractions is the Rizal Shrine, a relatively new building that stands on the site where Rizal, the founder of Philippine independence and a national hero, was imprisoned in December 1896. The building holds a number of Rizal mementos, including some of his clothes and medical tools, that shed light on his national and international importance. People today forget that Rizal was not only influential in his own country but throughout Europe as well.

The northwestern end of the fort held the infamous Baluarte de Santa Barbara, or the powder magazine. From the top of structure I watched boats—mostly tugs and barges—ply their trade from the bay and up the Pasig River, reminding me that this city was still a very important port. But I was not that interested in the river. It was the lower part of the baluarte that interested me. Here, one could peer into the heart of darkness.

As the Battle of Manila commenced, the Filipino men from Intramuros and any others considered guerrilla suspects—that is, in fact, anyone not Japanese—were taken and put into various cramped quarters. Systematically, the men were then taken out of their cells and out into the courtyard. There they were made to stand on a box in front of a galvanized iron wall. The iron wall had a tiny hole in it at about eye level. A voice with a Japanese accent would bark one of two English words: back or room. If the word was "back," the man was thrown back into the cell. If it were "room," it meant execution.

At first, the Japanese murdered the men with bayonets to the back, then dumped the victims into a pit. Apparently, however, the word choice approach was not quick enough. During the day and night of February 7, groups of men would be led out en masse, would be accused of being guerrillas, and would be shot. Later, witnesses saw assembled men kneeling in front of a bench. A Japanese officer came down the line and beheaded each civilian victim. Meanwhile, the Japanese had told the men's family members that they could leave food outside the fort's gate to be delivered to their husbands and fathers. After the women left, the Japanese soldiers would eat nearly all of the food.

As the U.S. troops explored the fallen fort on February 24 and 25, Santiago gave up its secrets. As soldiers attempted to locate the cause of a strong stench of decaying flesh, they found a room closed by a double steel door that was bolted and wired shut from the outside. They broke open the doors but found behind them iron bars. Behind the bars were thirty bodies— both men and women—in an advanced state of decomposition. Upon closer inspection, the soldiers determined that they had died of starvation.

The loathsome discoveries continued. In another building within the fort, troops found seventy-five bodies of people who had died from thirst and suffocation. In yet another room, forty to fifty Filipino and Chinese men were found with their hands tied, shot, and stabbed in the back. Authorities surmised that they had been brought in, made to face the wall, and then executed. As their bodies fell on previous victims, they formed a layered stack.

There are differing estimates of how many persons died in Fort Santiago. Some say as many as ten thousand, but the figure is probably closer to three thousand. Outside the Baluarte de Santa Barbara, two markers within ten feet of each other commemorate part of the atrocities. One is a granite cross, the other a National Historical Institute plaque. Both pay respects to the six hundred unknown bodies that were buried in a mass grave where the markers now stand.

The battles for Intramuros and Manila was over. The rest of the Philippines would be in American hands within a few months. It is almost impossible to comprehend the damage the battle caused, although the accounting of material losses is relatively easy. What it did to the psyche of the Philippine people and their relationship with the United States is more difficult to determine.

Twenty-two years after the battle, Carmen Guerrero Nakpil wrote of both the occupation and the liberation in these terms:

> Survival ruled our reflexes. It sharpened the mind, distorted the appetites and dulled the moral sense. The old values and ideas of order, decorum and limits were eroded. But starvelings cannot be moralists. . . . We survived by means of savage and ardent cunning. "Buy and sell" it was called, but it often was plain deceit, pimping, hoarding, looting, and furnishing the enemy with war material. We became a race of spies, thieves, sabateurs, informers and looters, callous and miserly and after three years when the American G.I.s swept in with their chocolate bars and their California apples they were appalled to find a country where the [American] mocking line went, "Anything that is not nailed down is stolen."[3]

Guerrero Nakpil's description is fascinating for a number of reasons.

302 ＊ THE MᴀᴄARTHUR HIGHWAY

It recalls the Spanish and American eras built on the notion of a traditional time, as perhaps reflected in the culture of Ermita and the classicism of the Burnham-Parsons buildings. But quaint Ermita and the buildings and the imperial dream were all now rubble. The people were roiling in not only physical catastrophe but in psychological disorder as well. The Filipinos, like MacArthur, had lost their compass. More importantly, neither the Filipinos nor the Americans would ever see themselves in quite the same terms again.

19
THE FILIPINAS HERITAGE LIBRARY, MEMORARE MANILA, 1945

C ompared to the other theaters of World War II, little has been written about the Philippines and almost nothing about the Battle of
Manila. There have been but three books, and parts or chapters
of others, dedicated to one of the most important battles of the conflict.
On the whole, however, the entire event is often misunderstood or misinter-
preted or, worse, explained to bolster a preexisting ideology. This ignorance
has resulted in some harsh debate. In 1995, the debate spilled into the Manila
newspapers.

As with the Leyte commemoration less than four months earlier, the
fiftieth anniversary of the Battle of Manila stirred up a cultural hornet's nest
and pretty much along the same lines as what happened in Tacloban. The
nationalists saw the ceremony as a dubious confirmation of U.S. benevolence.
How could the Battle of Manila be seen as a victory when a hundred thousand Filipinos died? Why was it necessary to use carpet shelling? Why did
there have to be a battle at all? At the heart of both positions was the role
MacArthur's forces played in the city's destruction.

In a review of the then just-released *The Battle of Manila* in the *Philippine
Star*, one writer said,

> Because the Japanese were incredibly sadistic conquerors, the arrogant
> Americans were seen in contrast as being the lesser evil. The thousands
> of Filipino deaths at the hands of the Americans were ignored in the

joy of the moment of liberation from the hated Japanese. (we could in-
sensitively compare the situation to a naïve married person that cannot
believe that his or her spouse could ever be unfaithful).[1]

Opposing this view were those who felt the United States was to be
commended for its action during the battle.

We see the nationalist charge that the United States destroyed Old
Manila needlessly so as to pulverize the foundation of a national consciousness for the bull it is. The historic and cultural parts of the city
were dynamited by the Japanese to destroy every vestige of a culture
and race they hated for being incorrigibly Western. Spanish Manila was
razed by the Japanese before the Americans were in view.[2]

So it went for weeks. Other issues were raised as well. Why have the
Japanese not accounted for the massacre of civilians in postwar Japan? Why
have the Japanese not monetarily compensated Filipina comfort women, or
sex slaves?

I sat reading clippings from the debate in the Filipinas Heritage Library,
or more simply the Ayala Library. The library itself is in the old Nielson airport tower. It was part of the first private airfield in the Philippines that was
built in 1937 and named after its entrepreneur builder, Laurie Nielson of New
Zealand. After the fall of Manila, because he was a British citizen, Nielson was
interned in Hong Kong, while his family went to Santo Tomas. He was never
heard from again. The Japanese commandeered the tower during the war,
and afterward, the airport only lasted a few years. The runways were turned
into Paseo de Roxas and Ayala avenues, and eventually, the tower passed to
the Ayala family.

The Nielson is a small but beautiful building. The reading room is down
the spiral staircase in the basement. For anyone studying the Battle of Manila,
here exists the research mother lode. Tucked on a neat shelf nearly behind
a computer terminal is a row of green document boxes all identified by the
words "Memorare Manila 1945." The boxes are variously titled "Memorare
Narratives," "Memorare Testimonies," and others. Critically, here rests the

most comprehensive attempt at understanding the civilian experience in Manila during February and March 1945.

The Memorare Manila 1945 is a group that formed in 1993 to remember the civilian dead of Manila. At the nucleus of the group were alumni of the American School in Manila; Johnny Rocha, the former Philippine ambassador to Spain; and Rod Hall and Consuelo Hall, the nephew and niece, respectively, of Mercedes McMicking. These people had lost loved ones in the Battle of Manila, and they themselves had witnessed its horrors. With the generous support of the Ayala Foundation, the group set out to do three things for the battle's fiftieth anniversary: establish an archive of the names and information of the dead, commission a sculpture in their memory, and have a Mass said for them on the anniversary of the battle. Looking at what was accomplished, one cannot help but be impressed.[3]

The green boxes in the library contained folders filled with questionnaires completed by survivors of the Battle of Manila or their descendants. Memorare Manila had printed the questionnaires in newspapers and also had them sent to different organizations in Manila. The questionnaires asked people for information on relatives and friends killed during the battle, such as their ages, nationalities, addresses, and so on. They also directed the respondent to describe how their loved ones died. As I sat in the air-conditioned comfort of the tower surrounded by fresh-faced college students, information, much of it written by hand, would leap out and suddenly drag me into a maelstrom of horror. Perhaps it was because of the declarative nature of the responses, simple, stark, often understated.

> Clara, 17 or 18 . . . raped and bayoneted . . . in front of De La Salle. . . .
>
> Henry Daland, approximately 60 years old . . . Burned in his family home. Gasoline was poured around the house, doors were bolted, the 3 people mentioned here (father, son, maid) were trapped and burned . . . [the son's] body was found cradling the body of a housemaid.
>
> Delfin de la Paz, 49, Math professor of University of the Philippines . . . killed by the Japanese together with 60 other male members of families in our block on suspicion that one of them killed a Japanese soldier. Machine gunned and burned.[4]

I read the account of the ninety-eight-year-old Spaniard killed by shrapnel in Malate. Another was from a doctor who described how his mother was killed by an errant U.S. bomb, and how he then lost his two brothers, then two sisters, and then his father to shooting and shelling. In these short accounts, the handwritten phrases repeat themselves with awful regularity: "machine gunned," "hand grenade thrown in," "buried alive."

In the quiet, cool comfort of the tower, I was often amazed. Around me were young people calmly reading a newspaper or studying for a science test while I was holding a chain to the inside of hell. Such simple pieces of paper revealed the tragic losses of family members sixty years ago. The writing was astonishing, and there were times when it was frankly difficult not to become emotional in public.

The Memorare Manila achieved its second objective: the memorial sculpture was built on fitting ground, in the Plaza de Santa Isabel, on the corner of Gen. Luna and Anda streets, behind the Manila Cathedral. On February 18, 1995, the monument was dedicated. The sculpture is of Saint Isabel caring for the sick, who lie prostrate before her. Below the figures a passage states that the monument is to all of the hundred thousand civilians who died in the liberation of Manila. After a promise never to forget what happened here, the passage concludes with the simple line: "May they rest in peace as part now of the sacred ground of this city: the Manila of our affections."

On the same day as the monument was dedicated, Cardinal Jaime Sin celebrated a requiem Mass dedicated as a "Commemoration of the Non-Combative Victims of the Battle of Liberation of Manila." Wolfgang Amadeus Mozart's *Requiem* was played. At one point during the Mass, the Prayer of the Faithful was said.

For those we loved, who suffered grievously and perished in the Battle of Manila, let us pray to the Lord.

For those victims who lie in unknown graves all over the city, let us pray to the Lord.

For our menfolk who were herded like cattle to die away from the comfort of their families, let us pray to the Lord.

For our women who were abused, and suffered every pain and indignity before being put to death, let us pray to the Lord.

For those who killed and raped and slaughtered that they may acknowledge their guilt and seek forgiveness, let us pray to the Lord.

For those of us who still weep and question in the night that we may find peace in the acceptance of your will, let us pray to the Lord.[5]

On February 18, 2006, sixty-one years after the battle and eleven years after Memorare Manila achieved its goals, Japanese ambassador Ryuichiro Yamazaki, standing at the Plaza de Santa Isabel monument, formerly apologized for atrocities committed in the battle. The ambassador said that the terror the citizens of Manila must have felt is beyond imagination. It was the first time the nation of Japan recognized its moral conduct in the battle.[6]

PART 5
MAKATI

20

EPILOGUE

It was one of my last days in the Philippines. I was in a taxicab. The radio was pumping out saccharin-laced pop music in Tagalog as I watched the area around Fort Bonafacio slip past. The driver was pleasant and courteous. His car smelled of a pine air freshener. He had posted a no-smoking warning and a phone number to report any complaints. I thought about how fifteen years ago it was a fifty-fifty chance the driver, whose meter would be mysteriously broken, would bargain for the fare, nearly always at least doubling the real cost. Now all the meters worked. Manila, or at least Makati, had become sanitized and predictable.

I had just been at the Manila American Cemetery. This land used to be Fort William McKinley in the prewar years. Now it is the largest cemetery in the Pacific for Americans killed in World War II with more than seventeen thousand graves. Filipino members of the illustrious Philippine Scouts are buried there as well. It was a vast, powerful place. The rows and rows of crosses and stars with their names of long-dead young men created a sobering sight. As I walked aimlessly through the rows, I tried to piece together history. Here was a man from New Jersey who died in April 1942; he must have been on Bataan. Next to him was someone from Tennessee who was killed in February 1945, surely during the Battle of Manila. Just as at the San Fernando train station, I marveled at the fact that people still cared for these long-dead heroes.

It was oppressively hot. The sun smacked off the white markers and memorials. The fire trees dotting the land were incredible, and their bright

311

orange-red leaves contrasted perfectly with the green grass and blue sky. As I went through a row of graves, up rolled a golf cart driven by the cemetery's American superintendent, who was an early middle-aged former Marine. We chatted about the number of dead, about the condition of the cemetery, about doing historical research in Manila. Mostly, though, we talked about the huge condominium towers that were rising all around us.

I had first seen the cemetery in the early 1990s. It then was an oasis of tranquility, a silent locale on a plateau removed from the energy of Makati and the decay of Ermita. Today the gentle green fields of the cemetery are becoming surrounded by the soaring apartment buildings of Global City. Their huge size cast shadows over the burial sites. Some buildings were not yet finished, and the din of construction overpowered any serious contemplation. The superintendent told me that the buildings were being financed mostly by investors out of Taipei and Shanghai. The Chinese, he said, think it is bad luck to live next to a cemetery, so they lease the condos facing the dead to Filipinos and foreigners. The condos with views in the other direction were kept for the owners.

Global City, for me, epitomized the new Philippines and the final remains of the American period. President Arroyo has embraced globalization with open arms. Foreign money is pouring in as Filipinos leave in the tens of thousands. I thought about the dead Americans and Philippine Scouts in the cemetery, their eternal bivouac now being cooled by the lengthening shadows of global investment, their peace harried by the jackhammers of construction. Perhaps it was good that the memory of the American period was being erased.

How far has American cultural influence declined? On the one hand, an American walking through the Philippines today would be constantly reminded of the United States. These cues, however, are visual or physical ones. Throughout my trip, I saw numerous structures the Americans had built during the colonial period, including provincial capitol buildings and Manila landmarks. Historical monuments, many dedicated to MacArthur and the war, abound. Cities, islands, and streets are still named after MacArthur and other Americans. Actual artifacts of the war, the guns of Corregidor, the airfield at Clark, the walls of Intramuros—all of them can still be seen. There are also the people in places such as the Manila Elks Club, where I spoke to elderly Americans who have lived in the islands for decades, breathing vestiges of another time.

The relics are also conceptual. The Philippine political system is built on the U.S. model, and throughout the provinces and large cities, one sees a strong dedication to democracy. Public education in the country is likewise copied from the American version, with English still being used as the language of instruction (as well as that of commerce and law). American cultural organizations such as the Rotary Club exist in almost every Philippine town. There is also the widespread Filipino belief, especially among older persons, that America is in some way still very much a part of these islands, even a pseudo-guardian. Perhaps this conviction stems from a decidedly pro-American educational system or, more likely, from the military agreements that still put U.S. troops on Filipino soil. In any event, Filipinos still have a pronounced affinity for America.

On the other hand, U.S. influence in the Philippines is eroding, not evolving. The fluency level of English now is lower than that of the 1950s. Philippine public schools are in a state of near collapse. The political system has recently seen one deposed dictator, another president removed from office and incarcerated, and nearly twenty coup attempts since 1986. In fact, since the election of Ferdinand Marcos in 1965, only one Philippine president has not faced an attempt to remove him or her from office. No president has been able to completely eradicate the communist movement in the Philippines; indeed, it is now one of the world's oldest armed revolutions. Within the past two decades, a potent Muslim secessionist movement has emerged, which uses terrorism to achieve its ends. Political assassinations are commonplace. The Philippines is usually ranked within the top five countries for murdered journalists, killings that normally have a political connection.

It would seem, then, that the agencies of U.S. nation building were either flawed to begin with or have just deteriorated over the years. Whatever the case, the grand neoclassic vision of both the Americans and the Filipinos during the prewar years has not panned out. Something else has taken its place, but what it is exactly has yet to be determined.

It was time for me to say my good-byes. I did so in Sid's Sports Bar, a Makati restaurant that catered to the international crowd. At a table sat four old men: three Filipinos and one white American. We greeted each other, ready to begin the Friday afternoon ritual of beer, salami, and cheese. I enjoyed this ceremony immensely because the men were excellent conversationalists.

The three well-dressed Filipinos, all in their late sixties or early seventies and with light complexions, were involved in a friendly banter about schools. Two of them were Ateneo de Manila alumni, while the third was from De la Salle. The De la Salle grad accused the Ateneo priests (a Jesuit university) of having José Rizal executed. The Ateneans demanded to know if De la Salle (a Christian Brothers university) was actually a Catholic institution. The conversation wound through hilarious country, stopping briefly at the *Iliad* and ending in an earnest contest attempting to see which man could speak Latin the most fluently.

Just as the men at the Elks Club, these were from another time, a time when schoolboys learned Latin and Homer. There were other historical wonders as well. One man revealed that his birth certificate states he was born in the Philippine Islands, then a commonwealth of the United States. The two others said their certificates read the same. As I sipped the cold San Miguel and sampled the imported salami, I marveled that here were living relics of American empire.

The conversation then touched on the war. One said he and his family were north of the city. He did not see any of the fighting but remembers the aftermath. Another man, when he was just a boy with his family in Pasay, near Malate, cowered with his parents and neighbors in a trench, hoping to escape the U.S. shelling. Two GIs heard their voices coming from the trench and, presumably thinking they were Japanese voices, threw in a grenade. With great animation he related how everyone in the trench screamed and climbed out, surprising the GIs. "We were twice lucky," he laughed, "because the grenade did not go off and the Americans were too dumbfounded to shoot."

The third Filipino simply said he was not in the country, and he missed the whole thing. I did not mention to him that the day before, sitting in the cool Filipinas Heritage Library, I had read the harrowing tale about how his father had died from a shrapnel wound, presumably from U.S. artillery, in Paco, quite near the Price house.

The pleasant exchange lasted several hours. The men spoke of Manila in the early 1960s, a seemingly frenzied phase of unrestrained booze and nightclubs and politicians with bodyguards and guns. They once knew the names of the best apartments and hotels and where to get a good meal. All of these places, they noted, were all now gone.

The American, Merv Simpson, quietly listened to the conversation. He was older than the Filipino men by at least a decade, and he smiled and chuckled at his companions' friendly gripes and jabs. I looked at his hands. They were hands that shook Douglas MacArthur's, hands that defeated General Sutherland in golf, hands that held a compass to chart his B-29 over Japan. They were steady hands.

The ritual was nearly over, and I prepared to get up and leave. I experienced a weakness in my knees and a lump in my throat; there was every possibility that I would not sit and chat with Merv Simpson again. I could not assume I would do the same with the three others. All phases must end or at least evolve.

I said my good-byes as quickly I could, promising I would call or send an e-mail. Then I went back out into the afternoon heat. My condo was but a few blocks away, and I walked down Jupiter Street. As I did, I thought of the cool sanctuary of Sid's behind me, where there were contests in Latin and navigator's hands.

NOTES

1. THE FUTURE AND THE PAST

1. My observations come from my personal notes taken during trips to the Philippines. Most of these occurred between 2004 and 2007, although some, as indicated, occurred earlier.

2. Carmen Nakpil Guerrero, *Myself, Elsewhere* (Metro Manila: Circe Communication, 2006), 43.

3. For the history and development of Makati, see Manuel D. Duldulao, *A Vision of Makati: The City* (Makati: Japuzinni Publishing, 1996); *History of Makati: A Report of the Research Department* (Filipinas Foundation, August 30, 1983); "Makati: A Planned City Blossoms in a Tropical Setting," *Engineering News Record*, November 17, 1966, 106; and "Makati: City of the Future," *Philippine Herald Magazine Special Issue*, March 14, 1964.

2. THE OAKWOOD MUTINY

1. The mutiny was covered extensively in the Manila media. A good resource for the mutiny and its aftermath can be found on GMA News, "Oakwood Mutiny," July 20, 2007, images.gmanews.tv/html/research/2007/11/oakwood_mutiny_timeline.html (accessed December 1, 2008).

2. The notion of a cacique system is the central tenet of the Philippine Left. For two of the most well-known examples, see Renato Constantino, *A History of the Philippines: From the Spanish Colonization to the Second World War* (New York: Monthly Review Press, 1975); and Amado (Jose Maria

Sison) Guerrero, *Philippine Society and Revolution* (Hong Kong: Ta Kung Pao, 1971).

3. THE ELKS CLUB

1. Walter Robb, *The Filipinos* (Manila: the author, 1939), 364, 368–70.
2. Florence Horn, *Orphans of the Pacific: The Philippines* (Cornwall, NY: Cornwall Press, 1941), 95–96.
3. Carlos P. Romulo, *I Walked with Heroes* (New York: Holt, Rinehart and Winston, 1961), 116–17.
4. See "Kapihan sa AmCham," *AmCham Business Journal,* June 2004, 20.
5. The interview with Merv Simpson was conducted by the author in Makati on July 2 and July 20, 2004.
6. Ibid.

4. THE RETURN

1. D. Clayton James, *The Years of MacArthur*, vol. 2, *1941–1945* (Boston: Houghton Mifflin, 1975), 66.
2. The discussion of MacArthur's return to Leyte relies on Samuel Eliot Morison, *History of the United States Naval Operations in World War II*, vol. 12, *Leyte, June 1944–January 1945* (Edison, NJ: Castle Books, 2001); M. Hamlin Cannon, *Leyte: The Return to the Philippines* (Washington, D.C.: Center of Military History, United States Army, 1987); James, *Years of MacArthur*; and Courtney Whitney, *MacArthur: His Rendezvous with History* (New York: Alfred A. Knopf, 1956). The population statistics on Leyte come from Cannon, *Leyte*, 13.
3. See Carlos Quirino, *Chick Parsons: America's Master Spy in the Philippines* (Manila: New Day, 1954); and William B. Brewer, *MacArthur's Undercover War: Spies, Saboteurs, Guerrillas, and Secret Missions* (New York: John Wiley and Sons, 1995).
4. Carlos P. Romulo, *I See the Philippines Rise* (New York: Doubleday, 1946), 11.
5. Douglas A. MacArthur, *Reminiscences* (New York: McGraw-Hill, 1964), 216.
6. Text of speech from U.S. Department of Defense, "60th Anniversary, Battle of Leyte Gulf, Liberation of the Philippines" (2004), www.de-

fenselink.mil/home/features/Leyte/ (accessed July 23, 2007).

7. The primary source for the MacArthur biography here is Carol Morris Petillo, *Douglas MacArthur: The Philippine Years* (Bloomington: Indiana University Press, 1981).

8. D. Clayton James, *The Years of MacArthur*, vol. 1, *1880–1941* (Boston: Houghton Mifflin, 1970), 42–44.

9. Petillo, *Douglas MacArthur*, 65–66.

10. Ibid., 69.

11. Michael Schaller, *Douglas MacArthur: The Far Eastern General* (New York: Oxford University Press, 1989), 127.

12. Jan Valtin, *Children of Yesterday: The 24th Infantry Division in WWII* (New York: The Readers' Press, 1946), 39, 40–42.

13. Ibid., 180.

14. For a representative account of this debate, see Antonio Abaya, "If There Had Been No Leyte Landing . . . ," *Philippine Star*, October 25, 1994; Dahli Aspillera, "I Shall Return," *Malaya*, August 18, 1994; Jose Antonio Custodio and Rino A. Francisco, "Perceptions of U.S. Presence in Asia," *Philippine Star*, December 2, 1994; and Ferdinand Llanes, "A Sham Celebration," *Manila Chronicle*, October 16, 1994.

15. "MacArthur Falls!" *Philippine Star*, October 21, 1994; and Johanna Son, "Philippines Holds Big Party for Its Own D-Day," *Manila Chronicle*, October 14, 1994.

5. THE KING OF LEYTE AND THE JUNKYARD OAKIE

1. National Statistics Office, Philippines, "2007 Census of Population" (2007), www.census.gov.ph/data/census2007/index.html (accessed December 21, 2008).

2. MacArthur's quote and the story of Osmeña can be found in Dale Pontius, "MacArthur and the Filipinos," *Asia and the Americas*, November 1946, 510.

3. Ralph Harrington Doane, "The Story of American Architecture in the Philippines," *Architectural Review* 8, old series vol. 25, no. 2 (May 1919): 25. For an analysis of American architecture as part of the colonial system, see David Brody, "Building Empire: Architecture and American Imperialism

in the Philippines," *Journal of Asian Studies* 4, no. 2 (June 2001): 123–45.

4. Doane, "The Story of American Architecture in the Philippines," 28.

5. Ibid., 116.

6. For accounts of MacArthur and the house, see James, *The Years of MacArthur*, 2:561–62, 583–86; and Weldon E. Rhoades, *Flying MacArthur to Victory* (College Station: Texas A&M University Press, 1987), 308. In particular, A. Jack Brown provides intimate details of the Joe Price family and the restoration of the house in 1979–1982. See his *Katakana Man: I Worked Only for Generals: The Most Secret of All Allied Operations in World War II in the Pacific* (Tuggeranong, Australia: Air Power Development Centre, 2006), 179, 181–84.

7. James, *The Years of MacArthur*, 2:585; and Geoffrey Perret, *Old Soldiers Never Die: The Life of Douglas MacArthur* (New York: Random House, 1996), 427.

8. The only known biographical treatment of Price is by Father Raymond Quetchenbach, SVD, "Walter Scott Price—'King of Leyte,'" *Leyte-Samar Studies* 8, no. 1 (1974): 33–38.

9. Ibid., 36.

10. A. V. H. Hartendorp, *The Japanese Occupation of the Philippines*, 2 vols. (Manila: Bookmark, 1967), 1:372 and 388 and 2:613.

11. This information was found in the University of Santo Tomas (UST) Internment Camp Papers, Census Report, roll calls 1943–44, kept in the American Historical Collection, the Rizal Library, Ateneo University of Manila.

12. Quetchenbach, "Walter Scott Price," 37.

13. All quotes of Woolbright's can be found in Joseph P. McCallus, *American Exiles in the Philippines, 1941–1996: A Collected Oral Narrative* (Quezon City: New Day Publishers, 1999); and Joseph P. McCallus, "Eddie Woolbright: A Biographical Sketch Drawn from an Oral Narrative," *Bulletin of the American Historical Collection* 25, no. 3 (July–September, 1997): 7–20.

14. For an update on Eddie's Log Cabin, see Honey Jarque Loop, "Cebu's Legendary Eddie's Log Cabin Gets a Makeover," *Philippine Headline News Online*, www.newsflash.org/2004/02/ht/ht006146.htm (accessed January 20, 2008).

15. "The Definitive History of Balut in the Far East," www.nuss.org.

6. THE SECOND BATTLE OF LEYTE

1. The discussion of the history of religion in the Philippines and the rise of Christian fundamentalism is drawn from Kenton J. Clymer, *Protestant Missionaries in the Philippines, 1898–1916: An Inquiry into the American Colonial Mentality* (Urbana: University of Illinois Press, 1986); Thelma F. Naraval, *The Southern Cross: A History of the Christian and Missionary Alliance Churches of the Philippines* (Cagayan de Oro, Philippines: Bustamante Press, 1977); Steve Brouwer, Paul Gifford, and Susan D. Rose, *Exporting the American Gospel: Global Christian Fundamentalism* (New York: Routledge, 1996); L. Shelton Woods, *A Broken Mirror: Protestant Fundamentalism in the Philippines* (Quezon City: New Day Press, 2002); and Working Group on New Religious Movements, ed., *Sects and New Religious Movements: An Anthology of Texts from the Catholic Church, 1986–1994* (Washington, DC: U.S. Catholic Conference, 1995).

2. From the Spanish-American War Centennial Website, "McKinley Gives His Reasons for the U.S. to Keep the Philippines," www.spanamwar.com/ McKinleyphilreasons.htm (accessed July 1, 2008).

3. Clymer, *Protestant Missionaries in the Philippines*, 154.

4. Ibid., 163.

5. The three quotes here are from ibid., 138, 139, and 140.

6. See ibid., 194; and Jack Miller, "Religion in the Philippines," *Asia Society's Focus on Asian Studies* 2, no. 1 (Fall 1982): 26–27.

7. Brouwer, Gifford, and Rose, *Exporting the American Gospel*, 77.

8. In McCallus, *American Exiles in the Philippines*, 128.

9. Brouwer, Gifford, and Rose, *Exporting the American Gospel*, 85.

10. Joseph Collins, *The Philippines: Fire on the Rim* (San Francisco: Institute for Food and Development Policy, 1989), 102.

11. The relationship between the Philippine military and fundamentalists can be found in Brouwer, Gifford, and Rose, *Exporting the American Gospel*, 95–96. See also Sterling Seagrave, *The Marcos Dynasty* (New York: Harper & Row, 1988), 401; and Stanley Karnow, *In Our Image: America's Empire in the Philippines* (New York: Ballantine Books, 1990), 406.

12. The Joshua Project, www.joshuaproject.net/index.php (accessed January 19, 2007).

13. The Christian Light Foundation, www.clfphils.org/aboutus.htm (accessed June 19, 2006).

14. Working Group, *Sects and New Religious Movements*, 49.

7. THE BALICUARTO ISLANDS

1. Background information on Samar was found on the province's website, "General Information," samar.lgu-ph.com/history.htm (accessed November 13, 2006).

2. To date, the best analysis of the affair is Rolando Borrinaga's *The Balangiga Conflict Revisited* (Quezon City: New Day Publishers, 2003).

3. See the Philippine Overseas Employment Administration's website at www.poea.gov.ph/stats/remittance_1997_2006.html (accessed July 2008).

4. See Martha Ann Overland, "A Nursing Crisis in the Philippines," *The Chronicle of Higher Education*, January 7, 2005, chronicle.com/weekly/v51/i18/18a04601.htm (accessed March 30, 2007); and PDI Research, "In the Know," *Philippine Daily Inquirer*, August 4, 2005. For more on the effects of OFWs and community change, see Luis H. Francia, *Eye of the Fish: A Personal Archipelago* (New York: Kaya Press, 2001).

5. Interview with municipal official, July 15, 2005.

6. All historical data regarding the military activities on Biri was taken from Francis D. Cronin, *Under the Southern Cross: The Saga of the Americal Division* (Washington, D.C.: Combat Forces Press, 1951), 248–57; and Robert R. Smith, *Triumph in the Philippines: The U.S. Army in WWII* (Washington, DC: Department of the Army, 1963), 436–437.

7. From S. J. Herbert Thurston and Donald Attwater, eds., *Butler's Lives of the Saints*, vol. 2 (New York: P. J. Kennedy and Sons, 1956), 32–33.

8. *Biri Fiesta 2005* (No publisher, 2005).

8. THE LINGAYEN BEACHES AND SOUTH

1. The historical details of the Lingayen landing are drawn from James, *The Years of MacArthur*, vol. 2; Morison, *History of the United States Naval Operations*, vol. 12; Samuel Eliot Morison, *History of the United States Naval Operations in World War II*, vol. 13, *The Liberation of the Philippines: Luzon, Mindanao, the Visayas, October 1944–August 1945* (Edison, NJ: Castle Books,

2002); Smith, *Triumph in the Philippines*; Whitney, *MacArthur*; *U.S. Army, 40th Infantry Division: The Years of World War II* (Nashville: The Battery Press, 1946); Richard Connaughton, John Pimlott, and Duncan Anderson, *The Battle for Manila: The Most Devastating Story of World War II* (Novato, CA: Presidio Press, 1995); and Rose Contey-Aillo, *The 50th Anniversary Commemorative Album of the Flying Column 1945–1995: The Liberation of Santo Tomas Internment Camp, February 1945* (Tarpon Springs, FL: Marrakech Express, 1995).

2. As found in Morison, *History of the United States Naval Operations*, 13:111.

3. From MacArthur, *Reminiscences*, 240.

4. See the coverage of MacArthur's visit in the *Manila Times*, July 7, 1961, 1 and 2.

5. Information on Dagupan was found on "Pangasinan History," www.pangasinan.gov.ph (accessed July 2008).

9. THE MacARTHUR HIGHWAY

1. The Philippine newspapers covered every moment of the general's trip. See, for instance, the "Independence Day MacArthur Special Issue," *Philippines Herald*, July 3, 1961. See also United States Information Service, *A Sentimental Journey: General Douglas MacArthur's Visit to the Philippines* (United States Information Service, no date, probably 1961).

10. HACIENDA LUISITA AND CAMP O'DONNELL

1. The discussion on MacArthur in this chapter uses the following sources: James D. Delk, *The Fighting Fortieth: In War and Peace* (Palm Springs, CA: ETC Publications, 1998); James, *The Years of MacArthur*, vol. 2; Morison, *History of the United States Naval Operations*, vol. 12; Ibid., vol. 13; and Smith, *Triumph in the Philippines*.

2. This story appears in numerous places. See, for instance, Perret, *Old Soldiers Never Die*, 442.

3. See Lino L. Dizon, *Mr. White: A "Thomasite" History of Tarlac Province, 1901–1913* (Tarlac City, Philippines: JDN Center for Kapampangan Studies, Holy Angel University, with Public Affairs Office, Embassy of the United States–Manila 2002); and W. Cameron Forbes, *The Philippine Islands*, rev.

ed. (Cambridge, MA: Harvard University Press, 1945). See also Glenn Anthony May, *Social Engineering in the Philippines: The Aims, Execution, and Impact of American Colonial Policy, 1900–1913* (Westport, CT: Greenwood Press, 1980); and Lewis E. Gleeck Jr., "Fulfillment in the Philippines (IV)," *Bulletin of the American Historical Collection* 19, no. 1 (January–March 1991): 44–69.

4. For information on the Thomasites and other American teachers of the 1900–1910 period, see Dizon, *Mr. White*; Encarnacion Alzona, *A History of Education in the Philippines, 1565–1930* (Manila: University of Philippines Press, 1932); Geromina T. Pecson and Maria Racelis, eds., *Tales of American Teachers in the Philippines* (Manila: Carmelo and Bauremann, 1959); and Arthur S. Pier, *American Apostles to the Philippines* (Boston: Beacon Press, 1950). Over the years the *Bulletin of the American Historical Collection* has published a number of articles on the Thomasites, often from primary sources. These include Helen P. Beattie, "American Teachers and the Filipinos," 12, no. 3 (July–September 1984): 70–81; Price W. Cooper, "The Life and Death of an Ilocos Public School Teacher (1901–1903): From the Letters of Price W. Cooper, 1875–1903," 10, no. 1 (January–March 1982): 36–41; Edilberto P. Dagot, "American Teachers in Paragua: Charles D. Hart (1871–1907)," 2, no. 1 (September 1973): 27–39; and Gilbert Perez, "From the Transport Thomas to Sto. Tomas," 1, no. 5 (September 1973): 13–26, and 2, no. 1 (January 1974): 59–74.

5. Forbes, *The Philippine Islands*, 175.

6. The early days of American education in the Philippines are described by the works in note 4 (above) as well as in the following: John Morgan Gates, *Schoolbooks and Krags: The United States Army in the Philippines, 1898–1902* (Westport, CT: Greenwood Press, 1973); May, *Social Engineering in the Philippines*; and Frank J. Swetz, "Mathematics for Social Change, 1898–1925," *Bulletin of the American Historical Collection* 27, no. 1 (January–March 1999): 61–80. For an account of more recent American involvement in Philippine education, including that of the Peace Corps, see the United States Information Service, *The American Contribution to Philippine Education, 1898–1998* (Washington, D.C.: United States Information Service, 1998).

7. Renato Constantino carried the flag for revising the history of American

education in the Philippines, and it has inspired a host of other writers. See Constantino, *A History of the Philippines*; and Renato Constantino, *Neocolonial Identity and Counter-consciousness: Essays in Cultural Decolonization* (New York: M. E. Sharpe, 1978).

8. Constantino, *A History of the Philippines*, 312–13.

9. For a discussion of the American emphasis on practical education, see Fred W. Atkinson, *The Philippine Islands* (Boston: Ginn, 1905); Alzona, *History of Education*; Dizon, *Mr. White*; May, *Social Engineering*; and Swetz, "Mathematics for Social Change."

10. Atkinson, *The Philippine Islands*, 14. Atkinson also wrote that the Filipinos were "incapable" of self-government (p. 5) and that "the Filipino people, taken as a body, are children and, childlike, do not know what is best for them" (p. 6). In drawing a direct comparison to the African Americans' situation in America, Atkinson proclaimed, "Thirty-nine years have now passed since the close of the civil war and the negro problem is still unsolved; at the end of a like period of time we shall be struggling with the Philippine question" (p. 14).

11. Tetch Torres, "Tutors Ask SC Not to Make English Primary Education Medium," *Philippine Inquirer.net*, April 27, 2007, newsinfo.inquirer.net/breakingnews/nation/view_article.php?article_id+62882 (accessed June 1, 2007).

12. For the effects of English on the Filipino culture, see Constantino, *Neocolonial Identity and Counter-consciousness*, 66–69. See also E. San Juan Jr., *Writing and National Liberation: Essays on Critical Practice* (Quezon City: University of the Philippines Press, 1991); and his *The Philippine Temptation: Dialectics of Philippine-U.S. Literary Relations* (Philadelphia: Temple University Press, 1996).

13. Katipunan ng mga Anak ng Bayan Citizen's Development Initiatives, Inc. (KAAKBAY CDI), "Philippine Public Education: A Situationer," June 05, 2006, qc.indymedia.org (accessed July 1, 2007).

14. Daniel Walfish, "Higher Education in the Philippines: Lots of Access, Little Quality," *The Chronicle of Higher Education* (September 7, 2001), A60. See also Cecil Morella, "Philippine Education in Crisis," *Philippine Inquirer. net*, July 5, 2004, www.inq7.net/brk/2004/jul/brkpol_4-1htm (accessed

June 26, 2006); and Mayen Jaymalin, "Over 1M[illion] College Graduates Jobless," *Philippine Star*, June 30, 2007, 1.

15. Yvonne T. Chua, *Robbed: An Investigation of Corruption in Philippine Education* (Manila: Philippine Center for Investigative Journalism, 1999).

16. Jo. Florendo B. Lontoc, "A Situationer on Philippine Education," *Forum Online Magazine* 6, no. 4 (July–August 2005), www.up.edu.ph/forum/2005/Jul-Aug05/situationer.html (accessed June 26, 2007).

17. KAAKBAY CDI, "Philippine Public Education."

18. John Dos Passos, *Tour of Duty* (New York: Houghton Mifflin, 1946), 169–70.

19. Ibid., 158–61.

20. For the history of the hacienda, see chapter 6, "Sugar and Salt," of Nick Joaquin's *The Aquinos of Tarlac: An Essay on History as Three Generations* (Manila: Cacho Hermanos, 1983).

21. Information on recent labor problems and Hacienda Luisita comes from a variety of sources, including Dabet Castañeda, "For Land and Wages: Half a Century of Peasant Struggle in Hacienda Luisita," *Bulatlat Report* 4, no. 46 (December 19–25, 2004), www.bulatlat.com/news/4-46/4-46-land.html (accessed July 6, 2006); Emilia Dapulang, "Trade Union Repression in the Philippines," *Kapatiran: Newsletter of Philippine Solidarity Network of Aotearoa*, www.converge.org.nz/psna/Kapatiran/KapNo22/Kap22Art/art87.htm (accessed July 6, 2006); Tony Dorono, "Hacienda Luisita Workers in the Philippines Celebrate Their Historic Victory," Asian Pacific American Labor Alliance, ALF-CIO (APALA), www.aplanet.org/ht/d/sp/i/5267/pid/5267 (accessed July 6, 2006); The Internationalist, "Massacre of Sugar Plantation Workers in the Philippines," December 2004, www.internationalist.org/philippineslu-isitamassacre0412html (accessed July 6, 2006); International Union of Food, Agricultural, Hotel, Restaurant, Catering, Tobacco and Allied Workers' Associations (IUF), "IUF Condemns Killing of Workers at Hacienda Luisita Sugar Mill and Plantation, Philippines," www.asian-foodworker.net/philippines/041126luisita.htm (accessed July 6, 2006); Bobby Tuazon, "The Hacienda Luisita Massacre, Landordism and State Terrorism," *Bulatlat News Analysis*, November 22, 2004, www.bulatlat.com/news/4-42/4-42-massacre.html (accessed July 6, 2006).

22. After thirty years, Benedict J. Kerkvliet's *The Huk Rebellion: A Study of Peasant Revolt in the Philippines* (Berkeley: University of California Press, 1977) is still the definitive work on the Huks. This discussion draws on his work, as well as Eduardo Lachica, *The Huks: Philippine Agrarian Society in Revolt* (New York: Praeger Publishers, 1971); William J. Pomeroy, *An American Made Tragedy: Neo-Colonialism and Dictatorship in the Philippines* (New York: International Publishers, 1974); and Alfredo B. Saulo, *Communism in the Philippines: An Introduction* (Quezon City: The Ateneo de Manila University Press, 1990).

23. Kerklivet, *The Huk Rebellion*, 93.

24. For the return of the landowners, see Hernando J. Abaya, *Betrayal in the Philippines* (New York: A. A. Wyn, 1946), 134–48; and Pontius, "MacArthur and the Filipinos," 510.

25. Because the insurgency has stretched for decades, its scholarship is wide. See Saulo, *Communism in the Philippines*; Patricio N. Abinales, ed., *The Revolution Falters: The Left in Philippine Politics after 1986* (Ithaca, NY: Southeast Asia Program Publications, Cornell University, 1996); William Chapman, *Inside the Philippine Revolution: The New People's Army and Its Struggle for Power* (New York: W. W. Norton, 1987); Gregg R. Jones, *Red Revolution: Inside the Philippine Guerrilla Movement* (Boulder, CO: Westview Press, 1989); and Kathleen Weekley, *The Communist Party of the Philippines, 1968–1993: A Story of Its Theory and Practice* (Quezon City: University of the Philippines Press, 2001).

26. Jones, *Red Revolution*, 265; and Abinales, *The Revolution Falters*, 154–79.

27. See Joseph P. McCallus, "The Propaganda of the National Democratic Front: A Study of Rhetorical Method in Liberation," *Pilipinas: A Journal of Philippine Studies* 20 (Spring 1993): 23–42.

28. Guerrero, *Philippine Society and Revolution*, 230.

29. See Stephen Rosskamm Shalom, *The United States and the Philippines: A Study in Neocolonialism* (Philadelphia: Institute for the Study of Human Issues, 1981).

30. Biographical details are taken from Lucy Komisar, *Corazon Aquino: The Story of a Revolution* (New York: George Braziller, 1987).

31. Ibid., 81–82.

32. There has been much written on the election and revolution. A sampling would include Raymond Bonner, *Waltzing with a Dictator: The Marcoses and the Making of American Policy* (New York: Times Books, 1987); Bryan Johnson, *The Four Days of Courage: The Untold Story of the People Who Brought Marcos Down* (New York: Free Press, 1987); Karnow, *In Our Image*; Monina Allarey Mercado, ed., *People Power: The Philippine Revolution of 1986: An Eyewitness History* (Manila: James B. Reuter, S. J., Foundation, 1986); and Beth Day Romulo, *Inside the Palace: The Rise and Fall of Ferdinand and Imelda Marcos* (New York: G. P. Putnam's Sons, 1987).

33. Karnow, *In Our Image*, 412.

34. For a recent discussion of the Aquino presidency, see Patricio N. Abinales and Donna J. Amoroso, *State and Society in the Philippines* (Lanham, MD: Rowman & Littlefield Publishers, 2005).

35. Pacita Pestano-Jacinto, *Living with the Enemy: A Diary of the Japanese Occupation* (Pasig City, Philippines: Anvil, 1999).

36. The camp was named after a nearby barrio, which got its name either from a member of the British engineering team that constructed the nearby railroad or from Leopoldo O'Donnell, a Spanish premier in the mid-nineteenth century, who was a direct descendant of the Irish flight of the earl's centuries before. Details of Camp O'Donnell during the war can be found in the following: William B. Breuer, *The Great Raid on Cabanatuan: Rescuing the Doomed Ghosts of Bataan and Corregidor* (New York: John Wiley and Sons, 1994); Donald Knox, *Death March: The Survivors of Bataan* (New York: Harcourt Brace Jovanovich, 1981); Antonio A. Nieva, *The Fight for Freedom: Remembering Bataan and Corregidor* (Quezon City: New Day Publishers, 1997); John E. Olson, *O'Donnell, Andersonville of the Pacific* (self-published, 1985); and Sidney Stewart, *Give Us This Day* (New York: W. W. Norton, 1956). For more on the camp today, see the following websites: "The Battling Bastards of Bataan," www.battlingbastards-bataan.com/capas1.htm (accessed April 28, 2007); "Battling Bastards of Bataan," home.pacbell.net/fbaldie/Battling_Bastards_of_Bataan.html (accessed April 28, 2007); and "Philippines and U.S. Commemorate the 60th Anniversary of the End of WWII," manila.usembassy.gov/ww-whr632.html.

37. Victor Buencamino, "Manila under Japanese Occupation," *Bulletin of the American Historical Collection* 7, no. 1 (January–March 1980): 39.

38. See John E. Olson, "Home at Last!" *Bulletin of the American Historical Collection* 28, no. 4 (October–December 2000): 59–62.

11. THE HILLS OF BAMBAN

1. The discussion of the battle of the Bamban Hills relies on the following sources: Delk, *The Fighting Fortieth*; James, *The Years of MacArthur*, vol. 2; Walter Krueger, *From Down Under to Nippon: The Story of the Sixth Army in World War II* (Washington, D.C.: Combat Forces Press, 1953); Morison, *History of the United States Naval Operations*, vol. 12; Ibid., vol. 13; and Smith, *Triumph in the Philippines*. The *Bamban Historical Society Journal* was especially helpful.

2. See Lino Dizon, "Bamban, Tarlac in 1899: A Cruz of the Philippine Revolution," *Center for Tarlaqueno Studies*, www.geocities.com/cts_tsu/web-BAMBAN.html (accessed August 1, 2007); and Rhonie Dela Cruz, "The Paruao (Bamban) River Line—1899: The Last Battle of the Republic," *Bamban Historical Society Journal* 1, no. 5 (August 14, 2004).

3. For a description of the Bamban at the outbreak of the war followed by its role within the resistance movement, see Rhonie Dela Cruz, "Vincit, Amor, Patriae: The USAFFE Guerrilla Movement in the Bamban Area," *Bamban Historical Society Journal* 2, no. 2 (May 22, 2005).

4. Duane P. Schultz, *Hero of Bataan: The Story of General Jonathan M. Wainwright* (New York: St. Martin's Press, 1981), 88.

5. McCallus, *American Exiles in the Philippines*, 189.

6. Malcom Decker, *On a Mountainside: The 155th Provisional Guerrilla Battalion against the Japanese on Luzon* (Las Cruces, NM: Yucca Tree Press, 2004). See also Millard E. Hileman and Paul Fridlund, *1051: An American POW's Remarkable Journey through World War II* (Walla Walla, WA: Words Worth Press, 1992), 357–59; and Chris Schaefer, *Bataan Diary: An American Family in World War II, 1941–1945* (Houston: Riverview Publishing, 2004), 80–81, 104–5.

7. Dela Cruz, "Vincit, Amor, Patriae," 7–8.

8. Rhonie Dela Cruz, "The Bamban Kamikaze Airfield of WWII: A

Comprehensive Historical Essay," *Bamban Historical Society Journal* 1, no. 6 (October 16, 2004).

9. Rhonie Dela Cruz, "Beneath the Sword of the Kempei-Tai: The Death of an American Pilot in Bamban Field," *Bamban Historical Society Journal* 1, no. 3 (June 25, 2004).

10. On the kamikaze operations in Bamban and for more on Ohnishi, see Dela Cruz, "The Bamban Kamikaze Airfield of WWII"; and Rhonie Dela Cruz, "Asahiyama: The Japanese Naval Headquarters in Bamban," *Bamban Historical Society Journal* 1, no. 1 (June 25, 2004).

11. For a background on the Aeta, see Tonette Orejas, "From 'Lubay' to Levi's," *Philippine Daily Inquirer*, June 14, 2006, A1.

12. Dela Cruz, "Vincit, Amor, Patriae," 4.

13. Orejas, "From 'Lubay' to Levi's."

14. For a discussion of the Aeta in the post-Pinatubo era, see Felicisimo H. Manalansan Jr., "Oust-GMA to End Mining Liberalization, Conference Declares," *Bulatlat* 5, no. 20 (June 26–July 2, 2005), www.bulatlat.com/news/5-20/5-20-mining.htm (accessed July 2, 2005); Tonette Orejas, "Aeta People Like Leaves on Water," *Philippine Daily Inquirer*, May 31, 2005, A19; and Gerardo Gobrin and Almira Andini, "Development Conflict: The Philippine Experience," Minority Rights Group International and KAMP, November 2002, www.minorityrights.org/929/macro-studies/development-conflict-the-philippine-experience.html (accessed June 20, 2006).

15. Mission to Unreached Peoples, "Overview of Ministries and Programs," www.mup.org/ministries/index.php (accessed June 20, 2006); and Nazarene Compassionate Ministries, www.ncm.org (accessed June 20, 2006).

16. A written account of the battle and the Society's climbing of the hill can be found in Rhonie Dela Cruz, "Revisiting the Bamban Hills: The Raising of the American Flag at Hill 1700," *Bamban Historical Society Journal* 1, no. 2 (May 31, 2004).

12. ANGELES CITY AND CLARK FIELD

1. Historical information on Angeles was drawn from the Tourist Center

Corporation Philippines, "Angeles, Pampanga," www.touristcenter.com. ph/philippines/information/angeles.html (accessed May 1, 2008). For a description of the events around Angeles in 1899, see Brian McCallister Linn, *The Philippine War, 1899–1902* (Lawrence: University of Kansas, 2000).

2. For a history of Clark, see Richard B. Meixsel, *Clark Field and the U.S. Army Air Corps in the Philippines, 1919–1942* (Quezon City: New Day Publishers, 2002).

3. See the various descriptions of the base and the military's interactions with the local population during the 1930s in Charles Willeford's *Something about a Soldier* (New York: Random House, 1986).

4. The debacle at Clark has been covered by many. See James, *The Years of MacArthur*, vol. 2.

5. See Bonner, *Waltzing with a Dictator*, 206.

6. Communist Party of the Philippines, "U.S. Military Bases: Outposts for Aggression," *Ang Bayan*, April 1983, 2.

7. See Tonette Orejas, "More Jobs Today in Subic and Clark," *Philippine Daily Inquirer*, June 26, 2007, 1.

8. The toxic waste controversy is well documented. See, for example, Greenpeace, "Toxic Alert: US Toxic Legacies: Toxic Hotspots in Clark and Subic," February 29, 2000, archive.greenpeace.org/toxics/toxfreeasia/documents/clarksubic.html (accessed December 10, 2008); and Christina Leaño's "Benzene and Butterflies: The Toxic Legacy of the U.S. Military in the Philippines," *Pax Christi USA*, Spring 2003. www.paxchristiusa.org/news_events_more.asp?id=567 (accessed October 20, 2008).

9. See McCallus, *American Exiles in the Philippines*, xx–xxi.

10. "Bonk . . . The Life Saver," www.clarkab.com/ck_stories_bonk.htm (accessed March 15, 2007).

11. Biographical information on Nick Rowe appears on a number of websites. See "Colonel James 'Nick' Rowe, February 8, 1938–April 21, 1989," www.psywarrior.com/rowe.html (accessed October 10, 2007); the Arlington National Cemetery Website, "James Nicholas Rowe," www. arlingtoncemetery.net/jamesnic.htm (accessed October 8, 2007); and

P.O.W. Network, "Case Synopsis: Rowe, James Nicholas 'Nick,'" www.pownetwork.org/bios/r/r077.htm (accessed October 3, 2007).

12. The Philippine counterinsurgency operations during the late 1980s and early 1990s were both effective and controversial. A sampling of the work produced would include Victor N. Corpus, *Silent War* (Quezon City: VNC Enterprises, 1989); and Lawyers Committee for Human Rights, *Out of Control: Militia Abuses in the Philippines* (New York: Lawyers Committee for Human Rights, 1990).

13. National Democratic Front, "NPA Punishes US 'LIC' Expert," *Liberation*, March–April 1989, 16.

14. See Communist Party of the Philippines (CPP), "CPP Warns against Use of Philippines as Staging Ground for U.S. War against DPRK," October 17, 2006, www.democraticunderground.com/discuss/duboard.php?az=view_all&address=132x2891393 (accessed March 20, 2007); Maoist International Movement (MIM), "Wimmin's Movement Leader from the Philippines Speaks Out against the Visiting Forces Agreement," *MIM Notes* 185 (May 1 ,1999), www.etext.org/Politics/MIM/cal/vfa.html (accessed March 8, 2007); and League of Filipino Students, "Cohen's Visit, a U.S. Pressure Tactic for the VFA!" August 3, 1998, www.geocities.com/CollegePark/Field/4927/lfs/stmts/cohen (accessed March 13, 2007). There are a great many other examples of leftist statements against the VFA.

15. "Target: 20M Signatures; CBCP Starts 50-day Protest against VFA," *Philippine Daily Inquirer*, July 26 1998, c26, www.hartford-hwp.com/archives/27c/477.html (accessed March 13, 2007).

16. Ecumenical Bishops' Forum, "Statement on Visiting Forces Agreement," *Critical Asian Studies* 38, no. 4 (December 2006), www.Bcasnet.org/campaigns/campaign5.htm (accessed March 8, 2007).

17. The discussion on Philippine terrorist groups relies on Thomas Lum and Larry A. Niksch, *The Republic of the Philippines: Background and U.S. Relations*, *CRS Report for Congress* (Washington, D.C.: Congressional Research Service, January 10, 2006).

18. Anthony Vargas, "DNA Testing Confirms Death of Janjalani," *Manila Times*, January 21, 2007, www.manilatimes.net/national/2007/jan21/

yehey/metro/20070121met1.html (accessed March 9, 2007); and Jaime Laude, "4 Informants vs Sayyaf Receive $10M from U.S.," *Philippine Star*, June 8, 2007, 6.

19. The case captivated the country and was covered exhaustively by the media. For a background on the rape case, see Cecil Morella, "Rape Trial in RP Revives 'Ugly American' Image," *Manila Times*, October 26, 2006, 6.

20. Ibid.

21. Emmi De Jesus, "Justice for Nicole Requires Abrogation of VFA," Gabriella Network, December 4, 2006, www.feministpeacenetwork. org/2006/12/05/analysis-of-the-subic-bay-rape-verdicts/ (accessed May 9, 2007).

22. For an overview of the resumption of the exercises, see Emily Vital, "Bayan Challenges Candidates to Junk VFA," *Bulatlat* 7, no. 3 (February 18–24, 2007), www.bulatlat.com/news/7-3/7-3-vfa.htm (accessed May 8, 2007); Francis Earl A. Cueto, Sam Mediavilla, Anthony Vargas, and AFP, "Balikatan on Again with Malacañang Cave In," *Manila Times*, January 3, 2007, www.manilatimes.net/national/2007/jan/03/yehey/top_stories (accessed May 8, 2007); and the U.S. Embassy, Manila, Philippines, "Exercise Balikatan 2007 Partners with Gawad Kalinga to Build Communities while Building Relationships," March 7, 2007, manila.usembassy.gov/wwwhs102.html (accessed March 8, 2007).

23. See Philip Bowring, "Criminal Rape or Philippine Nationalism?" *Asia Sentinel*, December 29, 2006, www.asiasentinel.com/index.php?option=com_content&task=view&id=319&Itemid=187 (May 8, 2007).

24. Rina Jimenez-David, "We Are All Nicole," *Philippine Daily Inquirer*, July 8, 2006, A13.

25. Representative reports include James Mananghaya, "US Pours $5-M Aid to Bicol," *Philippine Star*, July 5, 2007; Tarra Quismundo, "Fil-ams in US Navy Help in Typhoon Rehab," *Philippine Inquirer.net*, July 8, 2007, www.inquirer.net/specialfeatures/milenyo/view.php?db=1&article=20070708-75501; and John Unson, "US Envoy Adopted 'Darling' of S. Cotabato," *Philippine Star*, July 11, 2007.

26. See "Philippines Post Hits 1,100 Mark with Latest Life Member: VFW's Largest Overseas Post Just Got Larger in December—Membership—

VFW Post in Angeles City, Philippines," *VFW Magazine*, March 2003.
27. Interview with retired veteran, June 15, 2007. This person requested to remain anonymous.

13. SAN FERNANDO TO MANILA

1. The thumbnail of San Fernando was drawn from the city's official website www.cityofsanfernando.gov.ph. (accessed April 2, 2008).
2. For more on the Maywood parade, see the Maywood Bataan Day Organization's website at Mbdo.org (accessed January 3, 2008).

14. THE WAR YEARS

1. For a history of pre-American Manila, see Nick Joaquin, *Manila, My Manila* (Manila: Bookmark, 1999); and Alfonso J. Aluit, *By Sword and Fire: The Destruction of Manila in World War II, 3 February–3 March 1945* (Makati City, Philippines: Bookmark, 1995).
2. The history of the American development of Manila was informed by Joaquin, *Manila, My Manila*; Aluit, *By Sword and Fire*; and Connaughton, Pimlott, and Anderson, *The Battle for Manila*. Gleeck's *The Manila Americans* is also a valuable resource.
3. Joaquin, *Manila, My Manila*, 253.
4. Information on the Japanese occupation is taken from Connaughton, Pimlott, and Anderson, *The Battle for Manila*; Hartendorp, *The Japanese Occupation of the Philippines*; Ricardo Trota Jose and Lydia Yu-Jose, *The Japanese Occupation of the Philippines: A Pictorial History* (Makati, Philippines: Ayala Foundation, 1997); and the writers specifically cited in the following notes in this chapter. The discussion of the Battle of Manila was informed by Connaughton, Pimlott, and Anderson, *The Battle for Manila*; and Aluit's *By Sword and Fire*.
5. Marcial P. Lichauco, *Dear Mother Putnam: A Diary of the War in the Philippines* (Manila, 1949), 40–41.
6. Buencamino, "Manila under Japanese Occupation," 12–13.
7. Pestano-Jacinto, *Living with the Enemy*, 25.
8. Pedro M. Gimenez, *Under the Shadows of the "Kemp"* (Manila: A. Narvez Publishing House, 1946), 218, 252, 272.

9. Edgar Krohn Jr., text of speech given to Rotary Club, Makati, February 1995, in Memorare Manila collection, box titled "Narratives," Filipinas Heritage Library.
10. Aluit, *By Sword and Fire*, 381.

15. SANTO TOMAS

1. See both Connaughton, Pimlott, and Anderson, *The Battle for Manila*; and James, *The Years of MacArthur*, vol. 2, for the account of the drive to Manila.
2. There are many primary narratives of life inside Santo Tomas. Perhaps the most complete rendition can be found in A. V. H. Hartendorp's *The Santo Tomas Story* (New York: McGraw-Hill, 1964). See also Frederic Stevens, *The Santo Tomas Internment Camp* (Manila, 1946).
3. Emily Van Sickle, *The Iron Gates of Santo Tomas: The Firsthand Account of an American Couple Interned by the Japanese in Manila, 1942–1945* (Chicago: Academy Chicago Publishers, 1992), 293–94.
4. Leon D'Angelo in Contey-Aillo, *The 50th Anniversary Commemorative Album*, 140.
5. Robert B. Holland, *The Rescue of Santo Tomas, Manila WWII: The Flying Column: 100 Miles to Freedom* (Paducah, KY: Turner Publishing, 2003), 60.
6. Aluit, *By Sword and Fire*, 182.

16. ERMITA

1. For a prewar description of Ermita and Paco, see Aluit, *By Sword and Fire*; Joaquin, *Manila, My Manila*; and Guerrero Nakpil, *Myself, Elsewhere*.
2. See Aluit, *By Sword and Fire*, 242–43; and Jose Ma. Bonifacio M. Escoda, *Warsaw of Asia: The Rape of Manila* (Quezon City: Giraffe Books, 2001), 217–18.
3. Leticia Sta. Maria Rinongbayan, questionnaire in Memorare Manila collection, box titled "Narratives," Filipinas Heritage Library.
4. See Angus Campbell, "The Agoncillo Years," in *The Manila Club: A Social History of the British in Manila* (Manila: St Paul's Press, 1993), chap. 12.
5. Luis R. Estaban, "My War: A Personal Narrative," in Memorare Manila collection, box titled "Narratives," Filipinas Heritage Library, 27.

6. Ibid., 33.
7. See Thomas S. Hines for a description of the prewar hospital in "American Modernism in the Philippines: The Forgotten Architecture of William E. Parsons," *Journal of the Society of Architectural Historians* 32, no. 4 (December 1973): 316–26.
8. This incident relies on Aluit, *By Sword and Fire*, 228–232; and Connaughton, Pimlott, and Anderson, *The Battle for Manila*, 114–116.
9. Pacita Tapia, testimony from USA v. Tomoyuki Yamashita, in Memorare Manila collection, box titled "Memorare Testimonies," Filipinas Heritage Library.
10. The quotes here are from Escoda, Warsaw of Asia, 205; and Wilfrido Maria Guerreros, *The Guerreros of Ermita: Family History and Personal Memoirs* (Quezon City: New Day Press, 1988), 54.
11. See Connaughton, Pimlott, and Anderson, *The Battle for Manila*, 180.
12. Petillo, *Douglas MacArthur*, 226–27; and Aluit, *By Sword and Fire*, 367, both discuss this incident.

17. CORREGIDOR

1. Information on the island and the battle was obtained from James H. Belote and William M. Belote, *Corregidor: The Saga of a Fortress* (New York: Harper & Row, 1967); James, *The Years of MacArthur*, vol. 2; and Morison, *History of the United States Naval Operations*, vol. 13.
2. *Graphic* magazine provided excellent coverage of the event. See its editorial, "If the Administration Has No Skeletons to Hide, It Must Come Out with Truthful Answers," April 3, 1968, 1–2. In the same issue, Narciso Pimentel Jr. discussed the variety of potential explanations for the affair (including that it was part of a movie set) in "Behind the Corregidor Massacre," 18–19. A full discussion of the Senate committee hearings can be found in Manuel F. Almario, "The Murder of Truth on Corregidor," *Graphic*, July 3, 1968, 12, 55.

18. INTRAMUROS

1. The historical background on Intramuros was from Joaquin, *Manila, My Manila*; Esperanza B. Gatbonton, *Intramuros: A Historical Guide* (Manila:

Intramuros Administration, 1980); and Jaime C. Laya and Esperanza B. Gatbonton, *Intramuros of Memory* (Manila: Ministry of Human Settlements, Intramuros Administration, 1983). Accounts of the battle were taken from Aluit, *By Sword and Fire*; Escoda, *Warsaw of Asia*; Connaughton, Pimlott, and Anderson, *The Battle for Manila*; and Smith, *Triumph in the Philippines*.
2. Smith, *Triumph in the Philippines*, 294.
3. Carmen Guerrero Nakpil, "The Watershed," *Sunday Times Magazine*, April 16, 1967, 10.

19. THE FILIPINAS HERITAGE LIBRARY, MEMORARE MANILA, 1945
1. The Memorare Manila 1945 collection holds numerous clippings that document the controversy such as the quote from Isagani R. Cruz, "Poor Manilans," *Philippine Star*, April 27, 1995; as well as Custodio and Francisco, "Perceptions on U.S. Presence in Asia"; former Huk leader Jesus B. Lava, "Was Destruction of Manila during WWII Necessary: Liberation or Reoccupation?" *Philippine Daily Inquirer*, February 2, 1995; and Benito Legarda, "War and Forgetfulness," *Philippine Daily Inquirer*, March 23, 1995.
2. Teodoro L. Locsin Jr., "The Moral Score," *Today*, February 20, 1995.
3. The history of the group can be found in *Bamboo Bridge: (the official publication of the American School Alumni Association)* 5, no. 1 (September 1995): 1–2, found in the Memorare Manila collection.
4. From various Memorare Manila questionnaires.
5. From the Memorare Manila Mass program.
6. See David Cagahastian, "Japan Apologizes over Battle of Manila," *Manila Bulletin Online*, February 19, 2006. www.mb.com.ph/issues/2006/02/19/MTNN2006021956705.html (accessed June 30, 2007).

SELECTED BIBLIOGRAPHY

BOOKS

Abaya, Hernando J. *Betrayal in the Philippines*. New York: A. A. Wyn, 1946.

Abinales, Patricio N., ed. *The Revolution Falters: The Left in Philippine Politics after 1986*. Ithaca, NY: Southeast Asia Program Publications, Cornell University, 1996.

Abinales, Patricio N., and Donna J. Amoroso. *State and Society in the Philippines*. Lanham, MD: Rowman & Littlefield Publishers, 2005.

Aluit, Alfonso J. *By Sword and Fire: The Destruction of Manila in World War II, 3 February–3 March 1945*. Makati City: Bookmark, 1995.

Alzona, Encarnacion. *A History of Education in the Philippines, 1565–1930*. Manila: University of Philippines Press, 1932.

Atkinson, Fred. *The Philippine Islands*. Boston: Ginn, 1905.

Belote, James H., and William M. Belote. *Corregidor: The Saga of a Fortress*. New York: Harper & Row, 1967.

Bonner, Raymond. *Waltzing with a Dictator: The Marcoses and the Making of American Policy*. New York: Times Books, 1987.

Borrinaga, Rolando O. *The Balangiga Conflict Revisited*. Quezon City: New Day Publishers, 2003.

Brands, H. W. *Bound to Empire: The United States and the Philippines*. New York: Oxford University Press, 1992.

Breuer, William B. *The Great Raid on Cabanatuan: Rescuing the Doomed Ghosts of Bataan and Corregidor*. New York: John Wiley and Sons, 1994.

Brewer, William B. *MacArthur's Undercover War: Spies, Saboteurs, Guerrillas, and Secret Missions*. New York: John Wiley and Sons, 1995.

Brouwer, Steve, Paul Gifford, and Susan D. Rose. *Exporting the American Gospel: Global Christian Fundamentalism*. New York: Routledge, 1996.

Brown, A. Jack. *Katakana Man: I Worked Only for Generals: The Most Secret of All Allied Operations in World War II in the Pacific*. Tuggeranong, Australia: Air Power Development Centre, 2006.

Campbell, Angus. *The Manila Club: A Social History of the British in Manila*. Manila: St. Paul's Press, 1993.

Cannon, M. Hamlin. *Leyte: The Return to the Philippines*. Washington, D.C.: Center of Military History, United States Army, 1987.

Chapman, William. *Inside the Philippine Revolution: The New People's Army and Its Struggle for Power*. New York: W. W. Norton, 1987.

Chua, Yvonne T. *Robbed: An Investigation of Corruption in Philippine Education*. Manila: Philippine Center for Investigative Journalism, 1999.

Clymer, Kenton J. *Protestant Missionaries in the Philippines, 1898–1916: An Inquiry into the American Colonial Mentality*. Urbana: University of Illinois Press, 1986.

Collins, Joseph. *The Philippines: Fire on the Rim*. San Francisco: Institute for Food and Development Policy, 1989.

Connaughton, Richard, John Pimlott, and Duncan Anderson. *The Battle for Manila: The Most Devastating Story of World War II*. Novato, CA: Presidio Press, 1995.

Constantino, Renato. *A History of the Philippines: From the Spanish Colonization to the Second World War*. New York: Monthly Review Press, 1975.

———. *Neo-colonial Identity and Counter-consciousness: Essays in Cultural Decolonization*. New York: M. E. Sharpe, 1978.

Contey-Aiello, Rose. *The 50th Anniversary Commemorative Album of the Flying Column 1945–1995: The Liberation of Santo Tomas Internment Camp, February 1945*. Tarpon Springs, FL: Marrakech Express, 1995.

Corpus, Victor N. *Silent War*. Quezon City: VNC Enterprises, 1989.

Cronin, Francis D. *Under the Southern Cross: The Saga of the American Division*. Washington, D.C.: Combat Forces Press, 1951.

Davis, Leonard. *The Philippines: People, Poverty, and Politics*. New York: St. Martin's Press, 1987.

Day, Beth. *The Manila Hotel: The Heart and Memory of a City.* N.p., n.d.

Decker, Malcom. *On a Mountainside: The 155th Provisional Guerrilla Battalion Against the Japanese on Luzon.* Las Cruces, NM: Yucca Tree Press, 2004.

Delk, James D. *The Fighting Fortieth in War and Peace.* Palm Springs, CA: ETC Publications, 1998.

Dizon, Lino L. *Mr. White: A "Thomasite" History of Tarlac Province, 1901–1913: In Honor of Frank Russell White.* Tarlac City, Philippines: JDN Center for Kapampangan Studies, Holy Angel University, with Public Affairs Office, Embassy of the United States–Manila, 2002.

Dos Passos, John. *Tour of Duty.* New York: Houghton Mifflin, 1946.

Escoda, Jose Ma. Bonifacio M. *Warsaw of Asia: The Rape of Manila.* Quezon City: Giraffe Books, 2001.

Forbes, W. Cameron. *The Philippine Islands.* Rev. ed. Cambridge, MA: Harvard University Press, 1945.

Francia, Luis H. *Eye of the Fish: A Personal Archipelago.* New York: Kaya Press, 2001.

Gatbonton, Esperanza B. *Intramuros: A Historical Guide.* Manila: Intramuros Administration, 1980.

Gates, John Morgan. *Schoolbooks and Krags: The United States Army in the Philippines, 1898–1902.* Westport, CT: Greenwood Press, 1973.

Gimenez, Pedro M. *Under the Shadows of the "Kemp."* Manila: A. Narvez Publishing House, 1946.

Gleeck, Lewis E., Jr. *The Manila Americans (1901–1964).* Manila: Carmelo and Bauermann, 1977.

Guerrero, Amado (Jose Maria Sison). *Philippine Society and Revolution.* Hong Kong: Ta Kung Pao, 1971.

Guerreros, Wilfrido Maria. *The Guerreros of Ermita: Family History and Personal Memoirs.* Quezon City: New Day Press, 1988.

Hartendorp, A. V. H. *The Japanese Occupation of the Philippines.* 2 vols. Manila: Bookmark, 1967.

———. *The Santo Tomas Story.* New York: McGraw-Hill, 1964.

Hileman, Millard E., and Paul Fridlund. *1051: An American POW's Remarkable Journey through World War II.* Walla Walla, WA: Words Worth Press, 1992.

Holland, Robert B. *The Rescue of Santo Tomas, Manila, WWII: The Flying Column:*

100 Miles to Freedom. Paducah, KY: Turner Publishing, 2003.

Horn, Florence. *Orphans of the Pacific: The Philippines.* Cornwall, NY: Cornwall Press, 1941.

James, D. Clayton. *The Years of MacArthur.* Vol. 1, *1880–1940.* Boston: Houghton Mifflin, 1970.

———. *The Years of MacArthur.* Vol. 2, *1941–1945.* Boston: Houghton Mifflin, 1975.

Joaquin, Nick. *The Aquinos of Tarlac: An Essay on History as Three Generations.* Manila: Cacho Hermanos, 1983.

———. *Manila, My Manila.* Manila: Bookmark, 1999.

Johnson, Bryan. *The Four Days of Courage: The Untold Story of the People Who Brought Marcos Down.* New York: Free Press, 1987.

Jones, Gregg R. *Red Revolution: Inside the Philippine Guerrilla Movement.* Boulder, CO: Westview Press, 1989.

Jose, Ricardo Trota, and Lydia Yu-Jose. *The Japanese Occupation of the Philippines: A Pictorial History.* Makati, Philippines: Ayala Foundation, 1997.

Karnow, Stanley. *In Our Image: America's Empire in the Philippines.* New York: Ballantine Books, 1990.

Kerkvliet, Benedict J. *The Huk Rebellion: A Study of Peasant Revolt in the Philippines.* Berkeley: University of California Press, 1977.

Knox, Donald. *Death March: The Survivors of Bataan.* New York: Harcourt Brace Jovanovich, 1981.

Komisar, Lucy. *Corazon Aquino: The Story of a Revolution.* New York: George Braziller, 1987.

Krueger, Walter. *From Down Under to Nippon: The Story of the Sixth Army in World War II.* Washington, D.C.: Combat Forces Press, 1953.

Lachica, Eduardo. *The Huks: Philippine Agrarian Society in Revolt.* New York: Praeger Publishers, 1977.

Lawyers Committee for Human Rights. *Out of Control: Militia Abuses in the Philippines.* New York: Lawyers Committee for Human Rights, 1990.

Laya, Jaime C., and Esperanza B. Gatbonton. *Intramuros of Memory.* Manila: Ministry of Human Settlements, Intramuros Administration, 1983.

Lichauco, Marcial P. *Dear Mother Putnam: A Diary of the War in the Philippines.* Manila, 1949.

Linn, Brian McCallister. *The Philippine War, 1899–1902*. Lawrence: University of Kansas, 2000.

MacArthur, Douglas A. *Reminiscences*. New York: McGraw-Hill, 1964.

May, Glenn Anthony. *Social Engineering in the Philippines: The Aims, Execution, and Impact of American Colonial Policy, 1900–1913*. Westport, CT: Greenwood Press, 1980.

McCallus, Joseph P. *American Exiles in the Philippines, 1941–1996: A Collected Oral Narrative*. Quezon City: New Day Publishers, 1999.

Meixsel, Richard B. *Clark Field and the U.S. Army Air Corps in the Philippines, 1919–1942*. Quezon City: New Day Publishers, 2002.

Mercado, Monina Allarey, ed. *People Power: The Philippine Revolution of 1986: An Eyewitness History*. Manila: James B. Reuter, S. J., Foundation, 1986.

Morison, Samuel Eliot. *History of the United States Naval Operations in World War II*. Vol. 12, *Leyte, June 1944–January 1945*. Edison, NJ: Castle Books, 2001.

———. *History of the United States Naval Operations in World War II*. Vol. 13, *The Liberation of the Philippines: Luzon, Mindanao, the Visayas, October 1944–August 1945*. Edison, NJ: Castle Books, 2002.

Nakpil, Carmen Guerrero. *Myself, Elsewhere*. Metro Manila: Nakpil Publishers, 2006.

———. *A Question of Identity: Selected Essays*. Manila: Vessel Books, 1973.

Naraval, Thelma F. *The Southern Cross: A History of the Christian and Missionary Alliance Churches of the Philippines, Inc.* Vol 1. Cagayan de Oro, Philippines: Bustamante Press, 1977.

Nieva, Antonio A. *The Fight for Freedom: Remembering Bataan and Corregidor*. Quezon City: New Day Publishers, 1997.

O'Brien, Niall. *Revolution from the Heart*. New York: Oxford University Press, 1987.

Olson, John E. *O'Donnell, Andersonville of the Pacific*. Self-published, 1985.

Owens, William A. *Eye-Deep in Hell: A Memoir of the Liberation of the Philippines, 1944–45*. Dallas: Southern Methodist University Press, 1989.

Pecson, Geromina T., and Maria Racelis, eds. *Tales of American Teachers in the Philippines*. Manila: Carmelo and Bauremann, 1959.

Perret, Geoffrey. *Old Soldiers Never Die: The Life of Douglas MacArthur*. New York: Random House, 1996.

Pestano-Jacinto, Pacita. *Living with the Enemy: A Diary of the Japanese Occupation.* Pasig City, Philippines: Anvil, 1999.

Petillo, Carol Morris. *Douglas MacArthur: The Philippine Years.* Bloomington: Indiana University Press, 1981.

Pier, Arthur S. *American Apostles to the Philippines.* Boston: Beacon Press, 1950.

Pomeroy, William J. *An American Made Tragedy: Neo-Colonialism and Dictatorship in the Philippines.* New York: International Publishers, 1974.

Quirino, Carlos. *Chick Parsons: America's Master Spy in the Philippines.* Manila: New Day, 1954.

Rhoades, Weldon E. *Flying MacArthur to Victory.* College Station: Texas A&M University Press, 1987.

Robb, Walter. *The Filipinos.* Manila: the author, 1939.

Romulo, Beth Day. *Inside the Palace: The Rise and Fall of Ferdinand and Imelda Marcos.* New York: G. P. Putnam's Sons, 1987.

Romulo, Carlos P. *I See the Philippines Rise.* New York: Doubleday, 1946.

———. *I Walked with Heroes.* New York: Holt, Rinehart and Winston, 1961.

San Juan, E., Jr. *The Philippine Temptation: Dialectics of Philippines-U.S. Literary Relations.* Philadelphia: Temple University Press, 1996.

———. *Writing and National Liberation: Essays in Critical Practice.* Quezon City: University of the Philippines Press, 1991.

Saulo, Alfredo B. *Communism in the Philippines: An Introduction.* Quezon City: The Ateneo de Manila University Press, 1990.

Schaefer, Chris. *Bataan Diary: An American Family in World War II, 1941–1945.* Houston: Riverview Publishing, 2004.

Schaller, Michael. *Douglas MacArthur: The Far Eastern General.* New York: Oxford University Press, 1989.

Schultz, Duane P. *Hero of Bataan: The Story of General Jonathan M. Wainwright.* New York: St. Martin's Press, 1981.

Seagrave, Stirling. *The Marcos Dynasty.* New York: Harper & Row, 1988.

Shalom, Stephen Rosskamm. *The United States and the Philippines: A Study in Neocolonialism.* Philadelphia: Institute for the Study of Human Issues, 1981.

Smith, Robert R. *Triumph in the Philippines: The U.S. Army in WWII.* Washington, D.C.: Department of the Army, 1963.

Steinberg, Rafael, ed. *Return to the Philippines.* New York: Time-Life Books, 1979.

Stevens, Frederic H. *The Santo Tomas Internment Camp*. New York, 1946.

Stewart, Sidney. *Give Us This Day*. New York: W. W. Norton, 1956.

Swinson, Arthur. *Four Samurai: A Quartet of Japanese Army Commanders in the Second World War*. London: Hutchinson, 1968.

Thurston, Herbert, S. J., and Donald Attwater, eds. *Butler's Lives of the Saints*. Vol 2. New York: P. J. Kennedy and Sons, 1956.

Timberman, David G. *A Changeless Land: Continuity and Change in Philippine Politics*. New York: M. E. Sharpe, 1991.

U.S. Army. *40th Infantry Division: The Years of World War II*. Nashville: The Battery Press, 1946.

United States Information Service. *A Sentimental Journey: General Douglas MacArthur's Visit to the Philippines*. United States Information Service, no date, probably 1961.

Valtin, Jan. *Children of Yesterday: The 24th Infantry Division in WWII*. New York: The Readers' Press, 1946.

Van Sickle, Emily. *The Iron Gates of Santo Tomas: The Firsthand Account of an American Couple Interned by the Japanese in Manila, 1942–1945*. Chicago: Academy Chicago Publishers, 1992.

Weekley, Kathleen. *The Communist Party of the Philippines, 1968–1993: A Story of Its Theory and Practice*. Quezon City: University of the Philippines Press, 2001.

Whitney, Courtney. *MacArthur: His Rendezvous with History*. New York: Alfred A. Knopf, 1956.

Willeford, Charles. *Something About a Soldier*. New York: Random House, 1986.

Woods, L. Shelton. *A Broken Mirror: Protestant Fundamentalism in the Philippines*. Quezon City: New Day Press, 2002.

Working Group on New Religious Movements, ed. *Sects and New Religious Movements: An Anthology of Texts from the Catholic Church, 1986–1994*. Washington, DC: U.S. Catholic Conference, 1995.

DOCUMENTS

Biri Fiesta 2005. No publisher. 2005.

Lum, Thomas, and Larry A. Niksch. *The Republic of the Philippines: Background and U.S. Relations*. CRS Report for Congress. Washington, DC: Congressional Research Service, January 10, 2006.

Memorare Manila 1945. "Memorare Manila 1945. In Commemoration of the Non-Combative Victims of the Battle of Liberation of Manila, February 3–March 3, 1945," ceremony program, 1995. Kept at Filipinas Heritage Library.

United States Information Service. *The American Contribution to Philippine Education, 1898–1998.* Washington, DC: United States Information Service, 1998.

United States Senate, Committee on Military Affairs. *The Sack of Manila.* Washington, D.C.: Government Printing Office, 1945.

UNPUBLISHED DOCUMENTS

Estaban, Luis R. "My War: A Personal Narrative." In Memorare Manila collection, box titled "Narratives," Filipinas Heritage Library, 27.

Krohn, Edgar, Jr. Text of speech given to Rotary Club, Makati, February 1995. Found in Memorare Manila collection, box titled "Narratives," Filipinas Heritage Library.

Oral Reminiscences of Frederic S. Marquardt, interviewed by D. Clayton James, September 5, 1971. Norfolk, VA: MacArthur Archives, 27.

Rinongbayan, Leticia Sta. Maria. Questionnaire in Memorare Manila collection, box titled "Narratives," Filipinas Heritage Library.

Tapia, Pacita. Testimony from *USA v. Tomoyuki Yamashita,* in Memorare Manila collection, box titled "Memorare Testimonies," Filipinas Heritage Library.

University of Santo Tomas Internment Camp Papers, American Historical Collection, Rizal Library, Ateneo University of Manila, from 1942–1945.

ARTICLES

Abaya, Antonio. "If There Had Been No Leyte Landing. . . ." *Philippine Star,* October 25, 1994.

Almario, Manuel F. "The Murder of Truth on Corregidor." *Graphic,* July 3, 1968, 12, 55.

American School Alumni Association. *Bamboo Bridge* 5, no. 1 (September 1995): 1.

Antiporda, Jefferson, and James Konstantin Galvez. "God Knows the Truth:

Smith Gets 40 for Nicole's Rape; 3 Pals Acquitted." *Manila Times Internet Edition*, December 5, 2006.

Aspillera, Dahli. "I Shall Return." *Malaya*, August 18, 1994.

Beattie, Helen B. "American Teachers and the Filipinos." *Bulletin of the American Historical Collection* 12, no. 3 (July–September 1984): 70–81.

Belote, W. M. "The Rock in the 'Tween War Years." *Bulletin of the American Historical Collection* 19, no. 1 (January–March 1991): 26–43.

Bowring, Philip. "Criminal Rape or Philippine Nationalism?" *Asia Sentinel*, December 29, 2006. www.asiasentinel.com/index.php?option=com_con tent&task=view&id=319&Itemid=187 (accessed May 8, 2007).

Brody, David. "Building Empire: Architecture and American Imperialism in the Philippines." *Journal of Asian Studies* 4, no. 2 (June 2001): 123–45.

Buencamino, Victor. "Manila under Japanese Occupation." *Bulletin of the American Historical Collection* 7, no. 3 (July–Sept 1979): 7–29; and 8, no. 1 (January–March 1980): 23–44.

Cagahastian, David. "Japan Apologizes over Battle of Manila." *Manila Bulletin Online*, February 19, 2006. www.mb.com.ph/issues/2006/02/19/ MTNN2006021956705.html (accessed June 30, 2007).

Communist Party of the Philippines. "U.S. Military Bases: Outposts for Aggression." *Ang Bayan*, April 1983, 2.

Communist Party of the Philippines Information Bureau. "CPP Warns against Use of Philippines as Staging Ground for U.S. War against DPRK." Press release, October 17, 2006.

Cooper, Price W. "The Life and Death of an Ilocos Public School Teacher (1901–1903): From the Letters of Price W. Cooper, 1875–1903." *Bulletin of the American Historical Collection* 10, no. 1 (January–March 1982): 36–41.

Cruz, Isagani R. "Poor Manilans." *Philippine Star*, April 27, 1995.

Cueto, Francis Earl A., Sam Mediavilla, Anthony Vargas, and AFP. "Balikatan on Again with Malacañang Cave In." *Manila Times*, January 3, 2007. www.manilatimes.net/national/2007/jan/03/yehey/top_stories (accessed May 8, 2007).

Custodio, Jose Antonio, and Rino A. Francisco. "Perceptions on U.S. Presence in Asia." *Philippine Star*, December 2, 1994.

Dagot, Edilberto P. "American Teachers in Paragua: Charles D. Hart (1871–

1907)." *Bulletin of the American Historical Collection* 2, no. 1 (September 1973): 27–39.

Dela Cruz, Rhonie. "Asahiyama: The Japanese Naval Headquarters in Bamban." *Bamban Historical Society Journal* 1, no. 1 (June 25, 2004).

———. "The Bamban Kamikaze Airfield of WWII: A Comprehensive Historical Essay." *Bamban Historical Society Journal* 1, no. 6 (October 16, 2004).

———. "Beneath the Sword of the Kempei-Tai: The Death of an American Pilot in Bamban Field." *Bamban Historical Society Journal* 1, no. 3 (June 25, 2004).

———. "The Paruao (Bamban) River Line—1899: The Last Battle of the Republic." *Bamban Historical Society Journal* 1, no. 5 (August 14, 2004).

———. "Revisiting the Bamban Hills: The Raising of the American Flag at Hill 1700." *Bamban Historical Society Journal* 1, no. 2 (May 31, 2004).

———. "Vincit, Amor, Patriae: The USAFFE Guerrilla Movement in the Bamban Area." *Bamban Historical Society Journal* 2, no. 2 (May 22, 2005).

Doane, Ralph Harrington. "The Story of American Architecture in the Philippines." *Architectural Review* 8, old series vol. 25, no. 2 (February 1919): 25–32; and no. 5 (May 1919): 115–22.

Esguerra, Christian V. *Philippine Daily Inquirer*, August 4, 2005, A1.

Gleek, Lewis E., Jr. "Fulfillment in the Philippines (IV)." *Bulletin of the American Historical Collection* 19, no. 1 (January–March 1991): 44–69.

Hines, Thomas S. "American Modernism in the Philippines: The Forgotten Architecture of William E. Parsons." *Journal of the Society of Architectural Historians* 32, no. 4 (December 1973): 316–26.

"If the Administration Has No Skeletons to Hide, It Must Come Out with Truthful Answers." *Graphic*, April 3, 1968, 1–2.

"Independence Day MacArthur Special Issue." *Philippines Herald*, July 3, 1961.

Jaymalin, Mayen. "Over 1M[illion] College Graduates Jobless." *Philippine Star*, June 30, 2007, 1.

Jimenez-David, Rina. "We Are All Nicole." *Philippine Daily Inquirer*, July 8, 2006, A13.

"Kapihan sa AmCham." *AmCham Business Journal*, June 2004, 20.

Laude, Jaime. "4 Informants vs Sayyaf Receive $10M from U.S." *Philippine Star*, June 8, 2007, 6.

Lava, Jesus B. "Was Destruction of Manila during WWII Necessary: Liberation or Reoccupation?" *Philippine Daily Inquirer*, February 2, 1995.

Leaño, Christina. "Benzene and Butterflies: The Toxic Legacy of the U.S. Military in the Philippines." *Pax Christi USA*, Spring 2003. www.paxchristiusa.org/news_events_more.asp?id=567 (accessed October 20, 2008).

Legarda, Benito. "War and Forgetfulness." *Philippine Daily Inquirer*, March 23, 1995.

Llanes, Ferdinand. "A Sham Celebration." *Manila Chronicle*, October 16, 1994.

Locsin, Teodoro L., Jr. "The Moral Score." *Today*, February 20, 1995.

"MacArthur Falls!" *Philippine Star*, October 21, 1994.

Mananghaya, James. "US Pours $5-M Aid to Bicol." *Philippine Star*, July 5, 2007, 1, 8.

Manila Times, July 7, 1961, 1–2.

McCallus, Joseph P. "Eddie Woolbright: A Biographical Sketch Drawn from an Oral Narrative." *Bulletin of the American Historical Collection* 25, no. 3 (July–September 1997): 7–20.

———. "The Propaganda of the National Democratic Front: A Study of Rhetorical Method in Liberation." *Pilipinas: A Journal of Philippine Studies* 20 (Spring 1993): 23–42.

Miller, Jack. "Religion in the Philippines." *Asia Society's Focus on Asian Studies* 2, no. 1 (Fall 1982): 26–27.

Morella, Cecil. "Philippine Education in Crisis." *Philippine Inquirer.net*, July 5, 2004. www.inq7net/brk/2004/jul/05/brkpol_4-1.htm (accessed June 26, 2006).

———. "Rape Trial in RP Revives 'Ugly American' Image." *Manila Times*, October 26, 2006, 6.

Nakpil, Carmen Guerrero. "The Watershed." *Sunday Times Magazine*, April 16, 1967, 10.

National Democratic Front. "NPA Punishes U.S. 'LIC' Expert." *Liberation*, March–April 1989, 16.

Olson, John E. "Home at Last!" *Bulletin of the American Historical Collection* 28, no. 4 (October–December 2000): 59–62.

Orejas, Tonette. "Aeta People Like Leaves on Water." *Philippine Daily Inquirer*, May 31, 2005, A19.

———. "From 'Lubay' to Levi's." *Philippine Daily Inquirer*, June 14, 2006, A1.

———. "More Jobs Today in Subic and Clark." *Philippine Daily Inquirer*, June 26, 2007, 1.

Overland, Martha Ann. "A Nursing Crisis in the Philippines." *The Chronicle of Higher Education*, January 7, 2005. chronicle.com/weekly/v51/i18/18a04601.htm (accessed March 30, 2007).

PDI Research. "In the Know." *Philippine Daily Inquirer*, August 4, 2005, A6.

Perez, Gilbert. "From the Transport Thomas to Sto. Tomas." *Bulletin of the American Historical Collection* 1, no. 5 (September 1973): 13–26; and 2, no. 1 (January 1974): 59–74.

"Philippines Post Hits 1,100 Mark with Latest Life Member: VFW's Largest Overseas Post Just Got Larger in December—Membership—VFW Post in Angeles City, Philippines," *VFW Magazine*, March 2003.

Pimentel, Narciso, Jr. "Behind the Corregidor Massacre," *Graphic*, April 3, 1968, 18–19.

Pontius, Dale. "MacArthur and the Filipinos." *Asia and the Americas*, October 1946, 436, and November 1946, 509–12.

Quetchenbach, Raymond, SVD. "Walter Scott Price—'King of Leyte.'" *Leyte-Samar Studies* 8, no. 1 (1974): 33–38.

Quismundo, Tarra. "Fil-ams in US Navy Help in Typhoon Rehab." *Philippine Inquirer.net*, July 8, 2007. www.inquirer.net/specialfeatures/milenyo/view.php?db=1&article=20070708-75501 (accessed July 20, 2007).

Solivan, Max V. *Philippine Star*, August 11, 2004, 10–11.

Son, Johanna. "Philippines Holds Big Party for Its Own D-Day." *Manila Chronicle*, October 14, 1994.

Swetz, Frank J. "Mathematics for Social Change, 1898–1925." *Bulletin of the American Historical Collection* 27, no. 1 (January–March 1999): 61–80.

"Target: 20M Signatures; CBCP Starts 50-day Protest against VFA." *Philippine Daily Inquirer*, July 26, 1998, 26. www.hartford-hwp.com/archives/27c/477.html (accessed March 13, 2007).

Torres, Tetch. "Tutors Ask SC Not to Make English Primary Education Medium." *Philippine Inquirer.net*, April 27, 2007. newsinfo.inquirer.net/breakingnews/nation/view_article.php?article_id+62882 (accessed June 1, 2007).

Unson, John. "US Envoy Adopted 'Darling' of S. Cotabato." *Philippine Star*, July 11, 2007, 9.

Vargas, Anthony. "DNA Testing Confirms Death of Janjalani." *Manila Times*, January 21, 2007. www.manilatimes.net/national/2007/jan21/yehey/metro/20070121metl.html (accessed March 9, 2007).

Walfish, Daniel. "Higher Education in the Philippines: Lots of Access, Little Quality." *The Chronicle of Higher Education*, September 7, 2001, A60.

WEBSITES

Arlington National Cemetery Website, "James Nicholas Rowe." www.arlingtoncemetery.net/jamesnic.htm (accessed October 8, 2007).

"Battling Bastards of Bataan." home.pacbell.net/fbaldie/Battling_Bastards_of_Bataan.html (accessed April 28, 2007).

"The Battling Bastards of Bataan." www.battlingbastardsbataan.com/capas1.htm (accessed April 28 2007).

"Bonk . . . The Life Saver." www.clarkab.com/ck_stories_bonk.htm (accessed March 15, 2007).

Casteñeda, Dabet. "For Land and Wages: Half a Century of Peasant Struggle in Hacienda Luisita." *Bulatlat Report* 4, no. 46 (December 19–25, 2004). www.bulatlat.com/news/4-46/4-46-land.html. (accessed July 6, 2006).

Christian Light Foundation. www.clfphils.org/aboutus.htm (accessed June 19, 2006).

"Colonel James 'Nick' Rowe, February 8, 1938–April 21, 1989." www.psy-warrior.com/rowe.html (accessed October 10, 2007).

Communist Party of the Philippines (CPP). "CPP Warns against Use of Philippines as Staging Ground for U.S. War against DPRK," October 17, 2006. ww.democraticunderground.com/discuss/duboard.php?az=view_all&address=132x2891393 (accessed March 20, 2007).

Dapulang, Emilia. "Trade Union Repression in the Philippines." *Kapatiran: Newsletter of Philippine Solidarity Network of Aotearoa*. www.converge.org.nz/psna/Kapatiran/KapNo22/Kap22Art/art87.htm (accessed July 6, 2006).

"The Definitive History of Balut in the Far East." www.nuss.org (accessed December 1, 2007).

De Jesus, Emmi. "Justice for Nicole Requires Abrogation of VFA." *Gabriela Network*, December 4, 2006. www.feministpeacenetwork.org/2006/12/05/analysis-of-the-subic-bay-rape-verdicts (accessed May 9, 2007).

Dizon, Lino. "Bamban, Tarlac in 1899: A Cruz of the Philippine Revolution." Center for Tarlaqueño Studies. www.geocities.com/cts_tsu/webBAMBAN.html (accessed August 1, 2007).

Dorono, Tony. "Hacienda Luisita Workers in the Philippines Celebrate Their Historic Victory." Asian Pacific American Labor Alliance, ALF-CIO (APALA). www.aplanet.org/ht/d/sp/i/5267/pid/5267 (accessed July 6, 2006).

Ecumenical Bishops' Forum. "Statement on Visiting Forces Agreement." *Critical Asian Studies* 38, no. 4 (December 2006). www.Bcasnet.org/campaigns/campaign5.htm (accessed March 8, 2007).

GMA News. "Oakwood Mutiny," July 20, 2007. images.gmanews.tv/html/research/2007/11/oakwood_mutiny_timeline.html (accessed December 1, 2008).

Gobrin, Gerardo, and Almira Andin. "Development Conflict: The Philippine Experience." www.minorityrights.org/929/macro-studies/development-conflict-the-philippine-experience.html (accessed June 20, 2006).

Greenpeace. "Toxic Alert: US Toxic Legacies: Toxic Hotspots in Clark and Subic," February 29, 2000. archive.greenpeace.org/toxics/toxfreeasia/documents/clarksubic.html (accessed December 10, 2008).

Internationalist, The. "Massacre of Sugar Plantation Workers in the Philippines," December 2004. www.internationalist.org/philippinesluisitamassacre0412.html (accessed July 6, 2006).

International Union of Food, Agricultural, Hotel, Restaurant, Catering, Tobacco and Allied Workers' Associations (IUF). "IUF Condemns Killing of Workers at Hacienda Luisita Sugar Mill and Plantation, Philippines." www.asianfoodworker.net/philippines/041126luisita.htm (accessed July 6, 2006).

Joshua Project. www.joshuaproject.net/index.php (accessed January 19, 2007).

Katipunan ng mga Anak ng Bayan Citizen's Development Initiatives, Inc. (KAAKBAY CDI). "Philippine Public Education: A Situationer," June 05, 2006. qc.indymedia.org (accessed July 1, 2007).

League of Filipino Students. "Cohen's Visit a U.S. Pressure Tactic for the VFA!" August 3, 1998. www.geocities.com/CollegePark/Field/4927/lfs/stmts/cohen (accessed March 13, 2007).

Lontoc, Jo. Florendo B. "A Situationer on Philippine Education." Forum Online Magazine 6, no. 4 (July–August 2005). www.up.edu.ph/oldforum/2005/Jul-Aug05/situationer.html (accessed June 26, 2007).

Loop, Honey Jarque. "Cebu's Legendary Eddie's Log Cabin Gets a Makeover." *Philippine Headline News Online*, April 19, 2006. www.newsflash.org/2004/02/ht/ht006146.htm (accessed January 20, 2008).

Manalansan, Felicisimo H., Jr. "Oust-GMA to End Mining Liberalization, Conference Declares." *Bulatlat* 5, no. 20 (June 26–July 2, 2005). www.bulatlat.com/news/5-20/5-20-mining.htm (accessed July 2, 2005).

Maoist International Movement (MIM). "Wimmin's Movement Leader from the Philippines Speaks Out against the Visiting Forces Agreement." *MIM Notes* 185 May 1, 1999. www.prisoncensorship.info/archive/etext/cal/vfa.html (accessed March 8, 2007).

Maywood Bataan Day Organization. Mbdo.org. (accessed January 3, 2008).

Mission to Unreached Peoples. "Overview of Ministries and Programs." www.mup.org/ministries/index.php (last accessed June 20, 2006).

National Statistics Office, Philippines. "2007 Census of Population" (2007). www.census.gov.ph/data/census2007/index.html (accessed December 21, 2008).

Nazarene Compassionate Ministries. www.ncm.org (accessed June 20, 2006).

Office of the Provost Marshal General. "Camp O'Donnell." *Report on American Prisoners of War Interned by the Japanese in the Philippines*, November 19, 1945. www.mansell.com/pow_resources/camplists/philippines/odonnell/provost_rpt.html#anchor35881 (accessed June 28, 2006).

"Pangasinan History." www.pangasinan.gov.ph (accessed July 2008).

Philippine Overseas Employment Administration. "OFW Remittances." www.poea.gov.ph/stats/remittance_1997_2006.html (accessed July 2008).

P.O.W. Network. "Case Synopsis: Rowe, James Nicholas 'Nick.'" www.pownetwork.org/bios/r/r077.htm (accessed October 3, 2007).

Samar, Province of. "General Information." samar.lgu-ph.com/history.htm (accessed November 13, 2006).

San Fernando, City of. www.cityofsanfernando.gov.ph (accessed April 2, 2008).

The Spanish-American War Centennial Website. "McKinley Gives His Reasons for the U.S. to Keep the Philippines." www.spanamwar.com/McKinleyphilreasons.htm (accessed July 1, 2008).

Tourist Center Corporation Philippines. "Angeles, Pampanga." www.tourist-center.com.ph/philippines/information/angeles.html (accessed May 1, 2008).

Tuazon, Bobby. "The Hacienda Luisita Massacre, Landordism and State Terrorism." *Bulatlat News Analysis*, November 22, 2004. www.bulatlat.com/news/4-42/4-42-massacre.html (accessed July 6, 2006).

University of the Philippines System, Diliman, Quezon City. "A Response to President Gloria Macapagal Arroyo Directing the Department of Education to 'Return English as Primary Medium of Instruction.'" February 2003. www.up.edu.ph/oldsystem/proenglish.htm (accessed June 26, 2006).

U.S. Department of Defense. "60th Anniversary, Battle of Leyte Gulf, Liberation of the Philippines" (2004). www.defenselink.mil/home/features/Leyte/ (accessed July 23, 2007).

U.S. Embassy, Manila, Philippines. "Philippines and U.S. Commemorate the 60th Anniversary of the End of WWII." http://manila.usembassy.gov/wwwhr632.html (last accessed April 28, 2007).

———. "Exercise Balikatan 2007 Partners with Gawad Kalinga to Build Communities while Building Relationships," March 7, 2007. manila.usembassy.gov/wwwhs102.html (accessed March 8, 2007).

Vital, Emily. "Bayan Challenges Candidates to Junk VFA," *Bulatlat* 7, no. 3 (February 18–24, 2007). www.bulatlat.com/news/7-3/7-3-vfa.htm (accessed May 8, 2007).

INTERVIEW

Simpson, Mervyn. Discussion with the author. Manila, Philippines, July 2 and July 20, 2004.

INDEX

241, 249, 312; advance through
the Luzon plain, 144–45; attack on
Clark Air Field, 195; at Bamban
Airfield, 180; and Christianity, 40; on
Corregidor, 282, 290; at Dagupan,
137–38, 143; defeat at Bataan,
27–28; denying air support, 293;
interview with Dos Passos, 152–53;
at Leyte landing, 33–35; at Lingayen,
126, 143; "Manila has fallen," 257;
Mindoro invasion, 121–22; 1961
visit to the Philippines, 142–43;
the Philippines and his development, 38–40; planning Philippine
campaign, 28–29; plans to capture
Manila, 127–28; at the Price house in
Tacloban, 52–54; on seeing Manila,
124; on seeing the Manila Hotel,
276–77; speech at Malacanang, 280;
visit to Santo Tomas, 253–54
MacArthur Highway (Highway 3), 127,
128, 129, 142–43, 144, 167, 171, 173,
174, 177, 184, 186, 218, 220, 221,
222, 230, 235
MacArthur Island, Tampipi, 91, 97–98,
113, 104–10; foreigners on, 97–98,
109–10
Mactan Island, 67
Magalang, 177
Magallanes Drive, 297
Magellan, Ferdinand, 12, 279
Magsaysay, Ramon, 156
Makapili, 243, 244
Makati, 6–7, 107, 215
Makino-san, 182
Malacanang Palace, 49, 143, 162, 249, 280
Malate, 6, 284, 306, 314
Malinta Tunnel, 282, 286, 288
Malolos, 235
Manalo, Felix, of Iglesia ni Cristo, 76
Manglapus, Raul, 198
Manila (city), 174, 177, 235; history of,
239–41; Insular Life Building, 291;

Japanese occupation of, 239–48; Jones
Bridge, 291, 295. *See also* Ermita
Manila American Cemetery, 311–12
Manila-Dagupan railway, 127, 136–37,
144, 173, 193, 232
Manila Fire Department, 240
Manila Hotel, 35, 127, 221, 241, 273,
276–77, 280
Marcos, Ferdinand, 10, 11, 20, 66, 79–80,
82, 153–54, 157, 160, 164; fall from
power, 162–64; and U.S. bases,
196–97
Marcos, Imelda, 10, 11, 66; née Imelda
Romualdez, 48–49, 65
Mariula River, 186
Mariveles, 167
Masbate, 117
Massello, William "Wild Bill," Jr., 285
Maywood Bataan Day Organization,
233–34
McFie, John, 16, 17, 18, 19, 254, 256
McGuire, James, 57
McKinley, William, 72–73
McMicking, Joseph R., 6–7
McMicking, Mercedes, 305
McSeveny, Major, 187
Melvin, John, 15
Memorare Manila 1945, 304–7
Mennonite Church, 197
Merritt, Wesley, 36
Methodist Church, 74, 197
Military Bases Agreement (1947), 196
Mills, Samuel Meyers, 281
Mimosa Leisure Estate, 200
Mindanao, 5, 28, 31, 64, 71, 74, 79, 106,
158, 195, 210–13, 218
Mindoro, invasion, 121–22
Mission of the Disciples of Christ, 74
Mission to Unreached Peoples, 190
Mitchell, William "Billy," 194
M. L. Quezon Avenue, 203
Moro Islamic Liberation Front, 212
Moro National Liberation Front, 212

ABOUT THE AUTHOR

Dr. Joseph P. McCallus is a professor of English at Columbus State University, Columbus, Georgia, and he has been a frequent visitor to the Philippines for more than twenty years. He is the author of *American Exiles in the Philippines, 1941–1996: A Collected Oral Narrative* and editor of *Gentleman Soldier: John Clifford Brown and the Philippine-American War*. He has also produced propaganda studies of the Marcos regime and both the Philippine communist and anticommunist movements.